Calibre Manual

A catalogue record for this book is available from the Hong Kong Public Libraries.

Published in Hong Kong by Samurai Media Limited.

Email: info@samuraimedia.org

ISBN 978-988-8381-17-3

Contents

calibre is an ebook library manager. It can view, convert and catalog ebooks in most of the major ebook formats. It can also talk to many ebook reader devices. It can go out to the Internet and fetch metadata for your books. It can download newspapers and convert them into ebooks for convenient reading. It is cross platform, running on Linux, Windows and OS X.

You've just started calibre. What do you do now? Before calibre can do anything with your ebooks, it first has to know about them. Drag and drop a few ebook files into calibre, or click the "Add books" button and browse for the ebooks you want to work with. Once you've added the books, they will show up in the main view looking something like this:

110	The Trouble With Physics	Lee Smolin	18 Mar 2011	0.9	★★★★★
111	The Wise Man's Fear	Patrick Rothfuss	08 Mar 2011	1.4	★★★★
112	The Heroes	Joe Abercrombie	08 Mar 2011	1.2	★★★

Once you've admired the list of books you just added to your heart's content, you'll probably want to read one. In order to do that you'll have to convert the book to a format your reader understands. When first running calibre, the Welcome Wizard starts and will set up calibre for your reader device. Conversion is a breeze. Just select the book you want to convert then click the "Convert books" button. Ignore all the options for now and click "OK". The little icon in the bottom right corner will start spinning. Once it's finished spinning, your converted book is ready. Click the "View" button to read the book.

If you want to read the book on your reader, connect it to the computer, wait till calibre detects it (10-20 seconds) and then click the "Send to device" button. Once the icon stops spinning again, disconnect your reader and read away! If you didn't convert the book in the previous step, calibre will auto convert it to the format your reader device understands.

To get started with more advanced usage, you should read about The Graphical User Interface (page 3). For even more power and versatility, learn the Command Line Interface (page 271). You will find the list of Frequently Asked Questions (page 104) useful as well.

Contents 1

Contents

Sections

1.1 The Graphical User Interface

The Graphical User Interface *(GUI)* provides access to all library management and ebook format conversion features. The basic workflow for using calibre is to first add books to the library from your hard disk. calibre will automatically try to read metadata from the books and add them to its internal database. Once they are in the database, you can perform various *Actions* (page 3) on them that include conversion from one format to another, transfer to the reading device, viewing on your computer, and editing metadata. The latter includes modifying the cover, description, and tags among other details. Note that calibre creates copies of the files you add to it. Your original files are left untouched.

The interface is divided into various sections:

- *Actions* (page 3)
- *Preferences* (page 10)
- *Catalogs* (page 10)
- *Search & Sort* (page 11)
- *The Search Interface* (page 11)
- *Saving searches* (page 13)
- *Virtual Libraries* (page 15)
- *Guessing metadata from file names* (page 15)
- *Book Details* (page 16)
- *Tag Browser* (page 18)
- *Cover Grid* (page 20)
- *Cover Browser* (page 21)
- *Quickview* (page 21)
- *Jobs* (page 22)
- *Keyboard Shortcuts* (page 22)

1.1.1 Actions

The actions toolbar provides convenient shortcuts to commonly used actions. If you right-click the buttons, you can perform variations on the default action. Please note that the actions toolbar will look slightly different depending on whether you have an ebook reader attached to your computer.

Add books

The *Add books* action has seven variations accessed by doing a right-click on the button.

1. **Add books from a single directory**: Opens a file chooser dialog and allows you to specify which books in a directory should be added. This action is *context sensitive*, i.e. it depends on which *catalog* (page 10) you have selected. If you have selected the *Library*, books will be added to the library. If you have selected the ebook reader device, the books will be uploaded to the device, and so on.

2. **Add books from directories, including sub-directories (One book per directory, assumes every ebook file is the same book in a different format)**: Allows you to choose a directory. The directory and all its sub-directories are scanned recursively, and any ebooks found are added to the library. calibre assumes that each directory contains a single book. All ebook files in a directory are assumed to be the same book in different formats. This action is the inverse of the *Save to disk* (page 8) action, i.e. you can *Save to disk*, delete the books and re-add them with no lost information except for the date (this assumes you have not changed any of the setting for the Save to disk action).

3. **Add books from directories, including sub-directories (Multiple books per directory, assumes every ebook file is a different book)**: Allows you to choose a directory. The directory and all its sub-directories are scanned recursively and any ebooks found are added to the library. calibre assumes that each directory contains many books. All ebook files with the same name in a directory are assumed to be the same book in different formats. Ebooks with different names are added as different books.

4. **Add multiple books from archive (ZIP/RAR)**: Allows you to add multiple ebooks that are stored inside the selected ZIP or RAR files. It is a convenient shortcut that avoids having to first unzip the archive and then add the books via one of the above two options.

5. **Add empty book. (Book Entry with no formats)**: Allows you to create a blank book record. This can be used to then manually fill out the information about a book that you may not have yet in your collection.

6. **Add from ISBN**: Allows you to add one or more books by entering their ISBNs.

7. **Add files to selected book records**: Allows you to add or update the files associated with an existing book in your library.

The *Add books* action can read metadata from a wide variety of ebook formats. In addition, it tries to guess metadata from the filename. See the *Guessing metadata from file names* (page 15) section, to learn how to configure this.

To add an additional format for an existing book you can do any of three things:

1. Drag and drop the file onto the book details panel on the right side of the main window

2. Right click the Add books button and choose *Add files to selected books*.

3. Click the red add books button in the top right area of the *Edit Metadata* dialog, accessed by the *Edit metadata* (page 5) action.

Edit metadata

 The *Edit metadata* action has four variations which can be accessed by doing a right-click on the button.

1. **Edit metadata individually**: Allows you to edit the metadata of books one-by-one with the option of fetching metadata, including covers, from the Internet. It also allows you to add or remove particular ebook formats from a book.

2. **Edit metadata in bulk**: Allows you to edit common metadata fields for large numbers of books simultaneously. It operates on all the books you have selected in the *Library view* (page 11).

3. **Download metadata and covers**: Downloads metadata and covers (if available) for the books that are selected in the book list.

4. **Merge book records**: Gives you the capability of merging the metadata and formats of two or more book records. You can choose to either delete or keep the records that were not clicked first.

For more details see *Editing Ebook Metadata* (page 101).

Convert books

 Ebooks can be converted from a number of formats into whatever format your ebook reader prefers. Many ebooks available for purchase will be protected by Digital Rights Management[1] *(DRM)* technology. calibre will not convert these ebooks. It is easy to remove the DRM from many formats, but as this may be illegal, you will have to find tools to liberate your books yourself and then use calibre to convert them.

For most people, conversion should be a simple one-click affair. If you want to learn more about the conversion process, see *Ebook Conversion* (page 54).

The *Convert books* action has three variations, accessed by doing a right-click on the button.

1. **Convert individually**: Allows you to specify conversion options to customize the conversion of each selected ebook.

2. **Bulk convert**: Allows you to specify options only once to convert a number of ebooks in bulk.

---

[1] http://drmfree.calibre-ebook.com/about#drm

3. **Create a catalog of the books in your calibre library**: Allows you to generate a complete listing of the books in your library, including all metadata, in several formats such as XML, CSV, BiBTeX, EPUB and MOBI. The catalog will contain all the books currently showing in the library view. This allows you to use the search features to limit the books to be catalogued. In addition, if you select multiple books using the mouse, only those books will be added to the catalog. If you generate the catalog in an ebook format such as EPUB, MOBI or AZW3, the next time you connect your ebook reader the catalog will be automatically sent to the device. For more information on how catalogs work, read the *Creating AZW3 • EPUB • MOBI Catalogs* (page 230).

View

 The *View* action displays the book in an ebook viewer program. calibre has a built-in viewer for many ebook formats. For other formats it uses the default operating system application. You can configure which formats should open with the internal viewer via Preferences->Behavior. If a book has more than one format, you can view a particular format by doing a right-click on the button.

Send to device

The *Send to device* action has eight variations, accessed by doing a right-click on the button.

1. **Send to main memory**: The selected books are transferred to the main memory of the ebook reader.

2. **Send to card (A)**: The selected books are transferred to the storage card (A) on the ebook reader.

3. **Send to card (B)**: The selected books are transferred to the storage card (B) on the ebook reader.

4. **Send specific format to**: The selected books are transferred to the selected storage location on the device, in the format that you specify.

5. **Eject device**: Detaches the device from calibre.

6. **Set default send to device action**: Allows you to specify which of the options, 1 through 5 above or 7 below, will be the default action when you click the main button.

7. **Send and delete from library**: The selected books are transferred to the selected storage location on the device and then **deleted** from the Library.

8. **Fetch Annotations (experimental)**: Transfers annotations you may have made on an ebook on your device to the comments metadata of the book in the calibre library.

You can control the file name and folder structure of files sent to the device by setting up a template in *Preferences->Import/Export->Sending books to devices*. Also see *The calibre template language* (page 161).

Fetch news

The *Fetch news* action downloads news from various websites and converts it into an ebook that can be read on your ebook reader. Normally, the newly created ebook is added to your ebook library, but if an ebook reader is connected at the time the download finishes, the news is also uploaded to the reader automatically.

The *Fetch news* action uses simple recipes (10-15 lines of code) for each news site. To learn how to create recipes for your own news sources, see *Adding your favorite news website* (page 125).

The *Fetch news* action has three variations, accessed by doing a right-click on the button.

1. **Schedule news download**: Allows you to schedule the download of of your selected news sources from a list of hundreds available. Scheduling can be set individually for each news source you select and the scheduling is flexible allowing you to select specific days of the week or a frequency of days between downloads.

2. **Add a custom news source**: Allows you to create a simple recipe for downloading news from a custom news site that you wish to access. Creating the recipe can be as simple as specifying an RSS news feed URL, or you can be more prescriptive by creating Python-based code for the task. For more information see *Adding your favorite news website* (page 125).

3. **Download all scheduled news sources**: Causes calibre to immediately begin downloading all news sources that you have scheduled.

Library

The *Library* action allows you to create, switch between, rename or remove a Library. calibre allows you to create as many libraries as you wish. You could, for instance, create a fiction library, a non-fiction library, a foreign language library, a project library, or any structure that suits your needs. Libraries are the highest organizational structure within calibre. Each library has its own set of books, tags, categories and base storage location.

1. **Switch/create library...**: Allows you to; a) connect to a pre-existing calibre library at another location, b) create an empty library at a new location or, c) move the current library to a newly specified location.

2. **Quick switch**: Allows you to switch between libraries that have been registered or created within calibre.

3. **Rename library**: Allows you to rename a Library.

4. **Delete library**: Allows you to unregister a library from calibre.

5. **<library name>**: Actions 5, 6 etc... give you immediate switch access between multiple libraries that you have created or attached to. This list contains only the 5 most frequently used libraries. For the complete list, use the Quick Switch menu.

6. **Library maintenance**: Allows you to check the current library for data consistency issues and restore the current library's database from backups.

Note: Metadata about your ebooks, e.g. title, author, and tags, is stored in a single file in your calibre library folder called metadata.db. If this file gets corrupted (a very rare event), you can lose the metadata. Fortunately, calibre automatically backs up the metadata for every individual book in the book's folder as an OPF file. By using the Restore database action under Library Maintenance described above, you can have calibre rebuild the metadata.db file from the individual OPF files for you.

You can copy or move books between different libraries (once you have more than one library setup) by right clicking on the book and selecting the action *Copy to library*.

Device

The *Device* action allows you to view the books in the main memory or storage cards of your device, or to eject the device (detach it from calibre). This icon shows up automatically on the main calibre toolbar when you connect a supported device. You can click on it to see the books on your device. You can also drag and drop books from your calibre library onto the icon to transfer them to your device. Conversely, you can drag and drop books from your device onto the library icon on the toolbar to transfer books from your device to the calibre library.

Save to disk

The *Save to disk* action has five variations, accessed by doing a right-click on the button.

1. **Save to disk**: Saves the selected books to disk organized in directories. The directory structure looks like:

```
Author_(sort)
    Title
        Book Files
```

You can control the file name and folder structure of files saved to disk by setting up a template in *Preferences->Import/Export->Saving books to disk*. Also see *The calibre template language* (page 161).

2. **Save to disk in a single directory**: Saves the selected books to disk in a single directory.

For 1. and 2., all available formats, as well as metadata, are stored to disk for each selected book. Metadata is stored in an OPF file. Saved books can be re-imported to the library without any loss of information by using the *Add books* (page 4) action.

3. **Save only *<your preferred>* format to disk**: Saves the selected books to disk in the directory structure as shown in (1.) but only in your preferred ebook format. You can set your preferred format in *Preferences->Behaviour->Preferred output format*

4. **Save only *<your preferred>* format to disk in a single directory**: Saves the selected books to disk in a single directory but only in your preferred ebook format. You can set your preferred format in *Preferences->Behaviour->Preferred output format*

5. **Save single format to disk...**: Saves the selected books to disk in the directory structure as shown in (1.) but only in the format you select from the pop-out list.

Connect/Share

 The *Connect/Share* action allows you to manually connect to a device or folder on your computer. It also allows you to set up you calibre library for access via a web browser or email.

The *Connect/Share* action has four variations, accessed by doing a right-click on the button.

1. **Connect to folder**: Allows you to connect to any folder on your computer as though it were a device and use all the facilities calibre has for devices with that folder. Useful if your device cannot be supported by calibre but is available as a USB disk.

2. **Connect to iTunes**: Allows you to connect to your iTunes books database as though it were a device. Once the books are sent to iTunes, you can use iTunes to make them available to your various iDevices.

3. **Start Content Server**: Starts calibre's built-in web server. When started, your calibre library will be accessible via a web browser from the Internet (if you choose). You can configure how the web server is accessed by setting preferences at *Preferences->Sharing->Sharing over the net*

4. **Setup email based sharing of books**: Allows sharing of books and news feeds by email. After setting up email addresses for this option, calibre will send news updates and book updates to the entered email addresses. You can configure how calibre sends email by setting preferences at *Preferences->Sharing->Sharing books by email*. Once you have set up one or more email addresses, this menu entry will be replaced by menu entries to send books to the configured email addresses.

Remove books

The *Remove books* action **deletes books permanently**, so use it with care. It is *context sensitive*, i.e. it depends on which *catalog* (page 10) you have selected. If you have selected the *Library*, books will be removed from the library. If you have selected the ebook reader device, books will be removed from the device. To remove only a particular format for a given book use the *Edit metadata* (page 5) action. Remove books also has five variations which can be accessed by doing a right-click on the button.

1. **Remove selected books**: Allows you to **permanently** remove all books that are selected in the book list.

2. **Remove files of a specific format from selected books...**: Allows you to **permanently** remove ebook files of a specified format from books that are selected in the book list.

3. **Remove all formats from selected books, except...**: Allows you to **permanently** remove ebook files of any format except a specified format from books that are selected in the book list.

4. **Remove all formats from selected books**: Allows you to **permanently** remove all ebook files from books that are selected in the book list. Only the metadata will remain.

5. **Remove covers from selected books**: Allows you to **permanently** remove cover image files from books that are selected in the book list.

6. **Remove matching books from device**: Allows you to remove ebook files from a connected device that match the books that are selected in the book list.

Note: Note that when you use Remove books to delete books from your calibre library, the book record is permanently deleted, but on Windows and OS X the files are placed into the recycle bin. This allows you to recover them if you change your mind.

1.1.2 Preferences

 The *Preferences* action allows you to change the way various aspects of calibre work. It has four variations, accessed by doing a right-click on the button.

1. **Preferences**: Allows you to change the way various aspects of calibre work. Clicking the button also performs this action.

2. **Run welcome wizard**: Allows you to start the Welcome Wizard which appeared the first time you started calibre.

3. **Get plugins to enhance calibre**: Opens a new windows that shows plugins for calibre. These plugins are developed by third parties to extend calibre's functionality.

4. **Restart in debug mode**: Allows you to enable a debugging mode that can assist the calibre developers in solving problems you encounter with the program. For most users this should remain disabled unless instructed by a developer to enable it.

1.1.3 Catalogs

A *catalog* is a collection of books. calibre can manage two types of different catalogs:

1. **Library**: This is a collection of books stored in your calibre library on your computer.

2. **Device**: This is a collection of books stored in your ebook reader. It will be available when you connect the reader to your computer.

Many operations, such as adding books, deleting, viewing, etc., are context sensitive. So, for example, if you click the View button when you have the **Device** catalog selected, calibre will open the files on the device to view. If you have the **Library** catalog selected, files in your calibre library will be opened instead.

1.1.4 Search & Sort

The Search & Sort section allows you to perform several powerful actions on your book collections.

- You can sort them by title, author, date, rating, etc. by clicking on the column titles. You can also sub-sort, i.e. sort on multiple columns. For example, if you click on the title column and then the author column, the book will be sorted by author and then all the entries for the same author will be sorted by title.

- You can search for a particular book or set of books using the search bar. More on that below.

- You can quickly and conveniently edit metadata by double-clicking the entry you want changed in the list.

- You can perform *Actions* (page 3) on sets to books. To select multiple books you can either:

  – Keep the `Ctrl` key pressed and click on the books you want selected.

  – Keep the `Shift` key pressed and click on the starting and ending book of a range of books you want selected.

- You can configure which fields you want displayed by using the *Preferences* (page 10) dialog.

1.1.5 The Search Interface

You can search all the metadata by entering search terms in the search bar. Searches are case insensitive. For example:

```
Asimov Foundation format:lrf
```

This will match all books in your library that have `Asimov` and `Foundation` in their metadata and are available in the LRF format. Some more examples:

```
author:Asimov and not series:Foundation
title:"The Ring" or "This book is about a ring"
format:epub publisher:feedbooks.com
```

Searches are by default 'contains'. An item matches if the search string appears anywhere in the indicated metadata. Two other kinds of searches are available: equality search and search using regular expressions[2].

---

[2]http://en.wikipedia.org/wiki/Regular_expression

Equality searches are indicated by prefixing the search string with an equals sign (=). For example, the query `tag:"=science"` will match "science", but not "science fiction" or "hard science". Regular expression searches are indicated by prefixing the search string with a tilde (~). Any python-compatible regular expression[3] can be used. Note that backslashes used to escape special characters in regular expressions must be doubled because single backslashes will be removed during query parsing. For example, to match a literal parenthesis you must enter `\ \ (`. Regular expression searches are 'contains' searches unless the expression contains anchors.

Should you need to search for a string with a leading equals or tilde, prefix the string with a backslash.

Enclose search strings with quotes (") if the string contains parenthesis or spaces. For example, to search for the tag `Science Fiction` you would need to search for `tag:"=science fiction"`. If you search for `tag:=science fiction` you will find all books with the tag 'science' and containing the word 'fiction' in any metadata.

You can build advanced search queries easily using the *Advanced Search Dialog* accessed by clicking the button

 .

Available fields for searching are: `tag`, `title`, `author`, `publisher`, `series`, `series_index`, `rating`, `cover`, `comments`, `format`, `identifiers`, `date`, `pubdate`, `search`, `size` and custom columns. If a device is plugged in, the `ondevice` field becomes available, when searching the calibre library view. To find the search name (actually called the *lookup name*) for a custom column, hover your mouse over the column header in the library view.

The syntax for searching for dates is:

```
pubdate:>2000-1 Will find all books published after Jan, 2000
date:<=2000-1-3 Will find all books added to calibre before 3 Jan, 2000
pubdate:=2009 Will find all books published in 2009
```

If the date is ambiguous, the current locale is used for date comparison. For example, in an mm/dd/yyyy locale 2/1/2009 is interpreted as 1 Feb 2009. In a dd/mm/yyyy locale it is interpreted as 2 Jan 2009. Some special date strings are available. The string `today` translates to today's date, whatever it is. The strings `yesterday` and `thismonth` (or the translated equivalent in the current language) also work. In addition, the string `daysago` (also translated) can be used to compare to a date some number of days ago. For example:

```
date:>10daysago
date:<=45daysago
```

To avoid potential problems with translated strings when using a non-English version of calibre, the strings `_today`, `_yesterday`, `_thismonth`, and `_daysago` are always available. They are not translated.

You can search for books that have a format of a certain size like this:

```
size:>1.1M Will find books with a format larger than 1.1MB
size:<=1K  Will find books with a format smaller than 1KB
```

Dates and numeric fields support the relational operators = (equals), > (greater than), >= (greater than or equal to), < (less than), <= (less than or equal to), and ! = (not equal to). Rating fields are considered to be numeric. For example, the search `rating:>=3` will find all books rated 3 or higher.

You can search for the number of items in multiple-valued fields such as tags. These searches begin with the character #, then use the same syntax as numeric fields. For example, to find all books with more than 4 tags use `tags:#>4`. To find all books with exactly 10 tags use `tags:#=10`.

Series indices are searchable. For the standard series, the search name is 'series_index'. For custom series columns, use the column search name followed by _index. For example, to search the indices for a custom series column named

---

[3] https://docs.python.org/2/library/re.html

#my_series, you would use the search name #my_series_index. Series indices are numbers, so you can use the relational operators described above.

The special field search is used for saved searches. So if you save a search with the name "My spouse's books" you can enter search:"My spouse's books" in the search bar to reuse the saved search. More about saving searches below.

You can search for the absence or presence of a field using the special "true" and "false" values. For example:

```
cover:false will give you all books without a cover
series:true will give you all books that belong to a series
comments:false will give you all books with an empty comment
format:false will give you all books with no actual files (empty records)
```

Yes/no custom columns are searchable. Searching for false, empty, or blank will find all books with undefined values in the column. Searching for true will find all books that do not have undefined values in the column. Searching for yes or checked will find all books with Yes in the column. Searching for no or unchecked will find all books with No in the column. Note that the words yes, no, blank, empty, checked and unchecked are translated; you can use either the current language's equivalent word or the English word. The words true and false and the special values _yes, _no, and _empty are not translated.

Hierarchical items (e.g. A.B.C) use an extended syntax to match initial parts of the hierarchy. This is done by adding a period between the exact match indicator (=) and the text. For example, the query tags:=.A will find the tags A and A.B, but will not find the tags AA or AA.B. The query tags:=.A.B will find the tags A.B and A.B.C, but not the tag A.

Identifiers (e.g., isbn, doi, lccn etc) also use an extended syntax. First, note that an identifier has the form type:value, as in isbn:123456789. The extended syntax permits you to specify independently which type and value to search for. Both the type and the value parts of the query can use *equality*, *contains*, or *regular expression* matches. Examples:

- identifiers:true will find books with any identifier.
- identifiers:false will find books with no identifier.
- identifiers:123 will search for books with any type having a value containing *123*.
- identifiers:=123456789 will search for books with any type having a value equal to *123456789*.
- identifiers:=isbn: and identifiers:isbn:true will find books with a type equal to isbn having any value
- identifiers:=isbn:false will find books with no type equal to isbn.
- identifiers:=isbn:123 will find books with a type equal to isbn having a value containing *123*.
- identifiers:=isbn:=123456789 will find books with a type equal to isbn having a value equal to *123456789*.
- identifiers:i:1 will find books with a type containing an *i* having a value containing a *1*.

1.1.6 Saving searches

calibre allows you to save a frequently used search under a special name and then reuse that search with a single click. To do this, create your search either by typing it in the search bar or using the Tag Browser. Then type the name you would like to give to the search in the Saved Searches box next to the search bar. Click the plus icon next to the saved searches box to save the search.

Now you can access your saved search in the Tag Browser under "Searches". A single click will allow you to reuse any arbitrarily complex search easily, without needing to re-create it.

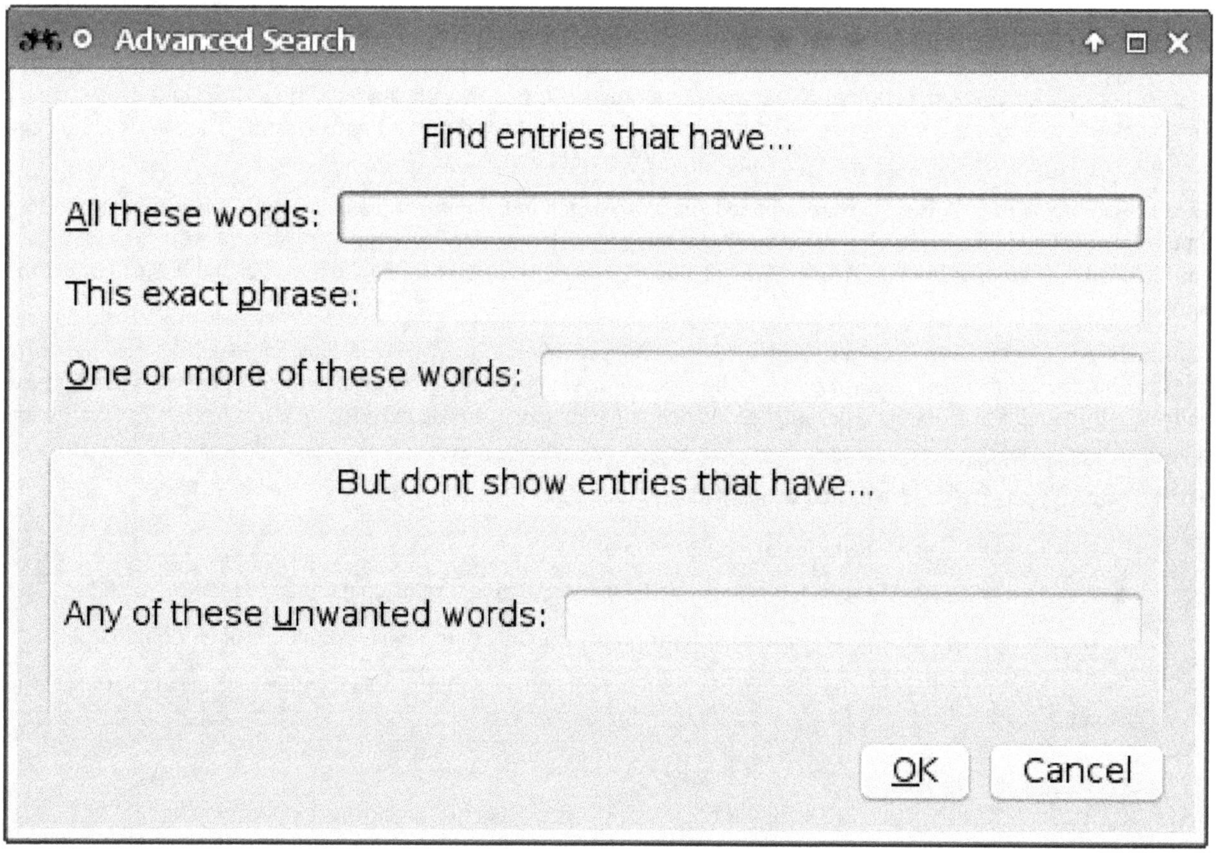

Fig. 1.1: *Advanced Search Dialog*

1.1.7 Virtual Libraries

A *Virtual Library* is a way to pretend that your calibre library has only a few books instead of its full collection. This is an excellent way to partition your large collection of books into smaller, manageable chunks. To learn how to create and use virtual libraries, see the tutorial: *Virtual Libraries* (page 234).

1.1.8 Guessing metadata from file names

Normally, calibre reads metadata from inside the book file. However, it can be configured to read metadata from the file name instead, via *Preferences->Adding Books->Read metadata from file contents*.

You can also control how metadata is read from the filename using regular expressions (see All about using regular expressions in calibre (page 205)). In the *Adding Books* section of the configuration dialog, you can specify a regular expression that calibre will use to try and guess metadata from the names of ebook files that you add to the library. The default regular expression is:

```
title - author
```

that is, it assumes that all characters up to the first − are the title of the book and subsequent characters are the author of the book. For example, the filename:

```
Foundation and Earth - Isaac Asimov.txt
```

will be interpreted to have the title: Foundation and Earth and author: Isaac Asimov

Tip: If the filename does not contain the hyphen, the above regular expression will fail.

1.1.9 Book Details

Authors: Oscar Wilde

Formats: EPUB

Ids: 9781580495806

Tags: lit 101 homework

Path: Click to open

SUMMARY:
This Prestwick House Literary
Touchstone Edition includes a
glossary and reader's notes to help
the modern reader appreciate
Wilde's wry wit and elaborate plot
twists. Oscar Wilde's madcap farce
about mistaken identities, secret
engagements, and lovers?
entanglements still delights readers

The Book Details display shows the cover and all the metadata for the currently selected book. It can be hidden via the button in the lower right corner of the main calibre window. The author names shown in the Book Detail panel are clickable, they will by default take you to the Wikipedia page for the author. This can be customized by right clicking on the author name and selecting Manage this author.

Similarly, if you download metadata for the book, the Book details panel will automatically show you links pointing to the web pages for the book on amazon, worldcat, etc. from where the metadata was downloaded.

You can right click on individual ebook formats in the Book Details panel to delete them, compare them to their original versions, save them to disk, open them with an external program, etc.

You can change the cover of the book by simply drag and dropping an image onto the book details panel. If you wish to edit the cover image in an external program, simply right click on it and choose *Open With*.

You can also add ebook files to the current book by drag and dropping the files onto the book details panel.

Double clicking the book details panel will open it up in a separate popup window.

Finally, you can customize exactly what information is displayed in the Book Details panel via *Preferences->Look & Feel->Book Details*.

1.1.10 Tag Browser

The Tag Browser allows you to easily browse your collection by Author/Tags/Series/etc. If you click on any item in the Tag Browser, for example the author name Isaac Asimov, then the list of books to the right is restricted to showing books by that author. You can click on category names as well. For example, clicking on "Series" will show you all books in any series.

The first click on an item will restrict the list of books to those that contain or match the item. Continuing the above example, clicking on Isaac Asimov will show books by that author. Clicking again on the item will change what is shown, depending on whether the item has children (see sub-categories and hierarchical items below). Continuing the Isaac Asimov example, clicking again on Isaac Asimov will restrict the list of books to those not by Isaac Asimov. A third click will remove the restriction, showing all books. If you hold down the Ctrl or Shift keys and click on multiple items, then restrictions based on multiple items are created. For example you could hold Ctrl and click on the tags History and Europe for finding books on European history. The Tag Browser works by constructing search expressions that are automatically entered into the Search bar. Looking at what the Tag Browser generates is a good way to learn how to construct basic search expressions.

Items in the Tag browser have their icons partially colored. The amount of color depends on the average rating of the books in that category. So for example if the books by Isaac Asimov have an average of four stars, the icon for Isaac Asimov in the Tag Browser will be 4/5th colored. You can hover your mouse over the icon to see the average rating.

The outer-level items in the tag browser, such as Authors and Series, are called categories. You can create your own categories, called User Categories, which are useful for organizing items. For example, you can use the User Categories Editor (click *Alter Tag Browser->Manage authors, series, etc->Manage User Categories*) to create a user category called Favorite Authors, then put the items for your favorites into the category. User categories can have sub-categories. For example, the user category Favorites.Authors is a sub-category of Favorites. You might also have Favorites.Series, in which case there will be two sub-categories under Favorites. Sub-categories can be created by right-clicking on a user category, choosing "Add sub-category to ...", and entering the sub-category name; or by using the User Categories Editor by entering names like the Favorites example above.

You can search user categories in the same way as built-in categories, by clicking on them. There are four different sea

1. "everything matching an item in the category" indicated by a single green plus sign.

2. "everything matching an item in the category or its sub-categories" indicated by two green plus signs.

3. "everything not matching an item in the category" shown by a single red minus sign.

4. "everything not matching an item in the category or its sub-categories" shown by two red minus signs.

It is also possible to create hierarchies inside some of the text categories such as tags, series, and custom columns. These hierarchies show with the small triangle, permitting the sub-items to be hidden. To use hierarchies of items in a category, you must first go to Preferences->Look & Feel and enter the category name(s) into the "Categories with hierarchical items" box. Once this is done, items in that category that contain periods will be shown using the small triangle. For example, assume you create a custom column called "Genre" and indicate that it contains hierarchical items. Once done, items such as Mystery.Thriller and Mystery.English will display as Mystery with the small triangle next to it. Clicking on the triangle will show Thriller and English as sub-items. See *Managing subgroups of books, for example "genre"* (page 154) for more information.

Hierarchical items (items with children) use the same four 'click-on' searches as user categories. Items that do not have children use two of the searches: "everything matching" and "everything not matching".

You can drag and drop items in the Tag browser onto user categories to add them to that category. If the source is a user category, holding the shift key while dragging will move the item to the new category. You can also drag and drop books from the book list onto items in the Tag Browser; dropping a book on an item causes that item to be automatically applied to the dropped books. For example, dragging a book onto Isaac Asimov will set the author of that book to Isaac Asimov. Dropping it onto the tag History will add the tag History to the book's tags.

There is a search bar at the top of the Tag Browser that allows you to easily find any item in the Tag Browser. In addition, you can right click on any item and choose one of several operations. Some examples are to hide it, rename it, or open a "Manage x" dialog that allows you to manage items of that kind. For example, the "Manage Authors" dialog allows you to rename authors and control how their names are sorted.

You can control how items are sorted in the Tag browser via the *Alter Tag Browser* button at the bottom of the Tag Browser. You can choose to sort by name, average rating or popularity (popularity is the number of books with an item in your library; for example, the popularity of Isaac Asimov is the number of books in your library by Isaac Asimov).

1.1.11 Cover Grid

You can have calibre display a grid of book covers instead of a list of books, if you prefer to browse your collection by covers instead. The *Cover Grid* is activated by clicking the grid button in the bottom right corner of the main calibre window. You can customize the cover sizes and the background of the cover grid via *Preferences->Look & Feel->Cover Grid*. You can even have calibre display any specified field under the covers, such as title or authors or rating or a custom column of your own devising.

1.1.12 Cover Browser

In addition to the cover grid described above, you can also have calibre display covers in the single row. This is activated via a button in the lower right corner of the main window. In *Preferences->Look & Feel->Cover Browser* you can change the number of covers displayed, and even have the cover browser display itself in a separate popup window.

1.1.13 Quickview

Sometimes you want to select a book and quickly get a list of books with the same value in some category (authors, tags, publisher, series, etc) as the currently selected book, but without changing the current view of the library. You can do this with Quickview. Quickview opens a second window showing the list of books matching the value of interest.

For example, assume you want to see a list of all the books with the same author of the currently-selected book. Click in the author cell you are interested in and press the 'Q' key. A window will open with all the authors for that book on the left, and all the books by the selected author on the right.

Some example Quickview usages: quickly seeing what other books:

- have some tag that is applied to the currently selected book,

- are in the same series as the current book

- have the same values in a custom column as the current book

- are written by one of the same authors of the current book

without changing the contents of the library view.

The Quickview window opens on top of the calibre window and will stay open until you explicitly close it. You can use Quickview and the calibre library view at the same time. For example, if in the calibre library view you click on a category column (tags, series, publisher, authors, etc) for a book, the Quickview window contents will change to show you in the left-hand side pane the items in that category for the selected book (e.g., the tags for that book). The first item in that list will be selected, and Quickview will show you on the right-hand side pane all the books in your library that reference that item. Click on an different item in the left-hand pane to see the books with that different item.

Double-click on a book in the Quickview window to select that book in the library view. This will also change the items display in the QuickView window(the left-hand pane) to show the items in the newly-selected book.

Shift- (or Ctrl-) double-click on a book in the Quickview window to open the edit metadata dialog on that book in the calibre window.

You can see if a column can be Quickview'ed by hovering your mouse over the column heading and looking at the tooltip for that heading. You can also know by right-clicking on the column heading to see of the "Quickview" option is shown in the menu, in which case choosing that Quickview option is equivalent to pressing 'Q' in the current cell.

Quickview respects the virtual library setting, showing only books in the current virtual library.

1.1.14 Jobs

The Jobs panel shows the number of currently running jobs. Jobs are tasks that run in a separate process. They include converting ebooks and talking to your reader device. You can click on the jobs panel to access the list of jobs. Once a job has completed you can see a detailed log from that job by double-clicking it in the list. This is useful to debug jobs that may not have completed successfully.

1.1.15 Keyboard Shortcuts

Calibre has several keyboard shortcuts to save you time and mouse movement. These shortcuts are active in the book list view (when you're not editing the details of a particular book), and most of them affect the title you have selected. The calibre ebook viewer has its own shortcuts which can be customised by clicking the Preferences button in the viewer.

Note: Note: The Calibre keyboard shortcuts do not require a modifier key (Command, Option, Control, etc.), unless specifically noted. You only need to press the letter key, e.g. E to edit.

Table 1.1: Keyboard Shortcuts

Keyboard Shortcut	Action
F2 (Enter in OS X)	Edit the metadata of the currently selected field in the book list.
A	Add Books
Shift+A	Add Formats to the selected books
C	Convert selected Books
D	Send to device
Del	Remove selected Books
E	Edit metadata of selected books
G	Get Books
I	Show book details
K	Edit Table of Contents
M	Merge selected records
Alt+M	Merge selected records, keeping originals
O	Open containing folder
P	Polish books
S	Save to Disk
T	Edit Book
V	View
Alt+V/Cmd+V in OS X	View specific format
Alt+Shift+J	Toggle jobs list

Table 1.1 – continued from previous page

Keyboard Shortcut	Action
Alt+Shift+B	Toggle Cover Browser
Alt+Shift+D	Toggle Book Details panel
Alt+Shift+T	Toggle Tag Browser
Alt+Shift+G	Toggle Cover Grid
Alt+A	Show books by the same author as the current book
Alt+T	Show books with the same tags as current book
Alt+P	Show books by the same publisher as current book
Alt+Shift+S	Show books in the same series as current book
/, Ctrl+F	Focus the search bar
Shift+Ctrl+F	Open the advanced search dialog
Esc	Clear the current search
Shift+Esc	Focus the book list
Ctrl+Esc	Clear the virtual library
Alt+Esc	Clear the additional restriction
Ctrl+*	Create a temporary virtual library based on the current search
Ctrl+Right	Select the next virtual library tab
Ctrl+Left	Select the previous virtual library tab
N or F3	Find the next book that matches the current search (only works if search highlighting is turne
Shift+N or Shift+F3	Find the previous book that matches the current search (only works if search highlighting is t
Ctrl+D	Download metadata and covers
Ctrl+R	Restart calibre
Ctrl+Shift+R	Restart calibre in debug mode
Shift+Ctrl+E	Add empty books to calibre
Ctrl+M	Toggle Mark/unmarked status on selected books
Q	Open the Quick View popup for viewing books in related series/tags/etc.
Shift+Q	Focus the opened Quick View panel
Shift+S	Perform a search in the Quick View panel
Ctrl+Q	Quit calibre

1.2 Adding your favorite news website

calibre has a powerful, flexible and easy-to-use framework for downloading news from the Internet and converting it into an ebook. The following will show you, by means of examples, how to get news from various websites.

To gain an understanding of how to use the framework, follow the examples in the order listed below:

1.2.1 Completely automatic fetching

If your news source is simple enough, calibre may well be able to fetch it completely automatically, all you need to do is provide the URL. calibre gathers all the information needed to download a news source into a *recipe*. In order to tell calibre about a news source, you have to create a *recipe* for it. Let's see some examples:

The calibre blog

The calibre blog is a blog of posts that describe many useful calibre features in a simple and accessible way for new calibre users. In order to download this blog into an ebook, we rely on the *RSS* feed of the blog:

```
http://blog.calibre-ebook.com/feeds/posts/default
```

I got the RSS URL by looking under "Subscribe to" at the bottom of the blog page and choosing *Posts->Atom*. To make calibre download the feeds and convert them into an ebook, you should right click the *Fetch news* button and then the *Add a custom news source* menu item and then the *New Recipe* button. A dialog similar to that shown below should open up.

First enter `calibre Blog` into the *Recipe title* field. This will be the title of the ebook that will be created from the articles in the above feeds.

The next two fields (*Oldest article* and *Max. number of articles*) allow you some control over how many articles should be downloaded from each feed, and they are pretty self explanatory.

To add the feeds to the recipe, enter the feed title and the feed URL and click the *Add feed* button. Once you have added the feed, simply click the *Save* button and you're done! Close the dialog.

To test your new *recipe*, click the *Fetch news* button and in the *Custom news sources* sub-menu click *calibre Blog*. After a couple of minutes, the newly downloaded ebook of blog posts will appear in the main library view (if you have your reader connected, it will be put onto the reader instead of into the library). Select it and hit the *View* button to read!

The reason this worked so well, with so little effort is that the blog provides *full-content RSS* feeds, i.e., the article content is embedded in the feed itself. For most news sources that provide news in this fashion, with *full-content* feeds, you don't need any more effort to convert them to ebooks. Now we will look at a news source that does not provide full content feeds. In such feeds, the full article is a webpage and the feed only contains a link to the webpage with a short summary of the article.

bbc.co.uk

Lets try the following two feeds from *The BBC*:

1. News Front Page: http://newsrss.bbc.co.uk/rss/newsonline_world_edition/front_page/rss.xml

2. Science/Nature: http://newsrss.bbc.co.uk/rss/newsonline_world_edition/science/nature/rss.xml

Follow the procedure outlined in *The calibre blog* (page 126) above to create a recipe for *The BBC* (using the feeds above). Looking at the downloaded ebook, we see that calibre has done a creditable job of extracting only the content you care about from each article's webpage. However, the extraction process is not perfect. Sometimes it leaves in undesirable content like menus and navigation aids or it removes content that should have been left alone, like article headings. In order, to have perfect content extraction, we will need to customize the fetch process, as described in the next section.

1.2.2 Customizing the fetch process

When you want to perfect the download process, or download content from a particularly complex website, you can avail yourself of all the power and flexibility of the *recipe* framework. In order to do that, in the *Add custom news sources* dialog, simply click the *Switch to Advanced mode* button.

The easiest and often most productive customization is to use the print version of the online articles. The print version typically has much less cruft and translates much more smoothly to an ebook. Let's try to use the print version of the articles from *The BBC*.

Using the print version of bbc.co.uk

The first step is to look at the ebook we downloaded previously from *bbc.co.uk* (page 128). At the end of each article, in the ebook is a little blurb telling you where the article was downloaded from. Copy and paste that URL into a browser. Now on the article webpage look for a link that points to the "Printable version". Click it to see the print version of the article. It looks much neater! Now compare the two URLs. For me they were:

Article URL http://news.bbc.co.uk/2/hi/science/nature/7312016.stm

Print version URL http://newsvote.bbc.co.uk/mpapps/pagetools/print/news.bbc.co.uk/2/hi/science/nature/7312016.stm

So it looks like to get the print version, we need to prefix every article URL with:

newsvote.bbc.co.uk/mpapps/pagetools/print/

Now in the *Advanced Mode* of the Custom news sources dialog, you should see something like (remember to select *The BBC* recipe before switching to advanced mode):

```
Recipe source code (python)

class AdvancedUserRecipe1206418393(BasicNewsRecipe):
    title           = u'The BBC'
    oldest_article = 7
    max_articles_per_feed = 100

    feeds           = [(u'News Front Page', u'http://newsrss.bbc.co.uk/rss/newsonli
```

You can see that the fields from the *Basic mode* have been translated to python code in a straightforward manner. We need to add instructions to this recipe to use the print version of the articles. All that's needed is to add the following two lines:

```
def print_version(self, url):
    return url.replace('http://', 'http://newsvote.bbc.co.uk/mpapps/pagetools/print/')
```

This is python, so indentation is important. After you've added the lines, it should look like:

```
Recipe source code (python)

class AdvancedUserRecipe1206418393(BasicNewsRecipe):
    title           = u'The BBC'
    oldest_article = 7
    max_articles_per_feed = 100

    feeds           = [(u'News Front Page', u'http://newsrss.bbc.co.uk/rss/newsonli

    def print_version(self, url):
        return url.replace('http://', 'http://newsvote.bbc.co.uk/mpapps/pagetools/p
```

In the above, `def print_version(self, url)` defines a *method* that is called by calibre for every article. `url` is the URL of the original article. What `print_version` does is take that url and replace it with the new URL that points to the print version of the article. To learn about python[4] see the tutorial[5].

Now, click the *Add/update recipe* button and your changes will be saved. Re-download the ebook. You should have a much improved ebook. One of the problems with the new version is that the fonts on the print version webpage are too small. This is automatically fixed when converting to an ebook, but even after the fixing process, the font size of the menus and navigation bar to become too large relative to the article text. To fix this, we will do some more customization, in the next section.

Replacing article styles

In the previous section, we saw that the font size for articles from the print version of *The BBC* was too small. In most websites, *The BBC* included, this font size is set by means of *CSS* stylesheets. We can disable the fetching of such

---

[4]https://www.python.org
[5]https://docs.python.org/2/tutorial/

stylesheets by adding the line:

```
no_stylesheets = True
```

The recipe now looks like:

```
Recipe source code (python)

class AdvancedUserRecipe1206419520(BasicNewsRecipe):
    title          = u'The BBC'
    oldest_article = 7
    max_articles_per_feed = 100
    no_stylesheets = True

    feeds          = [(u'News Front Page', u'http://newsrss.bbc.co.uk/rss/newsonli

    def print_version(self, url):
        return url.replace('http://', 'http://newsvote.bbc.co.uk/mpapps/pagetools/
```

The new version looks pretty good. If you're a perfectionist, you'll want to read the next section, which deals with actually modifying the downloaded content.

Slicing and dicing

calibre contains very powerful and flexible abilities when it comes to manipulating downloaded content. To show off a couple of these, let's look at our old friend the *The BBC* (page 129) recipe again. Looking at the source code (*HTML*) of a couple of articles (print version), we see that they have a footer that contains no useful information, contained in

```
<div class="footer">
...
</div>
```

This can be removed by adding:

```
remove_tags    = [dict(name='div', attrs={'class':'footer'})]
```

to the recipe. Finally, lets replace some of the *CSS* that we disabled earlier, with our own *CSS* that is suitable for conversion to an ebook:

```
extra_css      = '.headline {font-size: x-large;} \n .fact { padding-top: 10pt   }'
```

With these additions, our recipe has become "production quality", indeed it is very close to the actual recipe used by calibre for the *BBC*, shown below:

```
##
## Title:       BBC News, Sport, and Blog Calibre Recipe
## Contact:     mattst - jmstanfield@gmail.com
##
## License:     GNU General Public License v3 - http://www.gnu.org/copyleft/gpl.html
## Copyright:   mattst - jmstanfield@gmail.com
##
## Written:     November 2011
## Last Edited: 2011-11-19
##

__license__    = 'GNU General Public License v3 - http://www.gnu.org/copyleft/gpl.html
```

```
__copyright__    = 'mattst - jmstanfield@gmail.com'


'''
BBC News, Sport, and Blog Calibre Recipe
'''

# Import the regular expressions module.
import re

# Import the BasicNewsRecipe class which this class extends.
from calibre.web.feeds.recipes import BasicNewsRecipe

class BBCNewsSportBlog(BasicNewsRecipe):

    #
    #     **** IMPORTANT USERS READ ME ****
    #
    #  First select the feeds you want then scroll down below the feeds list
    #  and select the values you want for the other user preferences, like
    #  oldest_article and such like.
    #
    #
    #  Select the BBC rss feeds which you want in your ebook.
    #  Selected feed have NO '#' at their start, de-selected feeds begin with a '#'.
    #
    #  Eg.  ("News Home", "http://feeds.bbci.co.uk/... - include feed.
    #  Eg. #("News Home", "http://feeds.bbci.co.uk/... - do not include feed.
    #
    # There are 68 feeds below which constitute the bulk of the available rss
    # feeds on the BBC web site. These include 5 blogs by editors and
    # correspondants, 16 sports feeds, 15 'sub' regional feeds (Eg. North West
    # Wales, Scotland Business), and 7 Welsh language feeds.
    #
    # Some of the feeds are low volume (Eg. blogs), or very low volume (Eg. Click)
    # so if "oldest_article = 1.5" (only articles published in the last 36 hours)
    # you may get some 'empty feeds' which will not then be included in the ebook.
    #
    # The 15 feeds currently selected below are simply my default ones.
    #
    # Note: With all 68 feeds selected, oldest_article set to 2,
    # max_articles_per_feed set to 100, and simultaneous_downloads set to 10,
    # the ebook creation took 29 minutes on my speedy 100 mbps net connection,
    # fairly high-end desktop PC running Linux (Ubuntu Lucid-Lynx).
    # More realistically with 15 feeds selected, oldest_article set to 1.5,
    # max_articles_per_feed set to 100, and simultaneous_downloads set to 20,
    # it took 6 minutes. If that's too slow increase 'simultaneous_downloads'.
    #
    # Select / de-select the feeds you want in your ebook.
    #
    feeds = [
             ("News Home", "http://feeds.bbci.co.uk/news/rss.xml"),
             ("UK", "http://feeds.bbci.co.uk/news/uk/rss.xml"),
             ("World", "http://feeds.bbci.co.uk/news/world/rss.xml"),
             #("England", "http://feeds.bbci.co.uk/news/england/rss.xml"),
             #("Scotland", "http://feeds.bbci.co.uk/news/scotland/rss.xml"),
             #("Wales", "http://feeds.bbci.co.uk/news/wales/rss.xml"),
             #("N. Ireland", "http://feeds.bbci.co.uk/news/northern_ireland/rss.xml"),
```

```
#("Africa", "http://feeds.bbci.co.uk/news/world/africa/rss.xml"),
#("Asia", "http://feeds.bbci.co.uk/news/world/asia/rss.xml"),
#("Europe", "http://feeds.bbci.co.uk/news/world/europe/rss.xml"),
#("Latin America", "http://feeds.bbci.co.uk/news/world/latin_america/rss.xml"),
#("Middle East", "http://feeds.bbci.co.uk/news/world/middle_east/rss.xml"),
("US & Canada", "http://feeds.bbci.co.uk/news/world/us_and_canada/rss.xml"),
("Politics", "http://feeds.bbci.co.uk/news/politics/rss.xml"),
("Science/Environment", "http://feeds.bbci.co.uk/news/science_and_environment/rs
("Technology", "http://feeds.bbci.co.uk/news/technology/rss.xml"),
("Magazine", "http://feeds.bbci.co.uk/news/magazine/rss.xml"),
("Entertainment/Arts", "http://feeds.bbci.co.uk/news/entertainment_and_arts/rss.
#("Health", "http://feeds.bbci.co.uk/news/health/rss.xml"),
#("Education/Family", "http://feeds.bbci.co.uk/news/education/rss.xml"),
("Business", "http://feeds.bbci.co.uk/news/business/rss.xml"),
("Special Reports", "http://feeds.bbci.co.uk/news/special_reports/rss.xml"),
("Also in the News", "http://feeds.bbci.co.uk/news/also_in_the_news/rss.xml"),
#("Newsbeat", "http://www.bbc.co.uk/newsbeat/rss.xml"),
#("Click", "http://newsrss.bbc.co.uk/rss/newsonline_uk_edition/programmes/click_
("Blog: Nick Robinson (Political Editor)", "http://feeds.bbci.co.uk/news/corresp
#("Blog: Mark D'Arcy (Parliamentary Correspondent)", "http://feeds.bbci.co.uk/ne
#("Blog: Robert Peston (Business Editor)", "http://feeds.bbci.co.uk/news/corresp
#("Blog: Stephanie Flanders (Economics Editor)", "http://feeds.bbci.co.uk/news/c
("Blog: Rory Cellan-Jones (Technology correspondent)", "http://feeds.bbci.co.uk/
("Sport Front Page", "http://newsrss.bbc.co.uk/rss/sportonline_uk_edition/front_
#("Football", "http://newsrss.bbc.co.uk/rss/sportonline_uk_edition/football/rss.
#("Cricket", "http://newsrss.bbc.co.uk/rss/sportonline_uk_edition/cricket/rss.xr
#("Rugby Union", "http://newsrss.bbc.co.uk/rss/sportonline_uk_edition/rugby_unic
#("Rugby League", "http://newsrss.bbc.co.uk/rss/sportonline_uk_edition/rugby_lea
#("Tennis", "http://newsrss.bbc.co.uk/rss/sportonline_uk_edition/tennis/rss.xml
#("Golf", "http://newsrss.bbc.co.uk/rss/sportonline_uk_edition/golf/rss.xml"),
#("Motorsport", "http://newsrss.bbc.co.uk/rss/sportonline_uk_edition/motorsport,
#("Boxing", "http://newsrss.bbc.co.uk/rss/sportonline_uk_edition/boxing/rss.xml
#("Athletics", "http://newsrss.bbc.co.uk/rss/sportonline_uk_edition/athletics/r:
#("Snooker", "http://newsrss.bbc.co.uk/rss/sportonline_uk_edition/other_sports/:
#("Horse Racing", "http://newsrss.bbc.co.uk/rss/sportonline_uk_edition/other_spc
#("Cycling", "http://newsrss.bbc.co.uk/rss/sportonline_uk_edition/other_sports/c
#("Disability Sport", "http://newsrss.bbc.co.uk/rss/sportonline_uk_edition/othe:
#("Other Sport", "http://newsrss.bbc.co.uk/rss/sportonline_uk_edition/other_spo:
#("Olympics 2012", "http://newsrss.bbc.co.uk/rss/sportonline_uk_edition/other_s;
#("N. Ireland Politics", "http://feeds.bbci.co.uk/news/northern_ireland/northeri
#("Scotland Politics", "http://feeds.bbci.co.uk/news/scotland/scotland_politics,
#("Scotland Business", "http://feeds.bbci.co.uk/news/scotland/scotland_business,
#("E. Scotland, Edinburgh & Fife", "http://feeds.bbci.co.uk/news/scotland/edinbu
#("W. Scotland & Glasgow", "http://feeds.bbci.co.uk/news/scotland/glasgow_and_we
#("Highlands & Islands", "http://feeds.bbci.co.uk/news/scotland/highlands_and_i:
#("NE. Scotland, Orkney & Shetland", "http://feeds.bbci.co.uk/news/scotland/nort
#("South Scotland", "http://feeds.bbci.co.uk/news/scotland/south_scotland/rss.xr
#("Central Scotland & Tayside", "http://feeds.bbci.co.uk/news/scotland/tayside_a
#("Wales Politics", "http://feeds.bbci.co.uk/news/wales/wales_politics/rss.xml",
#("NW. Wales", "http://feeds.bbci.co.uk/news/wales/north_west_wales/rss.xml"),
#("NE. Wales", "http://feeds.bbci.co.uk/news/wales/north_east_wales/rss.xml"),
#("Mid. Wales", "http://feeds.bbci.co.uk/news/wales/mid_wales/rss.xml"),
#("SW. Wales", "http://feeds.bbci.co.uk/news/wales/south_west_wales/rss.xml"),
#("SE. Wales", "http://feeds.bbci.co.uk/news/wales/south_east_wales/rss.xml"),
#("Newyddion - News in Welsh", "http://feeds.bbci.co.uk/newyddion/rss.xml"),
#("Gwleidyddiaeth", "http://feeds.bbci.co.uk/newyddion/gwleidyddiaeth/rss.xml"),
#("Gogledd-Ddwyrain", "http://feeds.bbci.co.uk/newyddion/gogledd-ddwyrain/rss.xr
#("Gogledd-Orllewin", "http://feeds.bbci.co.uk/newyddion/gogledd-orllewin/rss.xr
```

```
            #("Canolbarth", "http://feeds.bbci.co.uk/newyddion/canolbarth/rss.xml"),
            #("De-Ddwyrain", "http://feeds.bbci.co.uk/newyddion/de-ddwyrain/rss.xml"),
            #("De-Orllewin", "http://feeds.bbci.co.uk/newyddion/de-orllewin/rss.xml"),
        ]


    #    **** SELECT YOUR USER PREFERENCES ****

    # Title to use for the ebook.
    #
    title = 'BBC News'

    # A brief description for the ebook.
    #
    description = u'BBC web site ebook created using rss feeds.'

    # The max number of articles which may be downloaded from each feed.
    # I've never seen more than about 70 articles in a single feed in the
    # BBC feeds.
    #
    max_articles_per_feed = 100

    # The max age of articles which may be downloaded from each feed. This is
    # specified in days - note fractions of days are allowed, Eg. 2.5 (2 and a
    # half days). My default of 1.5 days is the last 36 hours, the point at
    # which I've decided 'news' becomes 'old news', but be warned this is not
    # so good for the blogs, technology, magazine, etc., and sports feeds.
    # You may wish to extend this to 2-5 but watch out ebook creation time will
    # increase as well. Setting this to 30 will get everything (AFAICT) as long
    # as max_articles_per_feed remains set high (except for 'Click' which is
    # v. low volume and its currently oldest article is 4th Feb 2011).
    #
    oldest_article = 1.5

    # Number of simultaneous downloads. 20 is consistantly working fine on the
    # BBC News feeds with no problems. Speeds things up from the defualt of 5.
    # If you have a lot of feeds and/or have increased oldest_article above 2
    # then you may wish to try increasing simultaneous_downloads to 25-30,
    # Or, of course, if you are in a hurry. [I've not tried beyond 20.]
    #
    simultaneous_downloads = 20

    # Timeout for fetching files from the server in seconds. The default of
    # 120 seconds, seems somewhat excessive.
    #
    timeout = 30

    # The format string for the date shown on the ebook's first page.
    # List of all values: http://docs.python.org/library/time.html
    # Default in news.py has a leading space so that's mirrored here.
    # As with 'feeds' select/de-select by adding/removing the initial '#',
    # only one timefmt should be selected, here's a few to choose from.
    #
    timefmt = ' [%a, %d %b %Y]'              # [Fri, 14 Nov 2011] (Calibre default)
    #timefmt = ' [%a, %d %b %Y %H:%M]'        # [Fri, 14 Nov 2011 18:30]
    #timefmt = ' [%a, %d %b %Y %I:%M %p]'     # [Fri, 14 Nov 2011 06:30 PM]
    #timefmt = ' [%d %b %Y]'                  # [14 Nov 2011]
    #timefmt = ' [%d %b %Y %H:%M]'            # [14 Nov 2011 18.30]
```

```
#timefmt = ' [%Y-%m-%d]'                    # [2011-11-14]
#timefmt = ' [%Y-%m-%d-%H-%M]'              # [2011-11-14-18-30]




#
#    **** IMPORTANT ****
#
#    DO NOT EDIT BELOW HERE UNLESS YOU KNOW WHAT YOU ARE DOING.
#
#    DO NOT EDIT BELOW HERE UNLESS YOU KNOW WHAT YOU ARE DOING.
#
#    I MEAN IT, YES I DO, ABSOLUTELY, AT YOU OWN RISK. :)
#
#    **** IMPORTANT ****
#



# Author of this recipe.
__author__ = 'mattst'

# Specify English as the language of the RSS feeds (ISO-639 code).
language = 'en_GB'

# Set tags.
tags = 'news, sport, blog'

# Set publisher and publication type.
publisher = 'BBC'
publication_type = 'newspaper'

# Disable stylesheets from site.
no_stylesheets = True

# Specifies an override encoding for sites that have an incorrect charset
# specified. Default of 'None' says to auto-detect. Some other BBC recipes
# use 'utf8', which works fine (so use that if necessary) but auto-detecting
# with None is working fine, so stick with that for robustness.
encoding = None

# Sets whether a feed has full articles embedded in it. The BBC feeds do not.
use_embedded_content = False

# Removes empty feeds - why keep them!?
remove_empty_feeds = True

# Create a custom title which fits nicely in the Kindle title list.
# Requires "import time" above class declaration, and replacing
# title with custom_title in conversion_options (right column only).
# Example of string below: "BBC News - 14 Nov 2011"
#
# custom_title = "BBC News - " + time.strftime('%d %b %Y')

'''

# Conversion options for advanced users, but don't forget to comment out the
# current conversion_options below. Avoid setting 'linearize_tables' as that
# plays havoc with the 'old style' table based pages.
```

```
    #
    conversion_options = { 'title'            : title,
                           'comments'         : description,
                           'tags'             : tags,
                           'language'         : language,
                           'publisher'        : publisher,
                           'authors'          : publisher,
                           'smarten_punctuation' : True
                         }
    '''

    conversion_options = { 'smarten_punctuation' : True }

    # Specify extra CSS - overrides ALL other CSS (IE. Added last).
    extra_css = 'body { font-family: verdana, helvetica, sans-serif; } \
                .introduction, .first { font-weight: bold; } \
                .cross-head { font-weight: bold; font-size: 125%; } \
                .cap, .caption { display: block; font-size: 80%; font-style: italic; } \
                .cap, .caption, .caption img, .caption span { display: block; text-align: cer
                .byl, .byd, .byline img, .byline-name, .byline-title, .author-name, .author-r
                    .correspondent-portrait img, .byline-lead-in, .name, .bbc-role { display:
                    text-align: center; font-size: 80%; font-style: italic; margin: 1px auto;
                .story-date, .published { font-size: 80%; } \
                table { width: 100%; } \
                td img { display: block; margin: 5px auto; } \
                ul { padding-top: 10px; } \
                ol { padding-top: 10px; } \
                li { padding-top: 5px; padding-bottom: 5px; } \
                h1 { text-align: center; font-size: 175%; font-weight: bold; } \
                h2 { text-align: center; font-size: 150%; font-weight: bold; } \
                h3 { text-align: center; font-size: 125%; font-weight: bold; } \
                h4, h5, h6 { text-align: center; font-size: 100%; font-weight: bold; }'

    # Remove various tag attributes to improve the look of the ebook pages.
    remove_attributes = [ 'border', 'cellspacing', 'align', 'cellpadding', 'colspan',
                          'valign', 'vspace', 'hspace', 'alt', 'width', 'height' ]

    # Remove the (admittedly rarely used) line breaks, "<br />", which sometimes
    # cause a section of the ebook to start in an unsightly fashion or, more
    # frequently, a "<br />" will muck up the formatting of a correspondant's byline.
    # "<br />" and "<br clear/>" are far more frequently used on the table formatted
    # style of pages, and really spoil the look of the ebook pages.
    preprocess_regexps      = [(re.compile(r'<br[ ]*/>', re.IGNORECASE), lambda m: ''),
                               (re.compile(r'<br[ ]*clear.*/>', re.IGNORECASE), lambda m: '')]


    # Create regular expressions for tag keeping and removal to make the matches more
    # robust against minor changes and errors in the HTML, Eg. double spaces, leading
    # and trailing spaces, missing hyphens, and such like.
    # Python regular expression ('re' class) page: http://docs.python.org/library/re.html

    # ****************************************
    # Regular expressions for keep_only_tags:
    # ****************************************

    # The BBC News HTML pages use variants of 'storybody' to denote the section of a HTML
    # page which contains the main text of the article. Match storybody variants: 'storybody',
    # 'story-body', 'story body','storybody ', etc.
```

```
storybody_reg_exp = '^.*story[_ -]*body.*$'

# The BBC sport and 'newsbeat' (features) HTML pages use 'blq_content' to hold the title
# and published date. This is one level above the usual news pages which have the title
# and date within 'story-body'. This is annoying since 'blq_content' must also be kept,
# resulting in a lot of extra things to be removed by remove_tags.
blq_content_reg_exp = '^.*blq[_ -]*content.*$'

# The BBC has an alternative page design structure, which I suspect is an out-of-date
# design but which is still used in some articles, Eg. 'Click' (technology), 'FastTrack'
# (travel), and in some sport pages. These alternative pages are table based (which is
# why I think they are an out-of-date design) and account for -I'm guesstimaking- less
# than 1% of all articles. They use a table class 'storycontent' to hold the article
# and like blq_content (above) have required lots of extra removal by remove_tags.
story_content_reg_exp = '^.*story[_ -]*content.*$'

# Keep the sections of the HTML which match the list below. The HTML page created by
# Calibre will fill <body> with those sections which are matched. Note that the
# blq_content_reg_exp must be listed before storybody_reg_exp in keep_only_tags due to
# it being the parent of storybody_reg_exp, that is to say the div class/id 'story-body'
# will be inside div class/id 'blq_content' in the HTML (if 'blq_content' is there at
# all). If they are the other way around in keep_only_tags then blq_content_reg_exp
# will end up being discarded.
keep_only_tags = [ dict(name='table', attrs={'class':re.compile(story_content_reg_exp, re.
                   dict(name='div',   attrs={'class':re.compile(blq_content_reg_exp, re.IGNOF
                   dict(name='div',   attrs={'id':re.compile(blq_content_reg_exp, re.IGNOF
                   dict(name='div',   attrs={'class':re.compile(storybody_reg_exp, re.IGNC
                   dict(name='div',   attrs={'id':re.compile(storybody_reg_exp, re.IGNOREC

# ***************************************
# Regular expressions for remove_tags:
# ***************************************

# Regular expression to remove share-help and variant tags. The share-help class
# is used by the site for a variety of 'sharing' type links, Eg. Facebook, delicious,
# twitter, email. Removed to avoid page clutter.
share_help_reg_exp = '^.*share[_ -]*help.*$'

# Regular expression to remove embedded-hyper and variant tags. This class is used to
# display links to other BBC News articles on the same/similar subject.
embedded_hyper_reg_exp = '^.*embed*ed[_ -]*hyper.*$'

# Regular expression to remove hypertabs and variant tags. This class is used to
# display a tab bar at the top of an article which allows the user to switch to
# an article (viewed on the same page) providing further info., 'in depth' analysis,
# an editorial, a correspondant's blog entry, and such like. The ability to handle
# a tab bar of this nature is currently beyond the scope of this recipe and
# possibly of Calibre itself (not sure about that - TO DO - check!).
hypertabs_reg_exp = '^.*hyper[_ -]*tabs.*$'

# Regular expression to remove story-feature and variant tags. Eg. 'story-feature',
# 'story-feature related narrow', 'story-feature wide', 'story-feature narrow'.
# This class is used to add additional info. boxes, or small lists, outside of
# the main story. TO DO: Work out a way to incorporate these neatly.
story_feature_reg_exp = '^.*story[_ -]*feature.*$'

# Regular expression to remove video and variant tags, Eg. 'videoInStoryB',
# 'videoInStoryC'. This class is used to embed video.
```

```
video_reg_exp = '^.*video.*$'

# Regular expression to remove audio and variant tags, Eg. 'audioInStoryD'.
# This class is used to embed audio.
audio_reg_exp = '^.*audio.*$'

# Regular expression to remove pictureGallery and variant tags, Eg. 'pictureGallery'.
# This class is used to embed a photo slideshow. See also 'slideshow' below.
picture_gallery_reg_exp = '^.*picture.*$'

# Regular expression to remove slideshow and variant tags, Eg. 'dslideshow-enclosure'.
# This class is used to embed a slideshow (not necessarily photo) but both
# 'slideshow' and 'pictureGallery' are used for slideshows.
slideshow_reg_exp = '^.*slide[_ -]*show.*$'

# Regular expression to remove social-links and variant tags. This class is used to
# display links to a BBC bloggers main page, used in various columnist's blogs
# (Eg. Nick Robinson, Robert Preston).
social_links_reg_exp = '^.*social[_ -]*links.*$'

# Regular expression to remove quote and (multi) variant tags, Eg. 'quote',
# 'endquote', 'quote-credit', 'quote-credit-title', etc. These are usually
# removed by 'story-feature' removal (as they are usually within them), but
# not always. The quotation removed is always (AFAICT) in the article text
# as well but a 2nd copy is placed in a quote tag to draw attention to it.
# The quote class tags may or may not appear in div's.
quote_reg_exp = '^.*quote.*$'

# Regular expression to remove hidden and variant tags, Eg. 'hidden'.
# The purpose of these is unclear, they seem to be an internal link to a
# section within the article, but the text of the link (Eg. 'Continue reading
# the main story') never seems to be displayed anyway. Removed to avoid clutter.
# The hidden class tags may or may not appear in div's.
hidden_reg_exp = '^.*hidden.*$'

# Regular expression to remove comment and variant tags, Eg. 'comment-introduction'.
# Used on the site to display text about registered users entering comments.
comment_reg_exp = '^.*comment.*$'

# Regular expression to remove form and variant tags, Eg. 'comment-form'.
# Used on the site to allow registered BBC users to fill in forms, typically
# for entering comments about an article.
form_reg_exp = '^.*form.*$'

# Extra things to remove due to the addition of 'blq_content' in keep_only_tags.

#<div class="story-actions"> Used on sports pages for 'email' and 'print'.
story_actions_reg_exp = '^.*story[_ -]*actions.*$'

#<div class="bookmark-list"> Used on sports pages instead of 'share-help' (for
# social networking links).
bookmark_list_reg_exp = '^.*bookmark[_ -]*list.*$'

#<div id="secondary-content" class="content-group">
# NOTE: Don't remove class="content-group" that is needed.
# Used on sports pages to link to 'similar stories'.
secondary_content_reg_exp = '^.*secondary[_ -]*content.*$'
```

```
#<div id="featured-content" class="content-group">
# NOTE: Don't remove class="content-group" that is needed.
# Used on sports pages to link to pages like 'tables', 'fixtures', etc.
featured_content_reg_exp = '^.*featured[_ -]*content.*$'

#<div id="navigation">
# Used on sports pages to link to pages like 'tables', 'fixtures', etc.
# Used sometimes instead of "featured-content" above.
navigation_reg_exp = '^.*navigation.*$'

#<a class="skip" href="#blq-container-inner">Skip to top</a>
# Used on sports pages to link to the top of the page.
skip_reg_exp = '^.*skip.*$'

# Extra things to remove due to the addition of 'storycontent' in keep_only_tags,
# which are the alterative table design based pages. The purpose of some of these
# is not entirely clear from the pages (which are a total mess!).

# Remove mapping based tags, Eg. <map id="world_map">
# The dynamic maps don't seem to work during ebook creation. TO DO: Investigate.
map_reg_exp = '^.*map.*$'

# Remove social bookmarking variation, called 'socialBookMarks'.
social_bookmarks_reg_exp = '^.*social[_ -]bookmarks.*$'

# Remove page navigation tools, like 'search', 'email', 'print', called 'blq-mast'.
blq_mast_reg_exp = '^.*blq[_ -]*mast.*$'

# Remove 'sharesb', I think this is a generic 'sharing' class. It seems to appear
# alongside 'socialBookMarks' whenever that appears. I am removing it as well
# under the assumption that it can appear alone as well.
sharesb_reg_exp = '^.*sharesb.*$'

# Remove class 'o'. The worst named user created css class of all time. The creator
# should immediately be fired. I've seen it used to hold nothing at all but with
# 20 or so empty lines in it. Also to hold a single link to another article.
# Whatever it was designed to do it is not wanted by this recipe. Exact match only.
o_reg_exp = '^o$'

# Remove 'promotopbg' and 'promobottombg', link lists. Have decided to
# use two reg expressions to make removing this (and variants) robust.
promo_top_reg_exp = '^.*promotopbg.*$'
promo_bottom_reg_exp = '^.*promobottombg.*$'

# Remove 'nlp', provides heading for link lists. Requires an exact match due to
# risk of matching those letters in something needed, unless I see a variation
# of 'nlp' used at a later date.
nlp_reg_exp = '^nlp$'

# Remove 'mva', provides embedded floating content of various types. Variant 'mvb'
# has also now been seen. Requires an exact match of 'mva' or 'mvb' due to risk of
# matching those letters in something needed.
mva_or_mvb_reg_exp = '^mv[ab]$'

# Remove 'mvtb', seems to be page navigation tools, like 'blq-mast'.
mvtb_reg_exp = '^mvtb$'

# Remove 'blq-toplink', class to provide a link to the top of the page.
```

```
    blq_toplink_reg_exp = '^.*blq[_ -]*top[_ -]*link.*$'

    # Remove 'products and services' links, Eg. desktop tools, alerts, and so on.
    # Eg. Class="servicev4 ukfs_services" - what a mess of a name. Have decided to
    # use two reg expressions to make removing this (and variants) robust.
    prods_services_01_reg_exp = '^.*servicev4.*$'
    prods_services_02_reg_exp = '^.*ukfs[_ -]*services.*$'

    # Remove -what I think is- some kind of navigation tools helper class, though I am
    # not sure, it's called: 'blq-rst blq-new-nav'. What I do know is it pops up
    # frequently and it is not wanted. Have decided to use two reg expressions to make
    # removing this (and variants) robust.
    blq_misc_01_reg_exp = '^.*blq[_ -]*rst.*$'
    blq_misc_02_reg_exp = '^.*blq[_ -]*new[_ -]*nav.*$'

    # Remove 'puffbox' - this may only appear inside 'storyextra', so it may not
    # need removing - I have no clue what it does other than it contains links.
    # Whatever it is - it is not part of the article and is not wanted.
    puffbox_reg_exp = '^.*puffbox.*$'

    # Remove 'sibtbg' and 'sibtbgf' - some kind of table formatting classes.
    sibtbg_reg_exp = '^.*sibtbg.*$'

    # Remove 'storyextra' - links to relevant articles and external sites.
    storyextra_reg_exp = '^.*story[_ -]*extra.*$'


    remove_tags = [ dict(name='div',   attrs={'class':re.compile(story_feature_reg_exp, re.IGN(
                    dict(name='div',   attrs={'class':re.compile(share_help_reg_exp, re.IGNORE(
                    dict(name='div',   attrs={'class':re.compile(embedded_hyper_reg_exp, re.IGI
                    dict(name='div',   attrs={'class':re.compile(hypertabs_reg_exp, re.IGNORECA
                    dict(name='div',   attrs={'class':re.compile(video_reg_exp, re.IGNORECASE)
                    dict(name='div',   attrs={'class':re.compile(audio_reg_exp, re.IGNORECASE)
                    dict(name='div',   attrs={'class':re.compile(picture_gallery_reg_exp, re.I(
                    dict(name='div',   attrs={'class':re.compile(slideshow_reg_exp, re.IGNORECA
                    dict(name='div',   attrs={'class':re.compile(quote_reg_exp, re.IGNORECASE)
                    dict(name='div',   attrs={'class':re.compile(hidden_reg_exp, re.IGNORECASE)
                    dict(name='div',   attrs={'class':re.compile(comment_reg_exp, re.IGNORECASE
                    dict(name='div',   attrs={'class':re.compile(story_actions_reg_exp, re.IGN(
                    dict(name='div',   attrs={'class':re.compile(bookmark_list_reg_exp, re.IGN(
                    dict(name='div',   attrs={'id':re.compile(secondary_content_reg_exp, re.IGI
                    dict(name='div',   attrs={'id':re.compile(featured_content_reg_exp, re.IGN(
                    dict(name='div',   attrs={'id':re.compile(navigation_reg_exp, re.IGNORECASE
                    dict(name='form', attrs={'id':re.compile(form_reg_exp, re.IGNORECASE)}),
                    dict(attrs={'class':re.compile(quote_reg_exp, re.IGNORECASE)}),
                    dict(attrs={'class':re.compile(hidden_reg_exp, re.IGNORECASE)}),
                    dict(attrs={'class':re.compile(social_links_reg_exp, re.IGNORECASE)}),
                    dict(attrs={'class':re.compile(comment_reg_exp, re.IGNORECASE)}),
                    dict(attrs={'class':re.compile(skip_reg_exp, re.IGNORECASE)}),
                    dict(name='map', attrs={'id':re.compile(map_reg_exp, re.IGNORECASE)}),
                    dict(name='map', attrs={'name':re.compile(map_reg_exp, re.IGNORECASE)}),
                    dict(name='div',   attrs={'id':re.compile(social_bookmarks_reg_exp, re.IGNOI
                    dict(name='div',   attrs={'id':re.compile(blq_mast_reg_exp, re.IGNORECASE)})
                    dict(name='div',   attrs={'class':re.compile(sharesb_reg_exp, re.IGNORECASE)
                    dict(name='div',   attrs={'class':re.compile(o_reg_exp, re.IGNORECASE)}),
                    dict(name='div',   attrs={'class':re.compile(promo_top_reg_exp, re.IGNORECA
                    dict(name='div',   attrs={'class':re.compile(promo_bottom_reg_exp, re.IGNOI
                    dict(name='div',   attrs={'class':re.compile(nlp_reg_exp, re.IGNORECASE)}),
```

```
                    dict(name='div',   attrs={'class':re.compile(mva_or_mvb_reg_exp, re.IGNORE(
                    dict(name='div',   attrs={'class':re.compile(mvtb_reg_exp, re.IGNORECASE)})
                    dict(name='div',   attrs={'class':re.compile(blq_toplink_reg_exp, re.IGNOR]
                    dict(name='div',   attrs={'class':re.compile(prods_services_01_reg_exp, re.
                    dict(name='div',   attrs={'class':re.compile(prods_services_02_reg_exp, re.
                    dict(name='div',   attrs={'class':re.compile(blq_misc_01_reg_exp, re.IGNOR]
                    dict(name='div',   attrs={'class':re.compile(blq_misc_02_reg_exp, re.IGNOR]
                    dict(name='div',   attrs={'class':re.compile(puffbox_reg_exp, re.IGNORECASH
                    dict(attrs={'class':re.compile(sibtbg_reg_exp, re.IGNORECASE)}),
                    dict(attrs={'class':re.compile(storyextra_reg_exp, re.IGNORECASE)})
                    ]

# Uses url to create and return the 'printer friendly' version of the url.
# In other words the 'print this page' address of the page.
#
# There are 3 types of urls used in the BBC site's rss feeds. There is just
# 1 type for the standard news while there are 2 used for sports feed urls.
# Note: Sports urls are linked from regular news feeds (Eg. 'News Home') when
# there is a major story of interest to 'everyone'. So even if no BBC sports
# feeds are added to 'feeds' the logic of this method is still needed to avoid
# blank / missing / empty articles which have an index title and then no body.
def print_version(self, url):

    # Handle sports page urls type 01:
    if (url.find("go/rss/-/sport1/") != -1):
        temp_url = url.replace("go/rss/-/", "")

    # Handle sports page urls type 02:
    elif (url.find("go/rss/int/news/-/sport1/") != -1):
        temp_url = url.replace("go/rss/int/news/-/", "")

    # Handle regular news page urls:
    else:
        temp_url = url.replace("go/rss/int/news/-/", "")

    # Always add "?print=true" to the end of the url.
    print_url = temp_url + "?print=true"

    return print_url


# Remove articles in feeds based on a string in the article title or url.
#
# Code logic written by: Starson17 - posted in: "Recipes - Re-usable code"
# thread, in post with title: "Remove articles from feed", see url:
# http://www.mobileread.com/forums/showpost.php?p=1165462&postcount=6
# Many thanks and all credit to Starson17.
#
# Starson17's code has obviously been altered to suite my requirements.
def parse_feeds(self):

    # Call parent's method.
    feeds = BasicNewsRecipe.parse_feeds(self)

    # Loop through all feeds.
    for feed in feeds:

        # Loop through all articles in feed.
```

```
        for article in feed.articles[:]:

            # Match key words and remove article if there's a match.

            # Most BBC rss feed video only 'articles' use upper case 'VIDEO'
            # as a title prefix. Just match upper case 'VIDEO', so that
            # articles like 'Video game banned' won't be matched and removed.
            if 'VIDEO' in article.title:
                feed.articles.remove(article)

            # Most BBC rss feed audio only 'articles' use upper case 'AUDIO'
            # as a title prefix. Just match upper case 'AUDIO', so that
            # articles like 'Hi-Def audio...' won't be matched and removed.
            elif 'AUDIO' in article.title:
                feed.articles.remove(article)

            # Most BBC rss feed photo slideshow 'articles' use 'In Pictures',
            # 'In pictures', and 'in pictures', somewhere in their title.
            # Match any case of that phrase.
            elif 'IN PICTURES' in article.title.upper():
                feed.articles.remove(article)

            # As above, but user contributed pictures. Match any case.
            elif 'YOUR PICTURES' in article.title.upper():
                feed.articles.remove(article)

            # 'Sportsday Live' are articles which contain a constantly and
            # dynamically updated 'running commentary' during a live sporting
            # event. Match any case.
            elif 'SPORTSDAY LIVE' in article.title.upper():
                feed.articles.remove(article)

            # Sometimes 'Sportsday Live' (above) becomes 'Live - Sport Name'.
            # These are being matched below using 'Live - ' because removing all
            # articles with 'live' in their titles would remove some articles
            # that are in fact not live sports pages. Match any case.
            elif 'LIVE - ' in article.title.upper():
                feed.articles.remove(article)

            # 'Quiz of the week' is a Flash player weekly news quiz. Match only
            # the 'Quiz of the' part in anticipation of monthly and yearly
            # variants. Match any case.
            elif 'QUIZ OF THE' in article.title.upper():
                feed.articles.remove(article)

            # Remove articles with 'scorecards' in the url. These are BBC sports
            # pages which just display a cricket scorecard. The pages have a mass
            # of table and css entries to display the scorecards nicely. Probably
            # could make them work with this recipe, but might take a whole day
            # of work to sort out all the css - basically a formatting nightmare.
            elif 'scorecards' in article.url:
                feed.articles.remove(article)

        return feeds

# End of class and file.
```

This *recipe* explores only the tip of the iceberg when it comes to the power of calibre. To explore more of the abilities of calibre we'll examine a more complex real life example in the next section.

Real life example

A reasonably complex real life example that exposes more of the *API* of `BasicNewsRecipe` is the *recipe* for *The New York Times*

```
import string, re
from calibre import strftime
from calibre.web.feeds.recipes import BasicNewsRecipe
from calibre.ebooks.BeautifulSoup import BeautifulSoup

class NYTimes(BasicNewsRecipe):

    title       = 'The New York Times'
    __author__  = 'Kovid Goyal'
    description = 'Daily news from the New York Times'
    timefmt = ' [%a, %d %b, %Y]'
    needs_subscription = True
    remove_tags_before = dict(id='article')
    remove_tags_after  = dict(id='article')
    remove_tags = [dict(attrs={'class':['articleTools', 'post-tools', 'side_tool', 'nextArtic
                  dict(id=['footer', 'toolsRight', 'articleInline', 'navigation', 'archive', 's
                  dict(name=['script', 'noscript', 'style'])]
    encoding = 'cp1252'
    no_stylesheets = True
    extra_css = 'h1 {font: sans-serif large;}\n.byline {font:monospace;}'

    def get_browser(self):
        br = BasicNewsRecipe.get_browser()
        if self.username is not None and self.password is not None:
            br.open('http://www.nytimes.com/auth/login')
            br.select_form(name='login')
            br['USERID']   = self.username
            br['PASSWORD'] = self.password
            br.submit()
        return br

    def parse_index(self):
        soup = self.index_to_soup('http://www.nytimes.com/pages/todayspaper/index.html')

        def feed_title(div):
            return ''.join(div.findAll(text=True, recursive=False)).strip()

        articles = {}
        key = None
        ans = []
        for div in soup.findAll(True,
            attrs={'class':['section-headline', 'story', 'story headline']}):

            if div['class'] == 'section-headline':
                key = string.capwords(feed_title(div))
                articles[key] = []
                ans.append(key)

            elif div['class'] in ['story', 'story headline']:
                a = div.find('a', href=True)
                if not a:
```

```
                 continue
             url = re.sub(r'\?.*', '', a['href'])
             url += '?pagewanted=all'
             title = self.tag_to_string(a, use_alt=True).strip()
             description = ''
             pubdate = strftime('%a, %d %b')
             summary = div.find(True, attrs={'class':'summary'})
             if summary:
                 description = self.tag_to_string(summary, use_alt=False)

             feed = key if key is not None else 'Uncategorized'
             if not articles.has_key(feed):
                 articles[feed] = []
             if not 'podcasts' in url:
                 articles[feed].append(
                          dict(title=title, url=url, date=pubdate,
                               description=description,
                               content=''))
     ans = self.sort_index_by(ans, {'The Front Page':-1, 'Dining In, Dining Out':1, 'Obitua
     ans = [(key, articles[key]) for key in ans if articles.has_key(key)]
     return ans

 def preprocess_html(self, soup):
     refresh = soup.find('meta', {'http-equiv':'refresh'})
     if refresh is None:
         return soup
     content = refresh.get('content').partition('=')[2]
     raw = self.browser.open('http://www.nytimes.com'+content).read()
     return BeautifulSoup(raw.decode('cp1252', 'replace'))
```

We see several new features in this *recipe*. First, we have:

```
timefmt = ' [%a, %d %b, %Y]'
```

This sets the displayed time on the front page of the created ebook to be in the format, `Day, Day_Number Month, Year`. See `timefmt` (page 333).

Then we see a group of directives to cleanup the downloaded *HTML*:

```
remove_tags_before = dict(name='h1')
remove_tags_after  = dict(id='footer')
remove_tags = ...
```

These remove everything before the first `<h1>` tag and everything after the first tag whose id is `footer`. See `remove_tags` (page 332), `remove_tags_before` (page 332), `remove_tags_after` (page 332).

The next interesting feature is:

```
needs_subscription = True
...
def get_browser(self):
    ...
```

`needs_subscription = True` tells calibre that this recipe needs a username and password in order to access the content. This causes, calibre to ask for a username and password whenever you try to use this recipe. The code in `calibre.web.feeds.news.BasicNewsRecipe.get_browser()` (page 325) actually does the login into the NYT website. Once logged in, calibre will use the same, logged in, browser instance to fetch all content. See mechanize[6] to understand the code in `get_browser`.

---

[6]http://wwwsearch.sourceforge.net/mechanize/

Chapter 1. Sections

The next new feature is the *calibre.web.feeds.news.BasicNewsRecipe.parse_index()* (page 327) method. Its job is to go to http://www.nytimes.com/pages/todayspaper/index.html and fetch the list of articles that appear in *todays* paper. While more complex than simply using *RSS*, the recipe creates an ebook that corresponds very closely to the days paper. `parse_index` makes heavy use of BeautifulSoup[7] to parse the daily paper webpage. You can also use other, more modern parsers if you dislike BeatifulSoup. calibre comes with lxml[8] and html5lib[9], which are the recommended parsers. To use them, replace the call to `index_to_soup()` with the following:

```
raw = self.index_to_soup(url, raw=True)
# For html5lib
import html5lib
root = html5lib.parse(raw, namespaceHTMLElements=False, treebuilder='lxml')
# For the lxml html 4 parser
from lxml import html
root = html.fromstring(raw)
```

The final new feature is the *calibre.web.feeds.news.BasicNewsRecipe.preprocess_html()* (page 328) method. It can be used to perform arbitrary transformations on every downloaded HTML page. Here it is used to bypass the ads that the nytimes shows you before each article.

1.2.3 Tips for developing new recipes

The best way to develop new recipes is to use the command line interface. Create the recipe using your favorite python editor and save it to a file say `myrecipe.recipe`. The *.recipe* extension is required. You can download content using this recipe with the command:

```
ebook-convert myrecipe.recipe .epub --test -vv --debug-pipeline debug
```

The command **ebook-convert** will download all the webpages and save them to the EPUB file `myrecipe.epub`. The `-vv` makes ebook-convert spit out a lot of information about what it is doing. The `--test` makes it download only a couple of articles from at most two feeds. In addition, ebook-convert will put the downloaded HTML into the `debug/input` directory, where debug is the directory you specified in the `--debug-pipeline` option.

Once the download is complete, you can look at the downloaded *HTML* by opening the file `debug/input/index.html` in a browser. Once you're satisfied that the download and preprocessing is happening correctly, you can generate ebooks in different formats as shown below:

```
ebook-convert myrecipe.recipe myrecipe.epub
ebook-convert myrecipe.recipe myrecipe.mobi
...
```

If you're satisfied with your recipe, and you feel there is enough demand to justify its inclusion into the set of built-in recipes, post your recipe in the calibre recipes forum[10] to share it with other calibre users.

Note: On OS X, the command line tools are inside the calibre bundle, for example, if you installed calibre in `/Applications` the command line tools are in `/Applications/calibre.app/Contents/console.app/Contents/MacOS/`.

See also:

ebook-convert (page 288) The command line interface for all ebook conversion.

---

[7]http://www.crummy.com/software/BeautifulSoup/documentation.html
[8]http://lxml.de/
[9]https://github.com/html5lib/html5lib-python
[10]http://www.mobileread.com/forums/forumdisplay.php?f=228

1.2.4 Further reading

To learn more about writing advanced recipes using some of the facilities, available in `BasicNewsRecipe` you should consult the following sources:

API Documentation **(page 324)** Documentation of the `BasicNewsRecipe` class and all its important methods and fields.

BasicNewsRecipe[11] The source code of `BasicNewsRecipe`

Built-in recipes[12] The source code for the built-in recipes that come with calibre

The calibre recipes forum[13] Lots of knowledgeable calibre recipe writers hang out here.

1.2.5 API documentation

API Documentation for recipes

The API for writing recipes is defined by the *BasicNewsRecipe* (page 324)

class `calibre.web.feeds.news.`**BasicNewsRecipe** (*options*, *log*, *progress_reporter*)
Base class that contains logic needed in all recipes. By overriding progressively more of the functionality in this class, you can make progressively more customized/powerful recipes. For a tutorial introduction to creating recipes, see Adding your favorite news website (page 125).

abort_article (*msg=None*)
Call this method inside any of the preprocess methods to abort the download for the current article. Useful to skip articles that contain inappropriate content, such as pure video articles.

abort_recipe_processing (*msg*)
Causes the recipe download system to abort the download of this recipe, displaying a simple feedback message to the user.

add_toc_thumbnail (*article*, *src*)
Call this from populate_article_metadata with the src attribute of an <img> tag from the article that is appropriate for use as the thumbnail representing the article in the Table of Contents. Whether the thumbnail is actually used is device dependent (currently only used by the Kindles). Note that the referenced image must be one that was successfully downloaded, otherwise it will be ignored.

classmethod adeify_images (*soup*)
If your recipe when converted to EPUB has problems with images when viewed in Adobe Digital Editions, call this method from within *postprocess_html()* (page 327).

canonicalize_internal_url (*url*, *is_link=True*)
Return a set of canonical representations of `url`. The default implementation uses just the server hostname and path of the URL, ignoring any query parameters, fragments, etc. The canonical representations must be unique across all URLs for this news source. If they are not, then internal links may be resolved incorrectly.

> **Parameters is_link** – Is True if the URL is coming from an internal link in an HTML file. False if the URL is the URL used to download an article.

cleanup ()
Called after all articles have been download. Use it to do any cleanup like logging out of subscription sites, etc.

clone_browser (*br*)
Clone the browser br. Cloned browsers are used for multi-threaded downloads, since mechanize is not

thread safe. The default cloning routines should capture most browser customization, but if you do something exotic in your recipe, you should override this method in your recipe and clone manually.

Cloned browser instances use the same, thread-safe CookieJar by default, unless you have customized cookie handling.

default_cover (*cover_file*)
Create a generic cover for recipes that don't have a cover

download ()
Download and pre-process all articles from the feeds in this recipe. This method should be called only once on a particular Recipe instance. Calling it more than once will lead to undefined behavior. :return: Path to index.html

extract_readable_article (*html, url*)
Extracts main article content from 'html', cleans up and returns as a (article_html, extracted_title) tuple. Based on the original readability algorithm by Arc90.

get_article_url (*article*)
Override in a subclass to customize extraction of the *URL* that points to the content for each article. Return the article URL. It is called with *article*, an object representing a parsed article from a feed. See feedparser[14]. By default it looks for the original link (for feeds syndicated via a service like feedburner or pheedo) and if found, returns that or else returns article.link[15].

get_browser (**args, **kwargs*)
Return a browser instance used to fetch documents from the web. By default it returns a mechanize[16] browser instance that supports cookies, ignores robots.txt, handles refreshes and has a mozilla firefox user agent.

If your recipe requires that you login first, override this method in your subclass. For example, the following code is used in the New York Times recipe to login for full access:

```python
def get_browser(self):
    br = BasicNewsRecipe.get_browser(self)
    if self.username is not None and self.password is not None:
        br.open('http://www.nytimes.com/auth/login')
        br.select_form(name='login')
        br['USERID']   = self.username
        br['PASSWORD'] = self.password
        br.submit()
    return br
```

get_cover_url ()
Return a *URL* to the cover image for this issue or *None*. By default it returns the value of the member *self.cover_url* which is normally *None*. If you want your recipe to download a cover for the e-book override this method in your subclass, or set the member variable *self.cover_url* before this method is called.

get_feeds ()
Return a list of *RSS* feeds to fetch for this profile. Each element of the list must be a 2-element tuple of the form (title, url). If title is None or an empty string, the title from the feed is used. This method is useful if your recipe needs to do some processing to figure out the list of feeds to download. If so, override in your subclass.

get_masthead_title ()
Override in subclass to use something other than the recipe title

---

[14] https://pythonhosted.org/feedparser/
[15] https://pythonhosted.org/feedparser/reference-entry-link.html
[16] http://wwwsearch.sourceforge.net/mechanize/

get_masthead_url()

> Return a *URL* to the masthead image for this issue or *None*. By default it returns the value of the member *self.masthead_url* which is normally *None*. If you want your recipe to download a masthead for the e-book override this method in your subclass, or set the member variable *self.masthead_url* before this method is called. Masthead images are used in Kindle MOBI files.

get_obfuscated_article(*url*)

> If you set *articles_are_obfuscated* this method is called with every article URL. It should return the path to a file on the filesystem that contains the article HTML. That file is processed by the recursive HTML fetching engine, so it can contain links to pages/images on the web.
>
> This method is typically useful for sites that try to make it difficult to access article content automatically.

classmethod image_url_processor(*baseurl*, *url*)

> Perform some processing on image urls (perhaps removing size restrictions for dynamically generated images, etc.) and return the precessed URL.

index_to_soup(*url_or_raw*, *raw=False*, *as_tree=False*)

> Convenience method that takes an URL to the index page and returns a BeautifulSoup[17] of it.
>
> *url_or_raw*: Either a URL or the downloaded index page as a string

is_link_wanted(*url*, *tag*)

> Return True if the link should be followed or False otherwise. By default, raises NotImplementedError which causes the downloader to ignore it.
>
> **Parameters**
>
> - **url** – The URL to be followed
> - **tag** – The Tag from which the URL was derived

javascript_login(*browser*, *username*, *password*)

> This method is used to login to a website that uses javascript for its login form. After the login is complete, the cookies returned from the website are copied to a normal (non-javascript) browser and the download proceeds using those cookies.
>
> An example implementation:

```
def javascript_login(self, browser, username, password):
    browser.visit('http://some-page-that-has-a-login')
    form = browser.select_form(nr=0) # Select the first form on the page
    form['username'] = username
    form['password'] = password
    browser.submit(timeout=120) # Submit the form and wait at most two minutes for lc
```

> Note that you can also select forms with CSS2 selectors, like this:

```
browser.select_form('form#login_form')
browser.select_from('form[name="someform"]')
```

parse_feeds()

> Create a list of articles from the list of feeds returned by *BasicNewsRecipe.get_feeds()* (page 326). Return a list of Feed objects.

parse_index()

> This method should be implemented in recipes that parse a website instead of feeds to generate a list of articles. Typical uses are for news sources that have a "Print Edition" webpage that lists all the articles in the current print edition. If this function is implemented, it will be used in preference to *BasicNewsRecipe.parse_feeds()* (page 327).

---

[17] http://www.crummy.com/software/BeautifulSoup/bs3/documentation.html

It must return a list. Each element of the list must be a 2-element tuple of the form (`'feed title'`, `list of articles`).

Each list of articles must contain dictionaries of the form:

```
{
'title'       : article title,
'url'         : URL of print version,
'date'        : The publication date of the article as a string,
'description' : A summary of the article
'content'     : The full article (can be an empty string). Obsolete
                do not use, instead save the content to a temporary
                file and pass a file:///path/to/temp/file.html as
                the URL.
}
```

For an example, see the recipe for downloading *The Atlantic*. In addition, you can add 'author' for the author of the article.

If you want to abort processing for some reason and have calibre show the user a simple message instead of an error, call *abort_recipe_processing()* (page 324).

populate_article_metadata (*article, soup, first*)

Called when each HTML page belonging to article is downloaded. Intended to be used to get article metadata like author/summary/etc. from the parsed HTML (soup). :param article: A object of class `calibre.web.feeds.Article`. If you change the summary, remember to also change the text_summary :param soup: Parsed HTML belonging to this article :param first: True iff the parsed HTML is the first page of the article.

postprocess_book (*oeb, opts, log*)

Run any needed post processing on the parsed downloaded e-book.

Parameters

- **oeb** – An OEBBook object
- **opts** – Conversion options

postprocess_html (*soup, first_fetch*)

This method is called with the source of each downloaded *HTML* file, after it is parsed for links and images. It can be used to do arbitrarily powerful post-processing on the *HTML*. It should return *soup* after processing it.

Parameters

- **soup** – A BeautifulSoup[18] instance containing the downloaded *HTML*.
- **first_fetch** – True if this is the first page of an article.

preprocess_html (*soup*)

This method is called with the source of each downloaded *HTML* file, before it is parsed for links and images. It is called after the cleanup as specified by remove_tags etc. It can be used to do arbitrarily powerful pre-processing on the *HTML*. It should return *soup* after processing it.

soup: A BeautifulSoup[19] instance containing the downloaded *HTML*.

preprocess_raw_html (*raw_html, url*)

This method is called with the source of each downloaded *HTML* file, before it is parsed into an object tree. raw_html is a unicode string representing the raw HTML downloaded from the web. url is the URL from which the HTML was downloaded.

---

[18] http://www.crummy.com/software/BeautifulSoup/bs3/documentation.html
[19] http://www.crummy.com/software/BeautifulSoup/bs3/documentation.html

Note that this method acts *before* preprocess_regexps.

This method must return the processed raw_html as a unicode object.

classmethod print_version (*url*)

Take a *url* pointing to the webpage with article content and return the *URL* pointing to the print version of the article. By default does nothing. For example:

```
def print_version(self, url):
    return url + '?&pagewanted=print'
```

skip_ad_pages (*soup*)

This method is called with the source of each downloaded *HTML* file, before any of the cleanup attributes like remove_tags, keep_only_tags are applied. Note that preprocess_regexps will have already been applied. It is meant to allow the recipe to skip ad pages. If the soup represents an ad page, return the HTML of the real page. Otherwise return None.

soup: A BeautifulSoup[20] instance containing the downloaded *HTML*.

sort_index_by (*index*, *weights*)

Convenience method to sort the titles in *index* according to *weights*. *index* is sorted in place. Returns *index*.

index: A list of titles.

weights: A dictionary that maps weights to titles. If any titles in index are not in weights, they are assumed to have a weight of 0.

classmethod tag_to_string (*tag*, *use_alt=True*, *normalize_whitespace=True*)

Convenience method to take a BeautifulSoup[21] *Tag* and extract the text from it recursively, including any CDATA sections and alt tag attributes. Return a possibly empty unicode string.

use_alt: If *True* try to use the alt attribute for tags that don't have any textual content

tag: BeautifulSoup[22] *Tag*

articles_are_obfuscated = False

Set to True and implement `get_obfuscated_article()` (page 326) to handle websites that try to make it difficult to scrape content.

auto_cleanup = False

Automatically extract all the text from downloaded article pages. Uses the algorithms from the readability project. Setting this to True, means that you do not have to worry about cleaning up the downloaded HTML manually (though manual cleanup will always be superior).

auto_cleanup_keep = None

Specify elements that the auto cleanup algorithm should never remove. The syntax is a XPath expression. For example:

```
auto_cleanup_keep = '//div[@id="article-image"]' will keep all divs with
                                         id="article-image"
auto_cleanup_keep = '//*[@class="important"]' will keep all elements
                                     with class="important"
auto_cleanup_keep = '//div[@id="article-image"]|//span[@class="important"]'
                will keep all divs with id="article-image" and spans
                with class="important"
```

center_navbar = True

If True the navigation bar is center aligned, otherwise it is left aligned

---

[20] http://www.crummy.com/software/BeautifulSoup/bs3/documentation.html
[21] http://www.crummy.com/software/BeautifulSoup/bs3/documentation.html
[22] http://www.crummy.com/software/BeautifulSoup/bs3/documentation.html

`compress_news_images = False`
> Set this to False to ignore all scaling and compression parameters and pass images through unmodified. If True and the other compression parameters are left at their default values, jpeg images will be scaled to fit in the screen dimensions set by the output profile and compressed to size at most (w * h)/16 where w x h are the scaled image dimensions.

`compress_news_images_auto_size = 16`
> The factor used when auto compressing jpeg images. If set to None, auto compression is disabled. Otherwise, the images will be reduced in size to (w * h)/compress_news_images_auto_size bytes if possible by reducing the quality level, where w x h are the image dimensions in pixels. The minimum jpeg quality will be 5/100 so it is possible this constraint will not be met. This parameter can be overridden by the parameter compress_news_images_max_size which provides a fixed maximum size for images. Note that if you enable scale_news_images_to_device then the image will first be scaled and then its quality lowered until its size is less than (w * h)/factor where w and h are now the *scaled* image dimensions. In other words, this compression happens after scaling.

`compress_news_images_max_size = None`
> Set jpeg quality so images do not exceed the size given (in KBytes). If set, this parameter overrides auto compression via compress_news_images_auto_size. The minimum jpeg quality will be 5/100 so it is possible this constraint will not be met.

`conversion_options = {}`
> Recipe specific options to control the conversion of the downloaded content into an e-book. These will override any user or plugin specified values, so only use if absolutely necessary. For example:

```
conversion_options = {
  'base_font_size'   : 16,
  'tags'             : 'mytag1,mytag2',
  'title'            : 'My Title',
  'linearize_tables' : True,
}
```

`cover_margins = (0, 0, '#ffffff')`
> By default, the cover image returned by get_cover_url() will be used as the cover for the periodical. Overriding this in your recipe instructs calibre to render the downloaded cover into a frame whose width and height are expressed as a percentage of the downloaded cover. cover_margins = (10, 15, '#ffffff') pads the cover with a white margin 10px on the left and right, 15px on the top and bottom. Color names defined at http://www.imagemagick.org/script/color.php Note that for some reason, white does not always work on windows. Use #ffffff instead

`delay = 0`
> Delay between consecutive downloads in seconds. The argument may be a floating point number to indicate a more precise time.

`description = u''`
> A couple of lines that describe the content this recipe downloads. This will be used primarily in a GUI that presents a list of recipes.

`encoding = None`
> Specify an override encoding for sites that have an incorrect charset specification. The most common being specifying `latin1` and using `cp1252`. If None, try to detect the encoding. If it is a callable, the callable is called with two arguments: The recipe object and the source to be decoded. It must return the decoded source.

`extra_css = None`
> Specify any extra *CSS* that should be added to downloaded *HTML* files. It will be inserted into *<style>* tags, just before the closing *</head>* tag thereby overriding all *CSS* except that which is declared using the style attribute on individual *HTML* tags. For example:

```
            extra_css = '.heading { font: serif x-large }'
```

feeds = None

> List of feeds to download. Can be either [url1, url2, ...] or [('title1', url1), ('title2', url2),...]

filter_regexps = []

> List of regular expressions that determines which links to ignore. If empty it is ignored. Used only if is_link_wanted is not implemented. For example:

```
    filter_regexps = [r'ads\.doubleclick\.net']
```

> will remove all URLs that have *ads.doubleclick.net* in them.
>
> Only one of *BasicNewsRecipe.match_regexps* (page 331) or *BasicNewsRecipe.filter_regexps* (page 330) should be defined.

ignore_duplicate_articles = None

> Ignore duplicates of articles that are present in more than one section. A duplicate article is an article that has the same title and/or URL. To ignore articles with the same title, set this to:

```
    ignore_duplicate_articles = {'title'}
```

> To use URLs instead, set it to:

```
    ignore_duplicate_articles = {'url'}
```

> To match on title or URL, set it to:

```
    ignore_duplicate_articles = {'title', 'url'}
```

keep_only_tags = []

> Keep only the specified tags and their children. For the format for specifying a tag see *BasicNewsRecipe.remove_tags* (page 332). If this list is not empty, then the *<body>* tag will be emptied and re-filled with the tags that match the entries in this list. For example:

```
    keep_only_tags = [dict(id=['content', 'heading'])]
```

> will keep only tags that have an *id* attribute of *"content"* or *"heading"*.

language = 'und'

> The language that the news is in. Must be an ISO-639 code either two or three characters long

masthead_url = None

> By default, calibre will use a default image for the masthead (Kindle only). Override this in your recipe to provide a url to use as a masthead.

match_regexps = []

> List of regular expressions that determines which links to follow. If empty, it is ignored. Used only if is_link_wanted is not implemented. For example:

```
    match_regexps = [r'page=[0-9]+']
```

> will match all URLs that have *page=some number* in them.
>
> Only one of *BasicNewsRecipe.match_regexps* (page 331) or *BasicNewsRecipe.filter_regexps* (page 330) should be defined.

max_articles_per_feed = 100

> Maximum number of articles to download from each feed. This is primarily useful for feeds that don't have article dates. For most feeds, you should use *BasicNewsRecipe.oldest_article* (page 331)

needs_subscription = False

If True the GUI will ask the user for a username and password to use while downloading. If set to "optional" the use of a username and password becomes optional

no_stylesheets = False

Convenient flag to disable loading of stylesheets for websites that have overly complex stylesheets unsuitable for conversion to ebooks formats. If True stylesheets are not downloaded and processed

oldest_article = 7.0

Oldest article to download from this news source. In days.

preprocess_regexps = []

List of *regexp* substitution rules to run on the downloaded *HTML*. Each element of the list should be a two element tuple. The first element of the tuple should be a compiled regular expression and the second a callable that takes a single match object and returns a string to replace the match. For example:

```
preprocess_regexps = [
    (re.compile(r'<!--Article ends here-->.*</body>', re.DOTALL|re.IGNORECASE),
     lambda match: '</body>'),
]
```

will remove everything from *<!–Article ends here–>* to *</body>*.

publication_type = 'unknown'

Publication type Set to newspaper, magazine or blog. If set to None, no publication type metadata will be written to the opf file.

recipe_disabled = None

Set to a non empty string to disable this recipe. The string will be used as the disabled message

recursions = 0

Number of levels of links to follow on article webpages

remove_attributes = []

List of attributes to remove from all tags. For example:

```
remove_attributes = ['style', 'font']
```

remove_empty_feeds = False

If True empty feeds are removed from the output. This option has no effect if parse_index is overridden in the sub class. It is meant only for recipes that return a list of feeds using *feeds* or `get_feeds()` (page 326). It is also used if you use the ignore_duplicate_articles option.

remove_javascript = True

Convenient flag to strip all javascript tags from the downloaded HTML

remove_tags = []

List of tags to be removed. Specified tags are removed from downloaded HTML. A tag is specified as a dictionary of the form:

```
{
 name    : 'tag name',   #e.g. 'div'
 attrs   : a dictionary, #e.g. {class: 'advertisment'}
}
```

All keys are optional. For a full explanation of the search criteria, see Beautiful Soup[23] A common example:

---

[23] http://www.crummy.com/software/BeautifulSoup/bs3/documentation.html#Searching%20the%20Parse%20Tree

```
remove_tags = [dict(name='div', attrs={'class':'advert'})]
```

This will remove all *<div class="advert">* tags and all their children from the downloaded *HTML*.

remove_tags_after = None
> Remove all tags that occur after the specified tag. For the format for specifying a tag see *BasicNewsRecipe.remove_tags* (page 332). For example:

```
remove_tags_after = [dict(id='content')]
```

will remove all tags after the first element with *id="content"*.

remove_tags_before = None
> Remove all tags that occur before the specified tag. For the format for specifying a tag see *BasicNewsRecipe.remove_tags* (page 332). For example:

```
remove_tags_before = dict(id='content')
```

will remove all tags before the first element with *id="content"*.

requires_version = (0, 6, 0)
> Minimum calibre version needed to use this recipe

resolve_internal_links = False
> If set to True then links in downloaded articles that point to other downloaded articles are changed to point to the downloaded copy of the article rather than its original web URL. If you set this to True, you might also need to implement *canonicalize_internal_url()* (page 325) to work with the URL scheme of your particular website.

reverse_article_order = False
> Reverse the order of articles in each feed

scale_news_images = None
> Maximum dimensions (w,h) to scale images to. If scale_news_images_to_device is True this is set to the device screen dimensions set by the output profile unless there is no profile set, in which case it is left at whatever value it has been assigned (default None).

scale_news_images_to_device = True
> Rescale images to fit in the device screen dimensions set by the output profile. Ignored if no output profile is set.

simultaneous_downloads = 5
> Number of simultaneous downloads. Set to 1 if the server is picky. Automatically reduced to 1 if *BasicNewsRecipe.delay* (page 329) > 0

summary_length = 500
> Max number of characters in the short description

template_css = u'\n .article_date {\n color: gray; font-family: monospace;\n }\n\n .article_description {\n text
> The CSS that is used to style the templates, i.e., the navigation bars and the Tables of Contents. Rather than overriding this variable, you should use *extra_css* in your recipe to customize look and feel.

timefmt = '[%a, %d %b %Y]'
> The format string for the date shown on the first page. By default: Day_Name, Day_Number Month_Name Year

timeout = 120.0
> Timeout for fetching files from server in seconds

title = u'Unknown News Source'
> The title to use for the ebook

use_embedded_content = None

> Normally we try to guess if a feed has full articles embedded in it based on the length of the embedded content. If *None*, then the default guessing is used. If *True* then the we always assume the feeds has embedded content and if *False* we always assume the feed does not have embedded content.

use_javascript_to_login = False

> If you set this True, then calibre will use javascript to login to the website. This is needed for some websites that require the use of javascript to login. If you set this to True you must implement the *javascript_login()* (page 326) method, to do the actual logging in.

1.3 The Ebook Viewer

calibre includes a built-in ebook viewer that can view all the major ebook formats. The viewer is highly customizable and has many advanced features.

- *Starting the viewer* (page 51)
- *Navigating around an ebook* (page 51)
- *Customizing the look and feel of your reading experience* (page 54)
- *Dictionary lookup* (page 54)
- *Copying text and images* (page 54)

1.3.1 Starting the viewer

You can view any of the books in your calibre library by selecting the book and pressing the View button. This will open up the book in the ebook viewer. You can also launch the viewer by itself from the Start menu in Windows or using the command **ebook-viewer** in Linux and OS X (you have to install the command line tools on OS X first by going to *Preferences->Advanced->Miscellaneous*).

1.3.2 Navigating around an ebook

You can "turn pages" in a book by using the *Page Next* and *Page Previous* buttons , or by pressing the Page Down/Page Up keys. Unlike most ebook viewers, calibre does not force you to view books in paged mode. You can scroll by amounts less than a page by using the scroll bar or various customizable keyboard shortcuts.

Bookmarks

When you are in the middle of a book and close the viewer, it will remember where you stopped reading and return there the next time you open the book. You can also set bookmarks in the book by using the Bookmark button

. When viewing EPUB format books, these bookmarks are actually saved in the EPUB file itself. You can add bookmarks, then send the file to a friend. When they open the file, they will be able to see your bookmarks.

Table of Contents

If the book you are reading defines a Table of Contents, you can access it by pressing the Table of Contents button

. This will bring up a list of sections in the book. You can click on any of them to jump to that portion of the book.

Navigating by location

Ebooks, unlike paper books, have no concept of pages. Instead, as you read through the book, you will notice that

your position in the book is displayed in the upper left corner in a box like this . This is both your current position and the total length of the book. These numbers are independent of the screen size and font size you are viewing the book at, and they play a similar role to page numbers in paper books. You can enter any number you like to go to the corresponding location in the book.

calibre also has a very handy reference mode. You can turn it on by clicking the Reference Mode button . Once you do this, every time you move your mouse over a paragraph, calibre will display a unique number made up of the section and paragraph numbers.

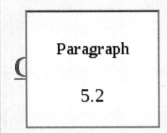

November 1918, Hobson, Lancashire

She stood in front of the cheval glass, the long mirror that Peter had given her on their second anniversary, and considered herself. Her hair had faded from shimmering English fair to almost the color of straw, and her face was lined from working in the vegetable beds throughout the war, though she'd worn a hat and gloves. Her skin, once like silk—he'd always told her that —was showing faint lines, and her eyes, though still very blue, stared back at her from some other woman's old face.

Four years—have I really aged that much in four years? she asked her image.

With a sigh she accepted the fact that she wouldn't see forty-four again. But he'd have aged too. Probably more than she had—war was no seaside picnic on a summer's afternoon.

You can use this number to unambiguously refer to parts of the books when discussing it with friends or referring to it in other works. You can enter these numbers in the box marked Go to at the top of the window to go to a particular reference location.

If you click on links inside the ebook to take you to different parts of the book, such as an endnote, you can use the back and forward buttons in the top left corner to return to where you were. These buttons behave just like those in a web browser.

1.3.3 Customizing the look and feel of your reading experience

You can change font sizes on the fly by using the font size buttons ____. You can also make the viewer full

screen by pressing the Full Screen button ____. By clicking the Preferences button ____, you can change the default fonts used by the viewer to ones you like as well as the default font size when the viewer starts up.

More advanced customization can be achieved by the User Stylesheet setting. This is a stylesheet you can set that will be applied to every book. Using it you can do things like have white text on a black background, change paragraph styles, text justification, etc. For examples of custom stylesheets used by calibre's users, see the forums[24].

1.3.4 Dictionary lookup

You can look up the meaning of words in the current book by right clicking on a word. calibre uses the publicly available dictionary server at `dict.org` to look up words. The definition is displayed in a small box at the bottom of the screen.

1.3.5 Copying text and images

You can select text and images by dragging the content with your mouse and then right clicking to copy to the clipboard. The copied material can be pasted into another application as plain text and images.

1.4 Ebook Conversion

calibre has a conversion system that is designed to be very easy to use. Normally, you just add a book to calibre, click convert and calibre will try hard to generate output that is as close as possible to the input. However, calibre accepts a very large number of input formats, not all of which are as suitable as others for conversion to ebooks. In the case of such input formats, or if you just want greater control over the conversion system, calibre has a lot of options to fine tune the conversion process. Note however that calibre's conversion system is not a substitute for a full blown ebook editor. To edit ebooks, I recommend first converting them to EPUB or AZW3 using calibre and then using the Edit Book feature to get them into perfect shape. You can then use the edited ebook as input for conversion into other formats in calibre.

This document will refer mainly to the conversion settings as found in the conversion dialog, pictured below. All these settings are also available via command line interface to conversion, documented at ebook-convert (page 288). In calibre, you can obtain help on any individual setting by holding your mouse over it, a tooltip will appear describing the setting.

---

[24] http://www.mobileread.com/forums/showthread.php?t=51500

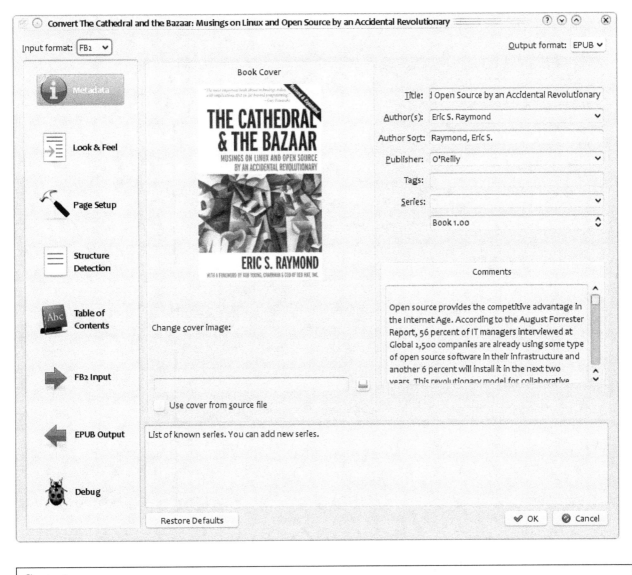

1.4.1 Introduction

The first thing to understand about the conversion system is that it is designed as a pipeline. Schematically, it looks like this:

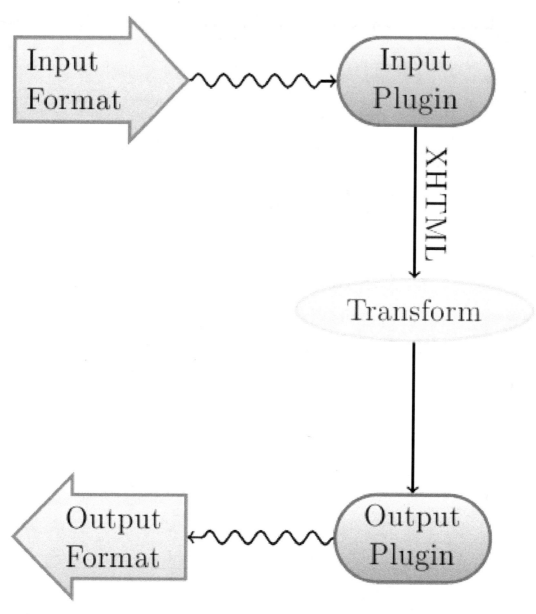

The input format is first converted to XHTML by the appropriate *Input Plugin*. This HTML is then *transformed*. In the last step, the processed XHTML is converted to the specified output format by the appropriate *Output Plugin*. The results of the conversion can vary greatly, based on the input format. Some formats convert much better than others. A list of the best source formats for conversion is available *here* (page 105).

The transforms that act on the XHTML output are where all the work happens. There are various transforms, for example, to insert book metadata as a page at the start of the book, to detect chapter headings and automatically create a Table of Contents, to proportionally adjust font sizes, et cetera. It is important to remeber that all the transforms act on the XHTML output by the *Input Plugin*, not on the input file itself. So, for example, if you ask calibre to convert an RTF file to EPUB, it will first be converted to XHTML internally, the various transforms will be applied to the XHTML and then the *Output Plugin* will create the EPUB file, automatically generating all metadata, Table of Contents, et cetera.

You can see this process in action by using the debug option . Just specify the path to a directory for the debug output. During conversion, calibre will place the XHTML generated by the various stages of the conversion pipeline in different sub-directories. The four sub-directories are:

Table 1.2: Stages of the conversion pipeline

Direc-tory	Description
input	This contains the HTML output by the Input Plugin. Use this to debug the Input Plugin.
parsed	The result of pre-processing and converting to XHTML the output from the Input Plugin. Use to debug structure detection.
struc-ture	Post structure detection, but before CSS flattening and font size conversion. Use to debug font size conversion and CSS transforms.
pro-cessed	Just before the ebook is passed to the output plugin. Use to debug the Output Plugin.

If you want to edit the input document a little before having calibre convert it, the best thing to do is edit the files in the `input` sub-directory, then zip it up, and use the zip file as the input format for subsequent conversions. To do this use the *Edit meta information* dialog to add the zip file as a format for the book and then, in the top left corner of the conversion dialog, select ZIP as the input format.

This document will deal mainly with the various transforms that operate on the intermediate XHTML and how to control them. At the end are some tips specific to each Input/Output format.

1.4.2 Look & Feel

Contents

- *Font size rescaling* (page 57)
- *Paragraph spacing* (page 58)
- *Extra CSS* (page 59)
- *Miscellaneous* (page 59)

This group of options controls various aspects of the look and feel of the converted ebook.

Font size rescaling

One of the nicest features of the e-reading experience is the ability to easily adjust font sizes to suit individual needs and lighting conditions. calibre has sophisticated algorithms to ensure that all the books it outputs have a consistent font sizes, no matter what font sizes are specified in the input document.

The base font size of a document is the most common font size in that document, i.e., the size of the bulk of text in that document. When you specify a *Base font size*, calibre automatically rescales all font sizes in the document proportionately, so that the most common font size becomes the specified base font size and other font sizes are rescaled appropriately. By choosing a larger base font size, you can make the fonts in the document larger and vice versa. When you set the base font size, for best results, you should also set the font size key.

Normally, calibre will automatically choose a base font size appropriate to the Output Profile you have chosen (see *Page Setup* (page 59)). However, you can override this here in case the default is not suitable for you.

The *Font size key* option lets you control how non-base font sizes are rescaled. The font rescaling algorithm works using a font size key, which is simply a comma-separated list of font sizes. The font size key tells calibre how many "steps" bigger or smaller a given font size should be compared to the base font size. The idea is that there should be a limited number of font sizes in a document. For example, one size for the body text, a couple of sizes for different levels of headings and a couple of sizes for super/sub scripts and footnotes. The font size key allows calibre to compartmentalize the font sizes in the input documents into separate "bins" corresponding to the different logical font sizes.

Let's illustrate with an example. Suppose the source document we are converting was produced by someone with excellent eyesight and has a base font size of 8pt. That means the bulk of the text in the document is sized at 8pts, while headings are somewhat larger (say 10 and 12pt) and footnotes somewhat smaller at 6pt. Now if we use the following settings:

```
Base font size : 12pt
Font size key  : 7, 8, 10, 12, 14, 16, 18, 20
```

The output document will have a base font size of 12pt, headings of 14 and 16pt and footnotes of 8pt. Now suppose we want to make the largest heading size stand out more and make the footnotes a little larger as well. To achieve this, the font key should be changed to:

```
New font size key : 7, 9, 12, 14, 18, 20, 22
```

The largest headings will now become 18pt, while the footnotes will become 9pt. You can play with these settings to try and figure out what would be optimum for you by using the font rescaling wizard, which can be accessed by clicking the little button next to the *Font size key* setting.

All the font size rescaling in the conversion can also be disabled here, if you would like to preserve the font sizes in the input document.

A related setting is *Line height*. Line height controls the vertical height of lines. By default, (a line height of 0), no manipulation of line heights is performed. If you specify a non-default value, line heights will be set in all locations that don't specify their own line heights. However, this is something of a blunt weapon and should be used sparingly. If you want to adjust the line heights for some section of the input, it's better to use the *Extra CSS* (page 59).

Paragraph spacing

Normally, paragraphs in XHTML are rendered with a blank line between them and no leading text indent. calibre has a couple of options to control this. *Remove spacing between paragraphs* forcefully ensure that all paragraphs have no inter paragraph spacing. It also sets the text indent to 1.5em (can be changed) to mark the start of every paragraph. *Insert blank line* does the opposite, guaranteeing that there is exactly one blank line between each pair of paragraphs. Both these options are very comprehensive, removing spacing, or inserting it for *all* paragraphs (technically <p> and <div> tags). This is so that you can just set the option and be sure that it performs as advertised, irrespective of how messy the input file is. The one exception is when the input file uses hard line breaks to implement inter-paragraph spacing.

If you want to remove the spacing between all paragraphs, except a select few, don't use these options. Instead add the following CSS code to *Extra CSS* (page 59):

```
p, div { margin: 0pt; border: 0pt; text-indent: 1.5em }
.spacious { margin-bottom: 1em; text-indent: 0pt; }
```

Then, in your source document, mark the paragraphs that need spacing with *class="spacious"*. If your input document is not in HTML, use the Debug option, described in the Introduction to get HTML (use the `input` sub-directory).

Extra CSS

This option allows you to specify arbitrary CSS that will be applied to all HTML files in the input. This CSS is applied with very high priority and so should override most CSS present in the **input document** itself. You can use this setting to fine tune the presentation/layout of your document. For example, if you want all paragraphs of class *endnote* to be right aligned, just add:

```
.endnote { text-align: right }
```

or if you want to change the indentation of all paragraphs:

```
p { text-indent: 5mm; }
```

Extra CSS is a very powerful option, but you do need an understanding of how CSS works to use it to its full potential. You can use the debug pipeline option described above to see what CSS is present in your input document.

Miscellaneous

There are a few more options in this section.

No text justification Normally, if the output format supports it, calibre will force the output ebook to have *justified* text (i.e., a smooth right margin). This option will turn off this behavior, in which case whatever justification is specified in the input document will be used instead.

Linearize tables Some badly designed documents use tables to control the layout of text on the page. When converted these documents often have text that runs off the page and other artifacts. This option will extract the content from the tables and present it in a linear fashion. Note that this option linearizes *all* tables, so only use it if you are sure the input document does not use tables for legitimate purposes, like presenting tabular information.

Transliterate unicode characters Transliterate unicode characters to an ASCII representation. Use with care because this will replace unicode characters with ASCII. For instance it will replace "Михаил Горбачёв" with "Mikhail Gorbachiov". Also, note that in cases where there are multiple representations of a character (characters shared by Chinese and Japanese for instance) the representation used by the largest number of people will be used (Chinese in the previous example). This option is mainly useful if you are going to view the ebook on a device that does not have support for unicode.

Input character encoding Older documents sometimes don't specify their character encoding. When converted, this can result in non-English characters or special characters like smart quotes being corrupted. calibre tries to auto-detect the character encoding of the source document, but it does not always succeed. You can force it to assume a particular character encoding by using this setting. *cp1252* is a common encoding for documents produced using windows software. You should also read *How do I convert my file containing non-English characters, or smart quotes?* (page 105) for more on encoding issues.

1.4.3 Page Setup

The Page Setup options are for controlling screen layout, like margins and screen sizes. There are options to setup page margins, which will be used by the Output Plugin, if the selected Output Format supports page margins. In addition, you should choose an Input profile and an Output profile. Both sets of profiles basically deal with how to interpret measurements in the input/output documents, screen sizes and default font rescaling keys.

If you know that the file you are converting was intended to be used on a particular device/software platform, choose the corresponding input profile, otherwise just choose the default input profile. If you know the files you are producing are meant for a particular device type, choose the corresponding Output profile. In particular, for MOBI Output files, you should choose the Kindle, for LIT the Microsoft Reader and for EPUB the Sony Reader. In the case of EPUB, the Sony Reader profile will result in EPUB files that will work everywhere. However, it has some side effects, like inserting artificial section breaks to keep internal components below the size threshold, needed for SONY devices. In particular for the iPhone/Android phones, choose the SONY output profile. If you know your EPUB files will not be read on a SONY or similar device, use the default output profile. If you are producing MOBI files that are not intended for the Kindle, choose the Mobipocket books output profile.

The Output profile also controls the screen size. This will cause, for example, images to be auto-resized to be fit to the screen in some output formats. So choose a profile of a device that has a screen size similar to your device.

1.4.4 Heuristic Processing

Heuristic Processing provides a variety of functions which can be used to try and detect and correct common problems in poorly formatted input documents. Use these functions if your input document suffers from poor formatting. Because these functions rely on common patterns, be aware that in some cases an option may lead to worse results, so use with care. As an example, several of these options will remove all non-breaking-space entities, or may include false positive matches relating to the function.

Enable heuristic processing This option activates calibre's Heuristic Processing stage of the conversion pipeline. This must be enabled in order for various sub-functions to be applied

Unwrap lines Enabling this option will cause calibre to attempt to detect and correct hard line breaks that exist within a document using punctuation clues and line length. calibre will first attempt to detect whether hard line breaks exist, if they do not appear to exist calibre will not attempt to unwrap lines. The line-unwrap factor can be reduced if you want to 'force' calibre to unwrap lines.

Line-unwrap factor This option controls the algorithm calibre uses to remove hard line breaks. For example, if the value of this option is 0.4, that means calibre will remove hard line breaks from the end of lines whose lengths are less than the length of 40% of all lines in the document. If your document only has a few line breaks which need correction, then this value should be reduced to somewhere between 0.1 and 0.2.

Detect and markup unformatted chapter headings and sub headings If your document does not have chapter headings and titles formatted differently from the rest of the text, calibre can use this option to attempt detection them and surround them with heading tags. <h2> tags are used for chapter headings; <h3> tags are used for any titles that are detected.

This function will not create a TOC, but in many cases it will cause calibre's default chapter detection settings to correctly detect chapters and build a TOC. Adjust the XPath under Structure Detection if a TOC is not automatically created. If there are no other headings used in the document then setting "//h:h2" under Structure Detection would be the easiest way to create a TOC for the document.

The inserted headings are not formatted, to apply formatting use the *Extra CSS* option under the Look and Feel conversion settings. For example, to center heading tags, use the following:

```
h2, h3 { text-align: center }
```

Renumber sequences of <h1> or <h2> tags Some publishers format chapter headings using multiple <h1> or <h2> tags sequentially. calibre's default conversion settings will cause such titles to be split into two pieces. This option will re-number the heading tags to prevent splitting.

Delete blank lines between paragraphs This option will cause calibre to analyze blank lines included within the document. If every paragraph is interleaved with a blank line, then calibre will remove all those blank paragraphs. Sequences of multiple blank lines will be considered scene breaks and retained as a single paragraph. This option differs from the 'Remove Paragraph Spacing' option under 'Look and Feel' in that it actually modifies the HTML content, while the other option modifies the document styles. This option can also remove paragraphs which were inserted using calibre's 'Insert blank line' option.

Ensure scene breaks are consistently formatted With this option calibre will attempt to detect common scene-break markers and ensure that they are center aligned. 'Soft' scene break markers, i.e. scene breaks only defined by extra white space, are styled to ensure that they will not be displayed in conjunction with page breaks.

Replace scene breaks If this option is configured then calibre will replace scene break markers it finds with the replacement text specified by the user. Please note that some ornamental characters may not be supported across all reading devices.

In general you should avoid using html tags, calibre will discard any tags and use pre-defined markup. <hr /> tags, i.e. horizontal rules, and <img> tags are exceptions. Horizontal rules can optionally be specified with styles, if you choose to add your own style be sure to include the 'width' setting, otherwise the style information will be discarded. Image tags can used, but calibre does not provide the ability to add the image during conversion, this must be done after the fact using the 'Edit Book' feature.

Example image tag (place the image within an 'Images' folder inside the epub after conversion):
<img style="width:10%" src="../Images/scenebreak.png" />

Example horizontal rule with styles: <hr style="width:20%;padding-top: 1px;border-top: 2px ridge black;border-bottom: 2px groove black;"/>

Remove unnecessary hyphens calibre will analyze all hyphenated content in the document when this option is enabled. The document itself is used as a dictionary for analysis. This allows calibre to accurately remove hyphens for any words in the document in any language, along with made-up and obscure scientific words. The primary drawback is words appearing only a single time in the document will not be changed. Analysis happens in two passes, the first pass analyzes line endings. Lines are only unwrapped if the word exists with or without a hyphen in the document. The second pass analyzes all hyphenated words throughout the document, hyphens are removed if the word exists elsewhere in the document without a match.

Italicize common words and patterns When enabled, calibre will look for common words and patterns that denote italics and italicize them. Examples are common text conventions such as ~word~ or phrases that should generally be italicized, e.g. latin phrases like 'etc.' or 'et cetera'.

Replace entity indents with CSS indents Some documents use a convention of defining text indents using non-breaking space entities. When this option is enabled calibre will attempt to detect this sort of formatting and convert them to a 3% text indent using css.

1.4.5 Search & Replace

These options are useful primarily for conversion of PDF documents or OCR conversions, though they can also be used to fix many document specific problems. As an example, some conversions can leaves behind page headers and footers in the text. These options use regular expressions to try and detect headers, footers, or other arbitrary text and remove or replace them. Remember that they operate on the intermediate XHTML produced by the conversion pipeline. There is a wizard to help you customize the regular expressions for your document. Click the magic wand beside the expression box, and click the 'Test' button after composing your search expression. Successful matches will be highlighted in Yellow.

The search works by using a python regular expression. All matched text is simply removed from the document or replaced using the replacement pattern. The replacement pattern is optional, if left blank then text matching the search pattern will be deleted from the document. You can learn more about regular expressions and their syntax at *All about using regular expressions in calibre* (page 205).

1.4.6 Structure Detection

Structure detection involves calibre trying its best to detect structural elements in the input document, when they are not properly specified. For example, chapters, page breaks, headers, footers, etc. As you can imagine, this process varies widely from book to book. Fortunately, calibre has very powerful options to control this. With power comes complexity, but if once you take the time to learn the complexity, you will find it well worth the effort.

Chapters and page breaks

calibre has two sets of options for *chapter detection* and *inserting page breaks*. This can sometimes be slightly confusing, as by default, calibre will insert page breaks before detected chapters as well as the locations detected by the page breaks option. The reason for this is that there are often location where page breaks should be inserted that are not chapter boundaries. Also, detected chapters can be optionally inserted into the auto generated Table of Contents.

calibre uses *XPath*, a powerful language to allow the user to specify chapter boundaries/page breaks. XPath can seem a little daunting to use at first, fortunately, there is a *XPath tutorial* (page 159) in the User Manual. Remember that Structure Detection operates on the intermediate XHTML produced by the conversion pipeline. Use the debug option described in the *Introduction* (page 55) to figure out the appropriate settings for your book. There is also a button for a XPath wizard to help with the generation of simple XPath expressions.

By default, calibre uses the following expression for chapter detection:

```
//*[((name()='h1' or name()='h2') and re:test(., 'chapter|book|section|part\s+', 'i')) or @cl
```

This expression is rather complex, because it tries to handle a number of common cases simultaneously. What it means is that calibre will assume chapters start at either *<h1>* or *<h2>* tags that have any of the words *(chapter, book, section or part)* in them or that have the *class="chapter"* attribute.

A related option is *Chapter mark*, which allows you to control what calibre does when it detects a chapter. By default, it will insert a page break before the chapter. You can have it insert a ruled line instead of, or in addition to the page break. You can also have it do nothing.

The default setting for detecting page breaks is:

```
//*[name()='h1' or name()='h2']
```

which means that calibre will insert page breaks before every *<h1>* and *<h2>* tag by default.

Note: The default expressions may change depending on the input format you are converting.

Miscellaneous

There are a few more options in this section.

Insert metadata as page at start of book One of the great things about calibre is that it allows you to maintain very complete metadata about all of your books, for example, a rating, tags, comments, etc. This option will create a single page with all this metadata and insert it into the converted ebook, typically just after the cover. Think of it as a way to create your own customised book jacket.

Remove first image Sometimes, the source document you are converting includes the cover as part of the book, instead of as a separate cover. If you also specify a cover in calibre, then the converted book will have two covers. This option will simply remove the first image from the source document, thereby ensuring that the converted book has only one cover, the one specified in calibre.

1.4.7 Table of Contents

When the input document has a Table of Contents in its metadata, calibre will just use that. However, a number of older formats either do not support a metadata based Table of Contents, or individual documents do not have one. In these cases, the options in this section can help you automatically generate a Table of Contents in the converted ebook, based on the actual content in the input document.

Note: Using these options can be a little challenging to get exactly right. If you prefer creating/editing the Table of Contents by hand, convert to the EPUB or AZW3 formats and select the checkbox at the bottom of the Table of

Contents section of the conversion dialog that says *Manually fine-tune the Table of Contents after conversion*. This will launch the ToC Editor tool after the conversion. It allows you to create entries in the Table of Contents by simply clicking the place in the book where you want the entry to point. You can also use the ToC Editor by itself, without doing a conversion. Go to *Preferences->Toolbars* and add the ToC Editor to the main toolbar. Then just select the book you want to edit and click the ToC Editor button.

The first option is *Force use of auto-generated Table of Contents*. By checking this option you can have calibre override any Table of Contents found in the metadata of the input document with the auto generated one.

The default way that the creation of the auto generated Table of Contents works is that, calibre will first try to add any detected chapters to the generated table of contents. You can learn how to customize the detection of chapters in the *Structure Detection* (page 61) section above. If you do not want to include detected chapters in the generated table of contents, check the *Do not add detected chapters* option.

If less than the *Chapter threshold* number of chapters were detected, calibre will then add any hyperlinks it finds in the input document to the Table of Contents. This often works well many input documents include a hyperlinked Table of Contents right at the start. The *Number of links* option can be used to control this behavior. If set to zero, no links are added. If set to a number greater than zero, at most that number of links is added.

calibre will automatically filter duplicates from the generated Table of Contents. However, if there are some additional undesirable entries, you can filter them using the *TOC Filter* option. This is a regular expression that will match the title of entries in the generated table of contents. Whenever a match is found, it will be removed. For example, to remove all entries titles "Next" or "Previous" use:

```
Next|Previous
```

The *Level 1,2,3 TOC* options allow you to create a sophisticated multi-level Table of Contents. They are XPath expressions that match tags in the intermediate XHTML produced by the conversion pipeline. See the *Introduction* (page 55) for how to get access to this XHTML. Also read the *XPath Tutorial* (page 159), to learn how to construct XPath expressions. Next to each option is a button that launches a wizard to help with the creation of basic XPath expressions. The following simple example illustrates how to use these options.

Suppose you have an input document that results in XHTML that look like this:

```
<html xmlns="http://www.w3.org/1999/xhtml">
    <head>
        <title>Sample document</title>
    </head>
    <body>
        <h1>Chapter 1</h1>
        ...
        <h2>Section 1.1</h2>
        ...
        <h2>Section 1.2</h2>
        ...
        <h1>Chapter 2</h1>
        ...
        <h2>Section 2.1</h2>
        ...
    </body>
</html>
```

Then, we set the options as:

```
Level 1 TOC : //h:h1
Level 2 TOC : //h:h2
```

This will result in an automatically generated two level Table of Contents that looks like:

```
Chapter 1
    Section 1.1
    Section 1.2
Chapter 2
    Section 2.1
```

> **Warning:** Not all output formats support a multi level Table of Contents. You should first try with EPUB Output. If that works, then try your format of choice.

1.4.8 Using images as chapter titles when converting HTML input documents

Suppose you want to use an image as your chapter title, but still want calibre to be able to automatically generate a Table of Contents for you from the chapter titles. Use the following HTML markup to achieve this

```html
<html>
    <body>
        <h2>Chapter 1</h2>
        <p>chapter 1 text...</p>
        <h2 title="Chapter 2"><img src="chapter2.jpg" /></h2>
        <p>chapter 2 text...</p>
    </body>
</html>
```

Set the *Level 1 TOC* setting to `//h:h2`. Then, for chapter two, calibre will take the title from the value of the `title` attribute on the `<h2>` tag, since the tag has no text.

1.4.9 Using tag attributes to supply the text for entries in the Table of Contents

If you have particularly long chapter titles and want shortened versions in the Table of Contents, you can use the title attribute to achieve this, for example:

```html
<html>
    <body>
        <h2 title="Chapter 1">Chapter 1: Some very long title</h2>
        <p>chapter 1 text...</p>
        <h2 title="Chapter 2">Chapter 2: Some other very long title</h2>
        <p>chapter 2 text...</p>
    </body>
</html>
```

Set the *Level 1 TOC* setting to `//h:h2/@title`. Then calibre will take the title from the value of the `title` attribute on the `<h2>` tags, instead of using the text inside the tag. Note the trailing `/@title` on the XPath expression, you can use this form to tell calibre to get the text from any attribute you like.

1.4.10 How options are set/saved for Conversion

There are two places where conversion options can be set in calibre. The first is in Preferences->Conversion. These settings are the defaults for the conversion options. Whenever you try to convert a new book, the settings set here will be used by default.

You can also change settings in the conversion dialog for each book conversion. When you convert a book, calibre remembers the settings you used for that book, so that if you convert it again, the saved settings for the individual book will take precedence over the defaults set in Preferences. You can restore the individual settings to defaults by using the Restore to defaults button in the individual book conversion dialog. You can remove the saved settings for a group of books by selecting all the books and then clicking the edit metadata button to bring up the bulk metadata edit dialog, near the bottom of the dialog is an option to remove stored conversion settings.

When you Bulk Convert a set of books, settings are taken in the following order (last one wins):

- From the defaults set in Preferences->Conversion

- From the saved conversion settings for each book being converted (if any). This can be turned off by the option in the top left corner of the Bulk Conversion dialog.

- From the settings set in the Bulk conversion dialog

Note that the final settings for each book in a Bulk Conversion will be saved and re-used if the book is converted again. Since the highest priority in Bulk Conversion is given to the settings in the Bulk Conversion dialog, these will override any book specific settings. So you should only bulk convert books together that need similar settings. The exceptions are metadata and input format specific settings. Since the Bulk Conversion dialog does not have settings for these two categories, they will be taken from book specific settings (if any) or the defaults.

Note: You can see the actual settings used during any conversion by clicking the rotating icon in the lower right corner and then double clicking the individual conversion job. This will bring up a conversion log that will contain the actual settings used, near the top.

1.4.11 Format specific tips

Here you will find tips specific to the conversion of particular formats. Options specific to particular format, whether input or output are available in the conversion dialog under their own section, for example *TXT Input* or *EPUB Output*.

Convert Microsoft Word documents

calibre can automatically convert `.docx` files created by Microsoft Word 2007 and newer. Just add the file to calibre and click convert (make sure you are running the latest version of calibre as support for `.docx` files is very new).

Note: There is a demo .docx file[25] that demonstrates the capabilities of the calibre conversion engine. Just download it and convert it to EPUB or AZW3 to see what calibre can do.

---

calibre will automatically generate a Table of Contents based on headings if you mark your headings with the `Heading 1`, `Heading 2`, etc. styles in Word. Open the output ebook in the calibre viewer and click the Table of Contents button to view the generated Table of Contents.

Older .doc files

For older .doc files, you can save the document as HTML with Microsoft Word and then convert the resulting HTML file with calibre. When saving as HTML, be sure to use the "Save as Web Page, Filtered" option as this will produce clean HTML that will convert well. Note that Word produces really messy HTML, converting it can take a long time, so be patient. If you have a newer version of Word available, you can directly save it as docx as well.

Another alternative is to use the free OpenOffice. Open your .doc file in OpenOffice and save it in OpenOffice's format .odt. calibre can directly convert .odt files.

---

[25] http://calibre-ebook.com/downloads/demos/demo.docx

Convert TXT documents

TXT documents have no well defined way to specify formatting like bold, italics, etc, or document structure like paragraphs, headings, sections and so on, but there are a variety of conventions commonly used. By default calibre attempts automatic detection of the correct formatting and markup based on those conventions.

TXT input supports a number of options to differentiate how paragraphs are detected.

> ***Paragraph Style: Auto*** Analyzes the text file and attempts to automatically determine how paragraphs are defined. This option will generally work fine, if you achieve undesirable results try one of the manual options.

> ***Paragraph Style: Block*** Assumes one or more blank lines are a paragraph boundary:

```
This is the first.

This is the
second paragraph.
```

> ***Paragraph Style: Single*** Assumes that every line is a paragraph:

```
This is the first.
This is the second.
This is the third.
```

> ***Paragraph Style: Print*** Assumes that every paragraph starts with an indent (either a tab or 2+ spaces). Paragraphs end when the next line that starts with an indent is reached:

```
  This is the
first.
  This is the second.

  This is the
third.
```

> ***Paragraph Style: Unformatted*** Assumes that the document has no formatting, but does use hard line breaks. Punctuation and median line length are used to attempt to re-create paragraphs.

> ***Formatting Style: Auto*** Attempts to detect the type of formatting markup being used. If no markup is used then heuristic formatting will be applied.

> ***Formatting Style: Heuristic*** Analyzes the document for common chapter headings, scene breaks, and italicized words and applies the appropriate html markup during conversion.

> ***Formatting Style: Markdown*** calibre also supports running TXT input though a transformation preprocessor known as markdown. Markdown allows for basic formatting to be added to TXT documents, such as bold, italics, section headings, tables, lists, a Table of Contents, etc. Marking chapter headings with a leading # and setting the chapter XPath detection expression to "//h:h1" is the easiest way to have a proper table of contents generated from a TXT document. You can learn more about the markdown syntax at daringfireball[26].

> ***Formatting Style: None*** Applies no special formatting to the text, the document is converted to html with no other changes.

Convert PDF documents

PDF documents are one of the worst formats to convert from. They are a fixed page size and text placement format. Meaning, it is very difficult to determine where one paragraph ends and another begins. calibre will try to unwrap

---

[26] http://daringfireball.net/projects/markdown/syntax

paragraphs using a configurable, *Line Un-Wrapping Factor*. This is a scale used to determine the length at which a line should be unwrapped. Valid values are a decimal between 0 and 1. The default is 0.45, just under the median line length. Lower this value to include more text in the unwrapping. Increase to include less. You can adjust this value in the conversion settings under *PDF Input*.

Also, they often have headers and footers as part of the document that will become included with the text. Use the Search and Replace panel to remove headers and footers to mitigate this issue. If the headers and footers are not removed from the text it can throw off the paragraph unwrapping. To learn how to use the header and footer removal options, read *All about using regular expressions in calibre* (page 205).

Some limitations of PDF input are:

- Complex, multi-column, and image based documents are not supported.

- Extraction of vector images and tables from within the document is also not supported.

- Some PDFs use special glyphs to represent ll or ff or fi, etc. Conversion of these may or may not work depending on just how they are represented internally in the PDF.

- Links and Tables of Contents are not supported

- PDFs that use embedded non-unicode fonts to represent non-English characters will result in garbled output for those characters

- Some PDFs are made up of photographs of the page with OCRed text behind them. In such cases calibre uses the OCRed text, which can be very different from what you see when you view the PDF file

- PDFs that are used to display complex text, like right to left languages and math typesetting will not convert correctly

To re-iterate **PDF is a really, really bad** format to use as input. If you absolutely must use PDF, then be prepared for an output ranging anywhere from decent to unusable, depending on the input PDF.

Comic Book Collections

A comic book collection is a .cbc file. A .cbc file is a zip file that contains other CBZ/CBR files. In addition the .cbc file must contain a simple text file called comics.txt, encoded in UTF-8. The comics.txt file must contain a list of the comics files inside the .cbc file, in the form filename:title, as shown below:

```
one.cbz:Chapter One
two.cbz:Chapter Two
three.cbz:Chapter Three
```

The .cbc file will then contain:

```
comics.txt
one.cbz
two.cbz
three.cbz
```

calibre will automatically convert this .cbc file into a ebook with a Table of Contents pointing to each entry in comics.txt.

EPUB advanced formatting demo

Various advanced formatting for EPUB files is demonstrated in this demo file[27]. The file was created from hand coded HTML using calibre and is meant to be used as a template for your own EPUB creation efforts.

---

[27] http://calibre-ebook.com/downloads/demos/demo.epub

The source HTML it was created from is available demo.zip[28]. The settings used to create the EPUB from the ZIP file are:

```
ebook-convert demo.zip .epub -vv --authors "Kovid Goyal" --language en --level1-toc '//*[@clas
```

Note that because this file explores the potential of EPUB, most of the advanced formatting is not going to work on readers less capable than calibre's built-in EPUB viewer.

Convert ODT documents

calibre can directly convert ODT (OpenDocument Text) files. You should use styles to format your document and minimize the use of direct formatting. When inserting images into your document you need to anchor them to the paragraph, images anchored to a page will all end up in the front of the conversion.

To enable automatic detection of chapters, you need to mark them with the build-in styles called 'Heading 1', 'Heading 2', ..., 'Heading 6' ('Heading 1' equates to the HTML tag <h1>, 'Heading 2' to <h2> etc). When you convert in calibre you can enter which style you used into the 'Detect chapters at' box. Example:

- If you mark Chapters with style 'Heading 2', you have to set the 'Detect chapters at' box to `//h:h2`

- For a nested TOC with Sections marked with 'Heading 2' and the Chapters marked with 'Heading 3' you need to enter `//h:h2|//h:h3`. On the Convert - TOC page set the 'Level 1 TOC' box to `//h:h2` and the 'Level 2 TOC' box to `//h:h3`.

Well-known document properties (Title, Keywords, Description, Creator) are recognized and calibre will use the first image (not to small, and with good aspect-ratio) as the cover image.

There is also an advanced property conversion mode, which is activated by setting the custom property `opf.metadata` ('Yes or No' type) to Yes in your ODT document (File->Properties->Custom Properties). If this property is detected by calibre, the following custom properties are recognized (`opf.authors` overrides document creator):

```
opf.titlesort
opf.authors
opf.authorsort
opf.publisher
opf.pubdate
opf.isbn
opf.language
opf.series
opf.seriesindex
```

In addition to this, you can specify the picture to use as the cover by naming it `opf.cover` (right click, Picture->Options->Name) in the ODT. If no picture with this name is found, the 'smart' method is used. As the cover detection might result in double covers in certain output formats, the process will remove the paragraph (only if the only content is the cover!) from the document. But this works only with the named picture!

To disable cover detection you can set the custom property `opf.nocover` ('Yes or No' type) to Yes in advanced mode.

Converting to PDF

The first, most important, setting to decide on when converting to PDF is the page size. By default, calibre uses a page size defined by the current *Output profile*. So if your output profile is set to Kindle, calibre will create a PDF with page size suitable for viewing on the small kindle screen. However, if you view this PDF file on a computer screen, then

---

[28] http://calibre-ebook.com/downloads/demos/demo.zip

it will appear to have too large fonts. To create "normal" sized PDFs, use the *Override page size* option under *PDF Output* in the conversion dialog.

Headers and Footers

You can insert arbitrary headers and footers on each page of the PDF by specifying header and footer templates. Templates are just snippets of HTML code that get rendered in the header and footer locations. For example, to display page numbers centered at the bottom of every page, in green, use the following footer template:

```
<p style="text-align:center; color:green">Page _PAGENUM_</p>
```

calibre will automatically replace _PAGENUM_ with the current page number. You can even put different content on even and odd pages, for example the following header template will show the title on odd pages and the author on even pages:

```
<p style="text-align:right"><span class="even_page">_AUTHOR_</span><span class="odd_page"><i>_
```

calibre will automatically replace _TITLE_ and _AUTHOR_ with the title and author of the document being converted. You can also display text at the left and right edges and change the font size, as demonstrated with this header template:

```
<div style="font-size:x-small"><p style="float:left">_TITLE_</p><p style="float:right;"><i>_A
```

This will display the title at the left and the author at the right, in a font size smaller than the main text.

You can also use the current section in templates, as shown below:

```
<p style="text-align:right">_SECTION_</p>
```

SECTION is replaced by whatever the name of the current section is. These names are taken from the metadata Table of Contents in the document (the PDF Outline). If the document has no table of contents then it will be replaced by empty text. If a single PDF page has multiple sections, the first section on the page will be used.

You can even use javascript inside the header and footer templates, for example, the following template will cause page numbers to start at 4 instead of 1:

```
<p id="pagenum" style="text-align:center;"></p><script>document.getElementById("pagenum").inne
```

Note: When adding headers and footers make sure you set the page top and bottom margins to large enough values, under the Page Setup section of the conversion dialog.

Printable Table of Contents

You can also insert a printable Table of Contents at the end of the PDF that lists the page numbers for every section. This is very useful if you intend to print out the PDF to paper. If you wish to use the PDF on an electronic device, then the PDF Outline provides this functionality and is generated by default.

You can customize the look of the the generated Table of contents by using the Extra CSS conversion setting under the Look & Feel part of the conversion dialog. The default css used is listed below, simply copy it and make whatever changes you like.

```
.calibre-pdf-toc table { width: 100%% }

.calibre-pdf-toc table tr td:last-of-type { text-align: right }

.calibre-pdf-toc .level-0 {
    font-size: larger;
```

```
}
.calibre-pdf-toc .level-1 td:first-of-type { padding-left: 1.4em }
.calibre-pdf-toc .level-2 td:first-of-type { padding-left: 2.8em }
```

1.5 Editing E-books

calibre has an integrated e-book editor that can be used to edit books in the EPUB and AZW3 (Kindle) formats. The editor shows you the HTML and CSS that is used internally inside the book files, with a live preview that updates as you make changes. It also contains various automated tools to perform common cleanup and fixing tasks.

You can use this editor by right clicking on any book in calibre and selecting *Edit book*.

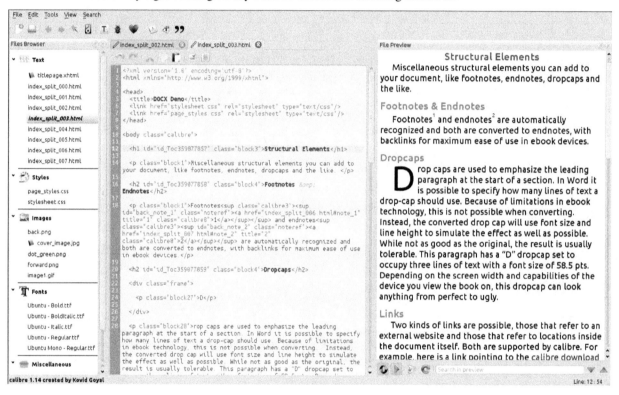

Contents

1.5.1 Basic workflow

Note: A video tour of the calibre editor is available here[29].

[29] http://calibre-ebook.com/demo#tutorials

When you first open a book with the Edit book tool, you will be presented with a list of files on the left. These are the individual HTML files, stylesheets, images, etc. that make up the content of the book. Simply double click on a file to start editing it. Note that if you want to do anything more sophisticated than making a few small tweaks, you will need to know HTML Tutorial[30] and CSS Tutorial[31].

As you make changes to the HTML or CSS in the editor, the changes will be previewed, live, in the preview panel to the right. When you are happy with how the changes you have made look, click the Save button or use *File->Save* to save your changes into the ebook.

One useful feature is *Checkpoints*. Before you embark on some ambitious set of edits, you can create a checkpoint. The checkpoint will preserve the current state of your book, then if in the future you decide you don't like the changes you have made to you can go back to the state when you created the checkpoint. To create a checkpoint, use *Edit->Create checkpoint*. Checkpoints will also be automatically created for you whenever you run any automated tool like global search and replace. The checkpointing functionality is in addition to the normal Undo/redo mechanism when editing individual files. Checkpoints are useful for when changes are spread over multiple files in the book.

That is the basic work flow for editing books – Open a file, make changes, preview and save. The rest of this manual will discuss the various tools and features present to allow you to perform specific tasks efficiently.

---

[30] http://html.net/tutorials/html/
[31] http://html.net/tutorials/css/

1.5.2 The Files Browser

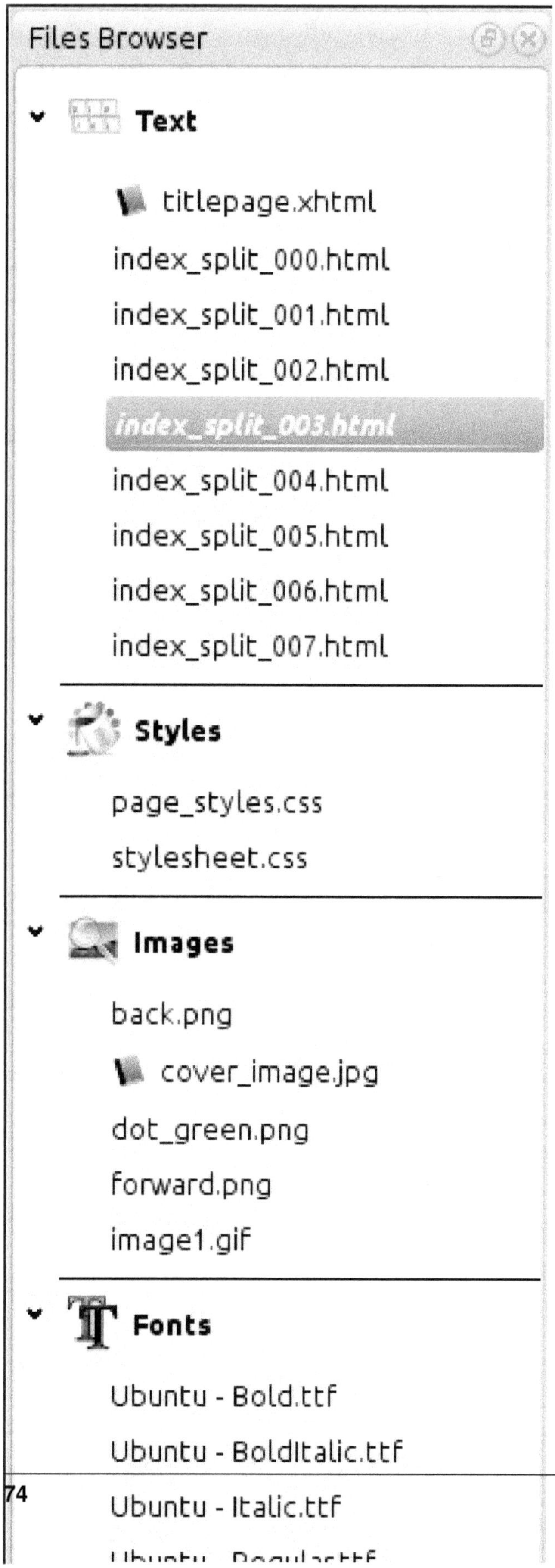

Files Browser

⌄ ⊞ **Text**

　　▌ titlepage.xhtml

　　index_split_000.html

　　index_split_001.html

　　index_split_002.html

　　index_split_003.html

　　index_split_004.html

　　index_split_005.html

　　index_split_006.html

　　index_split_007.html

⌄ **Styles**

　　page_styles.css

　　stylesheet.css

⌄ **Images**

　　back.png

　　▌ cover_image.jpg

　　dot_green.png

　　forward.png

　　image1.gif

⌄ **Fonts**

　　Ubuntu - Bold.ttf

　　Ubuntu - BoldItalic.ttf

　　Ubuntu - Italic.ttf

　　Ubuntu - Regular.ttf

The *Files Browser* gives you an overview of the various files inside the book you are editing. The files are arranged by category, with text (HTML) files at the top, followed by stylesheet (CSS) files, images and so on. Simply double click on a file to start editing it. Editing is supported for HTML, CSS and image files. The order of text files is the same order that they would be displayed in, if you were reading the book. All other files are arranged alphabetically.

By hovering your mouse over an entry, you can see its size, and also, at the bottom of the screen, the full path to the file inside the book. Note that files inside ebooks are compressed, so the size of the final book is not the sum of the individual file sizes.

Many files have special meaning, in the book. These will typically have an icon next to their names, indicating the special meaning. For example, in the picture to the left, you can see that the files *cover_image.jpg* and *titlepage.xhtml* have the icon of a cover next to them, this indicates they are the book cover image and titlepage. Similarly, the *content.opf* file has a metadata icon next to it, indicating the book metadata is present in it and the the *toc.ncx* file has a T icon next to it, indicating it is the Table of Contents.

You can perform many actions on individual files, by right clicking them.

Renaming files

You can rename an individual file by right clicking it and selecting *Rename*. Renaming a file automatically updates all links and references to it throughout the book. So all you have to do is provide the new name, calibre will take care of the rest.

You can also bulk rename many files at once. This is useful if you want the files to have some simple name pattern. For example you might want to rename all the HTML files to have names Chapter-1.html, Chapter-2.html and so on. Select the files you want bulk renamed by holding down the Shift or Ctrl key and clicking the files. Then right click and select *Bulk rename*. Enter a prefix and what number you would like the automatic numbering to start at, click OK and you are done.

Merging files

Sometimes, you may want to merge two HTML files or two CSS files together. It can sometimes be useful to have everything in a single file. Be wary, though, putting a lot of content into a single file will cause performance problems when viewing the book in a typical ebook reader.

To merge multiple files together, select them by holding the Ctrl key and clicking on them (make sure you only select files of one type, either all HTML files or all CSS files and so on). Then right click and select merge. That's all, calibre will merge the files, automatically taking care of migrating all links and references to the merged files. Note that merging files can sometimes cause text styling to change, since the individual files could have used different stylesheets.

Changing text file order

You can re-arrange the order in which text (HTML) files are opened when reading the book by simply dragging and dropping them in the Files browser. For the technically inclined, this is called re-ordering the book spine. Note that you have to drop the items *between* other items, not on top of them, this can be a little fiddly until you get used to it.

Marking the cover

E-books typically have a cover image. This image is indicated in the Files Browser by the icon of a brown book next to the image name. If you want to designate some other image as the cover, you can do so by right clicking on the file and choosing *Mark as cover*.

In addition, EPUB files has the concept of a *titlepage*. A title page is a HTML file that acts as the title page/cover for the book. You can mark an HTML file as the titlepage when editing EPUBs by right-clicking. Be careful that the file you mark contains only the cover information. If it contains other content, such as the first chapter, then that content will be lost if the user ever converts the EPUB file in calibre to another format. This is because when converting, calibre assumes that the marked title page contains only the cover and no other content.

Deleting files

You can delete files by either right clicking on them or by selecting them and pressing the Delete key. Deleting a file removes all references to the file from the OPF file, saving you that chore. However, references in other places are not removed, you can use the Check Book tool to easily find and remove/replace them.

Export of files

You can export a file from inside the book to somewhere else on your computer. This is useful if you want to work on the file in isolation, with specialised tools. To do this, simply right click on the file and choose *Export*.

Once you are done working on the exported file, you can re-import it into the book, by right clicking on the file again and choosing *Replace with file...* which will allow you to replace the file in the book with the previously exported file.

Adding new images/fonts/etc. or creating new blank files

You can add a new image, font, stylesheet, etc. from your computer into the book by clicking *File->New file*. This lets you either import a file by clicking the *Import resource file* button or create a new blank html file or stylesheet by simply entering the file name into the box for the new file.

You can also import multiple files into the book at once using File->Import files into book.

Replacing files

You can easily replace existing files in the book, by right clicking on the file and choosing replace. This will automatically update all links and references, in case the replacement file has a different name than the file being replaced.

Linking stylesheets to HTML files efficiently

As a convenience, you can select multiple HTML files in the Files Browser, right click and choose Link stylesheets to have calibre automatically insert the <link> tags for those stylesheets into all the selected HTML files.

1.5.3 Search & Replace

Edit Book has a very powerful search and replace interface that allows you to search and replace text in the current file, across all files and even in a marked region of the current file. You can search using a normal search or using regular expressions. To learn how to use regular expressions for advanced searching, see *All about using regular expressions in calibre* (page 205).

Start the search and replace via the *Search->Find/replace* menu entry (you must be editing an HTML or CSS file).

Type the text you want to find into the Find box and its replacement into the Replace box. You can the click the appropriate buttons to Find the next match, replace the current match and replace all matches.

Using the drop downs at the bottom of the box, you can have the search operate over the current file, all text files, all style files or all files. You can also choose the search mode to be a normal (string) search or a regular expression search.

You can count all the matches for a search expression via *Search->Count all*. The count will run over whatever files/regions you have selected in the dropdown box.

You can also go to a specific line in the currently open editor via *Search->Go to line*.

Note: Remember, to harness the full power of search and replace, you will need to use regular expressions. See *All about using regular expressions in calibre* (page 205).

Saved searches

You can save frequently used search/replace expressions and reuse them multiple times. To save a search simply right click in the Find box and select *Save current search*.

You can bring up the dialog of saved searches via *Search->Saved Searches*. This will present you with a list of search and replace expressions that you can apply. You can even select multiple entries in the list by holding down the Ctrl Key while clicking so as to run multiple search and replace expressions in a single operation.

Function mode

Function mode allows you to write arbitrarily powerful python functions that are run on every Find/replace. You can do pretty much any text manipulation you like in function mode. For more information, see Function Mode for Search & Replace in the Editor (page 89).

1.5.4 Automated tools

Edit book has various tools to help with common tasks. These are accessed via the *Tools* menu.

Edit the Table of Contents

There is a dedicated tool to ease editing of the Table of Contents. Launch it with *Tools->Table of Contents->Edit Table of Contents*.

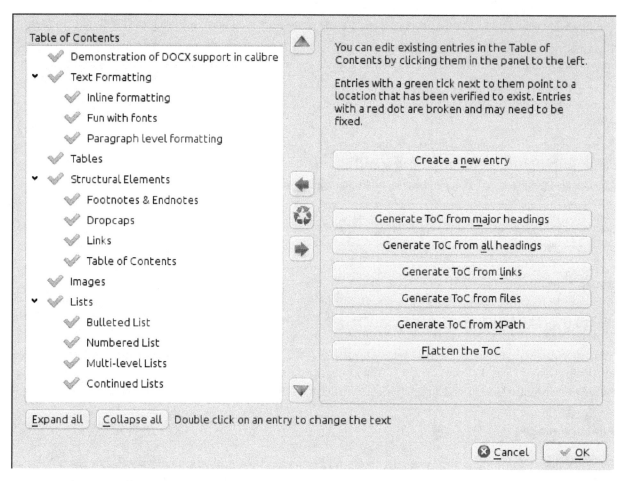

The Edit Table of Contents tool shows you the current Table of Contents (if any) on the left. Simply double click on any entry to change its text. You can also re-arrange entries by drag and drop or by using the buttons to the right.

For books that do not have a pre-existing Table of Contents, the tool gives you various options to auto-generate a Table of Contents from the text. You can generate from the headings in the document, from links, from individual files and so on.

You can edit individual entries by clicking on them and then clicking the *Change the location this entry points to* button. This will open up a mini-preview of the book, simply move the mouse cursor over the book view panel, and click where you want the entry to point to. A thick green line will show you the location. Click OK once you are happy with the location.

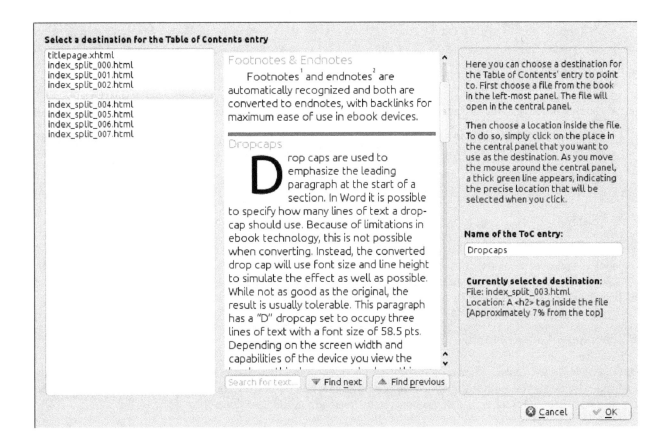

Check Book

The *Check Book* tool searches your book for problems that could prevent it working as intended on actual reader devices. Activate it via *Tools->Check Book*.

Any problems found are reported in a nice, easy to use list. Clicking any entry in the list shows you some help about that error as well as giving you the option to auto-fix that error, if the error can be fixed automatically. You can also double click the error to open the location of the error in an editor, so you can fix it yourself.

Some of the checks performed are:

- Malformed HTML markup. Any HTML markup that does not parse as well-formed XML is reported. Correcting it will ensure that your markup works as intended in all contexts. calibre can also auto-fix these errors, but auto-fixing can sometimes have unexpected effects, so use with care. As always, a checkpoint is created before auto-fixing so you can easily revert all changes. Auto-fixing works by parsing the markup using the HTML5 algorithm, which is highly fault tolerant and then converting to well formed XML.

- Malformed or unknown CSS styles. Any CSS that is not valid or that has properties not defined in the CSS 2.1 standard (plus a few from CSS 3) are reported. CSS is checked in all stylesheets, inline style attributes and <style> tags in HTML files.

- Broken links. Links that point to files inside the book that are missing are reported.

- Unreferenced files. Files in the book that are not referenced by any other file or are not in the spine are reported.

- Various common problems in OPF files such as duplicate spine or manifest items, broken idrefs or meta cover tags, missing required sections and so on.

- Various compatibility checks for known problems that can cause the book to malfunction on reader devices.

Add a cover

You can easily add a cover to the book via *Tools->Add cover*. This allows you to either choose an existing image in the book as the cover or import a new image into the book and make it the cover. When editing EPUB files, the HTML wrapper for the cover is automatically generated. If an existing cover in the book is found, it is replaced. The tool also automatically takes care of correctly marking the cover files as covers in the OPF.

Embedding referenced fonts

Accessed via *Tools->Embed reference fonts*, this tool finds all fonts referenced in the book and if they are not already embedded, searches your computer for them and embeds them into the book, if found. Please make sure that you have the necessary copyrights for embedding commercially licensed fonts, before doing this.

Subsetting embedded fonts

Accessed via *Tools->Subset embedded fonts*, this tool reduces all the fonts in the book to only contain glyphs for the text actually present in the book. This commonly reduces the size of the font files by ~ 50%. However, be aware that once the fonts are subset, if you add new text whose characters are not previously present in the subset font, the font will not work for the new text. So do this only as the last step in your workflow.

Smartening punctuation

Convert plain text dashes, ellipsis, quotes, multiple hyphens, etc. into their typographically correct equivalents. Note that the algorithm can sometimes generate incorrect results, especially when single quotes at the start of contractions are involved. Accessed via *Tools->Smarten punctuation*.

Removing unused CSS rules

Remove all unused CSS rules from stylesheets and <style> tags. Some books created from production templates can have a large number of extra CSS rules that don't match any actual content. These extra rules can slow down readers that need to process them all. Accessed via *Tools->Remove unused CSS*.

Fix HTML

This tool simply converts HTML that cannot be parsed as XML into well-formed XML. It is very common in ebooks to have non-well-formed XML, so this tool simply automates the process of fixing such HTML. The tool works by parsing the HTML using the HTML5 algorithm (the algorithm used in all modern browsers) and then converting the result into XML. Be aware that auto-fixing can sometimes have counter-intuitive results. If you prefer, you can use the Check Book tool discussed above to find and manually correct problems in the HTML. Accessed via *Tools->Fix HTML*.

Beautifying files

This tool is used to auto-format all HTML and CSS files so that they "look pretty". The code is auto-indented so that it lines up nicely, blank lines are inserted where appropriate and so on. Note that beautifying also auto-fixes broken HTML/CSS. Therefore, if you don't want any auto-fixing to be performed, first use the Check Book tool to correct all problems and only then run beautify. Accessed via *Tools->Beautify all files*.

Note: In HTML any text can have significant whitespace, via the CSS white-space directive. Therefore, beautification could potentially change the rendering of the HTML. To avoid this as far as possible, the beautify algorithm only beautifies block level tags that contain other block level tags. So, for example, text inside a <p> tag will not have its whitespace changed. But a <body> tag that contains only other <p> and <div> tags will be beautified. This can sometimes mean that a particular file will not be affected by beautify as it has no suitable block level tags. In such cases you can try different beautification tools, that are less careful, for example: HTML Tidy[32].

Insert inline Table of Contents

Normally in ebooks, the Table of Contents is separate from the main text and is typically accessed via a special Table of Contents button/menu in the ebook reading device. You can also have calibre automatically generate an *inline* Table of Contents that becomes part of the text of the book. It is generated based on the currently defined Table of Contents.

If you use this tool multiple times, each invocation will cause the previously created inline Table of Contents to be replaced. The tool can be accessed via *Tools->Table of Contents->Insert inline Table of Contents*.

Set Semantics

This tool is used to set *semantics* in EPUB files. Semantics are simply, links in the OPF file that identify certain locations in the book as having special meaning. You can use them to identify the foreword, dedication, cover, table of contents, etc. Simply choose the type of semantic information you want to specify and then select the location in the book the link should point to. This tool can be accessed via *Tools->Set semantics*.

Filter style information

This tool can be used to easily remove specified CSS style properties from the entire book. You can tell it what properties you want removed, for example, `color`, `background-color`, `line-height` and it will remove them from everywhere they occur — stylesheets, <style> tags and inline `style` attributes. After removing the style information, a summary of all the changes made is displayed so you can see exactly what was changed. The tool can be accessed via *Tools->Filter style information*.

1.5.5 Checkpoints

Checkpoints are a way to mark the current state of the book as "special". You can then go on to do whatever changes you want to the book and if you don't like the results, return to the checkpointed state. Checkpoints are automatically created every time you run any of the automated tools described in the previous section.

You can create a checkpoint via *Edit->Create checkpoint*. And go back to a previous checkpoint with *Edit->Revert to* ...

---

[32]http://infohound.net/tidy/

The checkpointing functionality is in addition to the normal Undo/redo mechanism when editing individual files. Checkpoints are particularly useful for when changes are spread over multiple files in the book or when you wish to be able to revert a large group of related changes as a whole.

You can see a list of available checkpoints via *View->Checkpoints*. You can compare the current state of the book to a specified checkpoint using the *Comparing E-books* (page 99) tool – by selecting the checkpoint of interest and clicking the *Compare* button. The *Revert to* button restores the book to the selected checkpoint, undoing all changes since that checkpoint was created.

1.5.6 The Live Preview panel

File Preview

Inline formatting

Here, we demonstrate various types of inline text formatting and the use of embedded fonts.

Here is some **bold,** *italic, **bold-italic,** underlined* and ~~struck out~~ text. Then, we have a super^script and a sub_script. Now we see some red, green and blue text. Some text with a yellow highlight. Some text in a box. Some text in inverse video.

A paragraph with styled text: *subtle emphasis* followed by **strong text** and *intense emphasis*. This paragraph uses document wide styles for styling rather than inline text properties as demonstrated in the previous paragraph — calibre can handle both with equal ease.

Fun with fonts

This document has embedded the Ubuntu font family. The body text is in the Ubuntu typeface, here is some text in the Ubuntu Mono typeface, notice how every letter has the same width, even i and m. Every embedded font will automatically be embedded in the output ebook during conversion.

The *File Preview* gives you an overview of the various files inside The live preview panel shows you the changes you are making live (with a second or two of delay). As you edit HTML or CSS files, the preview panel is updated automatically to reflect your changes. As you move the cursor around in the editor, the preview panel will track its location, showing you the corresponding location in the book. Clicking in the preview panel, will cause the cursor in the editor to be positioned over the element you clicked. If you click a link pointing to another file in the book, that file will be opened in the edit and the preview panel, automatically.

You can turn off the automatic syncing of position and live preview of changes – by buttons under the preview panel. The live update of the preview panel only happens when you are not actively typing in the editor, so as not to be distracting or slow you down, waiting for the preview to render.

The preview panel shows you how the text will look when viewed. However, the preview panel is not a substitute for actually testing your book an actual reader device. It is both more, and less capable than an actual reader. It will tolerate errors and sloppy markup much better than most reader devices. It will also not show you page margins, page breaks and embedded fonts that use font name aliasing. Use the preview panel while you are working on the book, but once you are done, review it in an actual reader device or software emulator.

Note: The preview panel does not support embedded fonts if the name of the font inside the font file does not match the name in the CSS @font-face rule. You can use the Check Book tool to quickly find and fix any such problem fonts.

Splitting HTML files

One, perhaps non-obvious, use of the preview panel is to split long HTML files. While viewing the file you want to

split, click the *split mode* button under the preview panel   . Then simply move your mouse to the place where you want to split the file and click. A thick green line will show you exactly where the split will happen as you move your mouse. Once you have found the location you want, simply click and the split will be performed.

Splitting the file will automatically update all links and references that pointed into the bottom half of the file and will open the newly split file in an editor.

You can also split a single HTML file at multiple locations automatically, by right clicking inside the file in the editor and choosing *Split at multiple locations*. This will allow you to easily split a large file at all heading tags or all tags having a certain class and so on.

1.5.7 The Live CSS panel

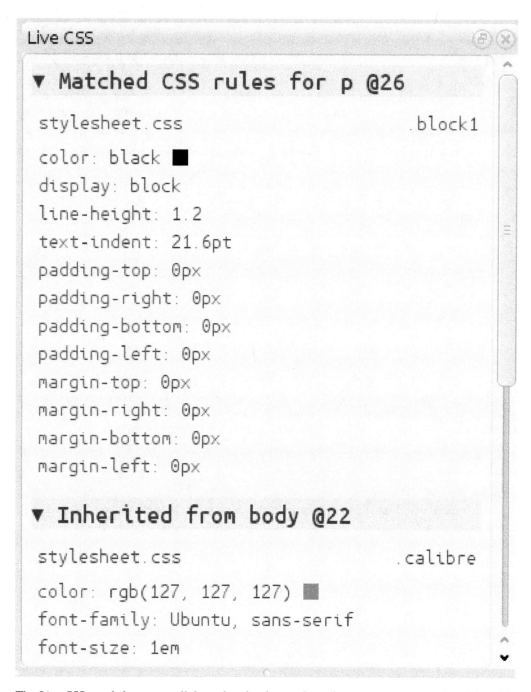

The *Live CSS* panel shows you all the style rules that apply to the tag you are currently editing. The name of tag, along with its line number in the editor are displayed, followed by a list of matching style rules.

It is a great way to quickly see which style rules apply to any tag. The view also has clickable links (in blue), which take you directly to the location where the style was defined, in case you wish to make any changes to the style rules. Style rules that apply directly to the tag, as well as rules that are inherited from parent tags are shown.

The panel also shows you what the finally calculated styles for the tag are. Properties in the list that are superseded by higher priority rules are shown with a line through them.

You can enable the Live CSS panel via *View->Live CSS*.

1.5.8 Miscellaneous Tools

There are a few more tools that can be useful while you edit the book.

The Table of Contents View

The Table of Contents view shows you the current table of contents in the book. Double clicking on any entry opens the place that entry points to in an editor. You can right click to edit the Table of Contents, refresh the view or expand/collapse all items. Access this view via *Views->Table of Contents*.

Checking the spelling of words in the book

You can run a spelling checker via *Tools->Check spelling*.

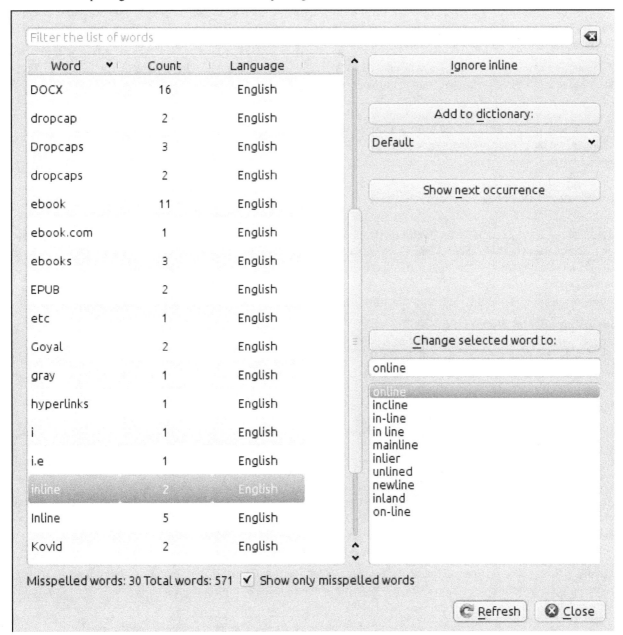

Words are shown with the number of times they occur in the book and the language the word belongs to. Language information is taken from the books metadata and from `lang` attributes in the HTML files. This allows the spell checker to work well even with books that contain text in multiple languages. For example, in the following HTML extract, the word color will be checked using American English and the word colour using British English:

```
<div lang="en_US">color <span lang="en_GB">colour</span></div>
```

Note: You can double click a word to highlight the next occurrence of that word in the editor. This is useful if you wish to manually edit the word, or see what context it is in.

To change a word, simply double click one of the suggested alternative spellings on the right, or type in your own corrected spelling and click the *Change selected word to* button. This will replace all occurrences of the word in the book. You can also right click on a word in the main word list to change the word conveniently from the right click menu.

You can have the spelling checker ignore a word for the current session by clicking the *Ignore* button. You can also add a word to the user dictionary by clicking the *Add to dictionary* button. The spelling checker supports multiple user dictionaries, so you can select the dictionary you want the word added to.

You can also have the spelling checker display all the words in your book, not just the incorrectly spelled ones. This is useful to see what words are most common in your book and to run a simple search and replace on individual words.

Note: If you make any changes to the book by editing files while the spell check tool is open, you should click the *Refresh* button in the spell check tool. If you do not do this and continue to use the spell check tool, you could lose the changes you have made in the editor.

Adding new dictionaries

The spelling checker comes with builtin dictionaries for the English and Spanish languages. You can install your own dictionaries via *Preferences->Editor->Manage spelling dictionaries*. The spell checker can use dictionaries from the LibreOffice program (in the .oxt format). You can download these dictionaries from The LibreOffice Extensions repository[33].

Inserting special characters

You can insert characters that are difficult to type by using the *Edit->Insert special character* tool. This shows you all unicode characters, simply click on the character you want to type. If you hold Ctrl while clicking, the window will close itself after inserting the selected character. This tool can be used to insert special characters into the main text or into any other area of the user interface, such as the Search and replace tool.

Because there are a lot of characters, you can define your own *Favorite* characters, that will be shown first. Simply right click on a character to mark it as favorite. You can also right click on a character in favorites to remove it from favorites. Finally, you can re-arrange the order of characters in favorites by clicking the *Re-arrange favorites* button and then drag and dropping the characters in favorites around.

You can also directly type in special characters using the keyboard. To do this, you type the unicode code for the character (in hexadecimal) and then press the *Alt+X* key which will convert the previously typed code into the corresponding character. For example, to type ÿ you would type ff and then Alt+X. To type a non-breaking space you would use a0 and then *Alt+X*, to type the horizontal ellipsis you would use 2026 and *Alt+X* and so on.

Finally, you can type in special characters by using HTML named entities. For example, typing   will be replaced by a non breaking space when you type the semi-colon. The replacement happens only when typing the semi-colon.

---

[33] http://extensions.libreoffice.org/extension-center?getCategories=Dictionary&getCompatibility=any&sort_on=positive_ratings

The code inspector view

This view shows you the HTML coding and CSS that applies to the current element of interest. You open it by right clicking a location in the preview panel and choosing *Inspect*. It allows you to see the HTML coding for that element and more importantly, the CSS styles that apply to it. You can even dynamically edit the styles and see what effect your changes have instantly. Note that editing the styles does not actually make changes to the book contents, it only allows for quick experimentation. The ability to live edit inside the Inspector is under development.

Checking external links

You can use this tool to check all links in your book that point to external websites. The tool will try to visit every externally linked website, and if the visit fails, it will report all broken links in a convenient format for you to fix.

Arrange files into folders by type

Often when editing EPUB files that you get from somewhere, you will find that the files inside the EPUB are arranged haphazardly, in different sub-folders. This tool allows you to automatically move all files into sub-folders based on their types. Access it via *Tools->Arrange into folders*. Note that this tool only changes how the files are arranged inside the EPUB, it does not change how they are displayed in the Files Browser.

Importing files in other e-book formats as EPUB

The editor includes the ability to import files in some other e-book formats directly as a new EPUB, without going through a full conversion. This is particularly useful to directly create EPUB files from your own hand-edited HTML files. You can do this via *File->Import an HTML or DOCX file as a new book*.

Function Mode for Search & Replace in the Editor

The Search & Replace tool in the editor support a *function mode*. In this mode, you can combine regular expressions (see All about using regular expressions in calibre (page 205)) with arbitrarily powerful python functions to do all sorts of advanced text processing.

In the standard *regexp* mode for search and replace, you specify both a regular expression to search for as well as a template that is used to replace all found matches. In function mode, instead of using a fixed template, you specify an arbitrary function, in the python programming language[34]. This allows you to do lots of things that are not possible with simple templates.

Techniques for using function mode and the syntax will be described by means of examples, showing you how to create functions to perform progressively more complex tasks.

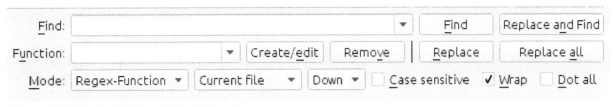

---

[34]https://docs.python.org/2.7/

Automatically fixing the case of headings in the document   Here, we will leverage one of the builtin functions in the editor to automatically change the case of all text inside heading tags to title case:

```
Find expression: <([Hh][1-6])[^>]*>.+?</\1>
```

For the function, simply choose the *Title-case text (ignore tags)* builtin function. The will change titles that look like: `<h1>some TITLE</h1>` to `<h1>Some Title</h1>`. It will work even if there are other HTML tags inside the heading tags.

Your first custom function - smartening hyphens   The real power of function mode comes from being able to create your own functions to process text in arbitrary ways. The Smarten Punctuation tool in the editor leaves individual hyphens alone, so you can use the this function to replace them with em-dashes.

To create a new function, simply click the Create/Edit button to create a new function and copy the python code from below.

```
def replace(match, number, file_name, metadata, dictionaries, data, functions, *args, **kwargs
    return match.group().replace('--', '––').replace('-', '––')
```

Every Search & Replace custom function must have a unique name and consist of a python function named replace, that accepts all the arguments shown above. For the moment, we wont worry about all the different arguments to `replace()` function. Just focus on the `match` argument. It represents a match when running a search and replace. Its full documentation in available here[35]. `match.group()` simply returns all the matched text and all we do is replace hyphens in that text with em-dashes, first replacing double hyphens and then single hyphens.

Use this function with the find regular expression:

```
>[^<>]+<
```

And it will replace all hyphens with em-dashes, but only in actual text and not inside HTML tag definitions.

The power of function mode - using a spelling dictionary to fix mis-hyphenated words   Often, ebooks created from scans of printed books contain mis-hyphenated words – words that were split at the end of the line on the printed page. We will write a simple function to automatically find and fix such words.

```
import regex
from calibre import replace_entities
from calibre import prepare_string_for_xml

def replace(match, number, file_name, metadata, dictionaries, data, functions, *args, **kwargs

    def replace_word(wmatch):
        # Try to remove the hyphen and replace the words if the resulting
        # hyphen free word is recognized by the dictionary
        without_hyphen = wmatch.group(1) + wmatch.group(2)
        if dictionaries.recognized(without_hyphen):
            return without_hyphen
        return wmatch.group()

    # Search for words split by a hyphen
    text = replace_entities(match.group()[1:-1])  # Handle HTML entities like &amp;
    corrected = regex.sub(r'(\w+)\s*-\s*(\w+)', replace_word, text, flags=regex.VERSION1 | re
    return '>%s<' % prepare_string_for_xml(corrected)  # Put back required entities
```

Use this function with the same find expression as before, namely:

---

[35]https://docs.python.org/2.7/library/re.html#match-objects

```
>[^<>]+<
```

And it will magically fix all mis-hyphenated words in the text of the book. The main trick is to use one of the useful extra arguments to the replace function, `dictionaries`. This refers to the dictionaries the editor itself uses to spell check text in the book. What this function does is look for words separated by a hyphen, remove the hyphen and check if the dictionary recognizes the composite word, if it does, the original words are replaced by the hyphen free composite word.

Note that one limitation of this technique is it will only work for mono-lingual books, because, by default, `dictionaries.recognized()` uses the main language of the book.

Auto numbering sections   Now we will see something a little different. Suppose your HTML file has many sections, each with a heading in an `<h2>` tag that looks like `<h2>Some text</h2>`. You can create a custom function that will automatically number these headings with consecutive section numbers, so that they look like `<h2>1.   Some text</h2>`.

```
def replace(match, number, file_name, metadata, dictionaries, data, functions, *args, **kwargs
    section_number = '%d. ' % number
    return match.group(1) + section_number + match.group(2)

# Ensure that when running over multiple files, the files are processed
# in the order in which they appear in the book
replace.file_order = 'spine'
```

Use it with the find expression:

```
(?s)(<h2[^<>]*>)(.+?</h2>)
```

Place the cursor at the top of the file and click *Replace all*.

This function uses another of the useful extra arguments to `replace()`: the `number` argument. When doing a *Replace All* number is automatically incremented for every successive match.

Another new feature is the use of `replace.file_order` – setting that to `'spine'` means that if this search is run on multiple HTML files, the files are processed in the order in which they appear in the book. See *Choose file order when running on multiple HTML files* (page 94) for details.

Auto create a Table of Contents   Finally, lets try something a little more ambitious. Suppose your book has headings in `h1` and `h2` tags that look like `<h1 id="someid">Some Text</h1>`. We will auto-generate an HTML Table of Contents based on these headings. Create the custom function below:

```
from calibre import replace_entities
from calibre.ebooks.oeb.polish.toc import TOC, toc_to_html
from calibre.gui2.tweak_book import current_container
from calibre.ebooks.oeb.base import xml2str

def replace(match, number, file_name, metadata, dictionaries, data, functions, *args, **kwargs
    if match is None:
        # All matches found, output the resulting Table of Contents.
        # The argument metadata is the metadata of the book being edited
        if 'toc' in data:
            toc = data['toc']
            root = TOC()
            for (file_name, tag_name, anchor, text) in toc:
                parent = root.children[-1] if tag_name == 'h2' and root.children else root
                parent.add(text, file_name, anchor)
            toc = toc_to_html(root, current_container(), 'toc.html', 'Table of Contents for '
```

```
            print (xml2str(toc))
        else:
            print ('No headings to build ToC from found')
    else:
        # Add an entry corresponding to this match to the Table of Contents
        if 'toc' not in data:
            # The entries are stored in the data object, which will persist
            # for all invocations of this function during a 'Replace All' operation
            data['toc'] = []
        tag_name, anchor, text = match.group(1), replace_entities(match.group(2)), replace_ent
        data['toc'].append((file_name, tag_name, anchor, text))
        return match.group()  # We don't want to make any actual changes, so return the origin

# Ensure that we are called once after the last match is found so we can
# output the ToC
replace.call_after_last_match = True
# Ensure that when running over multiple files, this function is called,
# the files are processed in the order in which they appear in the book
replace.file_order = 'spine'
```

And use it with the find expression:

```
<(h[12])  [^<>]*  id=['"]([^'"]+)['"][^<>]*>([^<>]+)
```

Run the search on *All text files* and at the end of the search, a window will popup with "Debug Output from your function" which will have the HTML Table of Contents, ready to be pasted into `toc.html`.

The function above is heavily commented, so it should be easy to follow. The key new feature is the use of another useful extra argument to the `replace()` function, the `data` object. The `data` object is a python *dict* that persists between all successive invocations of `replace()` during a single *Replace All* operation.

Another new feature is the use of `call_after_last_match` – setting that to `True` on the `replace()` function means that the editor will call `replace()` one extra time after all matches have been found. For this extra call, the match object will be `None`.

This was just a demonstration to show you the power of function mode, if you really needed to generate a Table of Contents from headings in your book, you would be better off using the dedicated Table of Contents tool in *Tools->Table of Contents*.

The API for the function mode All function mode functions must be python functions named replace, with the following signature:

```
def replace(match, number, file_name, metadata, dictionaries, data, functions, *args, *kwargs
    return a_string
```

When a find/replace is run, for every match that is found, the `replace()` function will be called, it must return the replacement string for that match. If no replacements are to be done, it should return `match.group()` which is the original string. The various arguments to the `replace()` function are documented below.

The match argument The `match` argument represents the currently found match. It is a python Match object[36]. It's most useful method is `group()` which can be used to get the matched text corresponding to individual capture groups in the search regular expression.

---

[36]https://docs.python.org/2.7/library/re.html#match-objects

The `number` argument The `number` argument is the number of the current match. When you run *Replace All*, every successive match will cause `replace()` to be called with an increasing number. The first match has number 1.

The `file_name` argument This is the filename of the file in which the current match was found. When searching inside marked text, the `file_name` is empty. The `file_name` is in canonical form, a path relative to the root of the book, using / as the path separator.

The `metadata` argument This represents the metadata of the current book, such as title, authors, language, etc. It is an object of class *calibre.ebooks.metadata.book.base.Metadata* (page 201). Useful attributes include, `title`, `authors` (a list of authors) and `language` (the language code).

The `dictionaries` argument This represents the collection of dictionaries used for spell checking the current book. It's most useful method is `dictionaries.recognized(word)` which will return `True` if the passed in word is recognized by the dictionary for the current book's language.

The `data` argument This a simple python `dict`. When you run *Replace All*, every successive match will cause `replace()` to be called with the same `dict` as data. You can thus use it to store arbitrary data between invocations of `replace()` during a *Replace All* operation.

The `functions` argument The `functions` argument gives you access to all other user defined functions. This is useful for code re-use. You can define utility functions in one place and re-use them in all your other functions. For example, suppose you create a function name `My Function` like this:

```
def utility():
    # do something

def replace(match, number, file_name, metadata, dictionaries, data, functions, *args, **kwargs
    ...
```

Then, in another function, you can access the `utility()` function like this:

```
def replace(match, number, file_name, metadata, dictionaries, data, functions, *args, **kwargs
    utility = functions['My Function']['utility']
    ...
```

You can also use the functions object to store persistent data, that can be re-used by other functions. For example, you could have one function that when run with *Replace All* collects some data and another function that uses it when it is run afterwards. Consider the following two functions:

```
# Function One
persistent_data = {}

def replace(match, number, file_name, metadata, dictionaries, data, functions, *args, **kwargs
    ...
    persistent_data['something'] = 'some data'

# Function Two
def replace(match, number, file_name, metadata, dictionaries, data, functions, *args, **kwargs
    persistent_data = functions['Function One']['persistent_data']
    ...
```

Debugging your functions   You can debug the functions you create by using the standard `print()` function from python. The output of print will be displayed in a popup window after the Find/replace has completed. You saw an example of using `print()` to output an entire table of contents above.

Choose file order when running on multiple HTML files   When you run a *Replace All* on multiple HTML files, the order in which the files are processes depends on what files you have open for editing. You can force the search to process files in the order in which the appear by setting the `file_order` attribute on your function, like this:

```
def replace(match, number, file_name, metadata, dictionaries, data, functions, *args, **kwargs
    ...

replace.file_order = 'spine'
```

`file_order` accepts two values, `spine` and `spine-reverse` which cause the search to process multiple files in the order they appear in the book, either forwards or backwards, respectively.

Having your function called an extra time after the last match is found   Sometimes, as in the auto generate table of contents example above, it is useful to have your function called an extra time after the last match is found. You can do this by setting the `call_after_last_match` attribute on your function, like this:

```
def replace(match, number, file_name, metadata, dictionaries, data, functions, *args, **kwargs
    ...

replace.call_after_last_match = True
```

Snippets

The calibre editor supports *snippets*. A snippet is a piece of text that is either re-used often or contains a lot of redundant text. The editor allows you to insert a snippet with only a few key strokes. For example, suppose you often find yourself inserting link tags when editing HTML files, then you can simply type <a in the editor and press `Control+J`. The editor will expand it to:

```
<a href="filename"></a>
```

Not only that, the word `filename` will be selected, with the cursor placed over it, so that you can easily type in the real filename, using the editor's nifty *Auto-complete* (page 98) feature. And once you are done typing the filename, press `Control+J` again and the cursor will jump to the position in between the <a> tags so you can easily type in the text for the link.

The snippets system in the editor is very sophisticated, there are a few built-in snippets and you can create your own to suit your editing style.

The following discussion of the built-in snippets should help illustrate the power of the snippets system.

Note: You can also use snippets in the text entry fields in the Search and Replace panel, however, placeholders (using `Control+J` to jump around) will not work.

The built-in snippets   The built-in snippets are described below. Note that you can override them by creating your own snippets with the same trigger text.

Inserting filler text [Lorem]   The first built-in snippet, and the simplest is used to insert filler text into a document. The filler text is taken from De finibus bonorum et malorum[37] a philosophical work by Cicero (translated to English). To use it simply type `Lorem` in an HTML file and press `Control+J`. It will be replaced by a couple of paragraphs of filler.

The definition of this snippet is very simple, the trigger text is defined as `Lorem` and the template is defined simply as the literal text to be inserted. You can easily customize it to use your favorite form of filler text.

Inserting a self-closing HTML tag [<>]   Now let's look at a simple example of the powerful concept of *placeholders*. Say you want to insert the self-closing tag `<hr/>`. Just type `<>`, and press `Control+J`, the editor will expand the snippet to:

```
<|/>
```

Here, the | symbol represents the current cursor position. You can then type `hr` and press `Control+J` to move the cursor to after the end of the tag. This snippet is defined as:

```
Trigger: <>
Template: <$1/>$2
```

Placeholders are simply the dollar ($) sign followed by a number. When the snippet is expanded by pressing `Control+J` the cursor is positioned at the first placeholder (the placeholder with the lowest number). When you press `Control+J` again the cursor jumps to the next placeholder (the placeholder with the next higher number).

Inserting an HTML link tag [<a]   HTML link tags all share a common structure. They have an `href` attribute and some text between the opening and closing tags. A snippet to make typing them more efficient will introduce us to some more features of placeholders. To use this snippet, simply type `<a` and press `Control+J`. The editor will expand this to:

```
<a href="filename|"></a>
```

Not only that, the word `filename` will be selected, with the cursor placed over it, so that you can easily type in the real filename, using the editor's nifty *Auto-complete* (page 98) feature. And once you are done typing the filename, press `Control+J` again and the cursor will jump to the position in between the `<a>` tags so you can easily type in the text for the link. After you are done typing the text, press `Control+J` again to jump to the point after the closing tag. This snippet is defined as:

```
Trigger: <a
Template: <a href="${1:filename}">${2*}</a>$3
```

There are a couple of new features here. First the `$1` placeholder has become more complex. It now includes some *default text* (the word `filename`. If a placeholder contains default text, the default text is substituted for the placeholder when the snippet is expanded. Also when you jump to a placeholder with default text using `Control+J`, the default text is selected. In this way, you can use default text to act as a reminder to you to fill in important parts of the template. You can specify default text for a placeholder by using the syntax: `${<number>:default text}`.

The other new feature is that the second placeholder has an asterisk after it (`${2*}`). This means that any text that was selected before expanding the template is substituted for the placeholder. To see this in action, select some text in the editor, press `Control+J`, type `<a` and press `Control+J` again, the template will be expanded to:

```
<a href="filename">whatever text you selected</a>
```

---

[37] http://en.wikipedia.org/wiki/De_finibus_bonorum_et_malorum

Inserting a HTML image tag [<i]   This is very similar to inserting an HTML link, as we saw above. It allows you to quickly input an `<img src="filename" alt="description" />` tag and jump between the `src` and `alt` attributes:

```
Trigger: <i
Template: <img src="${1:filename}" alt="${2*:description}" />$3
```

Insert an arbitrary HTML tag [<<]   This allows you to insert an arbitrary full HTML tag (or wrap previously selected text in the tag). To use it, simply type << and press `Control+J`.The editor will expand it to:

```
<|></>
```

Type the tag name, for example: `span` and press `Control+J`, that will result in:

```
<span>|</span>
```

You will note that the closing tag has been automatically filled with `span`. This is achieved with yet another feature of placeholders, *mirroring*. Mirroring simply means that if you specify the sample placeholder more than once in a template, the second and all later positions will be automatically filled in with whatever you type in the first position, when you press `Control+J`. The definition for this snippet is:

```
Trigger: <<
Template: <$1>${2*}</$1>$3
```

As you can see, the first placeholder ($1) has been specified twice, the second time in the closing tag, which will simply copy whatever you type in the opening tag.

Inserting an arbitrary HTML tag with a class attribute [<c]   This is very similar to the insert arbitrary tag example above, except that it assumes that you want to specify a class for the tag:

```
Trigger: <c
Template: <$1 class="${2:classname}">${3*}</$1>$4
```

This will allow you to first type the tag name, press `Control+J`, type the class name, press `Control+J` type the contents of the tag and press `Control+J` one last time to jump out of the tag. The closing tag will be auto-filled.

Creating your own snippets   Snippets really shine because you can create your own to suit your editing style. To create your own snippets go to *Edit->Preferences->Editor settings->Manage snippets* in the editor. This will pop-up an easy to use dialog to help you create your own snippets. Simply click the *Add snippet* button and you will see a dialog that looks like:

Create a snippet

For help with snippets, see the User Manual

Name: [The name of this snippet]

Trigger: [The text used to trigger this snippet]

Template: [   ]

File types: [✔ All] [css] [html] [javascript] [text] [xml]

Test: [   ]

[✔ OK] [⊗ Cancel]

First give your snippet a name, something descriptive, to help identify the snippet in the future. Then specify the *trigger*. A trigger is simply the text that you have to type in the editor before pressing `Control+J` in order to expand the snippet.

Then specify the snippet template. You should start with one of the example above and modify it to suit your needs. Finally, specify which file types you want the snippet to be active for. This way you can have multiple snippets with the same trigger text that work differently in different file types.

The next step is to test your newly created snippet. Use the *Test* box at the bottom. Type in the trigger text and press `Control+J` to expand the snippet and jump between placeholders.

The Reports tool

The editor includes a nice *Reports* tool (via *Tools->Reports*) that shows summaries of the files, images, links, words, characters and styles used in the book. Every line in the report is hot-linked. Double clicking a line jumps to the place in the book where that item is used or defined (as appropriate). For example, in the *Links* view, you can double click entries the *Source* column to jump to where the link is defined and entries in the *Target* column to jump to where the link points.

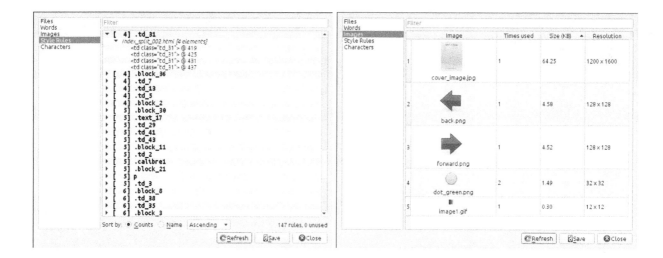

1.5.9 Special features in the code editor

The calibre HTML editor is very powerful. It has many features that make editing of HTML (and CSS) easier.

Syntax highlighting

The HTML editor has very sophisticated syntax highlighting. Features include:

- The text inside bold, italic and heading tags is made bold/italic
- As you move your cursor through the HTML, the matching HTML tags are highlighted
- Invalid HTML is highlighted with a red underline
- Spelling errors in the text inside HTML tags and attributes such as title are highlighted. The spell checking is language aware, based on the value of the lang attribute of the current tag and the overall book language.
- CSS embedded inside `<style>` tags is highlighted
- Special characters that can be hard to distinguish such as non-breaking spaces, different types of hyphens, etc. are highlighted.
- Links to other files in `<a>` tags, `<img>` and `<link>` tags all have the filenames highlighted. If the filename they point to does not exist, the filename is marked with a red underline.

Context sensitive help

You can right click on an HTML tag name or a CSS property name to get help for that tag or property.

You can also hold down the Ctrl key and click on any filename inside a link tag to open that file in the editor automatically.

Auto-complete

When editing an ebook, one of the most tedious tasks is creating links to other files inside the book, or to CSS stylesheets, or images. You have to figure out the correct filename and relative path to the file. The editor has auto-complete to make that easier.

As you type a filename, the editor automatically pops up suggestions. Simply use the Tab key to select the correct file name. The editor even offers suggestions for links pointing to an anchor inside another HTML file. After you type the # character, the editor will show you a list of all anchors in the target file, with a small snippet of text to help you choose the right anchor.

Note that unlike most other completion systems, the editor's completion system uses subsequence matching. This means that you can type just two or three letters from anywhere in the filename to complete the filename. For example, say you want the filename `../images/arrow1.png`, you can simply type `ia1` and press Tab to complete the filename. When searching for matches, the completion system prioritizes letters that are at the start of a word, or immediately after a path separator. Once you get used to this system, you will find it saves you a lot of time and effort.

Snippets

The calibre editor supports *snippets*. A snippet is a piece of text that is either re-used often or contains a lot of redundant text. The editor allows you to insert a snippet with only a few key strokes. The snippets are very powerful, with many features, such as placeholders you can jump between, automatic mirroring of repeated text and so on. For more information, see Snippets (page 94).

1.6 Comparing E-books

calibre includes an integrated e-book comparison tool that can be used to see what has changed inside an ebook after editing or converting it. It can compare books in the EPUB and AZW3 formats.

To use it, either open the ebook in the tool for *Editing E-books* (page 70) and then click *File->Compare to other book* or use the *Book Details* (page 16) panel. If you do a conversion from EPUB to EPUB, the original EPUB file will be saved as ORIGINAL_EPUB. Simply right click on the ORIGINAL_EPUB entry in the Book Details panel and choose *Compare to EPUB format*.

The comparison tool that opens will look like the screenshot below. It shows you the differences in text, styles and images in the chosen books.

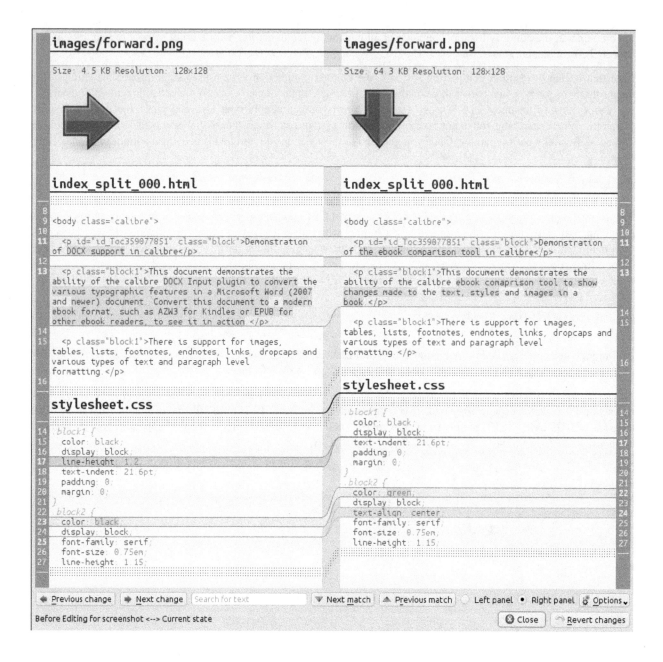

1.6.1 Understanding the comparison view

As can be seen in the screenshot above, the comparison view shows the differences between the two books side by side. Only the differences, with a few lines of context around them are shown. This makes it easy to see at a glance only what was changed inside a large document like a book.

Added text is shown with a green background, removed text with a red background and changed text with a blue background.

The line numbers of all changed text are show at the sides, making it easy to go to a particular change in the editor. When you open the comparison tool from within the editor, you can also double click on a line in the right panel to go to that line in the editor automatically.

One useful technique when comparing books is to tell the comparison tool to beautify the text and style files before calculating differences. This can often result in cleaner and easier to follow differences. To do this, click the *Options* button in the bottom right and choose *Beautify files before comparing*. Note that beautifying can sometimes have undesired effects, as it can cause invalid markup to be altered to make it valid. You can also change the number of lines of context shown around differences via the *Options* button.

You can search for any text in the differences via the search bar at the bottom. You will need to specify which panel to search, the *Left* or the *Right*.

1.6.2 How to launch the comparison tool

The comparison tool is most useful when you have two versions of the same book and you want to see what is different between them. To that end, there are several ways to launch the tool.

Comparing two ebook files

Open the first file in the *Editing E-books* (page 70) tool. Now click *File->Compare to another book* and choose the second file (it must be in the same format as the first). The comparison view will open with the file being edited on the right and the second file on the left.

Comparing the ORIGINAL_FMT to FMT

When you do a conversion in calibre from a FMT to itself, the original file is saved as ORIGINAL_FMT. You can see what was changed by the conversion, by right clicking on the ORIGINAL_FMT entry in the *Book Details* (page 16) panel in the main calibre window and selecting *Compare to FMT*. The comparison view will open with ORIGINAL_FMT on the left and FMT on the right.

Comparing a checkpoint to the current state of the book while editing

The *Editing E-books* (page 70) tool has a very useful feature, called *Checkpoints* (page 81). This allows you to save the current state of the book as a named *checkpoint*, to which you can revert if you do not like the changes you have made since creating the checkpoint. Checkpoints are also created automatically when you perform various automated actions in the editor. You can see the list of checkpoints by going to *View->Checkpoints* and then use the *Compare* button to compare the book at the selected checkpoint with the current state. The comparison tool will show the checkpoint on the left and the current state on the right.

1.7 Editing Ebook Metadata

Contents

Ebooks come in all shapes and sizes and more often than not, their metadata (things like title/author/series/publisher) is incomplete or incorrect. The simplest way to change metadata in calibre is to simply double click on an entry and type in the correct replacement. For more sophisticated, "power editing" use the edit metadata tools discussed below.

1.7.1 Editing the metadata of one book at a time

Click the book you want to edit and then click the *Edit metadata* button or press the E key. A dialog opens that allows you to edit all aspects of the metadata. It has various features to make editing faster and more efficient. A list of the commonly used tips:

- You can click the button in between title and authors to swap them automatically.

- You can click the button next to author sort to have calibre automatically fill it in using the sort values stored with each author. Use the *Manage authors* dialog to see and change the authors' sort values. This dialog can be opened by clicking and holding the button next to author sort.

- You can click the button next to tags to use the Tag Editor to manage the tags associated with the book.

- The ISBN box will have a red background if you enter an invalid ISBN. It will be green for valid ISBNs

- The author sort box will be red if the author sort value differs from what calibre thinks it should be.

Downloading metadata

The nicest feature of the edit metadata dialog is its ability to automatically fill in many metadata fields by getting metadata from various websites. Currently, calibre uses isbndb.com, Google Books, Amazon and Library Thing. The metadata download can fill in Title, author, series, tags, rating, description and ISBN for you.

To use the download, fill in the title and author fields and click the *Fetch metadata* button. calibre will present you with a list of books that most closely match the title and author. If you fill in the ISBN field first, it will be used in preference to the title and author. If no matches are found, try making your search a little less specific by including only some key words in the title and only the author last name.

Managing book formats

In calibre, a single book entry can have many different *formats* associated with it. For example you may have obtained the Complete Works of Shakespeare in EPUB format and later converted it to MOBI to read on your Kindle. calibre automatically manages multiple formats for you. In the *Available formats* section of the Edit metadata dialog, you can manage these formats. You can add a new format, delete an existing format and also ask calibre to set the metadata and cover for the book entry from the metadata in one of the formats.

All about covers

You can ask calibre to download book covers for you, provided the book has a known ISBN. Alternatively you can specify a file on your computer to use as the cover. calibre can even generate a default cover with basic metadata on it for you. You can drag and drop images onto the cover to change it and also right click to copy/paste cover images.

In addition, there is a button to automatically trim borders from the cover, in case your cover image has an ugly border.

1.7.2 Editing the metadata of many books at a time

First select the books you want to edit by holding Ctrl or Shift and clicking on them. If you select more than one book, clicking the *Edit metadata* button will cause a new *Bulk* metadata edit dialog to open. Using this dialog, you can quickly set the author/publisher/rating/tags/series etc of a bunch of books to the same value. This is particularly useful if you have just imported a number of books that have some metadata in common. This dialog is very powerful, for example, it has a Search and Replace tab that you can use to perform bulk operations on metadata and even copy metadata from one column to another.

The normal edit metadata dialog also has Next and Previous buttons that you can use to edit the metadata of several books one after the other.

Search and replace

The Bulk metadata edit dialog allows you to perform arbitrarily powerful search and replace operations on the selected books. By default it uses a simple text search and replace, but it also support *regular expressions*. For more on regular expressions, see *All about using regular expressions in calibre* (page 205).

As noted above, there are two search and replace modes: character match and regular expression. Character match will look in the *Search field* you choose for the characters you type in the *search for* box and replace those characters with what you type in the *replace with* box. Each occurance of the search characters in the field will be replaced. For example, assume the field being searched contains *a bad cat.* if you search for *a* to be replaced with *HELLO*, then the result will be *HELLO bHELLOd cHELLOt.*

If the field you are searching on is a *multiple* field like tags, then each tag is treated separately. For example, if your tags contain *Horror, Scary*, the search expression *r,* will not match anything because the expression will first be applied to *Horror* and then to *Scary*.

If you want the search to ignore upper/lowercase differences, uncheck the *Case sensitive* box.

You can have calibre change the case of the result (information after the replace has happened) by choosing one of the functions from the *Apply function after replace* box. The operations available are:

- *Lower case* – change all the characters in the field to lower case
- *Upper case* – change all the characters in the field to upper case
- *Title case* – capitalize each word in the result.

The *Your test* box is provided for you to enter text to check that search/replace is doing what you want. In the majority of cases the book test boxes will be sufficient, but it is possible that there is a case you want to check that isn't shown in these boxes. Enter that case into *Your test*.

Regular expression mode has some differences from character mode, beyond (of course) using regular expressions. The first is that functions are applied to the parts of the string matched by the search string, not the entire field. The second is that functions apply to the replacement string, not to the entire field.

The third and most important is that the replace string can make reference to parts of the search string by using backreferences. A backreference is \\n where n is an integer that refers to the n'th parenthesized group in the search expression. For example, given the same example as above, *a bad cat*, a search expression *a (...) (...)*, and a replace expression *a \2 \1*, the result will be *a cat bad*. Please see the *All about using regular expressions in calibre* (page 205) for more information on backreferences.

One useful pattern: assume you want to change the case of an entire field. The easiest way to do this is to use character mode, but lets further assume you want to use regular expression mode. The search expression should be *(.*)* the replace expression should be *\1*, and the desired case change function should be selected.

Finally, in regular expression mode you can copy values from one field to another. Simply make the source and destination field different. The copy can replace the destination field, prepend to the field (add to the front), or append to the field (add at the end). The 'use comma' checkbox tells calibre to (or not to) add a comma between the text and the destination field in prepend and append modes. If the destination is multiple (e.g., tags), then you cannot uncheck this box.

Search and replace is done after all the other metadata changes in the other tabs are applied. This can lead to some confusion, because the test boxes will show the information before the other changes, but the operation will be applied after the other changes. If you have any doubts about what is going to happen, do not mix search/replace with other changes.

Bulk downloading of metadata

If you want to download the metadata for multiple books at once, right-click the *Edit metadata* button and select *Download metadata*. You can choose to download only metadata, only covers, or both.

1.8 Frequently Asked Questions

Contents

1.8.1 Ebook Format Conversion

Contents

What formats does calibre support conversion to/from?

calibre supports the conversion of many input formats to many output formats. It can convert every input format in the following list, to every output format.

Input Formats: AZW, AZW3, AZW4, CBZ, CBR, CBC, CHM, DJVU, DOCX, EPUB, FB2, HTML, HTMLZ, LIT, LRF, MOBI, ODT, PDF, PRC, PDB, PML, RB, RTF, SNB, TCR, TXT, TXTZ

Output Formats: AZW3, EPUB, DOCX, FB2, HTMLZ, OEB, LIT, LRF, MOBI, PDB, PMLZ, RB, PDF, RTF, SNB, TCR, TXT, TXTZ, ZIP

Note: PRC is a generic format, calibre supports PRC files with TextRead and MOBIBook headers. PDB is also a generic format. calibre supports eReader, Plucker, PML and zTxt PDB files. DJVU support is only for converting DJVU files that contain embedded text. These are typically generated by OCR software. MOBI books can be of two types Mobi6 and KF8. calibre fully supports both. MOBI files often have .azw or .azw3 file extensions. DOCX files from Microsoft Word 2007 and newer are supported.

What are the best source formats to convert?

In order of decreasing preference: LIT, MOBI, AZW, EPUB, AZW3, FB2, DOCX, HTML, PRC, ODT, RTF, PDB, TXT, PDF

I converted a PDF file, but the result has various problems?

PDF is a terrible format to convert from. For a list of the various issues you will encounter when converting PDF, see: *Convert PDF documents* (page 66).

How do I convert my file containing non-English characters, or smart quotes?

There are two aspects to this problem:

1. Knowing the encoding of the source file: calibre tries to guess what character encoding your source files use, but often, this is impossible, so you need to tell it what encoding to use. This can be done in the GUI via the *Input character encoding* field in the *Look & Feel* section of the conversion dialog. The command-line tools all have an --input-encoding option.

2. When adding HTML files to calibre, you may need to tell calibre what encoding the files are in. To do this go to *Preferences->Plugins->File Type plugins* and customize the HTML2Zip plugin, telling it what encoding your HTML files are in. Now when you add HTML files to calibre they will be correctly processed. HTML files from different sources often have different encodings, so you may have to change this setting repeatedly. A common encoding for many files from the web is cp1252 and I would suggest you try that first. Note that when converting HTML files, leave the input encoding setting mentioned above blank. This is because the HTML2ZIP plugin automatically converts the HTML files to a standard encoding (utf-8).

What's the deal with Table of Contents in MOBI files?

The first thing to realize is that most ebooks have two tables of contents. One is the traditional Table of Contents, like the ToC you find in paper books. This Table of Contents is part of the main document flow and can be styled however you like. This ToC is called the *content ToC*.

Then there is the *metadata ToC*. A metadata ToC is a ToC that is not part of the book text and is typically accessed by some special button on a reader. For example, in the calibre viewer, you use the Show Table of Contents button to see this ToC. This ToC cannot be styled by the book creator. How it is represented is up to the viewer program.

In the MOBI format, the situation is a little confused. This is because the MOBI format, alone amongst mainstream ebook formats, *does not* have decent support for a metadata ToC. A MOBI book simulates the presence of a metadata ToC by putting an *extra* content ToC at the end of the book. When you click Goto Table of Contents on your Kindle, it is to this extra content ToC that the Kindle takes you.

Now it might well seem to you that the MOBI book has two identical ToCs. Remember that one is semantically a content ToC and the other is a metadata ToC, even though both might have exactly the same entries and look the same. One can be accessed directly from the Kindle's menus, the other cannot.

When converting to MOBI, calibre detects the *metadata ToC* in the input document and generates an end-of-file ToC in the output MOBI file. You can turn this off by an option in the MOBI Output settings. You can also tell calibre whether to put it and the start or the end of the book via an option in the MOBI Output settings. Remember this ToC is semantically a *metadata ToC*, in any format other than MOBI it *cannot not be part of the text*. The fact that it is part of the text in MOBI is an accident caused by the limitations of MOBI. If you want a ToC at a particular location in your document text, create one by hand. So we strongly recommend that you leave the default as it is, i.e. with the metadata ToC at the end of the book. Also note that if you disable the generation of the end-of-file ToC the resulting

MOBI file may not function correctly on a Kindle, since the Kindle's use the metadata ToC for many things, including the Page Flip feature.

If you have a hand edited ToC in the input document, you can use the ToC detection options in calibre to automatically generate the metadata ToC from it. See the conversion section of the User Manual for more details on how to use these options.

Finally, I encourage you to ditch the content ToC and only have a metadata ToC in your ebooks. Metadata ToCs will give the people reading your ebooks a much superior navigation experience (except on the Kindle, where they are essentially the same as a content ToC).

Note: The newer AZW3 format has proper support for a metadata ToC. However, the Kindle firmware tends to malfunction if you disable the generation of the end-of-file inline ToC. So it is recommended that you leave the generated ToC alone. If you create an AZW3 file with a metadata ToC and no end-of-file generated ToC, some features on the Kindle will not work, such as the Page Flip feature.

The covers for my MOBI files have stopped showing up in Kindle for PC/Kindle for Android/iPad etc.

This is caused by a bug in the Amazon software. You can work around it by going to *Preferences->Output Options->MOBI output* and setting the "Enable sharing of book content" option. If you are reconverting a previously converted book, you will also have to enable the option in the conversion dialog for that individual book (as per book conversion settings are saved and take precedence).

Note that doing this will mean that the generated MOBI will show up under personal documents instead of Books on the Kindle Fire and Amazon whispersync will not work, but the covers will. It's your choice which functionality is more important to you. I encourage you to contact Amazon and ask them to fix this bug.

The bug in Amazon's software is that when you put a MOBI file on a Kindle, unless the file is marked as a Personal document, Amazon assumes you bought the book from it and tries to download the cover thumbnail for it from its servers. When the download fails, it refuses to fallback to the cover defined in the MOBI file. This is likely deliberate on Amazon's part to try to force authors to sell only through them. In other words, Kindle's only display covers for books marked as Personal Documents or books bought directly from Amazon.

If you send a MOBI file to an e-ink Kindle with calibre using a USB connection, calibre works around this Amazon bug by uploading a cover thumbnail itself. However, that workaround is only possible when using a USB connection and sending with calibre. Note that if you send using email, Amazon will automatically mark the MOBI file as a Personal Document and the cover will work, but the book will show up in Personal Documents.

How do I convert a collection of HTML files in a specific order?

In order to convert a collection of HTML files in a specific order, you have to create a table of contents file. That is, another HTML file that contains links to all the other files in the desired order. Such a file looks like:

```
<html>
    <body>
      <h1>Table of Contents</h1>
      <p style="text-indent:0pt">
         <a href="file1.html">First File</a><br/>
         <a href="file2.html">Second File</a><br/>
         .
         .
         .
      </p>
    </body>
</html>
```

Then, just add this HTML file to the GUI and use the convert button to create your ebook. You can use the option in the Table of Contents section in the conversion dialog to control how the Table of Contents is generated.

Note: By default, when adding HTML files, calibre follows links in the files in *depth first* order. This means that if file A.html links to B.html and C.html and D.html, but B.html also links to D.html, then the files will be in the order A.html, B.html, D.html, C.html. If instead you want the order to be A.html, B.html, C.html, D.html then you must tell calibre to add your files in *breadth first* order. Do this by going to Preferences->Plugins and customizing the HTML to ZIP plugin.

The EPUB I produced with calibre is not valid?

calibre does not guarantee that an EPUB produced by it is valid. The only guarantee it makes is that if you feed it valid XHTML 1.1 + CSS 2.1 it will output a valid EPUB. calibre tries hard to ensure that EPUBs it produces actually work as intended on a wide variety of devices, a goal that is incompatible with producing valid EPUBs, and one that is far more important to the vast majority of its users. If you need a tool that always produces valid EPUBs, calibre is not for you. This means, that if you want to send a calibre produced EPUB to an online store that uses an EPUB validity checker, you have to make sure that the EPUB is valid yourself, calibre will not do it for you – in other words you must feed calibre valid XHTML + CSS as the input documents.

How do I use some of the advanced features of the conversion tools?

You can get help on any individual feature of the converters by mousing over it in the GUI or running `ebook-convert dummy.html .epub -h` at a terminal. A good place to start is to look at the following demo file that demonstrates some of the advanced features html-demo.zip[38]

1.8.2 Device Integration

Contents

---

[38] http://calibre-ebook.com/downloads/html-demo.zip

What devices does calibre support?

calibre can directly connect to all the major (and most of the minor) ebook reading devices, smarthphones, tablets, etc. In addition, using the *Connect to folder* function you can use it with any ebook reader that exports itself as a USB disk. You can even connect to Apple devices (via iTunes), using the *Connect to iTunes* function.

How can I help get my device supported in calibre?

If your device appears as a USB disk to the operating system, adding support for it to calibre is very easy. We just need some information from you:

- Complete list of ebook formats that your device supports.

- Is there a special directory on the device in which all ebook files should be placed? Also does the device detect files placed in sub-directories?

- We also need information about your device that calibre will collect automatically. First, if your device supports SD cards, insert them. Then connect your device to the computer. In calibre go to *Preferences->Miscellaneous* and click the "Debug device detection" button. This will create some debug output. Copy it to a file and repeat the process, this time with your device disconnected from your computer.

- Send both the above outputs to us with the other information and we will write a device driver for your device.

Once you send us the output for a particular operating system, support for the device in that operating system will appear in the next release of calibre. To send us the output, open a bug report and attach the output to it. See calibre bugs[39].

My device is not being detected by calibre?

Follow these steps to find the problem:

- Make sure that you are connecting only a single device to your computer at a time. Do not have another calibre supported device like an iPhone/iPad etc. at the same time.

- If you are connecting an Apple iDevice (iPad, iPod Touch, iPhone), use the 'Connect to iTunes' method in the 'Getting started' instructions in Calibre + Apple iDevices: Start here[40].

- Make sure you are running the latest version of calibre. The latest version can always be downloaded from the calibre website[41]. You can tell what version of calibre you are currently running by looking at the bottom line of the main calibre window.

- Ensure your operating system is seeing the device. That is, the device should show up in Windows Explorer (in Windows) or Finder (in OS X).

- In calibre, go to *Preferences->Ignored Devices* and check that your device is not being ignored

- If all the above steps fail, go to *Preferences->Miscellaneous* and click *Debug device detection* with your device attached and post the output as a ticket on the calibre bug tracker[42].

My device is non-standard or unusual. What can I do to connect to it?

In addition to the *Connect to Folder* function found under the Connect/Share button, calibre provides a `User Defined` device plugin that can be used to connect to any USB device that shows up as a disk drive in your

---

[39]http://calibre-ebook.com/bugs
[40]http://www.mobileread.com/forums/showthread.php?t=118559
[41]http://calibre-ebook.com/download
[42]https://bugs.launchpad.net/calibre

operating system. Note: on Windows, the device must have a drive letter for calibre to use it. See the device plugin `Preferences -> Plugins -> Device Plugins -> User Defined` and `Preferences -> Miscellaneous -> Get information to setup the user defined device` for more information. Note that if you are using the user defined plugin for a device normally detected by a builtin calibre plugin, you must disable the builtin plugin first, so that your user defined plugin is used instead.

How does calibre manage collections on my SONY reader?

When calibre connects with the reader, it retrieves all collections for the books on the reader. The collections of which books are members are shown on the device view.

When you send a book to the reader, calibre will add the book to collections based on the metadata for that book. By default, collections are created from tags and series. You can control what metadata is used by going to *Preferences->Plugins->Device Interface plugins* and customizing the SONY device interface plugin. If you remove all values, calibre will not add the book to any collection.

Collection management is largely controlled by the 'Metadata management' option found at *Preferences->Import/Export->Sending books to devices*. If set to 'Manual' (the default), managing collections is left to the user; calibre will not delete already existing collections for a book on your reader when you resend the book to the reader, but calibre will add the book to collections if necessary. To ensure that the collections for a book are based only on current calibre metadata, first delete the books from the reader, then resend the books. You can edit collections directly on the device view by double-clicking or right-clicking in the collections column.

If 'Metadata management' is set to 'Only on send', then calibre will manage collections more aggressively. Collections will be built using calibre metadata exclusively. Sending a book to the reader will correct the collections for that book so its collections exactly match the book's metadata, adding and deleting collections as necessary. Editing collections on the device view is not permitted, because collections not in the metadata will be removed automatically.

If 'Metadata management' is set to 'Automatic management', then calibre will update metadata and collections both when the reader is connected and when books are sent. When calibre detects the reader and generates the list of books on the reader, it will send metadata from the library to the reader for all books on the reader that are in the library (On device is True), adding and removing books from collections as indicated by the metadata and device customization. When a book is sent, calibre corrects the metadata for that book, adding and deleting collections. Manual editing of metadata on the device view is not allowed. Note that this option specifies sending metadata, not books. The book files on the reader are not changed.

In summary, choose 'manual management' if you want to manage collections yourself. Collections for a book will never be removed by calibre, but can be removed by you by editing on the device view. Choose 'Only on send' if you want calibre to manage collections when you send a book, adding books to and removing books from collections as needed. Choose 'Automatic management' if you want calibre to keep collections up to date whenever the reader is connected.

If you use multiple installations of calibre to manage your reader, then option 'Automatic management' may not be what you want. Connecting the reader to one library will reset the metadata to what is in that library. Connecting to the other library will reset the metadata to what is in that other library. Metadata in books found in both libraries will be flopped back and forth.

Can I use both calibre and the SONY software to manage my reader?

Yes, you can use both, provided you do not run them at the same time. That is, you should use the following sequence: Connect reader->Use one of the programs->Disconnect reader. Reconnect reader->Use the other program->disconnect reader.

The underlying reason is that the Reader uses a single file to keep track of 'meta' information, such as collections, and this is written to by both calibre and the Sony software when either updates something on the Reader. The file will be saved when the Reader is (safely) disconnected, so using one or the other is safe if there's a disconnection between

---

them, but if you're not the type to remember this, then the simple answer is to stick to one or the other for the transfer and just export/import from/to the other via the computers hard disk.

If you do need to reset your metadata due to problems caused by using both at the same time, then just delete the media.xml file on the Reader using your PC's file explorer and it will be recreated after disconnection.

With recent reader iterations, SONY, in all its wisdom has decided to try to force you to use their software. If you install it, it auto-launches whenever you connect the reader. If you don't want to uninstall it altogether, there are a couple of tricks you can use. The simplest is to simply re-name the executable file that launches the library program. More detail in the forums[43].

How do I use calibre with my iPad/iPhone/iPod touch?

Over the air

The easiest way to browse your calibre collection on your Apple device (iPad/iPhone/iPod) is by using the calibre content server, which makes your collection available over the net. First perform the following steps in calibre

- Set the Preferred Output Format in calibre to EPUB (The output format can be set under *Preferences->Interface->Behavior*)

- Set the output profile to iPad (this will work for iPhone/iPods as well), under *Preferences->Conversion->Common Options->Page Setup*

- Convert the books you want to read on your iDevice to EPUB format by selecting them and clicking the Convert button.

- Turn on the Content Server by clicking the *Connect/Share* button and leave calibre running. You can also tell calibre to automatically start the content server via *Preferences->Sharing over the net*.

There are many apps for your iDevice that can connect to calibre. Here we describe using two of them, iBooks and Stanza.

Using Stanza   You should be able to access your books on your iPhone by opening Stanza. Go to "Get Books" and then click the "Shared" tab. Under Shared you will see an entry "Books in calibre". If you don't, make sure your iPad/iPhone is connected using the WiFi network in your house, not 3G. If the calibre catalog is still not detected in Stanza, you can add it manually in Stanza. To do this, click the "Shared" tab, then click the "Edit" button and then click "Add book source" to add a new book source. In the Add Book Source screen enter whatever name you like and in the URL field, enter the following:

```
http://192.168.1.2:8080/
```

Replace `192.168.1.2` with the local IP address of the computer running calibre. If you have changed the port the calibre content server is running on, you will have to change `8080` as well to the new port. The local IP address is the IP address you computer is assigned on your home network. A quick Google search will tell you how to find out your local IP address. Now click "Save" and you are done.

If you get timeout errors while browsing the calibre catalog in Stanza, try increasing the connection timeout value in the stanza settings. Go to Info->Settings and increase the value of Download Timeout.

Using iBooks   Start the Safari browser and type in the IP address and port of the computer running the calibre server, like this:

```
http://192.168.1.2:8080/
```

---

[43] http://www.mobileread.com/forums/showthread.php?t=65809

Replace `192.168.1.2` with the local IP address of the computer running calibre. If you have changed the port the calibre content server is running on, you will have to change `8080` as well to the new port. The local IP address is the IP address you computer is assigned on your home network. A quick Google search will tell you how to find out your local IP address.

You will see a list of books in Safari, just click on the epub link for whichever book you want to read, Safari will then prompt you to open it with iBooks.

With the USB cable + iTunes

Use the 'Connect to iTunes' method in the 'Getting started' instructions in Calibre + Apple iDevices: Start here[44].

This method only works on Windows Vista and higher, and OS X up to 10.8. Linux is not supported (iTunes is not available in linux) and OS X newer than 10.8 is not supported, as Apple removed the facility to use iTunes to manage books, replacing it with iBooks.

How do I use calibre with my Android phone/tablet or Kindle Fire HD?

There are two ways that you can connect your Android device to calibre. Using a USB cable – or wirelessly, over the air. The first step to using an Android device is installing an ebook reading application on it. There are many free and paid ebook reading applications for Android: Some examples (in no particular order): FBReader[45], Moon+[46], Mantano[47], Aldiko[48], Kindle[49].

Using a USB cable

Simply plug your device into the computer with a USB cable. calibre should automatically detect the device and then you can transfer books to it by clicking the Send to Device button. calibre does not have support for every single android device out there, so if your device is not automatically detected, follow the instructions at *How can I help get my device supported in calibre?* (page 108) to get your device supported in calibre.

Note: With newer Android devices, the USB connection is not supported on Windows XP and OS X before Mavericks (10.9). If you are on Windows XP or old versions of OS X, you should use one of the wireless connection methods.

Over the air

The easiest way to transfer books wirelessly to your Android device is to use the Calibre Companion[50] Android app. This app is maintained by a core calibre developer and allows calibre to connect to your Android device wirelessly, just as though you plugged in the device with a USB cable. You can browse files on the device in calibre and use the *Send to device* button to transfer files to your device wirelessly.

calibre also has a builtin web server, the *Content Server*. You can browse your calibre collection on your Android device is by using the calibre content server, which makes your collection available over the net. First perform the following steps in calibre

- Set the *Preferred Output Format* in calibre to EPUB for normal Android devices or MOBI for Kindles (The output format can be set under *Preferences->Interface->Behavior*)

---

[44]http://www.mobileread.com/forums/showthread.php?t=118559
[45]https://play.google.com/store/apps/details?id=org.geometerplus.zlibrary.ui.android&hl=en
[46]https://play.google.com/store/apps/details?id=com.flyersoft.moonreader&hl=en
[47]https://play.google.com/store/apps/details?id=com.mantano.reader.android.lite&hl=en
[48]https://play.google.com/store/apps/details?id=com.aldiko.android&hl=en
[49]https://play.google.com/store/apps/details?id=com.amazon.kindle&feature=related_apps
[50]http://www.multipie.co.uk/calibre-companion/

- Convert the books you want to read on your device to EPUB/MOBI format by selecting them and clicking the Convert button.

- Turn on the Content Server in calibre's preferences and leave calibre running.

Now on your Android device, open the browser and browse to

  http://192.168.1.2:8080/

Replace 192.168.1.2 with the local IP address of the computer running calibre. If your local network supports the use of computer names, you can replace the IP address with the network name of the computer. If you have changed the port the calibre content server is running on, you will have to change 8080 as well to the new port.

The local IP address is the IP address you computer is assigned on your home network. A quick Google search will tell you how to find out your local IP address. You can now browse your book collection and download books from calibre to your device to open with whatever ebook reading software you have on your android device.

Some reading programs support browsing the calibre library directly. For example, in Aldiko, click My Catalogs, then + to add a catalog, then give the catalog a title such as "calibre" and provide the URL listed above. You can now browse the calibre library and download directly into the reading software.

Can I access my calibre books using the web browser in my Kindle or other reading device?

calibre has a *Content Server* that exports the books in calibre as a web page. You can turn it on under *Preferences->Sharing over the net*. Then just point the web browser on your device to the computer running the Content Server and you will be able to browse your book collection. For example, if the computer running the server has IP address 63.45.128.5, in the browser, you would type:

```
http://63.45.128.5:8080
```

Some devices, like the Kindle (1/2/DX), do not allow you to access port 8080 (the default port on which the content server runs. In that case, change the port in the calibre Preferences to 80. (On some operating systems, you may not be able to run the server on a port number less than 1024 because of security settings. In this case the simplest solution is to adjust your router to forward requests on port 80 to port 8080).

I get the error message "Failed to start content server: Port 8080 not free on '0.0.0.0'"?

The most likely cause of this is your antivirus program. Try temporarily disabling it and see if it does the trick.

I cannot send emails using calibre?

Because of the large amount of spam in email, sending email can be tricky, as different mail servers use different strategies to block email. The most common problem is if you are sending email directly (without a mail relay) in calibre. Many servers (for example, Amazon) block email that does not come from a well known relay. The most robust way to setup email sending in calibre is to do the following:

- Create a free GMX account at GMX[51].

- Goto *Preferences->Sharing by Email* in calibre and click the *Use GMX* button and fill in the information asked for.

- calibre will then use GMX to send the mail.

- If you are sending to your Kindle, remember to update the email preferences on your Amazon Kindle page to allow email sent from your GMX email address. Also note that Amazon does not allow email delivery of AZW3 and new style (KF8) MOBI files.

---

[51] http://www.gmx.com

Even after doing this, you may have problems. One common source of problems is that some poorly designed antivirus programs block calibre from opening a connection to send email. Try adding an exclusion for calibre in your antivirus program.

Note: Microsoft/Google/Gmx can disable your account if you use it to send large amounts of email. So, when using Hotmail/Gmail to send mail calibre automatically restricts itself to sending one book every five minutes. If you don't mind risking your account being blocked you can reduce this wait interval by going to Preferences->Tweaks in calibre.

Note: Google recently deliberately broke their email sending protocol (SMTP) support in an attempt to force everyone to use their web interface so they can show you more ads. They are trying to claim that SMTP is insecure, that is incorrect and simply an excuse. If you have trouble with gmail you will need to allow less secure apps as described here[52].

Note: If you are concerned about giving calibre access to your email account, simply create a new free email account with GMX or Hotmail and use it only for calibre.

Why is my device not detected in linux?

calibre needs your linux kernel to have been setup correctly to detect devices. If your devices are not detected, perform the following tests:

```
grep SYSFS_DEPRECATED /boot/config-`uname -r`
```

You should see something like `CONFIG_SYSFS_DEPRECATED_V2 is not set`. Also,

```
grep CONFIG_SCSI_MULTI_LUN /boot/config-`uname -r`
```

must return `CONFIG_SCSI_MULTI_LUN=y`. If you don't see either, you have to recompile your kernel with the correct settings.

My device is getting mounted read-only in linux, so calibre cannot connect to it?

Linux kernels mount devices read-only when their filesystems have errors. You can repair the filesystem with:

```
sudo fsck.vfat -y /dev/sdc
```

Replace /dev/sdc with the path to the device node of your device. You can find the device node of your device, which will always be under /dev by examining the output of:

```
mount
```

Why does calibre not support collections on the Kindle or shelves on the Nook?

Neither the Kindle nor the Nook provide any way to manipulate collections over a USB connection. If you really care about using collections, I would urge you to sell your Kindle/Nook and get a Kobo. Only Kobo seems to understand that life is too short to be entering collections one by one on an e-ink screen :)

Note that in the case of the Kindle, there is a way to manipulate collections via USB, but it requires that the Kindle be rebooted *every time* it is disconnected from the computer, for the changes to the collections to be recognized. As

---

[52] https://support.google.com/accounts/answer/6010255

such, it is unlikely that any calibre developers will ever feel motivated enough to support it. There is however, a calibre plugin that allows you to create collections on your Kindle from the calibre metadata. It is available from here[53].

Note: Amazon have removed the ability to manipulate collections completely in their newer models, like the Kindle Touch and Kindle Fire, making even the above plugin useless, unless you root your Kindle and install custom firmware.

I am getting an error when I try to use calibre with my Kobo Touch/Glo/etc.?

The Kobo has very buggy firmware. Connecting to it has been known to fail at random. Certain combinations of motherboard, USB ports/cables/hubs can exacerbate this tendency to fail. If you are getting an error when connecting to your touch with calibre try the following, each of which has solved the problem for *some* calibre users.

- Connect the Kobo directly to your computer, not via USB Hub

- Try a different USB cable and a different USB port on your computer

- Try a different computer, in particular the Kobo does not work well with some Windows XP machines. If you are on Windows XP, try a computer with a newer version of Windows.

- Try upgrading the firmware on your Kobo Touch to the latest

- Try resetting the Kobo (sometimes this cures the problem for a little while, but then it re-appears, in which case you have to reset again and again)

- Try only putting one or two books onto the Kobo at a time and do not keep large collections on the Kobo

I transferred some books to my Kindle using calibre and they did not show up?

Books sent to the Kindle only show up on the Kindle after they have been *indexed* by the Kindle. This can take some time. If the book still does not show up after some time, then it is likely that the Kindle indexer crashed. Sometimes a particular book can cause the indexer to crash. Unfortunately, Amazon has not provided any way to deduce which book is causing a crash on the Kindle. Your only recourse is to either reset the Kindle, or delete all files from its memory using Windows Explorer (or whatever file manager you use) and then send the books to it again, one by one, until you discover the problem book. Once you have found the problem book, delete it off the Kindle and do a MOBI to MOBI or MOBI to AZW3 conversion in calibre and then send it back. This will most likely take care of the problem.

1.8.3 Library Management

Contents

---

[53] http://www.mobileread.com/forums/showthread.php?t=244202

What formats does calibre read metadata from?

calibre reads metadata from the following formats: CHM, LRF, PDF, LIT, RTF, OPF, MOBI, PRC, EPUB, FB2, IMP, RB, HTML. In addition it can write metadata to: LRF, RTF, OPF, EPUB, PDF, MOBI

Where are the book files stored?

When you first run calibre, it will ask you for a folder in which to store your books. Whenever you add a book to calibre, it will copy the book into that folder. Books in the folder are nicely arranged into sub-folders by Author and Title. Note that the contents of this folder are automatically managed by calibre, **do not** add any files/folders manually to this folder, as they may be automatically deleted. If you want to add a file associated to a particular book, use the top right area of *Edit metadata* dialog to do so. Then, calibre will automatically put that file into the correct folder and move it around when the title/author changes.

Metadata about the books is stored in the file metadata.db at the top level of the library folder This file is is a sqlite database. When backing up your library make sure you copy the entire folder and all its sub-folders.

The library folder and all it's contents make up what is called a calibre library. You can have multiple such libraries. To manage the libraries, click the calibre icon on the toolbar. You can create new libraries, remove/rename existing ones and switch between libraries easily.

You can copy or move books between different libraries (once you have more than one library setup) by right clicking on a book and selecting the *Copy to library* action.

How does calibre manage author names and sorting?

Author names are complex, especially across cultures, see this note[54] for some of complexities. calibre has a very flexible strategy for managing author names. The first thing to understand is that books and authors are separate entities in calibre. A book can have more than one author, and an author can have more than one book. You can manage the authors of a book by the edit metadata dialog. You can manage individual authors by right clicking on the author in the Tag Browser on the left of the main calibre screen and selecting *Manage authors*. Using this dialog you can change the name of an author and also how that name is sorted. This will automatically change the name of the author in all the books of that author. When a book has multiple authors, separate their names using the & character.

Now coming to author name sorting:

- When a new author is added to calibre (this happens whenever a book by a new author is added), calibre automatically computes a sort string for both the book and the author.

- Authors in the Tag Browser are sorted by the sort value for the **authors**. Remember that this is different from the Author sort field for a book.

- By default, this sort algorithm assumes that the author name is in First name Last name format and generates a Last name, First name sort value.

- You can change this algorithm by going to Preferences->Tweaks and setting the *author_sort_copy_method* tweak.

- You can force calibre to recalculate the author sort values for every author by right clicking on any author and selecting *Manage authors*, then pushing the *Recalculate all author sort values* button. Do this after you have set the author_sort_copy_method tweak to what you want.

- You can force calibre to recalculate the author sort values for all books by using the bulk metadata edit dialog (select all books and click edit metadata, check the *Automatically set author sort* checkbox, then press OK.)

---

[54] http://www.w3.org/International/questions/qa-personal-names.en.php?changelang=en

- When recalculating the author sort values for books, calibre uses the author sort values for each individual author. Therefore, ensure that the individual author sort values are correct before recalculating the books' author sort values.

- You can control whether the Tag Browser display authors using their names or their sort values by setting the *categories_use_field_for_author_name* tweak in Preferences->Tweaks

Note that you can set an individual author's sort value to whatever you want using *Manage authors*. This is useful when dealing with names that calibre will not get right, such as complex multi-part names like Miguel de Cervantes Saavedra or when dealing with Asian names like Sun Tzu.

With all this flexibility, it is possible to have calibre manage your author names however you like. For example, one con

- Set the `author_sort_copy_method` tweak to `copy` as described above.

- Restart calibre. Do not change any book metadata before doing the remaining steps.

- Change all author names to LN, FN using the Manage authors dialog.

- After you have changed all the authors, press the *Recalculate all author sort values* button.

- Press OK, at which point calibre will change the authors in all your books. This can take a while.

Note:

When changing from FN LN to LN, FN, it is often the case that the values in author_sort are already in LN, FN format

- set the `author_sort_copy_method` tweak to `copy` as described above.

- restart calibre. Do not change any book metadata before doing the remaining steps.

- open the Manage authors dialog. Press the `copy all author sort values to author` button.

- Check through the authors to be sure you are happy. You can still press Cancel to abandon the changes. Once you press OK, there is no undo.

- Press OK, at which point calibre will change the authors in all your books. This can take a while.

Why doesn't calibre let me store books in my own directory structure?

The whole point of calibre's library management features is that they provide a search and sort based interface for locating books that is *much* more efficient than any possible directory scheme you could come up with for your collection. Indeed, once you become comfortable using calibre's interface to find, sort and browse your collection, you wont ever feel the need to hunt through the files on your disk to find a book again. By managing books in its own directory structure of Author -> Title -> Book files, calibre is able to achieve a high level of reliability and standardization. To illustrate why a search/tagging based interface is superior to folders, consider the following. Suppose your book collection is nicely sorted into folders with the following scheme:

```
Genre -> Author -> Series -> ReadStatus
```

Now this makes it very easy to find for example all science fiction books by Isaac Asimov in the Foundation series. But suppose you want to find all unread science fiction books. There's no easy way to do this with this folder scheme, you would instead need a folder scheme that looks like:

```
ReadStatus -> Genre -> Author -> Series
```

In calibre, you would instead use tags to mark genre and read status and then just use a simple search query like `tag:scifi and not tag:read`. calibre even has a nice graphical interface, so you don't need to learn its search language instead you can just click on tags to include or exclude them from the search.

To those of you that claim that you need access to the filesystem to so that you can have access to your books over the network, calibre has an excellent content server that gives you access to your calibre library over the net.

If you are worried that someday calibre will cease to be developed, leaving all your books marooned in its folder structure, explore the powerful "Save to Disk" feature in calibre that lets you export all your files into a folder structure of arbitrary complexity based on their metadata.

Finally, the reason there are numbers at the end of every title folder, is for *robustness*. That number is the id number of the book record in the calibre database. The presence of the number allows you to have multiple records with the same title and author names. It is also part of what allows calibre to magically regenerate the database with all metadata if the database file gets corrupted. Given that calibre's mission is to get you to stop storing metadata in filenames and stop using the filesystem to find things, the increased robustness afforded by the id numbers is well worth the uglier folder names.

If you are still not convinced, then I'm afraid calibre is not for you. Look elsewhere for your book cataloguing needs. Just so we're clear, **this is not going to change**. Kindly do not contact us in an attempt to get us to change this.

Why doesn't calibre have a column for foo?

calibre is designed to have columns for the most frequently and widely used fields. In addition, you can add any columns you like. Columns can be added via *Preferences->Interface->Add your own columns*. Watch the tutorial UI Power tips[55] to learn how to create your own columns, or read this blog post[56].

You can also create "virtual columns" that contain combinations of the metadata from other columns. In the add column dialog use the *Quick create* links to easily create columns to show the book ISBN or formats. You can use the powerful calibre template language to do much more with columns. For more details, see *The calibre template language* (page 161).

Can I have a column showing the formats or the ISBN?

Yes, you can. Follow the instructions in the answer above for adding custom columns.

How do I move my calibre library from one computer to another?

Simply copy the calibre library folder from the old to the new computer. You can find out what the library folder is by clicking the calibre icon in the toolbar. The very first item is the path to the library folder. Now on the new computer, start calibre for the first time. It will run the Welcome Wizard asking you for the location of the calibre library. Point it to the previously copied folder. If the computer you are transferring to already has a calibre installation, then the Welcome wizard wont run. In that case, right-click the calibre icon in the tooolbar and point it to the newly copied directory. You will now have two calibre libraries on your computer and you can switch between them by clicking the calibre icon on the toolbar. Transferring your library in this manner preserver all your metadata, tags, custom columns, etc.

Note that if you are transferring between different types of computers (for example Windows to OS X) then after doing the above you should also right-click the calibre icon on the tool bar, select Library Maintenance and run the Check Library action. It will warn you about any problems in your library, which you should fix by hand.

Note: A calibre library is just a folder which contains all the book files and their metadata. All the metadata is stored in a single file called metadata.db, in the top level folder. If this file gets corrupted, you may see an empty list of books in calibre. In this case you can ask calibre to restore your books by doing a right-click on the calibre icon in the toolbar and selecting Library Maintenance->Restore database

---

[55] http://calibre-ebook.com/demo#tutorials
[56] http://blog.calibre-ebook.com/2011/11/calibre-custom-columns.html

---

The list of books in calibre is blank!

In order to understand why that happened, you have to understand what a calibre library is. At the most basic level, a calibre library is just a folder. Whenever you add a book to calibre, that book's files are copied into this folder (arranged into sub folders by author and title). Inside the calibre library folder, at the top level, you will see a file called metadata.db. This file is where calibre stores the metadata like title/author/rating/tags etc. for *every* book in your calibre library. The list of books that calibre displays is created by reading the contents of this metadata.db file.

There can be two reasons why calibre is showing a empty list of books:

- Your calibre library folder changed its location. This can happen if it was on an external disk and the drive letter for that disk changed. Or if you accidentally moved the folder. In this case, calibre cannot find its library and so starts up with an empty library instead. To remedy this, do a right-click on the calibre icon in the calibre toolbar and select Switch/create library. Click the little blue icon to select the new location of your calibre library and click OK. If you don't know the new location search your computer for the file `metadata.db`.

- Your metadata.db file was deleted/corrupted. In this case, you can ask calibre to rebuild the metadata.db from its backups. Right click the calibre icon in the calibre toolbar and select Library maintenance->Restore database. calibre will automatically rebuild metadata.db.

I am getting errors with my calibre library on a networked drive/NAS?

Do not put your calibre library on a networked drive.

A filesystem is a complex beast. Most network filesystems lack various filesystem features that calibre uses. Some don't support file locking, some don't support hardlinking, some are just flaky. Additionally, calibre is a single user application, if you accidentally run two copies of calibre on the same networked library, bad things will happen. Finally, different OSes impose different limitations on filesystems, so if you share your networked drive across OSes, once again, bad things *will happen*.

Consider using the calibre Content Server to make your books available on other computers. Run calibre on a single computer and access it via the Content Server or a Remote Desktop solution.

If you must share the actual library, use a file syncing tool like DropBox or rsync instead of a networked drive. If you are using a file-syncing tool it is **essential** that you make sure that both calibre and the file syncing tool do not try to access the calibre library at the same time. In other words, **do not** run the file syncing tool and calibre at the same time.

Even with these tools there is danger of data corruption/loss, so only do this if you are willing to live with that risk. In particular, be aware that **Google Drive** is incompatible with calibre, if you put your calibre library in Google Drive, **you will suffer data loss**. See this thread[57] for details.

1.8.4 Miscellaneous

---

[57] http://www.mobileread.com/forums/showthread.php?t=205581

Contents

I want calibre to download news from my favorite news website.

If you are reasonably proficient with computers, you can teach calibre to download news from any website of your choosing. To learn how to do this see *Adding your favorite news website* (page 125).

Otherwise, you can request a particular news site by posting in the calibre Recipes forum[58].

Why the name calibre?

Take your pick:

- Convertor And LIBRary for Ebooks
- A high *calibre* product
- A tribute to the SONY Librie which was the first e-ink based ebook reader
- My wife chose it ;-)

calibre is pronounced as cal-i-ber *not* ca-li-bre. If you're wondering, calibre is the British/commonwealth spelling for caliber. Being Indian, that's the natural spelling for me.

Why does calibre show only some of my fonts on OS X?

calibre embeds fonts in ebook files it creates. Ebook files support embedding only TrueType and OpenType (.ttf and .otf) fonts. Most fonts on OS X systems are in .dfont format, thus they cannot be embedded. calibre shows only TrueType and OpenType fonts found on your system. You can obtain many such fonts on the web. Simply download the .ttf/.otf files and add them to the Library/Fonts directory in your home directory.

---

[58] http://www.mobileread.com/forums/forumdisplay.php?f=228

calibre is not starting on Windows?

There can be several causes for this:

- If you are on Windows XP, or on a computer with a processor that does not support SSE2 (such as AMD processors from before 2003) try installing calibre version 1.48[59]. calibre 2.0 and newer use Qt 5 which is known to be incompatible with Windows XP machines, and requires SSE2. Simply un-install calibre and then install version 1.48, doing so will not affect your books/settings.

- If you get an error about calibre not being able to open a file because it is in use by another program, do the following:

  - Uninstall calibre

  - Reboot your computer

  - Re-install calibre. But do not start calibre from the installation wizard.

  - Temporarily disable your antivirus program (disconnect from the Internet before doing so, to be safe)

  - Look inside the folder you chose for your calibre library. If you see a file named metadata.db, delete it.

  - Start calibre

  - From now on you should be able to start calibre normally.

- If you get an error about a Python function terminating unexpectedly after upgrading calibre, first uninstall calibre, then delete the folders (if they exists) `C:\Program Files\Calibre` and `C:\Program Files\Calibre2`. Now re-install and you should be fine.

- If you get an error in the welcome wizard on an initial run of calibre, try choosing a folder like `C:\library` as the calibre library (calibre sometimes has trouble with library locations if the path contains non-English characters, or only numbers, etc.)

- Try running it as Administrator (Right click on the icon and select "Run as Administrator")

If it still wont launch, start a command prompt (press the windows key and R; then type **cmd.exe** in the Run dialog that appears). At the command prompt type the following command and press Enter:

```
calibre-debug -g
```

Post any output you see in a help message on the Forum[60].

calibre freezes/crashes occasionally?

There are several possible things I know of, that can cause this:

- You recently connected an external monitor or TV to your computer. In this case, whenever calibre opens a new window like the edit metadata window or the conversion dialog, it appears on the second monitor where you don't notice it and so you think calibre has frozen. Disconnect your second monitor and restart calibre.

- If you use RoboForm, it is known to cause calibre to crash. Add calibre to the blacklist of programs inside RoboForm to fix this. Or uninstall RoboForm.

- The Logitech SetPoint Settings application causes random crashes in calibre when it is open. Close it before starting calibre.

- Constant Guard Protection by Xfinity causes crashes in calibre. You have to manually allow calibre in it or uninstall Constant Guard Protection.

---

[59]http://download.calibre-ebook.com/1.48.0/
[60]http://www.mobileread.com/forums/forumdisplay.php?f=166

- Spybot - Search & Destroy blocks calibre from accessing its temporary files breaking viewing and converting of books.

- You are using a Wacom branded USB mouse. There is an incompatibility between Wacom mice and the graphics toolkit calibre uses. Try using a non-Wacom mouse.

- On some 64 bit versions of Windows there are security software/settings that prevent 64-bit calibre from working properly. If you are using the 64-bit version of calibre try switching to the 32-bit version.

- If the crashes happen specifically when you are using a file open dialog, like clicking on the Add Books button or the Save to Disk button, then you may have an issue with the windows file open dialogs on your computer. Some calibre users have reported that uninstalling the SpiderOak encrypted backup software also fixes these crashes. If you do not wish to uninstall SpiderOak, you can also turn off "Enable OS integration" in the SpiderOak preferences.

If none of the above apply to you, then there is some other program on your computer that is interfering with calibre. First reboot your computer in safe mode, to have as few running programs as possible, and see if the crashes still happen. If they do not, then you know it is some program causing the problem. The most likely such culprit is a program that modifies other programs' behavior, such as an antivirus, a device driver, something like RoboForm (an automatic form filling app) or an assistive technology like Voice Control or a Screen Reader.

The only way to find the culprit is to eliminate the programs one by one and see which one is causing the issue. Basically, stop a program, run calibre, check for crashes. If they still happen, stop another program and repeat.

Using the viewer or doing any conversions results in a permission denied error on Windows

Something on your computer is preventing calibre from accessing its own temporary files. Most likely the permissions on your Temp folder are incorrect. Go to the folder file:*C:\Users\USERNAME\AppData\Local* in Windows Explorer and then right click on the file:*Temp* folder, select Properties and go to the Security tab. Make sure that your user account has full control for this folder.

Some users have reported that running the following command in an Administrator Command Prompt fixed their permissions. To get an Administrator Command Prompt search for cmd.exe in the start menu, then right click on the command prompt entry and select Run as Administrator. At the command prompt type the following command and press Enter:

```
icacls "%appdata%\..\Local\Temp" /reset /T
```

Alternately, you can run calibre as Administrator, but doing so will cause some functionality, such as drag and drop to not work.

Finally, some users have reported that disabling UAC fixes the problem.

calibre is not starting/crashing on OS X?

One common cause of failures on OS X is the use of accessibility technologies that are incompatible with the graphics toolkit calibre uses. Try turning off VoiceOver if you have it on. Also go to System Preferences->System->Universal Access and turn off the setting for enabling access for assistive devices in all the tabs. Another cause can be some third party apps that modify system behavior, such as Smart Scroll.

You can obtain debug output about why calibre is not starting by running *Console.app*. Debug output will be printed to it. If the debug output contains a line that looks like:

```
Qt: internal: -108: Error ATSUMeasureTextImage text/qfontengine_mac.mm
```

then the problem is probably a corrupted font cache. You can clear the cache by following these instructions[61]. If that doesn't solve it, look for a corrupted font file on your system, in ~/Library/Fonts or the like. An easy way to check

---

[61] http://www.macworld.com/article/1139383/fontcacheclear.html

for corrupted fonts in OS X is to start the "Font Book" application, select all fonts and then in the File menu, choose "Validate fonts".

I downloaded the installer, but it is not working?

Downloading from the Internet can sometimes result in a corrupted download. If the calibre installer you downloaded is not opening, try downloading it again. If re-downloading it does not work, download it from an alternate location[62]. If the installer still doesn't work, then something on your computer is preventing it from running.

- Try temporarily disabling your antivirus program (Microsoft Security Essentials, or Kaspersky or Norton or McAfee or whatever). This is most likely the culprit if the upgrade process is hanging in the middle.

- Try rebooting your computer and running a registry cleaner like Wise registry cleaner[63].

- Try a clean install. That is, uninstall calibre, delete C:\Program Files\Calibre2 (or wherever you previously chose to install calibre). Then re-install calibre. Note that uninstalling does not touch your books or settings.

- Try downloading the installer with an alternate browser. For example if you are using Internet Explorer, try using Firefox or Chrome instead.

- If you get an error about a missing DLL on Windows, then most likely, the permissions on your temporary folder are incorrect. Go to the folder C:\Users\USERNAME\AppData\Local in Windows explorer and then right click on the Temp folder and select *Properties* and go to the *Security* tab. Make sure that your user account has full control for this folder.

If you still cannot get the installer to work and you are on Windows, you can use the calibre portable install[64], which does not need an installer (it is just a zip file).

My antivirus program claims calibre is a virus/trojan?

The first thing to check is that you are downloading calibre from the official website: http://calibre-ebook.com/download. Make sure you are clicking the download links on the left, not the advertisements on the right. calibre is a very popular program and unscrupulous people try to setup websites offering it for download to fool the unwary.

If you have the official download and your antivirus program is still claiming calibre is a virus, then, your antivirus program is wrong. Antivirus programs use heuristics, patterns of code that "look suspicious" to detect viruses. It's rather like racial profiling. calibre is a completely open source product. You can actually browse the source code yourself (or hire someone to do it for you) to verify that it is not a virus. Please report the false identification to whatever company you buy your antivirus software from. If the antivirus program is preventing you from downloading/installing calibre, disable it temporarily, install calibre and then re-enable it.

How do I backup calibre?

The most important thing to backup is the calibre library folder, that contains all your books and metadata. This is the folder you chose for your calibre library when you ran calibre for the first time. You can get the path to the library folder by clicking the calibre icon on the main toolbar. You must backup this complete folder with all its files and sub-folders.

You can switch calibre to using a backed up library folder by simply clicking the calibre icon on the toolbar and choosing your backup library folder. A backed up library folder backs up your custom columns and saved searches as well as all your books and metadata.

---

[62]http://www.fosshub.com/Calibre.html/
[63]http://www.wisecleaner.com
[64]http://calibre-ebook.com/download_portable

If you want to backup the calibre configuration/plugins, you have to backup the config directory. You can find this config directory via *Preferences->Miscellaneous*. Note that restoring configuration directories is not officially supported, but should work in most cases. Just copy the contents of the backup directory into the current configuration directory to restore.

How do I use purchased EPUB books with calibre (or what do I do with .acsm files)?

Most purchased EPUB books have DRM[65]. This prevents calibre from opening them. You can still use calibre to store and transfer them to your ebook reader. First, you must authorize your reader on a windows machine with Adobe Digital Editions. Once this is done, EPUB books transferred with calibre will work fine on your reader. When you purchase an epub book from a website, you will get an ".acsm" file. This file should be opened with Adobe Digital Editions, which will then download the actual ".epub" ebook. The ebook file will be stored in the folder "My Digital Editions", from where you can add it to calibre.

I am getting a "Permission Denied" error?

A permission denied error can occur because of many possible reasons, none of them having anything to do with calibre.

- You can get permission denied errors if you are using an SD card with write protect enabled.
- If you, or some program you used changed the file permissions of the files in question to read only.
- If there is a filesystem error on the device which caused your operating system to mount the filesystem in read only mode or mark a particular file as read only pending recovery.
- If the files have their owner set to a user other than you.
- If your file is open in another program.
- If the file resides on a device, you may have reached the limit of a maximum of 256 files in the root of the device. In this case you need to reformat the device/sd card referred to in the error message with a FAT32 filesystem, or delete some files from the SD card/device memory.

You will need to fix the underlying cause of the permissions error before resuming to use calibre. Read the error message carefully, see what file it points to and fix the permissions on that file or its containing folders.

Can I have the comment metadata show up on my reader?

Most readers do not support this. You should complain to the manufacturer about it and hopefully if enough people complain, things will change. In the meantime, you can insert the metadata, including comments into a "Jacket page" at the start of the ebook, by using the option to "Insert metadata as page at start of book" during conversion. The option is found in the *Structure Detection* section of the conversion settings. Note that for this to have effect you have to *convert* the book. If your book is already in a format that does not need conversion, you can convert from that format to the same format.

Another alternative is to create a catalog in ebook form containing a listing of all the books in your calibre library, with their metadata. Click-and-hold the convert button to access the catalog creation tool. And before you ask, no you cannot have the catalog "link directly to" books on your reader.

---

[65] http://drmfree.calibre-ebook.com/about#drm

How do I get calibre to use my HTTP proxy?

By default, calibre uses whatever proxy settings are set in your OS. Sometimes these are incorrect, for example, on Windows if you don't use Internet Explorer then the proxy settings may not be up to date. You can tell calibre to use a particular proxy server by setting the `http_proxy` environment variable. The format of the variable is: `http://username:password@servername` you should ask your network administrator to give you the correct value for this variable. Note that calibre only supports HTTP proxies not SOCKS proxies. You can see the current proxies used by calibre in Preferences->Miscellaneous.

I want some feature added to calibre. What can I do?

You have two choices:

1. Create a patch by hacking on calibre and send it to me for review and inclusion. See Development[66].

2. Open a bug requesting the feature[67] . Remember that while you may think your feature request is extremely important/essential, calibre developers might not agree. Fortunately, calibre is open source, which means you always have the option of implementing your feature yourself, or hiring someone to do it for you. Furthermore, calibre has a comprehensive plugin architecture, so you might be able to develop your feature as a plugin, see *Writing your own plugins to extend calibre's functionality* (page 213).

Why doesn't calibre have an automatic update?

For many reasons:

- *There is no need to update every week.* If you are happy with how calibre works turn off the update notification and be on your merry way. Check back to see if you want to update once a year or so. There is a check box to turn off the update notification, on the update notification itself.

- calibre downloads currently use about 100TB of bandwidth a month[68]. Implementing automatic updates would greatly increase that and end up costing thousands of dollars a month, which someone has to pay.

- If I implement a dialog that downloads the update and launches it, instead of going to the website as it does now, that would save the most ardent calibre updater, *at most five clicks a week.* There are far higher priority things to do in calibre development.

- If you really, really hate downloading calibre every week but still want to be up to the latest, I encourage you to run from source, which makes updating trivial. Instructions are *available here* (page 317).

- There are third party automatic updaters for calibre made by calibre users in the calibre forum[69].

How is calibre licensed?

calibre is licensed under the GNU General Public License v3 (an open source license). This means that you are free to redistribute calibre as long as you make the source code available. So if you want to put calibre on a CD with your product, you must also put the calibre source code on the CD. The source code is available for download[70]. You are free to use the results of conversions from calibre however you want. You cannot use either code or libraries from calibre in your software without making your software open source. For details, see The GNU GPL v3[71].

---

[66] http://calibre-ebook.com/get-involved
[67] http://calibre-ebook.com/bugs
[68] http://calibre-ebook.com/dynamic/downloads
[69] http://www.mobileread.com/forums/forumdisplay.php?f=238
[70] http://download.calibre-ebook.com
[71] http://www.gnu.org/licenses/gpl.html

How do I run calibre from my USB stick?

A portable version of calibre is available here[72].

How do I run parts of calibre like news download and the content server on my own linux server?

First, you must install calibre onto your linux server. If your server is using a modern linux distro, you should have no problems installing calibre onto it.

Note: calibre needs GLIBC >= 2.13 and libstdc++ >= 6.0.17. If you have an older server, you will either need to compile these from source, or use calibre 1.48 which requires only GLIBC >= 2.10. In addition, although the calibre command line utilities do not need a running X server, some of them do require the X server libraries to be installed on your system. This is because the use Qt, which links against these libraries. If you get an ImportError about some Qt modules, you are likely missing some X libraries.

You can run the calibre server via the command:

```
/opt/calibre/calibre-server --with-library /path/to/the/library/you/want/to/share
```

You can download news and convert it into an ebook with the command:

```
/opt/calibre/ebook-convert "Title of news source.recipe" outputfile.epub
```

If you want to generate MOBI, use outputfile.mobi instead and use `--output-profile kindle`.

You can email downloaded news with the command:

```
/opt/calibre/calibre-smtp
```

I leave figuring out the exact command line as an exercise for the reader.

Finally, you can add downloaded news to the calibre library with:

```
/opt/calibre/calibredb add --with-library /path/to/library outfile.epub
```

Remember to read the command line documentation section of the calibre User Manual to learn more about these, and other commands.

1.9 Tutorials

Here you will find tutorials to get you started using calibre's more advanced features, such as XPath and templates.

1.9.1 Adding your favorite news website

calibre has a powerful, flexible and easy-to-use framework for downloading news from the Internet and converting it into an ebook. The following will show you, by means of examples, how to get news from various websites.

To gain an understanding of how to use the framework, follow the examples in the order listed below:

---

[72] http://calibre-ebook.com/download_portable

Completely automatic fetching

If your news source is simple enough, calibre may well be able to fetch it completely automatically, all you need to do is provide the URL. calibre gathers all the information needed to download a news source into a *recipe*. In order to tell calibre about a news source, you have to create a *recipe* for it. Let's see some examples:

The calibre blog

The calibre blog is a blog of posts that describe many useful calibre features in a simple and accessible way for new calibre users. In order to download this blog into an ebook, we rely on the *RSS* feed of the blog:

```
http://blog.calibre-ebook.com/feeds/posts/default
```

I got the RSS URL by looking under "Subscribe to" at the bottom of the blog page and choosing *Posts->Atom*. To make calibre download the feeds and convert them into an ebook, you should right click the *Fetch news* button and then the *Add a custom news source* menu item and then the *New Recipe* button. A dialog similar to that shown below should open up.

First enter `calibre Blog` into the *Recipe title* field. This will be the title of the ebook that will be created from the articles in the above feeds.

The next two fields (*Oldest article* and *Max. number of articles*) allow you some control over how many articles should be downloaded from each feed, and they are pretty self explanatory.

To add the feeds to the recipe, enter the feed title and the feed URL and click the *Add feed* button. Once you have added the feed, simply click the *Save* button and you're done! Close the dialog.

To test your new *recipe*, click the *Fetch news* button and in the *Custom news sources* sub-menu click *calibre Blog*. After a couple of minutes, the newly downloaded ebook of blog posts will appear in the main library view (if you have your reader connected, it will be put onto the reader instead of into the library). Select it and hit the *View* button to read!

The reason this worked so well, with so little effort is that the blog provides *full-content RSS* feeds, i.e., the article content is embedded in the feed itself. For most news sources that provide news in this fashion, with *full-content* feeds, you don't need any more effort to convert them to ebooks. Now we will look at a news source that does not provide full content feeds. In such feeds, the full article is a webpage and the feed only contains a link to the webpage with a short summary of the article.

bbc.co.uk

Lets try the following two feeds from *The BBC*:

1. News Front Page: http://newsrss.bbc.co.uk/rss/newsonline_world_edition/front_page/rss.xml

2. Science/Nature: http://newsrss.bbc.co.uk/rss/newsonline_world_edition/science/nature/rss.xml

Follow the procedure outlined in *The calibre blog* (page 126) above to create a recipe for *The BBC* (using the feeds above). Looking at the downloaded ebook, we see that calibre has done a creditable job of extracting only the content you care about from each article's webpage. However, the extraction process is not perfect. Sometimes it leaves in undesirable content like menus and navigation aids or it removes content that should have been left alone, like article headings. In order, to have perfect content extraction, we will need to customize the fetch process, as described in the next section.

Customizing the fetch process

When you want to perfect the download process, or download content from a particularly complex website, you can avail yourself of all the power and flexibility of the *recipe* framework. In order to do that, in the *Add custom news sources* dialog, simply click the *Switch to Advanced mode* button.

The easiest and often most productive customization is to use the print version of the online articles. The print version typically has much less cruft and translates much more smoothly to an ebook. Let's try to use the print version of the articles from *The BBC*.

Using the print version of bbc.co.uk

The first step is to look at the ebook we downloaded previously from *bbc.co.uk* (page 128). At the end of each article, in the ebook is a little blurb telling you where the article was downloaded from. Copy and paste that URL into a browser. Now on the article webpage look for a link that points to the "Printable version". Click it to see the print version of the article. It looks much neater! Now compare the two URLs. For me they were:

Article URL http://news.bbc.co.uk/2/hi/science/nature/7312016.stm

Print version URL http://newsvote.bbc.co.uk/mpapps/pagetools/print/news.bbc.co.uk/2/hi/science/nature/7312016.stm

So it looks like to get the print version, we need to prefix every article URL with:

newsvote.bbc.co.uk/mpapps/pagetools/print/

Now in the *Advanced Mode* of the Custom news sources dialog, you should see something like (remember to select *The BBC* recipe before switching to advanced mode):

```
 Recipe source code (python)

 class AdvancedUserRecipe1206418393(BasicNewsRecipe):
     title          = u'The BBC'
     oldest_article = 7
     max_articles_per_feed = 100

     feeds          = [(u'News Front Page', u'http://newsrss.bbc.co.uk/rss/newsonlir
```

You can see that the fields from the *Basic mode* have been translated to python code in a straightforward manner. We need to add instructions to this recipe to use the print version of the articles. All that's needed is to add the following two lines:

```
def print_version(self, url):
    return url.replace('http://', 'http://newsvote.bbc.co.uk/mpapps/pagetools/print/')
```

This is python, so indentation is important. After you've added the lines, it should look like:

```
Recipe source code (python)

class AdvancedUserRecipe1206418393(BasicNewsRecipe):
    title           = u'The BBC'
    oldest_article = 7
    max_articles_per_feed = 100

    feeds           = [(u'News Front Page', u'http://newsrss.bbc.co.uk/rss/newsonlin

    def print_version(self, url):
        return url.replace('http://', 'http://newsvote.bbc.co.uk/mpapps/pagetools/p
```

In the above, `def print_version(self, url)` defines a *method* that is called by calibre for every article. `url` is the URL of the original article. What `print_version` does is take that url and replace it with the new URL that points to the print version of the article. To learn about python[73] see the tutorial[74].

Now, click the *Add/update recipe* button and your changes will be saved. Re-download the ebook. You should have a much improved ebook. One of the problems with the new version is that the fonts on the print version webpage are too small. This is automatically fixed when converting to an ebook, but even after the fixing process, the font size of the menus and navigation bar to become too large relative to the article text. To fix this, we will do some more customization, in the next section.

Replacing article styles

In the previous section, we saw that the font size for articles from the print version of *The BBC* was too small. In most websites, *The BBC* included, this font size is set by means of *CSS* stylesheets. We can disable the fetching of such stylesheets by adding the line:

```
no_stylesheets = True
```

The recipe now looks like:

---

[73] https://www.python.org
[74] https://docs.python.org/2/tutorial/

```
Recipe source code (python)

class AdvancedUserRecipe1206419520(BasicNewsRecipe):
    title           = u'The BBC'
    oldest_article = 7
    max_articles_per_feed = 100
    no_stylesheets = True

    feeds           = [(u'News Front Page', u'http://newsrss.bbc.co.uk/rss/newsonli

    def print_version(self, url):
        return url.replace('http://', 'http://newsvote.bbc.co.uk/mpapps/pagetools/
```

The new version looks pretty good. If you're a perfectionist, you'll want to read the next section, which deals with actually modifying the downloaded content.

Slicing and dicing

calibre contains very powerful and flexible abilities when it comes to manipulating downloaded content. To show off a couple of these, let's look at our old friend the *The BBC* (page 129) recipe again. Looking at the source code (*HTML*) of a couple of articles (print version), we see that they have a footer that contains no useful information, contained in

```
<div class="footer">
...
</div>
```

This can be removed by adding:

```
remove_tags     = [dict(name='div', attrs={'class':'footer'})]
```

to the recipe. Finally, lets replace some of the *CSS* that we disabled earlier, with our own *CSS* that is suitable for conversion to an ebook:

```
extra_css       = '.headline {font-size: x-large;} \n .fact { padding-top: 10pt   }'
```

With these additions, our recipe has become "production quality", indeed it is very close to the actual recipe used by calibre for the *BBC*, shown below:

```
##
## Title:       BBC News, Sport, and Blog Calibre Recipe
## Contact:     mattst - jmstanfield@gmail.com
##
## License:     GNU General Public License v3 - http://www.gnu.org/copyleft/gpl.html
## Copyright:   mattst - jmstanfield@gmail.com
##
## Written:     November 2011
## Last Edited: 2011-11-19
##


__license__     = 'GNU General Public License v3 - http://www.gnu.org/copyleft/gpl.html
__copyright__   = 'mattst - jmstanfield@gmail.com'


'''
BBC News, Sport, and Blog Calibre Recipe
```

```
'''

# Import the regular expressions module.
import re

# Import the BasicNewsRecipe class which this class extends.
from calibre.web.feeds.recipes import BasicNewsRecipe

class BBCNewsSportBlog(BasicNewsRecipe):

    #
    #    **** IMPORTANT USERS READ ME ****
    #
    #  First select the feeds you want then scroll down below the feeds list
    #  and select the values you want for the other user preferences, like
    #  oldest_article and such like.
    #
    #
    #  Select the BBC rss feeds which you want in your ebook.
    #  Selected feed have NO '#' at their start, de-selected feeds begin with a '#'.
    #
    #  Eg.  ("News Home", "http://feeds.bbci.co.uk/... - include feed.
    #  Eg. #("News Home", "http://feeds.bbci.co.uk/... - do not include feed.
    #
    # There are 68 feeds below which constitute the bulk of the available rss
    # feeds on the BBC web site. These include 5 blogs by editors and
    # correspondants, 16 sports feeds, 15 'sub' regional feeds (Eg. North West
    # Wales, Scotland Business), and 7 Welsh language feeds.
    #
    # Some of the feeds are low volume (Eg. blogs), or very low volume (Eg. Click)
    # so if "oldest_article = 1.5" (only articles published in the last 36 hours)
    # you may get some 'empty feeds' which will not then be included in the ebook.
    #
    # The 15 feeds currently selected below are simply my default ones.
    #
    # Note: With all 68 feeds selected, oldest_article set to 2,
    # max_articles_per_feed set to 100, and simultaneous_downloads set to 10,
    # the ebook creation took 29 minutes on my speedy 100 mbps net connection,
    # fairly high-end desktop PC running Linux (Ubuntu Lucid-Lynx).
    # More realistically with 15 feeds selected, oldest_article set to 1.5,
    # max_articles_per_feed set to 100, and simultaneous_downloads set to 20,
    # it took 6 minutes. If that's too slow increase 'simultaneous_downloads'.
    #
    # Select / de-select the feeds you want in your ebook.
    #
    feeds = [
              ("News Home", "http://feeds.bbci.co.uk/news/rss.xml"),
              ("UK", "http://feeds.bbci.co.uk/news/uk/rss.xml"),
              ("World", "http://feeds.bbci.co.uk/news/world/rss.xml"),
              #("England", "http://feeds.bbci.co.uk/news/england/rss.xml"),
              #("Scotland", "http://feeds.bbci.co.uk/news/scotland/rss.xml"),
              #("Wales", "http://feeds.bbci.co.uk/news/wales/rss.xml"),
              #("N. Ireland", "http://feeds.bbci.co.uk/news/northern_ireland/rss.xml"),
              #("Africa", "http://feeds.bbci.co.uk/news/world/africa/rss.xml"),
              #("Asia", "http://feeds.bbci.co.uk/news/world/asia/rss.xml"),
              #("Europe", "http://feeds.bbci.co.uk/news/world/europe/rss.xml"),
              #("Latin America", "http://feeds.bbci.co.uk/news/world/latin_america/rss.xml"),
              #("Middle East", "http://feeds.bbci.co.uk/news/world/middle_east/rss.xml"),
```

```
   ("US & Canada", "http://feeds.bbci.co.uk/news/world/us_and_canada/rss.xml"),
   ("Politics", "http://feeds.bbci.co.uk/news/politics/rss.xml"),
   ("Science/Environment", "http://feeds.bbci.co.uk/news/science_and_environment/rs
   ("Technology", "http://feeds.bbci.co.uk/news/technology/rss.xml"),
   ("Magazine", "http://feeds.bbci.co.uk/news/magazine/rss.xml"),
   ("Entertainment/Arts", "http://feeds.bbci.co.uk/news/entertainment_and_arts/rss.
#  ("Health", "http://feeds.bbci.co.uk/news/health/rss.xml"),
#  ("Education/Family", "http://feeds.bbci.co.uk/news/education/rss.xml"),
   ("Business", "http://feeds.bbci.co.uk/news/business/rss.xml"),
   ("Special Reports", "http://feeds.bbci.co.uk/news/special_reports/rss.xml"),
   ("Also in the News", "http://feeds.bbci.co.uk/news/also_in_the_news/rss.xml"),
#  ("Newsbeat", "http://www.bbc.co.uk/newsbeat/rss.xml"),
#  ("Click", "http://newsrss.bbc.co.uk/rss/newsonline_uk_edition/programmes/click_
   ("Blog: Nick Robinson (Political Editor)", "http://feeds.bbci.co.uk/news/corresp
#  ("Blog: Mark D'Arcy (Parliamentary Correspondent)", "http://feeds.bbci.co.uk/ne
#  ("Blog: Robert Peston (Business Editor)", "http://feeds.bbci.co.uk/news/corresp
#  ("Blog: Stephanie Flanders (Economics Editor)", "http://feeds.bbci.co.uk/news/c
   ("Blog: Rory Cellan-Jones (Technology correspondent)", "http://feeds.bbci.co.uk
   ("Sport Front Page", "http://newsrss.bbc.co.uk/rss/sportonline_uk_edition/front_
#  ("Football", "http://newsrss.bbc.co.uk/rss/sportonline_uk_edition/football/rss.
#  ("Cricket", "http://newsrss.bbc.co.uk/rss/sportonline_uk_edition/cricket/rss.x
#  ("Rugby Union", "http://newsrss.bbc.co.uk/rss/sportonline_uk_edition/rugby_unic
#  ("Rugby League", "http://newsrss.bbc.co.uk/rss/sportonline_uk_edition/rugby_lea
#  ("Tennis", "http://newsrss.bbc.co.uk/rss/sportonline_uk_edition/tennis/rss.xml
#  ("Golf", "http://newsrss.bbc.co.uk/rss/sportonline_uk_edition/golf/rss.xml"),
#  ("Motorsport", "http://newsrss.bbc.co.uk/rss/sportonline_uk_edition/motorsport.
#  ("Boxing", "http://newsrss.bbc.co.uk/rss/sportonline_uk_edition/boxing/rss.xml
#  ("Athletics", "http://newsrss.bbc.co.uk/rss/sportonline_uk_edition/athletics/rs
#  ("Snooker", "http://newsrss.bbc.co.uk/rss/sportonline_uk_edition/other_sports/s
#  ("Horse Racing", "http://newsrss.bbc.co.uk/rss/sportonline_uk_edition/other_spc
#  ("Cycling", "http://newsrss.bbc.co.uk/rss/sportonline_uk_edition/other_sports/c
#  ("Disability Sport", "http://newsrss.bbc.co.uk/rss/sportonline_uk_edition/othei
#  ("Other Sport", "http://newsrss.bbc.co.uk/rss/sportonline_uk_edition/other_spoi
#  ("Olympics 2012", "http://newsrss.bbc.co.uk/rss/sportonline_uk_edition/other_sp
#  ("N. Ireland Politics", "http://feeds.bbci.co.uk/news/northern_ireland/northern
#  ("Scotland Politics", "http://feeds.bbci.co.uk/news/scotland/scotland_politics.
#  ("Scotland Business", "http://feeds.bbci.co.uk/news/scotland/scotland_business.
#  ("E. Scotland, Edinburgh & Fife", "http://feeds.bbci.co.uk/news/scotland/edinbu
#  ("W. Scotland & Glasgow", "http://feeds.bbci.co.uk/news/scotland/glasgow_and_we
#  ("Highlands & Islands", "http://feeds.bbci.co.uk/news/scotland/highlands_and_is
#  ("NE. Scotland, Orkney & Shetland", "http://feeds.bbci.co.uk/news/scotland/nort
#  ("South Scotland", "http://feeds.bbci.co.uk/news/scotland/south_scotland/rss.xr
#  ("Central Scotland & Tayside", "http://feeds.bbci.co.uk/news/scotland/tayside_c
#  ("Wales Politics", "http://feeds.bbci.co.uk/news/wales/wales_politics/rss.xml",
#  ("NW. Wales", "http://feeds.bbci.co.uk/news/wales/north_west_wales/rss.xml"),
#  ("NE. Wales", "http://feeds.bbci.co.uk/news/wales/north_east_wales/rss.xml"),
#  ("Mid. Wales", "http://feeds.bbci.co.uk/news/wales/mid_wales/rss.xml"),
#  ("SW. Wales", "http://feeds.bbci.co.uk/news/wales/south_west_wales/rss.xml"),
#  ("SE. Wales", "http://feeds.bbci.co.uk/news/wales/south_east_wales/rss.xml"),
#  ("Newyddion - News in Welsh", "http://feeds.bbci.co.uk/newyddion/rss.xml"),
#  ("Gwleidyddiaeth", "http://feeds.bbci.co.uk/newyddion/gwleidyddiaeth/rss.xml"),
#  ("Gogledd-Ddwyrain", "http://feeds.bbci.co.uk/newyddion/gogledd-ddwyrain/rss.xr
#  ("Gogledd-Orllewin", "http://feeds.bbci.co.uk/newyddion/gogledd-orllewin/rss.xr
#  ("Canolbarth", "http://feeds.bbci.co.uk/newyddion/canolbarth/rss.xml"),
#  ("De-Ddwyrain", "http://feeds.bbci.co.uk/newyddion/de-ddwyrain/rss.xml"),
#  ("De-Orllewin", "http://feeds.bbci.co.uk/newyddion/de-orllewin/rss.xml"),
   ]
```

```
#     **** SELECT YOUR USER PREFERENCES ****

# Title to use for the ebook.
#
title = 'BBC News'

# A brief description for the ebook.
#
description = u'BBC web site ebook created using rss feeds.'

# The max number of articles which may be downloaded from each feed.
# I've never seen more than about 70 articles in a single feed in the
# BBC feeds.
#
max_articles_per_feed = 100

# The max age of articles which may be downloaded from each feed. This is
# specified in days - note fractions of days are allowed, Eg. 2.5 (2 and a
# half days). My default of 1.5 days is the last 36 hours, the point at
# which I've decided 'news' becomes 'old news', but be warned this is not
# so good for the blogs, technology, magazine, etc., and sports feeds.
# You may wish to extend this to 2-5 but watch out ebook creation time will
# increase as well. Setting this to 30 will get everything (AFAICT) as long
# as max_articles_per_feed remains set high (except for 'Click' which is
# v. low volume and its currently oldest article is 4th Feb 2011).
#
oldest_article = 1.5

# Number of simultaneous downloads. 20 is consistantly working fine on the
# BBC News feeds with no problems. Speeds things up from the defualt of 5.
# If you have a lot of feeds and/or have increased oldest_article above 2
# then you may wish to try increasing simultaneous_downloads to 25-30,
# Or, of course, if you are in a hurry. [I've not tried beyond 20.]
#
simultaneous_downloads = 20

# Timeout for fetching files from the server in seconds. The default of
# 120 seconds, seems somewhat excessive.
#
timeout = 30

# The format string for the date shown on the ebook's first page.
# List of all values: http://docs.python.org/library/time.html
# Default in news.py has a leading space so that's mirrored here.
# As with 'feeds' select/de-select by adding/removing the initial '#',
# only one timefmt should be selected, here's a few to choose from.
#
timefmt = ' [%a, %d %b %Y]'                # [Fri, 14 Nov 2011] (Calibre default)
#timefmt = ' [%a, %d %b %Y %H:%M]'         # [Fri, 14 Nov 2011 18:30]
#timefmt = ' [%a, %d %b %Y %I:%M %p]'      # [Fri, 14 Nov 2011 06:30 PM]
#timefmt = ' [%d %b %Y]'                   # [14 Nov 2011]
#timefmt = ' [%d %b %Y %H:%M]'             # [14 Nov 2011 18.30]
#timefmt = ' [%Y-%m-%d]'                   # [2011-11-14]
#timefmt = ' [%Y-%m-%d-%H-%M]'             # [2011-11-14-18-30]

#
```

```
#     **** IMPORTANT ****
#
#     DO NOT EDIT BELOW HERE UNLESS YOU KNOW WHAT YOU ARE DOING.
#
#     DO NOT EDIT BELOW HERE UNLESS YOU KNOW WHAT YOU ARE DOING.
#
#     I MEAN IT, YES I DO, ABSOLUTELY, AT YOU OWN RISK. :)
#
#     **** IMPORTANT ****
#


# Author of this recipe.
__author__ = 'mattst'

# Specify English as the language of the RSS feeds (ISO-639 code).
language = 'en_GB'

# Set tags.
tags = 'news, sport, blog'

# Set publisher and publication type.
publisher = 'BBC'
publication_type = 'newspaper'

# Disable stylesheets from site.
no_stylesheets = True

# Specifies an override encoding for sites that have an incorrect charset
# specified. Default of 'None' says to auto-detect. Some other BBC recipes
# use 'utf8', which works fine (so use that if necessary) but auto-detecting
# with None is working fine, so stick with that for robustness.
encoding = None

# Sets whether a feed has full articles embedded in it. The BBC feeds do not.
use_embedded_content = False

# Removes empty feeds - why keep them!?
remove_empty_feeds = True

# Create a custom title which fits nicely in the Kindle title list.
# Requires "import time" above class declaration, and replacing
# title with custom_title in conversion_options (right column only).
# Example of string below: "BBC News - 14 Nov 2011"
#
# custom_title = "BBC News - " + time.strftime('%d %b %Y')

'''
# Conversion options for advanced users, but don't forget to comment out the
# current conversion_options below. Avoid setting 'linearize_tables' as that
# plays havoc with the 'old style' table based pages.
#
conversion_options = { 'title'        : title,
                       'comments'     : description,
                       'tags'         : tags,
                       'language'     : language,
                       'publisher'    : publisher,
```

```
                              'authors'     : publisher,
                              'smarten_punctuation' : True
                          }
    '''

    conversion_options = { 'smarten_punctuation' : True }

    # Specify extra CSS - overrides ALL other CSS (IE. Added last).
    extra_css = 'body { font-family: verdana, helvetica, sans-serif; } \
                .introduction, .first { font-weight: bold; } \
                .cross-head { font-weight: bold; font-size: 125%; } \
                .cap, .caption { display: block; font-size: 80%; font-style: italic; } \
                .cap, .caption, .caption img, .caption span { display: block; text-align: cer
                .byl, .byd, .byline img, .byline-name, .byline-title, .author-name, .author-r
                    .correspondent-portrait img, .byline-lead-in, .name, .bbc-role { display:
                    text-align: center; font-size: 80%; font-style: italic; margin: 1px auto;
                .story-date, .published { font-size: 80%; } \
                table { width: 100%; } \
                td img { display: block; margin: 5px auto; } \
                ul { padding-top: 10px; } \
                ol { padding-top: 10px; } \
                li { padding-top: 5px; padding-bottom: 5px; } \
                h1 { text-align: center; font-size: 175%; font-weight: bold; } \
                h2 { text-align: center; font-size: 150%; font-weight: bold; } \
                h3 { text-align: center; font-size: 125%; font-weight: bold; } \
                h4, h5, h6 { text-align: center; font-size: 100%; font-weight: bold; }'

    # Remove various tag attributes to improve the look of the ebook pages.
    remove_attributes = [ 'border', 'cellspacing', 'align', 'cellpadding', 'colspan',
                          'valign', 'vspace', 'hspace', 'alt', 'width', 'height' ]

    # Remove the (admittedly rarely used) line breaks, "<br />", which sometimes
    # cause a section of the ebook to start in an unsightly fashion or, more
    # frequently, a "<br />" will muck up the formatting of a correspondant's byline.
    # "<br />" and "<br clear/>" are far more frequently used on the table formatted
    # style of pages, and really spoil the look of the ebook pages.
    preprocess_regexps   = [(re.compile(r'<br[ ]*/>', re.IGNORECASE), lambda m: ''),
                            (re.compile(r'<br[ ]*clear.*/>', re.IGNORECASE), lambda m: '')]


    # Create regular expressions for tag keeping and removal to make the matches more
    # robust against minor changes and errors in the HTML, Eg. double spaces, leading
    # and trailing spaces, missing hyphens, and such like.
    # Python regular expression ('re' class) page: http://docs.python.org/library/re.html

    # ******************************************
    # Regular expressions for keep_only_tags:
    # ******************************************

    # The BBC News HTML pages use variants of 'storybody' to denote the section of a HTML
    # page which contains the main text of the article. Match storybody variants: 'storybody',
    # 'story-body', 'story body','storybody ', etc.
    storybody_reg_exp = '^.*story[_ -]*body.*$'

    # The BBC sport and 'newsbeat' (features) HTML pages use 'blq_content' to hold the title
    # and published date. This is one level above the usual news pages which have the title
    # and date within 'story-body'. This is annoying since 'blq_content' must also be kept,
    # resulting in a lot of extra things to be removed by remove_tags.
```

```
blq_content_reg_exp = '^.*blq[_ -]*content.*$'

# The BBC has an alternative page design structure, which I suspect is an out-of-date
# design but which is still used in some articles, Eg. 'Click' (technology), 'FastTrack'
# (travel), and in some sport pages. These alternative pages are table based (which is
# why I think they are an out-of-date design) and account for -I'm guesstimaking- less
# than 1% of all articles. They use a table class 'storycontent' to hold the article
# and like blq_content (above) have required lots of extra removal by remove_tags.
story_content_reg_exp = '^.*story[_ -]*content.*$'

# Keep the sections of the HTML which match the list below. The HTML page created by
# Calibre will fill <body> with those sections which are matched. Note that the
# blq_content_reg_exp must be listed before storybody_reg_exp in keep_only_tags due to
# it being the parent of storybody_reg_exp, that is to say the div class/id 'story-body'
# will be inside div class/id 'blq_content' in the HTML (if 'blq_content' is there at
# all). If they are the other way around in keep_only_tags then blq_content_reg_exp
# will end up being discarded.
keep_only_tags = [ dict(name='table', attrs={'class':re.compile(story_content_reg_exp, re.
                   dict(name='div',   attrs={'class':re.compile(blq_content_reg_exp, re.I(
                   dict(name='div',   attrs={'id':re.compile(blq_content_reg_exp, re.IGNO
                   dict(name='div',   attrs={'class':re.compile(storybody_reg_exp, re.IGN(
                   dict(name='div',   attrs={'id':re.compile(storybody_reg_exp, re.IGNORE(

# *************************************
# Regular expressions for remove_tags:
# *************************************

# Regular expression to remove share-help and variant tags. The share-help class
# is used by the site for a variety of 'sharing' type links, Eg. Facebook, delicious,
# twitter, email. Removed to avoid page clutter.
share_help_reg_exp = '^.*share[_ -]*help.*$'

# Regular expression to remove embedded-hyper and variant tags. This class is used to
# display links to other BBC News articles on the same/similar subject.
embedded_hyper_reg_exp = '^.*embed*ed[_ -]*hyper.*$'

# Regular expression to remove hypertabs and variant tags. This class is used to
# display a tab bar at the top of an article which allows the user to switch to
# an article (viewed on the same page) providing further info., 'in depth' analysis,
# an editorial, a correspondant's blog entry, and such like. The ability to handle
# a tab bar of this nature is currently beyond the scope of this recipe and
# possibly of Calibre itself (not sure about that - TO DO - check!).
hypertabs_reg_exp = '^.*hyper[_ -]*tabs.*$'

# Regular expression to remove story-feature and variant tags. Eg. 'story-feature',
# 'story-feature related narrow', 'story-feature wide', 'story-feature narrow'.
# This class is used to add additional info. boxes, or small lists, outside of
# the main story. TO DO: Work out a way to incorporate these neatly.
story_feature_reg_exp = '^.*story[_ -]*feature.*$'

# Regular expression to remove video and variant tags, Eg. 'videoInStoryB',
# 'videoInStoryC'. This class is used to embed video.
video_reg_exp = '^.*video.*$'

# Regular expression to remove audio and variant tags, Eg. 'audioInStoryD'.
# This class is used to embed audio.
audio_reg_exp = '^.*audio.*$'
```

```
# Regular expression to remove pictureGallery and variant tags, Eg. 'pictureGallery'.
# This class is used to embed a photo slideshow. See also 'slideshow' below.
picture_gallery_reg_exp = '^.*picture.*$'

# Regular expression to remove slideshow and variant tags, Eg. 'dslideshow-enclosure'.
# This class is used to embed a slideshow (not necessarily photo) but both
# 'slideshow' and 'pictureGallery' are used for slideshows.
slideshow_reg_exp = '^.*slide[_ -]*show.*$'

# Regular expression to remove social-links and variant tags. This class is used to
# display links to a BBC bloggers main page, used in various columnist's blogs
# (Eg. Nick Robinson, Robert Preston).
social_links_reg_exp = '^.*social[_ -]*links.*$'

# Regular expression to remove quote and (multi) variant tags, Eg. 'quote',
# 'endquote', 'quote-credit', 'quote-credit-title', etc. These are usually
# removed by 'story-feature' removal (as they are usually within them), but
# not always. The quotation removed is always (AFAICT) in the article text
# as well but a 2nd copy is placed in a quote tag to draw attention to it.
# The quote class tags may or may not appear in div's.
quote_reg_exp = '^.*quote.*$'

# Regular expression to remove hidden and variant tags, Eg. 'hidden'.
# The purpose of these is unclear, they seem to be an internal link to a
# section within the article, but the text of the link (Eg. 'Continue reading
# the main story') never seems to be displayed anyway. Removed to avoid clutter.
# The hidden class tags may or may not appear in div's.
hidden_reg_exp = '^.*hidden.*$'

# Regular expression to remove comment and variant tags, Eg. 'comment-introduction'.
# Used on the site to display text about registered users entering comments.
comment_reg_exp = '^.*comment.*$'

# Regular expression to remove form and variant tags, Eg. 'comment-form'.
# Used on the site to allow registered BBC users to fill in forms, typically
# for entering comments about an article.
form_reg_exp = '^.*form.*$'

# Extra things to remove due to the addition of 'blq_content' in keep_only_tags.

#<div class="story-actions"> Used on sports pages for 'email' and 'print'.
story_actions_reg_exp = '^.*story[_ -]*actions.*$'

#<div class="bookmark-list"> Used on sports pages instead of 'share-help' (for
# social networking links).
bookmark_list_reg_exp = '^.*bookmark[_ -]*list.*$'

#<div id="secondary-content" class="content-group">
# NOTE: Don't remove class="content-group" that is needed.
# Used on sports pages to link to 'similar stories'.
secondary_content_reg_exp = '^.*secondary[_ -]*content.*$'

#<div id="featured-content" class="content-group">
# NOTE: Don't remove class="content-group" that is needed.
# Used on sports pages to link to pages like 'tables', 'fixtures', etc.
featured_content_reg_exp = '^.*featured[_ -]*content.*$'

#<div id="navigation">
```

```
# Used on sports pages to link to pages like 'tables', 'fixtures', etc.
# Used sometimes instead of "featured-content" above.
navigation_reg_exp = '^.*navigation.*$'

#<a class="skip" href="#blq-container-inner">Skip to top</a>
# Used on sports pages to link to the top of the page.
skip_reg_exp = '^.*skip.*$'

# Extra things to remove due to the addition of 'storycontent' in keep_only_tags,
# which are the alterative table design based pages. The purpose of some of these
# is not entirely clear from the pages (which are a total mess!).

# Remove mapping based tags, Eg. <map id="world_map">
# The dynamic maps don't seem to work during ebook creation. TO DO: Investigate.
map_reg_exp = '^.*map.*$'

# Remove social bookmarking variation, called 'socialBookMarks'.
social_bookmarks_reg_exp = '^.*social[_ -]*bookmarks.*$'

# Remove page navigation tools, like 'search', 'email', 'print', called 'blq-mast'.
blq_mast_reg_exp = '^.*blq[_ -]*mast.*$'

# Remove 'sharesb', I think this is a generic 'sharing' class. It seems to appear
# alongside 'socialBookMarks' whenever that appears. I am removing it as well
# under the assumption that it can appear alone as well.
sharesb_reg_exp = '^.*sharesb.*$'

# Remove class 'o'. The worst named user created css class of all time. The creator
# should immediately be fired. I've seen it used to hold nothing at all but with
# 20 or so empty lines in it. Also to hold a single link to another article.
# Whatever it was designed to do it is not wanted by this recipe. Exact match only.
o_reg_exp = '^o$'

# Remove 'promotopbg' and 'promobottombg', link lists. Have decided to
# use two reg expressions to make removing this (and variants) robust.
promo_top_reg_exp = '^.*promotopbg.*$'
promo_bottom_reg_exp = '^.*promobottombg.*$'

# Remove 'nlp', provides heading for link lists. Requires an exact match due to
# risk of matching those letters in something needed, unless I see a variation
# of 'nlp' used at a later date.
nlp_reg_exp = '^nlp$'

# Remove 'mva', provides embedded floating content of various types. Variant 'mvb'
# has also now been seen. Requires an exact match of 'mva' or 'mvb' due to risk of
# matching those letters in something needed.
mva_or_mvb_reg_exp = '^mv[ab]$'

# Remove 'mvtb', seems to be page navigation tools, like 'blq-mast'.
mvtb_reg_exp = '^mvtb$'

# Remove 'blq-toplink', class to provide a link to the top of the page.
blq_toplink_reg_exp = '^.*blq[_ -]*top[_ -]*link.*$'

# Remove 'products and services' links, Eg. desktop tools, alerts, and so on.
# Eg. Class="servicev4 ukfs_services" - what a mess of a name. Have decided to
# use two reg expressions to make removing this (and variants) robust.
prods_services_01_reg_exp = '^.*servicev4.*$'
```

```
    prods_services_02_reg_exp = '^.*ukfs[_ -]*services.*$'

    # Remove -what I think is- some kind of navigation tools helper class, though I am
    # not sure, it's called: 'blq-rst blq-new-nav'. What I do know is it pops up
    # frequently and it is not wanted. Have decided to use two reg expressions to make
    # removing this (and variants) robust.
    blq_misc_01_reg_exp = '^.*blq[_ -]*rst.*$'
    blq_misc_02_reg_exp = '^.*blq[_ -]*new[_ -]*nav.*$'

    # Remove 'puffbox' - this may only appear inside 'storyextra', so it may not
    # need removing - I have no clue what it does other than it contains links.
    # Whatever it is - it is not part of the article and is not wanted.
    puffbox_reg_exp = '^.*puffbox.*$'

    # Remove 'sibtbg' and 'sibtbgf' - some kind of table formatting classes.
    sibtbg_reg_exp = '^.*sibtbg.*$'

    # Remove 'storyextra' - links to relevant articles and external sites.
    storyextra_reg_exp = '^.*story[_ -]*extra.*$'


    remove_tags = [ dict(name='div',  attrs={'class':re.compile(story_feature_reg_exp, re.IGN(
                    dict(name='div',  attrs={'class':re.compile(share_help_reg_exp, re.IGNORE(
                    dict(name='div',  attrs={'class':re.compile(embedded_hyper_reg_exp, re.IGI
                    dict(name='div',  attrs={'class':re.compile(hypertabs_reg_exp, re.IGNORECA
                    dict(name='div',  attrs={'class':re.compile(video_reg_exp, re.IGNORECASE)
                    dict(name='div',  attrs={'class':re.compile(audio_reg_exp, re.IGNORECASE)
                    dict(name='div',  attrs={'class':re.compile(picture_gallery_reg_exp, re.I(
                    dict(name='div',  attrs={'class':re.compile(slideshow_reg_exp, re.IGNORECA
                    dict(name='div',  attrs={'class':re.compile(quote_reg_exp, re.IGNORECASE)
                    dict(name='div',  attrs={'class':re.compile(hidden_reg_exp, re.IGNORECASE)
                    dict(name='div',  attrs={'class':re.compile(comment_reg_exp, re.IGNORECASI
                    dict(name='div',  attrs={'class':re.compile(story_actions_reg_exp, re.IGN(
                    dict(name='div',  attrs={'class':re.compile(bookmark_list_reg_exp, re.IGN(
                    dict(name='div',  attrs={'id':re.compile(secondary_content_reg_exp, re.IGI
                    dict(name='div',  attrs={'id':re.compile(featured_content_reg_exp, re.IGN(
                    dict(name='div',  attrs={'id':re.compile(navigation_reg_exp, re.IGNORECASI
                    dict(name='form', attrs={'id':re.compile(form_reg_exp, re.IGNORECASE)}),
                    dict(attrs={'class':re.compile(quote_reg_exp, re.IGNORECASE)}),
                    dict(attrs={'class':re.compile(hidden_reg_exp, re.IGNORECASE)}),
                    dict(attrs={'class':re.compile(social_links_reg_exp, re.IGNORECASE)}),
                    dict(attrs={'class':re.compile(comment_reg_exp, re.IGNORECASE)}),
                    dict(attrs={'class':re.compile(skip_reg_exp, re.IGNORECASE)}),
                    dict(name='map', attrs={'id':re.compile(map_reg_exp, re.IGNORECASE)}),
                    dict(name='map', attrs={'name':re.compile(map_reg_exp, re.IGNORECASE)}),
                    dict(name='div',  attrs={'id':re.compile(social_bookmarks_reg_exp, re.IGNO
                    dict(name='div',  attrs={'id':re.compile(blq_mast_reg_exp, re.IGNORECASE)})
                    dict(name='div',  attrs={'class':re.compile(sharesb_reg_exp, re.IGNORECASE)
                    dict(name='div',  attrs={'class':re.compile(o_reg_exp, re.IGNORECASE)}),
                    dict(name='div',  attrs={'class':re.compile(promo_top_reg_exp, re.IGNORECA
                    dict(name='div',  attrs={'class':re.compile(promo_bottom_reg_exp, re.IGNOI
                    dict(name='div',  attrs={'class':re.compile(nlp_reg_exp, re.IGNORECASE)}),
                    dict(name='div',  attrs={'class':re.compile(mva_or_mvb_reg_exp, re.IGNORE(
                    dict(name='div',  attrs={'class':re.compile(mvtb_reg_exp, re.IGNORECASE)})
                    dict(name='div',  attrs={'class':re.compile(blq_toplink_reg_exp, re.IGNORI
                    dict(name='div',  attrs={'class':re.compile(prods_services_01_reg_exp, re.
                    dict(name='div',  attrs={'class':re.compile(prods_services_02_reg_exp, re.
                    dict(name='div',  attrs={'class':re.compile(blq_misc_01_reg_exp, re.IGNORI
```

```
                            dict(name='div',   attrs={'class':re.compile(blq_misc_02_reg_exp, re.IGNORE
                            dict(name='div',   attrs={'class':re.compile(puffbox_reg_exp, re.IGNORECASE
                            dict(attrs={'class':re.compile(sibtbg_reg_exp, re.IGNORECASE)}),
                            dict(attrs={'class':re.compile(storyextra_reg_exp, re.IGNORECASE)})
                     ]

    # Uses url to create and return the 'printer friendly' version of the url.
    # In other words the 'print this page' address of the page.
    #
    # There are 3 types of urls used in the BBC site's rss feeds. There is just
    # 1 type for the standard news while there are 2 used for sports feed urls.
    # Note: Sports urls are linked from regular news feeds (Eg. 'News Home') when
    # there is a major story of interest to 'everyone'. So even if no BBC sports
    # feeds are added to 'feeds' the logic of this method is still needed to avoid
    # blank / missing / empty articles which have an index title and then no body.
    def print_version(self, url):

        # Handle sports page urls type 01:
        if (url.find("go/rss/-/sport1/") != -1):
            temp_url = url.replace("go/rss/-/", "")

        # Handle sports page urls type 02:
        elif (url.find("go/rss/int/news/-/sport1/") != -1):
            temp_url = url.replace("go/rss/int/news/-/", "")

        # Handle regular news page urls:
        else:
            temp_url = url.replace("go/rss/int/news/-/", "")

        # Always add "?print=true" to the end of the url.
        print_url = temp_url + "?print=true"

        return print_url


    # Remove articles in feeds based on a string in the article title or url.
    #
    # Code logic written by: Starson17 - posted in: "Recipes - Re-usable code"
    # thread, in post with title: "Remove articles from feed", see url:
    # http://www.mobileread.com/forums/showpost.php?p=1165462&postcount=6
    # Many thanks and all credit to Starson17.
    #
    # Starson17's code has obviously been altered to suite my requirements.
    def parse_feeds(self):

        # Call parent's method.
        feeds = BasicNewsRecipe.parse_feeds(self)

        # Loop through all feeds.
        for feed in feeds:

            # Loop through all articles in feed.
            for article in feed.articles[:]:

                # Match key words and remove article if there's a match.

                # Most BBC rss feed video only 'articles' use upper case 'VIDEO'
                # as a title prefix. Just match upper case 'VIDEO', so that
```

```
                    # articles like 'Video game banned' won't be matched and removed.
                    if 'VIDEO' in article.title:
                        feed.articles.remove(article)

                    # Most BBC rss feed audio only 'articles' use upper case 'AUDIO'
                    # as a title prefix. Just match upper case 'AUDIO', so that
                    # articles like 'Hi-Def audio...' won't be matched and removed.
                    elif 'AUDIO' in article.title:
                        feed.articles.remove(article)

                    # Most BBC rss feed photo slideshow 'articles' use 'In Pictures',
                    # 'In pictures', and 'in pictures', somewhere in their title.
                    # Match any case of that phrase.
                    elif 'IN PICTURES' in article.title.upper():
                        feed.articles.remove(article)

                    # As above, but user contributed pictures. Match any case.
                    elif 'YOUR PICTURES' in article.title.upper():
                        feed.articles.remove(article)

                    # 'Sportsday Live' are articles which contain a constantly and
                    # dynamically updated 'running commentary' during a live sporting
                    # event. Match any case.
                    elif 'SPORTSDAY LIVE' in article.title.upper():
                        feed.articles.remove(article)

                    # Sometimes 'Sportsday Live' (above) becomes 'Live - Sport Name'.
                    # These are being matched below using 'Live - ' because removing all
                    # articles with 'live' in their titles would remove some articles
                    # that are in fact not live sports pages. Match any case.
                    elif 'LIVE - ' in article.title.upper():
                        feed.articles.remove(article)

                    # 'Quiz of the week' is a Flash player weekly news quiz. Match only
                    # the 'Quiz of the' part in anticipation of monthly and yearly
                    # variants. Match any case.
                    elif 'QUIZ OF THE' in article.title.upper():
                        feed.articles.remove(article)

                    # Remove articles with 'scorecards' in the url. These are BBC sports
                    # pages which just display a cricket scorecard. The pages have a mass
                    # of table and css entries to display the scorecards nicely. Probably
                    # could make them work with this recipe, but might take a whole day
                    # of work to sort out all the css - basically a formatting nightmare.
                    elif 'scorecards' in article.url:
                        feed.articles.remove(article)

        return feeds

# End of class and file.
```

This *recipe* explores only the tip of the iceberg when it comes to the power of calibre. To explore more of the abilities of calibre we'll examine a more complex real life example in the next section.

Real life example

A reasonably complex real life example that exposes more of the *API* of `BasicNewsRecipe` is the *recipe* for *The New York Times*

```python
import string, re
from calibre import strftime
from calibre.web.feeds.recipes import BasicNewsRecipe
from calibre.ebooks.BeautifulSoup import BeautifulSoup

class NYTimes(BasicNewsRecipe):

    title       = 'The New York Times'
    __author__  = 'Kovid Goyal'
    description = 'Daily news from the New York Times'
    timefmt = ' [%a, %d %b, %Y]'
    needs_subscription = True
    remove_tags_before = dict(id='article')
    remove_tags_after  = dict(id='article')
    remove_tags = [dict(attrs={'class':['articleTools', 'post-tools', 'side_tool', 'nextArtic
                   dict(id=['footer', 'toolsRight', 'articleInline', 'navigation', 'archive', 's:
                   dict(name=['script', 'noscript', 'style'])]
    encoding = 'cp1252'
    no_stylesheets = True
    extra_css = 'h1 {font: sans-serif large;}\n.byline {font:monospace;}'

    def get_browser(self):
        br = BasicNewsRecipe.get_browser()
        if self.username is not None and self.password is not None:
            br.open('http://www.nytimes.com/auth/login')
            br.select_form(name='login')
            br['USERID']   = self.username
            br['PASSWORD'] = self.password
            br.submit()
        return br

    def parse_index(self):
        soup = self.index_to_soup('http://www.nytimes.com/pages/todayspaper/index.html')

        def feed_title(div):
            return ''.join(div.findAll(text=True, recursive=False)).strip()

        articles = {}
        key = None
        ans = []
        for div in soup.findAll(True,
            attrs={'class':['section-headline', 'story', 'story headline']}):

            if div['class'] == 'section-headline':
                key = string.capwords(feed_title(div))
                articles[key] = []
                ans.append(key)

            elif div['class'] in ['story', 'story headline']:
                a = div.find('a', href=True)
                if not a:
                    continue
                url = re.sub(r'\?.*', '', a['href'])
```

```
                url += '?pagewanted=all'
                title = self.tag_to_string(a, use_alt=True).strip()
                description = ''
                pubdate = strftime('%a, %d %b')
                summary = div.find(True, attrs={'class':'summary'})
                if summary:
                    description = self.tag_to_string(summary, use_alt=False)

                feed = key if key is not None else 'Uncategorized'
                if not articles.has_key(feed):
                    articles[feed] = []
                if not 'podcasts' in url:
                    articles[feed].append(
                              dict(title=title, url=url, date=pubdate,
                                   description=description,
                                   content=''))
        ans = self.sort_index_by(ans, {'The Front Page':-1, 'Dining In, Dining Out':1, 'Obitua
        ans = [(key, articles[key]) for key in ans if articles.has_key(key)]
        return ans

    def preprocess_html(self, soup):
        refresh = soup.find('meta', {'http-equiv':'refresh'})
        if refresh is None:
            return soup
        content = refresh.get('content').partition('=')[2]
        raw = self.browser.open('http://www.nytimes.com'+content).read()
        return BeautifulSoup(raw.decode('cp1252', 'replace'))
```

We see several new features in this *recipe*. First, we have:

```
timefmt = ' [%a, %d %b, %Y]'
```

This sets the displayed time on the front page of the created ebook to be in the format, Day, Day_Number Month, Year. See *timefmt* (page 333).

Then we see a group of directives to cleanup the downloaded *HTML*:

```
remove_tags_before = dict(name='h1')
remove_tags_after  = dict(id='footer')
remove_tags = ...
```

These remove everything before the first <h1> tag and everything after the first tag whose id is footer. See *remove_tags* (page 332), *remove_tags_before* (page 332), *remove_tags_after* (page 332).

The next interesting feature is:

```
needs_subscription = True
...
def get_browser(self):
    ...
```

needs_subscription = True tells calibre that this recipe needs a username and password in order to access the content. This causes, calibre to ask for a username and password whenever you try to use this recipe. The code in *calibre.web.feeds.news.BasicNewsRecipe.get_browser()* (page 325) actually does the login into the NYT website. Once logged in, calibre will use the same, logged in, browser instance to fetch all content. See mechanize[75] to understand the code in get_browser.

The next new feature is the *calibre.web.feeds.news.BasicNewsRecipe.parse_index()* (page 327) method. Its job is to go to http://www.nytimes.com/pages/todayspaper/index.html and fetch the list of articles that

---

[75] http://wwwsearch.sourceforge.net/mechanize/

appear in *todays* paper. While more complex than simply using *RSS*, the recipe creates an ebook that corresponds very closely to the days paper. `parse_index` makes heavy use of BeautifulSoup[76] to parse the daily paper webpage. You can also use other, more modern parsers if you dislike BeatifulSoup. calibre comes with lxml[77] and html5lib[78], which are the recommended parsers. To use them, replace the call to `index_to_soup()` with the following:

```
raw = self.index_to_soup(url, raw=True)
# For html5lib
import html5lib
root = html5lib.parse(raw, namespaceHTMLElements=False, treebuilder='lxml')
# For the lxml html 4 parser
from lxml import html
root = html.fromstring(raw)
```

The final new feature is the `calibre.web.feeds.news.BasicNewsRecipe.preprocess_html()` (page 328) method. It can be used to perform arbitrary transformations on every downloaded HTML page. Here it is used to bypass the ads that the nytimes shows you before each article.

Tips for developing new recipes

The best way to develop new recipes is to use the command line interface. Create the recipe using your favorite python editor and save it to a file say `myrecipe.recipe`. The *.recipe* extension is required. You can download content using this recipe with the command:

```
ebook-convert myrecipe.recipe .epub --test -vv --debug-pipeline debug
```

The command **ebook-convert** will download all the webpages and save them to the EPUB file `myrecipe.epub`. The `-vv` makes ebook-convert spit out a lot of information about what it is doing. The `--test` makes it download only a couple of articles from at most two feeds. In addition, ebook-convert will put the downloaded HTML into the `debug/input` directory, where `debug` is the directory you specified in the `--debug-pipeline` option.

Once the download is complete, you can look at the downloaded *HTML* by opening the file `debug/input/index.html` in a browser. Once you're satisfied that the download and preprocessing is happening correctly, you can generate ebooks in different formats as shown below:

```
ebook-convert myrecipe.recipe myrecipe.epub
ebook-convert myrecipe.recipe myrecipe.mobi
...
```

If you're satisfied with your recipe, and you feel there is enough demand to justify its inclusion into the set of built-in recipes, post your recipe in the calibre recipes forum[79] to share it with other calibre users.

Note: On OS X, the command line tools are inside the calibre bundle, for example, if you installed calibre in `/Applications` the command line tools are in `/Applications/calibre.app/Contents/console.app/Contents/MacOS/`.

See also:

ebook-convert (page 288) The command line interface for all ebook conversion.

---

[76]http://www.crummy.com/software/BeautifulSoup/documentation.html
[77]http://lxml.de/
[78]https://github.com/html5lib/html5lib-python
[79]http://www.mobileread.com/forums/forumdisplay.php?f=228

Further reading

To learn more about writing advanced recipes using some of the facilities, available in `BasicNewsRecipe` you should consult the following sources:

API Documentation **(page 324)** Documentation of the `BasicNewsRecipe` class and all its important methods and fields.

BasicNewsRecipe[80] The source code of `BasicNewsRecipe`

Built-in recipes[81] The source code for the built-in recipes that come with calibre

The calibre recipes forum[82] Lots of knowledgeable calibre recipe writers hang out here.

API documentation

API Documentation for recipes

The API for writing recipes is defined by the *BasicNewsRecipe* (page 324)

class `calibre.web.feeds.news.`**BasicNewsRecipe**(*options, log, progress_reporter*)
 Base class that contains logic needed in all recipes. By overriding progressively more of the functionality in this class, you can make progressively more customized/powerful recipes. For a tutorial introduction to creating recipes, see Adding your favorite news website (page 125).

 abort_article(*msg=None*)
  Call this method inside any of the preprocess methods to abort the download for the current article. Useful to skip articles that contain inappropriate content, such as pure video articles.

 abort_recipe_processing(*msg*)
  Causes the recipe download system to abort the download of this recipe, displaying a simple feedback message to the user.

 add_toc_thumbnail(*article, src*)
  Call this from populate_article_metadata with the src attribute of an <img> tag from the article that is appropriate for use as the thumbnail representing the article in the Table of Contents. Whether the thumbnail is actually used is device dependent (currently only used by the Kindles). Note that the referenced image must be one that was successfully downloaded, otherwise it will be ignored.

 classmethod adeify_images(*soup*)
  If your recipe when converted to EPUB has problems with images when viewed in Adobe Digital Editions, call this method from within *postprocess_html ()* (page 327).

 canonicalize_internal_url(*url, is_link=True*)
  Return a set of canonical representations of `url`. The default implementation uses just the server hostname and path of the URL, ignoring any query parameters, fragments, etc. The canonical representations must be unique across all URLs for this news source. If they are not, then internal links may be resolved incorrectly.

   Parameters is_link – Is True if the URL is coming from an internal link in an HTML file. False if the URL is the URL used to download an article.

 cleanup()
  Called after all articles have been download. Use it to do any cleanup like logging out of subscription sites, etc.

 clone_browser(*br*)
  Clone the browser br. Cloned browsers are used for multi-threaded downloads, since mechanize is not

thread safe. The default cloning routines should capture most browser customization, but if you do something exotic in your recipe, you should override this method in your recipe and clone manually.

Cloned browser instances use the same, thread-safe CookieJar by default, unless you have customized cookie handling.

default_cover(*cover_file*)

Create a generic cover for recipes that don't have a cover

download()

Download and pre-process all articles from the feeds in this recipe. This method should be called only once on a particular Recipe instance. Calling it more than once will lead to undefined behavior. :return: Path to index.html

extract_readable_article(*html*, *url*)

Extracts main article content from 'html', cleans up and returns as a (article_html, extracted_title) tuple. Based on the original readability algorithm by Arc90.

get_article_url(*article*)

Override in a subclass to customize extraction of the *URL* that points to the content for each article. Return the article URL. It is called with *article*, an object representing a parsed article from a feed. See feedparser[83]. By default it looks for the original link (for feeds syndicated via a service like feedburner or pheedo) and if found, returns that or else returns article.link[84].

get_browser(**args*, ***kwargs*)

Return a browser instance used to fetch documents from the web. By default it returns a mechanize[85] browser instance that supports cookies, ignores robots.txt, handles refreshes and has a mozilla firefox user agent.

If your recipe requires that you login first, override this method in your subclass. For example, the following code is used in the New York Times recipe to login for full access:

```
def get_browser(self):
    br = BasicNewsRecipe.get_browser(self)
    if self.username is not None and self.password is not None:
        br.open('http://www.nytimes.com/auth/login')
        br.select_form(name='login')
        br['USERID']   = self.username
        br['PASSWORD'] = self.password
        br.submit()
    return br
```

get_cover_url()

Return a *URL* to the cover image for this issue or *None*. By default it returns the value of the member *self.cover_url* which is normally *None*. If you want your recipe to download a cover for the e-book override this method in your subclass, or set the member variable *self.cover_url* before this method is called.

get_feeds()

Return a list of *RSS* feeds to fetch for this profile. Each element of the list must be a 2-element tuple of the form (title, url). If title is None or an empty string, the title from the feed is used. This method is useful if your recipe needs to do some processing to figure out the list of feeds to download. If so, override in your subclass.

get_masthead_title()

Override in subclass to use something other than the recipe title

---

[83] https://pythonhosted.org/feedparser/
[84] https://pythonhosted.org/feedparser/reference-entry-link.html
[85] http://wwwsearch.sourceforge.net/mechanize/

get_masthead_url ()

Return a *URL* to the masthead image for this issue or *None*. By default it returns the value of the member *self.masthead_url* which is normally *None*. If you want your recipe to download a masthead for the e-book override this method in your subclass, or set the member variable *self.masthead_url* before this method is called. Masthead images are used in Kindle MOBI files.

get_obfuscated_article (*url*)

If you set *articles_are_obfuscated* this method is called with every article URL. It should return the path to a file on the filesystem that contains the article HTML. That file is processed by the recursive HTML fetching engine, so it can contain links to pages/images on the web.

This method is typically useful for sites that try to make it difficult to access article content automatically.

classmethod image_url_processor (*baseurl*, *url*)

Perform some processing on image urls (perhaps removing size restrictions for dynamically generated images, etc.) and return the precessed URL.

index_to_soup (*url_or_raw*, *raw=False*, *as_tree=False*)

Convenience method that takes an URL to the index page and returns a BeautifulSoup[86] of it.

url_or_raw: Either a URL or the downloaded index page as a string

is_link_wanted (*url*, *tag*)

Return True if the link should be followed or False otherwise. By default, raises NotImplementedError which causes the downloader to ignore it.

Parameters

- **url** – The URL to be followed

- **tag** – The Tag from which the URL was derived

javascript_login (*browser*, *username*, *password*)

This method is used to login to a website that uses javascript for its login form. After the login is complete, the cookies returned from the website are copied to a normal (non-javascript) browser and the download proceeds using those cookies.

An example implementation:

```
def javascript_login(self, browser, username, password):
    browser.visit('http://some-page-that-has-a-login')
    form = browser.select_form(nr=0) # Select the first form on the page
    form['username'] = username
    form['password'] = password
    browser.submit(timeout=120) # Submit the form and wait at most two minutes for lc
```

Note that you can also select forms with CSS2 selectors, like this:

```
browser.select_form('form#login_form')
browser.select_from('form[name="someform"]')
```

parse_feeds ()

Create a list of articles from the list of feeds returned by *BasicNewsRecipe.get_feeds()* (page 326). Return a list of Feed objects.

parse_index ()

This method should be implemented in recipes that parse a website instead of feeds to generate a list of articles. Typical uses are for news sources that have a "Print Edition" webpage that lists all the articles in the current print edition. If this function is implemented, it will be used in preference to *BasicNewsRecipe.parse_feeds()* (page 327).

---

[86]http://www.crummy.com/software/BeautifulSoup/bs3/documentation.html

It must return a list. Each element of the list must be a 2-element tuple of the form (`'feed title'`, `list of articles`).

Each list of articles must contain dictionaries of the form:

```
{
'title'       : article title,
'url'         : URL of print version,
'date'        : The publication date of the article as a string,
'description' : A summary of the article
'content'     : The full article (can be an empty string). Obsolete
                do not use, instead save the content to a temporary
                file and pass a file:///path/to/temp/file.html as
                the URL.
}
```

For an example, see the recipe for downloading *The Atlantic*. In addition, you can add 'author' for the author of the article.

If you want to abort processing for some reason and have calibre show the user a simple message instead of an error, call *abort_recipe_processing()* (page 324).

populate_article_metadata (*article*, *soup*, *first*)

Called when each HTML page belonging to article is downloaded. Intended to be used to get article metadata like author/summary/etc. from the parsed HTML (soup). :param article: A object of class `calibre.web.feeds.Article`. If you change the summary, remember to also change the text_summary :param soup: Parsed HTML belonging to this article :param first: True iff the parsed HTML is the first page of the article.

postprocess_book (*oeb*, *opts*, *log*)

Run any needed post processing on the parsed downloaded e-book.

Parameters

- **oeb** – An OEBBook object

- **opts** – Conversion options

postprocess_html (*soup*, *first_fetch*)

This method is called with the source of each downloaded *HTML* file, after it is parsed for links and images. It can be used to do arbitrarily powerful post-processing on the *HTML*. It should return *soup* after processing it.

Parameters

- **soup** – A BeautifulSoup[87] instance containing the downloaded *HTML*.

- **first_fetch** – True if this is the first page of an article.

preprocess_html (*soup*)

This method is called with the source of each downloaded *HTML* file, before it is parsed for links and images. It is called after the cleanup as specified by remove_tags etc. It can be used to do arbitrarily powerful pre-processing on the *HTML*. It should return *soup* after processing it.

soup: A BeautifulSoup[88] instance containing the downloaded *HTML*.

preprocess_raw_html (*raw_html*, *url*)

This method is called with the source of each downloaded *HTML* file, before it is parsed into an object tree. raw_html is a unicode string representing the raw HTML downloaded from the web. url is the URL from which the HTML was downloaded.

---

[87] http://www.crummy.com/software/BeautifulSoup/bs3/documentation.html
[88] http://www.crummy.com/software/BeautifulSoup/bs3/documentation.html

Note that this method acts *before* preprocess_regexps.

This method must return the processed raw_html as a unicode object.

classmethod `print_version` *(url)*

Take a *url* pointing to the webpage with article content and return the *URL* pointing to the print version of the article. By default does nothing. For example:

```
def print_version(self, url):
    return url + '?&pagewanted=print'
```

`skip_ad_pages` *(soup)*

This method is called with the source of each downloaded *HTML* file, before any of the cleanup attributes like remove_tags, keep_only_tags are applied. Note that preprocess_regexps will have already been applied. It is meant to allow the recipe to skip ad pages. If the soup represents an ad page, return the HTML of the real page. Otherwise return None.

soup: A BeautifulSoup[89] instance containing the downloaded *HTML*.

`sort_index_by` *(index, weights)*

Convenience method to sort the titles in *index* according to *weights*. *index* is sorted in place. Returns *index*.

index: A list of titles.

weights: A dictionary that maps weights to titles. If any titles in index are not in weights, they are assumed to have a weight of 0.

classmethod `tag_to_string` *(tag, use_alt=True, normalize_whitespace=True)*

Convenience method to take a BeautifulSoup[90] *Tag* and extract the text from it recursively, including any CDATA sections and alt tag attributes. Return a possibly empty unicode string.

use_alt: If *True* try to use the alt attribute for tags that don't have any textual content

tag: BeautifulSoup[91] *Tag*

`articles_are_obfuscated` = **False**

Set to True and implement `get_obfuscated_article()` (page 326) to handle websites that try to make it difficult to scrape content.

`auto_cleanup` = **False**

Automatically extract all the text from downloaded article pages. Uses the algorithms from the readability project. Setting this to True, means that you do not have to worry about cleaning up the downloaded HTML manually (though manual cleanup will always be superior).

`auto_cleanup_keep` = **None**

Specify elements that the auto cleanup algorithm should never remove. The syntax is a XPath expression. For example:

```
auto_cleanup_keep = '//div[@id="article-image"]' will keep all divs with
                                        id="article-image"
auto_cleanup_keep = '//*[@class="important"]' will keep all elements
                                        with class="important"
auto_cleanup_keep = '//div[@id="article-image"]|//span[@class="important"]'
                will keep all divs with id="article-image" and spans
                with class="important"
```

`center_navbar` = **True**

If True the navigation bar is center aligned, otherwise it is left aligned

---

[89] http://www.crummy.com/software/BeautifulSoup/bs3/documentation.html
[90] http://www.crummy.com/software/BeautifulSoup/bs3/documentation.html
[91] http://www.crummy.com/software/BeautifulSoup/bs3/documentation.html

compress_news_images = False

Set this to False to ignore all scaling and compression parameters and pass images through unmodified. If True and the other compression parameters are left at their default values, jpeg images will be scaled to fit in the screen dimensions set by the output profile and compressed to size at most (w * h)/16 where w x h are the scaled image dimensions.

compress_news_images_auto_size = 16

The factor used when auto compressing jpeg images. If set to None, auto compression is disabled. Otherwise, the images will be reduced in size to (w * h)/compress_news_images_auto_size bytes if possible by reducing the quality level, where w x h are the image dimensions in pixels. The minimum jpeg quality will be 5/100 so it is possible this constraint will not be met. This parameter can be overridden by the parameter compress_news_images_max_size which provides a fixed maximum size for images. Note that if you enable scale_news_images_to_device then the image will first be scaled and then its quality lowered until its size is less than (w * h)/factor where w and h are now the *scaled* image dimensions. In other words, this compression happens after scaling.

compress_news_images_max_size = None

Set jpeg quality so images do not exceed the size given (in KBytes). If set, this parameter overrides auto compression via compress_news_images_auto_size. The minimum jpeg quality will be 5/100 so it is possible this constraint will not be met.

conversion_options = {}

Recipe specific options to control the conversion of the downloaded content into an e-book. These will override any user or plugin specified values, so only use if absolutely necessary. For example:

```
conversion_options = {
  'base_font_size'   : 16,
  'tags'             : 'mytag1,mytag2',
  'title'            : 'My Title',
  'linearize_tables' : True,
}
```

cover_margins = (0, 0, '#ffffff')

By default, the cover image returned by get_cover_url() will be used as the cover for the periodical. Overriding this in your recipe instructs calibre to render the downloaded cover into a frame whose width and height are expressed as a percentage of the downloaded cover. cover_margins = (10, 15, '#ffffff') pads the cover with a white margin 10px on the left and right, 15px on the top and bottom. Color names defined at http://www.imagemagick.org/script/color.php Note that for some reason, white does not always work on windows. Use #ffffff instead

delay = 0

Delay between consecutive downloads in seconds. The argument may be a floating point number to indicate a more precise time.

description = u''

A couple of lines that describe the content this recipe downloads. This will be used primarily in a GUI that presents a list of recipes.

encoding = None

Specify an override encoding for sites that have an incorrect charset specification. The most common being specifying latin1 and using cp1252. If None, try to detect the encoding. If it is a callable, the callable is called with two arguments: The recipe object and the source to be decoded. It must return the decoded source.

extra_css = None

Specify any extra *CSS* that should be added to downloaded *HTML* files. It will be inserted into *<style>* tags, just before the closing *</head>* tag thereby overriding all *CSS* except that which is declared using the style attribute on individual *HTML* tags. For example:

```
extra_css = '.heading { font: serif x-large }'
```

feeds = None

List of feeds to download. Can be either [url1, url2, ...] or [('title1', url1), ('title2', url2),...]

filter_regexps = []

List of regular expressions that determines which links to ignore. If empty it is ignored. Used only if is_link_wanted is not implemented. For example:

```
filter_regexps = [r'ads\.doubleclick\.net']
```

will remove all URLs that have *ads.doubleclick.net* in them.

Only one of *BasicNewsRecipe.match_regexps* (page 331) or *BasicNewsRecipe.filter_regexps* (page 330) should be defined.

ignore_duplicate_articles = None

Ignore duplicates of articles that are present in more than one section. A duplicate article is an article that has the same title and/or URL. To ignore articles with the same title, set this to:

```
ignore_duplicate_articles = {'title'}
```

To use URLs instead, set it to:

```
ignore_duplicate_articles = {'url'}
```

To match on title or URL, set it to:

```
ignore_duplicate_articles = {'title', 'url'}
```

keep_only_tags = []

Keep only the specified tags and their children. For the format for specifying a tag see *BasicNewsRecipe.remove_tags* (page 332). If this list is not empty, then the *<body>* tag will be emptied and re-filled with the tags that match the entries in this list. For example:

```
keep_only_tags = [dict(id=['content', 'heading'])]
```

will keep only tags that have an *id* attribute of *"content"* or *"heading"*.

language = 'und'

The language that the news is in. Must be an ISO-639 code either two or three characters long

masthead_url = None

By default, calibre will use a default image for the masthead (Kindle only). Override this in your recipe to provide a url to use as a masthead.

match_regexps = []

List of regular expressions that determines which links to follow. If empty, it is ignored. Used only if is_link_wanted is not implemented. For example:

```
match_regexps = [r'page=[0-9]+']
```

will match all URLs that have *page=some number* in them.

Only one of *BasicNewsRecipe.match_regexps* (page 331) or *BasicNewsRecipe.filter_regexps* (page 330) should be defined.

max_articles_per_feed = 100

Maximum number of articles to download from each feed. This is primarily useful for feeds that don't have article dates. For most feeds, you should use *BasicNewsRecipe.oldest_article* (page 331)

needs_subscription = False

If True the GUI will ask the user for a username and password to use while downloading. If set to "optional" the use of a username and password becomes optional

no_stylesheets = False

Convenient flag to disable loading of stylesheets for websites that have overly complex stylesheets unsuitable for conversion to ebooks formats. If True stylesheets are not downloaded and processed

oldest_article = 7.0

Oldest article to download from this news source. In days.

preprocess_regexps = []

List of *regexp* substitution rules to run on the downloaded *HTML*. Each element of the list should be a two element tuple. The first element of the tuple should be a compiled regular expression and the second a callable that takes a single match object and returns a string to replace the match. For example:

```
preprocess_regexps = [
    (re.compile(r'<!--Article ends here-->.*</body>', re.DOTALL|re.IGNORECASE),
     lambda match: '</body>'),
]
```

will remove everything from *<!–Article ends here–>* to *</body>*.

publication_type = 'unknown'

Publication type Set to newspaper, magazine or blog. If set to None, no publication type metadata will be written to the opf file.

recipe_disabled = None

Set to a non empty string to disable this recipe. The string will be used as the disabled message

recursions = 0

Number of levels of links to follow on article webpages

remove_attributes = []

List of attributes to remove from all tags. For example:

```
remove_attributes = ['style', 'font']
```

remove_empty_feeds = False

If True empty feeds are removed from the output. This option has no effect if parse_index is overridden in the sub class. It is meant only for recipes that return a list of feeds using *feeds* or `get_feeds()` (page 326). It is also used if you use the ignore_duplicate_articles option.

remove_javascript = True

Convenient flag to strip all javascript tags from the downloaded HTML

remove_tags = []

List of tags to be removed. Specified tags are removed from downloaded HTML. A tag is specified as a dictionary of the form:

```
{
 name       : 'tag name',   #e.g. 'div'
 attrs      : a dictionary, #e.g. {class: 'advertisment'}
}
```

All keys are optional. For a full explanation of the search criteria, see Beautiful Soup[92] A common example:

---

[92]http://www.crummy.com/software/BeautifulSoup/bs3/documentation.html#Searching%20the%20Parse%20Tree

```
remove_tags = [dict(name='div', attrs={'class':'advert'})]
```

This will remove all *<div class="advert">* tags and all their children from the downloaded *HTML*.

remove_tags_after = None
> Remove all tags that occur after the specified tag. For the format for specifying a tag see *BasicNewsRecipe.remove_tags* (page 332). For example:

```
remove_tags_after = [dict(id='content')]
```

will remove all tags after the first element with *id="content"*.

remove_tags_before = None
> Remove all tags that occur before the specified tag. For the format for specifying a tag see *BasicNewsRecipe.remove_tags* (page 332). For example:

```
remove_tags_before = dict(id='content')
```

will remove all tags before the first element with *id="content"*.

requires_version = (0, 6, 0)
> Minimum calibre version needed to use this recipe

resolve_internal_links = False
> If set to True then links in downloaded articles that point to other downloaded articles are changed to point to the downloaded copy of the article rather than its original web URL. If you set this to True, you might also need to implement *canonicalize_internal_url ()* (page 325) to work with the URL scheme of your particular website.

reverse_article_order = False
> Reverse the order of articles in each feed

scale_news_images = None
> Maximum dimensions (w,h) to scale images to. If scale_news_images_to_device is True this is set to the device screen dimensions set by the output profile unless there is no profile set, in which case it is left at whatever value it has been assigned (default None).

scale_news_images_to_device = True
> Rescale images to fit in the device screen dimensions set by the output profile. Ignored if no output profile is set.

simultaneous_downloads = 5
> Number of simultaneous downloads. Set to 1 if the server is picky. Automatically reduced to 1 if *BasicNewsRecipe.delay* (page 329) > 0

summary_length = 500
> Max number of characters in the short description

template_css = u'\n .article_date {\n color: gray; font-family: monospace;\n }\n\n .article_description {\n text
> The CSS that is used to style the templates, i.e., the navigation bars and the Tables of Contents. Rather than overriding this variable, you should use *extra_css* in your recipe to customize look and feel.

timefmt = ' [%a, %d %b %Y]'
> The format string for the date shown on the first page. By default: Day_Name, Day_Number Month_Name Year

timeout = 120.0
> Timeout for fetching files from server in seconds

title = u'Unknown News Source'
> The title to use for the ebook

use_embedded_content = None

> Normally we try to guess if a feed has full articles embedded in it based on the length of the embedded content. If *None*, then the default guessing is used. If *True* then the we always assume the feeds has embedded content and if *False* we always assume the feed does not have embedded content.

use_javascript_to_login = False

> If you set this True, then calibre will use javascript to login to the website. This is needed for some websites that require the use of javascript to login. If you set this to True you must implement the *javascript_login()* (page 326) method, to do the actual logging in.

1.9.2 Managing subgroups of books, for example "genre"

Some people wish to organize the books in their library into subgroups, similar to subfolders. The most commonly provided reason is to create genre hierarchies, but there are many others. One user asked for a way to organize textbooks by subject and course number. Another wanted to keep track of gifts by subject and recipient. This tutorial will use the genre example for the rest of this post.

Before going on, please note that we are not talking about folders on the hard disk. Subgroups are not file folders. Books will not be copied anywhere. Calibre's library file structure is not affected. Instead, we are presenting a way to organize and display subgroups of books within a calibre library.

- *Setup* (page 156)
- *Searching* (page 158)
- *Restrictions* (page 158)
- *Useful Template Functions* (page 159)

The commonly-provided requirements for subgroups such as genres are:

- A subgroup (e.g., a genre) must contain (point to) books, not categories of books. This is what distinguishes subgroups from calibre user categories.

- A book can be in multiple subgroups (genres). This distinguishes subgroups from physical file folders.

- Subgroups (genres) must form a hierarchy; subgroups can contain subgroups.

Tags give you the first two. If you tag a book with the genre then you can use the tag browser (or search) for find the books with that genre, giving you the first. Many books can have the same tag(s), giving you the second. The problem is that tags don't satisfy the third requirement. They don't provide a hierarchy.

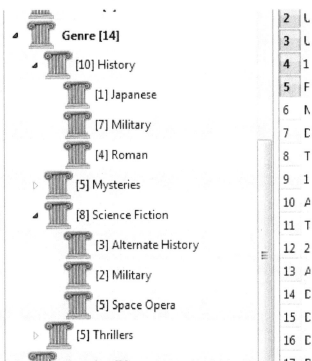

Calibre's hierarchy feature gives you the third, the ability to see the genres in a 'tree' and the ability to easily search for books in genre or sub-genre. For example, assume that your genre structure is similar to the following:

```
Genre
    . History
    .. Japanese
    .. Military
    .. Roman
    . Mysteries
    .. English
    .. Vampire
    . Science Fiction
    .. Alternate History
    .. Military
    .. Space Opera
    . Thrillers
    .. Crime
    .. Horror
    etc.
```

By using the hierarchy feature, you can see these genres in the tag browser in tree form, as shown in the screen image. In this example the outermost level (Genre) is a custom column that contains the genres. Genres containing sub-genres appear with a small triangle next to them. Clicking on that triangle will open the item and show the sub-genres, as you can see with History and Science Fiction.

Clicking on a genre can search for all books with that genre or children of that genre. For example, clicking on Science Fiction can give all three of the child genres, Alternate History, Military, and Space Opera. Clicking on Alternate History will give books in that genre, ignoring those in Military and Space Opera. Of course, a book can have multiple genres. If a book has both Space Opera and Military genres, then you will see that book if you click on either genre. Searching is discussed in more detail below.

Another thing you can see from the image is that the genre Military appears twice, once under History and once under Science Fiction. Because the genres are in a hierarchy, these are two separate genres. A book can be in one, the other, or (doubtfully in this case) both. For example, the books in Winston Churchill's "The Second World War" could be in

"History.Military". David Weber's Honor Harrington books could be in "Science Fiction.Military", and for that matter also in "Science Fiction.Space Opera."

Once a genre exists, that is at least one book has that genre, you can easily apply it to other books by dragging the books from the library view onto the genre you want the books to have. You can also apply genres in the metadata editors; more on this below.

Setup

By now, your question might be "How was all of this up?" There are three steps: 1) create the custom column, 2) tell calibre that the new column is to be treated as a hierarchy, and 3) add genres.

You create the custom column in the usual way, using Preferences -> Add your own columns. This example uses "#genre" as the lookup name and "Genre" as the column heading. The column type is "Comma-separated text, like tags, shown in the tag browser."

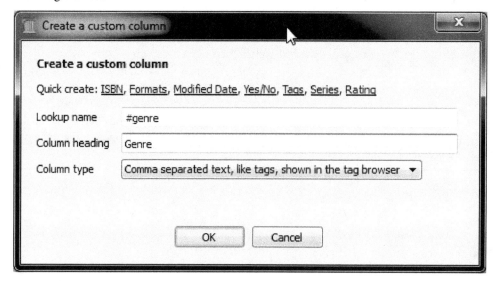

Then after restarting calibre, you must tell calibre that the column is to be treated as a hierarchy. Go to Preferences -> Look and Feel -> Tag Browser and enter the lookup name "#genre" into the "Categories with hierarchical items" box. Press Apply, and you are done with setting up.

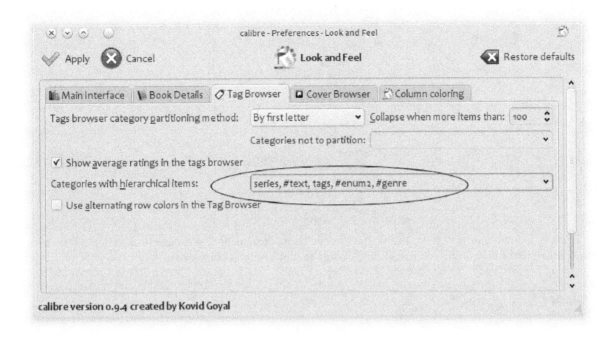

At the point there are no genres in the column. We are left with the last step: how to apply a genre to a book. A genre does not exist in calibre until it appears on at least one book. To learn how to apply a genre for the first time, we must go into some detail about what a genre looks like in the metadata for a book.

A hierarchy of 'things' is built by creating an item consisting of phrases separated by periods. Continuing the genre example, these items would "History.Military", "Mysteries.Vampire", "Science Fiction.Space Opera", etc. Thus to create a new genre, you pick a book that should have that genre, edit its metadata, and enter the new genre into the column you created. Continuing our example, if you want to assign a new genre "Comics" with a sub-genre "Superheroes" to a book, you would 'edit metadata' for that (comic) book, choose the Custom metadata tab, and then enter "Comics.Superheroes" as shown in the following (ignore the other custom columns):

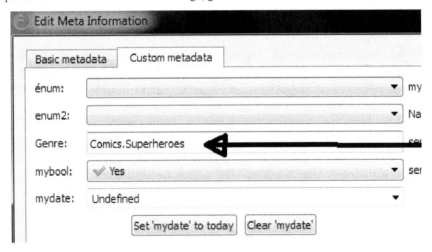

After doing the above, you see in the tag browser:

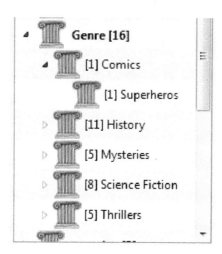

From here on, to apply this new genre to a book (a comic book, presumably), you can either drag the book onto the genre, or add it to the book using edit metadata in exactly the same way as done above.

Searching

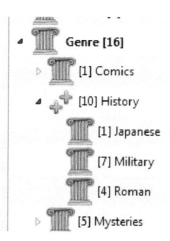

The easiest way to search for genres is using the tag browser, clicking on the genre you wish to see. Clicking on a genre with children will show you books with that genre and all child genres. However, this might bring up a question. Just because a genre has children doesn't mean that it isn't a genre in its own right. For example, a book can have the genre "History" but not "History.Military". How do you search for books with only "History"?

The tag browser search mechanism knows if an item has children. If it does, clicking on the item cycles through 5 searches instead of the normal three. The first is the normal green plus, which shows you books with that genre only (e.g., History). The second is a doubled plus (shown above), which shows you books with that genre and all sub-genres (e.g., History and History.Military). The third is the normal red minus, which shows you books without that exact genre. The fourth is a doubled minus, which shows you books without that genre or sub-genres. The fifth is back to the beginning, no mark, meaning no search.

Restrictions

If you search for a genre then create a saved search for it, you can use the 'restrict to' box to create a virtual library of books with that genre. This is useful if you want to do other searches within the genre or to manage/update metadata for books in the genre. Continuing our example, you can create a saved search named 'History.Japanese' by first clicking on the genre Japanese in the tag browser to get a search into the search box, entering History.Japanese into the saved search box, then pushing the "save search" button (the green box with the white plus, on the right-hand side).

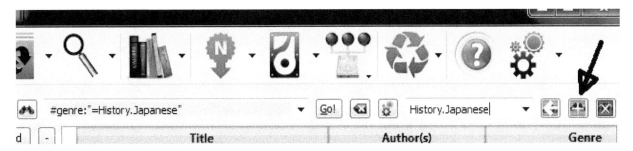

After creating the saved search, you can use it as a restriction.

Useful Template Functions

You might want to use the genre information in a template, such as with save to disk or send to device. The question might then be "How do I get the outermost genre name or names?" A calibre template function, subitems, is provided to make doing this easier.

For example, assume you want to add the outermost genre level to the save-to-disk template to make genre folders, as in "History/The Gathering Storm - Churchill, Winston". To do this, you must extract the first level of the hierarchy and add it to the front along with a slash to indicate that it should make a folder. The template below accomplishes this:

```
{#genre:subitems(0,1)||/}{title} - {authors}
```

See *The template language* (page 161) for more information about templates and the subitems() function.

1.9.3 XPath Tutorial

In this tutorial, you will be given a gentle introduction to XPath[93], a query language that can be used to select arbitrary parts of HTML[94] documents in calibre. XPath is a widely used standard, and googling it will yield a ton of information. This tutorial, however, focuses on using XPath for ebook related tasks like finding chapter headings in an unstructured HTML document.

---

[93] http://en.wikipedia.org/wiki/XPath
[94] http://en.wikipedia.org/wiki/HTML

Contents

Selecting by tagname

The simplest form of selection is to select tags by name. For example, suppose you want to select all the `<h2>` tags in a document. The XPath query for this is simply:

```
//h:h2          (Selects all <h2> tags)
```

The prefix `//` means *search at any level of the document*. Now suppose you want to search for `<span>` tags that are inside `<a>` tags. That can be achieved with:

```
//h:a/h:span     (Selects <span> tags inside <a> tags)
```

If you want to search for tags at a particular level in the document, change the prefix:

```
/h:body/h:div/h:p (Selects <p> tags that are children of <div> tags that are
                children of the <body> tag)
```

This will match only `<p>A very short ebook to demonstrate the use of XPath.</p>` in the *Sample ebook* (page 161) but not any of the other `<p>` tags. The `h:` prefix in the above examples is needed to match XHTML tags. This is because internally, calibre represents all content as XHTML. In XHTML tags have a *namespace*, and `h:` is the namespace prefix for HTML tags.

Now suppose you want to select both `<h1>` and `<h2>` tags. To do that, we need a XPath construct called *predicate*. A *predicate* is simply a test that is used to select tags. Tests can be arbitrarily powerful and as this tutorial progresses, you will see more powerful examples. A predicate is created by enclosing the test expression in square brackets:

```
//*[name()='h1' or name()='h2']
```

There are several new features in this XPath expression. The first is the use of the wildcard `*`. It means *match any tag*. Now look at the test expression `name()='h1' or name()='h2'`. *name()* is an example of a *built-in function*. It simply evaluates to the name of the tag. So by using it, we can select tags whose names are either *h1* or *h2*. Note that the *name()* function ignores namespaces so that there is no need for the `h:` prefix. XPath has several useful built-in functions. A few more will be introduced in this tutorial.

Selecting by attributes

To select tags based on their attributes, the use of predicates is required:

```
//*[@style]            (Select all tags that have a style attribute)
//*[@class="chapter"]    (Select all tags that have class="chapter")
//h:h1[@class="bookTitle"] (Select all h1 tags that have class="bookTitle")
```

Here, the `@` operator refers to the attributes of the tag. You can use some of the *XPath built-in functions* (page 161) to perform more sophisticated matching on attribute values.

Selecting by tag content

Using XPath, you can even select tags based on the text they contain. The best way to do this is to use the power of *regular expressions* via the built-in function *re:test()*:

```
//h:h2[re:test(., 'chapter|section', 'i')] (Selects <h2> tags that contain the words chapter ⟨
                                           section)
```

Here the `.` operator refers to the contents of the tag, just as the @ operator referred to its attributes.

Sample ebook

```
<html>
    <head>
        <title>A very short ebook</title>
        <meta name="charset" value="utf-8" />
    </head>
    <body>
        <h1 class="bookTitle">A very short ebook</h1>
        <p style="text-align:right">Written by Kovid Goyal</p>
        <div class="introduction">
            <p>A very short ebook to demonstrate the use of XPath.</p>
        </div>

        <h2 class="chapter">Chapter One</h2>
        <p>This is a truly fascinating chapter.</p>

        <h2 class="chapter">Chapter Two</h2>
        <p>A worthy continuation of a fine tradition.</p>
    </body>
</html>
```

XPath built-in functions

name()   The name of the current tag.

contains()   `contains(s1, s2)` returns *true* if s1 contains s2.

re:test()   `re:test(src, pattern, flags)` returns *true* if the string *src* matches the regular expression *pattern*. A particularly useful flag is `i`, it makes matching case insensitive. A good primer on the syntax for regular expressions can be found at regexp syntax[95]

1.9.4 The calibre template language

The calibre template language is used in various places. It is used to control the folder structure and file name when saving files from the calibre library to the disk or eBook reader. It is also used to define "virtual" columns that contain data from other columns and so on.

The basic template language is very simple, but has very powerful advanced features. The basic idea is that a template consists of text and names in curly brackets that are then replaced by the corresponding metadata from the book being processed. So, for example, the default template used for saving books to device in calibre is:

```
{author_sort}/{title}/{title} - {authors}
```

[95] https://docs.python.org/2.7/library/re.html

For the book "The Foundation" by "Isaac Asimov" it will become:

```
Asimov, Isaac/The Foundation/The Foundation - Isaac Asimov
```

The slashes are text, which is put into the template where it appears. For example, if your template is:

```
{author_sort} Some Important Text {title}/{title} - {authors}
```

For the book "The Foundation" by "Isaac Asimov" it will become:

```
Asimov, Isaac Some Important Text The Foundation/The Foundation - Isaac Asimov
```

You can use all the various metadata fields available in calibre in a template, including any custom columns you have created yourself. To find out the template name for a column simply hover your mouse over the column header. Names for custom fields (columns you have created yourself) always have a # as the first character. For series type custom fields, there is always an additional field named #seriesname_index that becomes the series index for that series. So if you have a custom series field named #myseries, there will also be a field named #myseries_index.

In addition to the column based fields, you also can use:

```
{formats} - A list of formats available in the calibre library for a book
{identifiers:select(isbn)} - The ISBN number of the book
```

If a particular book does not have a particular piece of metadata, the field in the template is automatically removed for that book. Consider, for example:

```
{author_sort}/{series}/{title} {series_index}
```

If a book has a series, the template will produce:

```
Asimov, Isaac/Foundation/Second Foundation 3
```

and if a book does not have a series:

```
Asimov, Isaac/Second Foundation
```

(calibre automatically removes multiple slashes and leading or trailing spaces).

Advanced formatting

You can do more than just simple substitution with the templates. You can also conditionally include text and control how the substituted data is formatted.

First, conditionally including text. There are cases where you might want to have text appear in the output only if a field is not empty. A common case is `series` and `series_index`, where you want either nothing or the two values with a hyphen between them. Calibre handles this case using a special field syntax.

For example, assume you want to use the template:

```
{series} - {series_index} - {title}
```

If the book has no series, the answer will be `- - title`. Many people would rather the result be simply `title`, without the hyphens. To do this, use the extended syntax `{field:|prefix_text|suffix_text}`. When you use this syntax, if field has the value SERIES then the result will be `prefix_textSERIESsuffix_text`. If field has no value, then the result will be the empty string (nothing); the prefix and suffix are ignored. The prefix and suffix can contain blanks. **Do not use subtemplates ('{ ... }') or functions (see below) as the prefix or the suffix.**

Using this syntax, we can solve the above series problem with the template:

```
{series}{series_index:| - | - }{title}
```

The hyphens will be included only if the book has a series index, which it will have only if it has a series.

Notes: you must include the : character if you want to use a prefix or a suffix. You must either use no | characters or both of them; using one, as in {field:| - }, is not allowed. It is OK not to provide any text for one side or the other, such as in {series:|| - }. Using {title:||} is the same as using {title}.

Second: formatting. Suppose you wanted to ensure that the series_index is always formatted as three digits with leading zeros. This would do the trick:

```
{series_index:0>3s} - Three digits with leading zeros
```

If instead of leading zeros you want leading spaces, use:

```
{series_index:>3s} - Three digits with leading spaces
```

For trailing zeros, use:

```
{series_index:0<3s} - Three digits with trailing zeros
```

If you use series indices with sub values (e.g., 1.1), you might want to ensure that the decimal points line up. For example, you might want the indices 1 and 2.5 to appear as 01.00 and 02.50 so that they will sort correctly. To do this, use:

```
{series_index:0>5.2f} - Five characters, consisting of two digits with leading zeros, a decima
```

If you want only the first two letters of the data, use:

```
{author_sort:.2} - Only the first two letter of the author sort name
```

The calibre template language comes from python and for more details on the syntax of these advanced formatting operations, look at the Python documentation[96].

Advanced features

Using templates in custom columns

There are sometimes cases where you want to display metadata that calibre does not normally display, or to display data in a way different from how calibre normally does. For example, you might want to display the ISBN, a field that calibre does not display. You can use custom columns for this by creating a column with the type 'column built from other columns' (hereafter called composite columns), and entering a template. Result: calibre will display a column showing the result of evaluating that template. To display the ISBN, create the column and enter {identifiers:select(isbn)} into the template box. To display a column containing the values of two series custom columns separated by a comma, use {#series1:||,}{#series2}.

Composite columns can use any template option, including formatting.

You cannot change the data contained in a composite column. If you edit a composite column by double-clicking on any item, you will open the template for editing, not the underlying data. Editing the template on the GUI is a quick way of testing and changing composite columns.

Using functions in templates - single-function mode

Suppose you want to display the value of a field in upper case, when that field is normally in title case. You can do this (and many more things) using the functions available for templates. For example, to display the title in upper case, use

---

[96]https://docs.python.org/2/library/string.html#format-string-syntax

{title:uppercase()}. To display it in title case, use {title:titlecase()}.

Function references appear in the format part, going after the : and before the first | or the closing }. If you have both a format and a function reference, the function comes after another :. Functions must always end with (). Some functions take extra values (arguments), and these go inside the ().

Functions are always applied before format specifications. See further down for an example of using both a format and a function, where this order is demonstrated.

The syntax for using functions is {field:function(arguments)}, or {field:function(arguments)|prefix|suffix}. Arguments are separated by commas. Commas inside arguments must be preceeded by a backslash ('\'). The last (or only) argument cannot contain a closing parenthesis (')'). Functions return the value of the field used in the template, suitably modified.

Important: If you have programming experience, please note that the syntax in this mode (single function) is not what you might expect. Strings are not quoted. Spaces are significant. All arguments must be constants; there is no sub-evaluation. **Do not use subtemplates ('{ ... }') as function arguments.** Instead, use *template program mode* (page 166) and *general program mode* (page 187).

Many functions use regular expressions. In all cases, regular expression matching is case-insensitive.

The functions available are listed below. Note that the definitive documentation for functions is available in the section *Function classification* (page 172):

- lowercase() – return value of the field in lower case.
- uppercase() – return the value of the field in upper case.
- titlecase() – return the value of the field in title case.
- capitalize() – return the value with the first letter upper case and the rest lower case.
- contains(pattern, text if match, text if not match) – checks if field contains matches for the regular expression *pattern*. Returns *text if match* if matches are found, otherwise it returns *text if no match*.
- count(separator) – interprets the value as a list of items separated by *separator*, returning the number of items in the list. Most lists use a comma as the separator, but authors uses an ampersand. Examples: *{tags:count(,)}, {authors:count(&)}*
- format_number(template) – interprets the value as a number and format that number using a python formatting template such as "{0:5.2f}" or "{0:,d}" or "${0:5,.2f}". The field_name part of the template must be a 0 (zero) (the "{0:" in the above examples). See the template language and python documentation for more examples. Returns the empty string if formatting fails.
- human_readable() – expects the value to be a number and returns a string representing that number in KB, MB, GB, etc.
- ifempty(text) – if the field is not empty, return the value of the field. Otherwise return *text*.
- in_list(separator, pattern, found_val, not_found_val) – interpret the field as a list of items separated by *separator*, comparing the *pattern* against each value in the list. If the pattern matches a value, return *found_val*, otherwise return *not_found_val*.
- language_codes(lang_strings) – return the language codes for the strings passed in *lang_strings*. The strings must be in the language of the current locale. *Lang_strings* is a comma-separated list.
- language_strings(lang_codes, localize) – return the strings for the language codes passed in *lang_codes*. If *localize* is zero, return the strings in English. If localize is not zero, return the strings in the language of the current locale. *Lang_codes* is a comma-separated list.
- list_item(index, separator) – interpret the field as a list of items separated by *separator*, returning the *index'th item. The first item is number zero. The last item can be returned using 'list_item(-1,separator). If*

the item is not in the list, then the empty value is returned. The separator has the same meaning as in the *count* function.

- `lookup(pattern, field, pattern, field, ..., else_field)` – like switch, except the arguments are field (metadata) names, not text. The value of the appropriate field will be fetched and used. Note that because composite columns are fields, you can use this function in one composite field to use the value of some other composite field. This is extremely useful when constructing variable save paths (more later).

- `re(pattern, replacement)` – return the field after applying the regular expression. All instances of *pattern* are replaced with *replacement*. As in all of calibre, these are python-compatible regular expressions.

- `select(key)` – interpret the field as a comma-separated list of items, with the items being of the form "id:value". Find the pair with the id equal to key, and return the corresponding value. This function is particularly useful for extracting a value such as an isbn from the set of identifiers for a book.

- `shorten(left chars, middle text, right chars)` – Return a shortened version of the field, consisting of *left chars* characters from the beginning of the field, followed by *middle text*, followed by *right chars* characters from the end of the string. *Left chars* and *right chars* must be integers. For example, assume the title of the book is *Ancient English Laws in the Times of Ivanhoe*, and you want it to fit in a space of at most 15 characters. If you use `{title:shorten(9,-,5)}`, the result will be *Ancient E-nhoe*. If the field's length is less than `left chars` + `right chars` + the length of `middle text`, then the field will be used intact. For example, the title *The Dome* would not be changed.

- `str_in_list(val, separator, string, found_val, not_found_val)` – treat val as a list of items separated by separator, comparing the string against each value in the list. If the string matches a value, return found_val, otherwise return not_found_val. If the string contains separators, then it is also treated as a list and each value is checked.

- `subitems(val, start_index, end_index)` – This function is used to break apart lists of tag-like hierarchical items such as genres. It interprets the value as a comma-separated list of tag-like items, where each item is a period-separated list. Returns a new list made by first finding all the period-separated tag-like items, then for each such item extracting the components from *start_index* to *end_index*, then combining the results back together. The first component in a period-separated list has an index of zero. If an index is negative, then it counts from the end of the list. As a special case, an end_index of zero is assumed to be the length of the list. Examples:

```
Assuming a #genre column containing "A.B.C":
    {#genre:subitems(0,1)} returns "A"
    {#genre:subitems(0,2)} returns "A.B"
    {#genre:subitems(1,0)} returns "B.C"
Assuming a #genre column containing "A.B.C, D.E":
    {#genre:subitems(0,1)} returns "A, D"
    {#genre:subitems(0,2)} returns "A.B, D.E"
```

- `sublist(val, start_index, end_index, separator)` – interpret the value as a list of items separated by *separator*, returning a new list made from the items from *start_index* 'to 'end_index*. The first item is number zero. If an index is negative, then it counts from the end of the list. As a special case, an end_index of zero is assumed to be the length of the list. Examples assuming that the tags column (which is comma-separated) contains "A, B ,C":

```
{tags:sublist(0,1,\,)} returns "A"
{tags:sublist(-1,0,\,)} returns "C"
{tags:sublist(0,-1,\,)} returns "A, B"
```

- `swap_around_comma(val)` `` -- given a value of the form ``B, A, return A B. This is most useful for converting names in LN, FN format to FN LN. If there is no comma, the function returns val unchanged.

- `switch(pattern, value, pattern, value, ..., else_value)` – for each `pattern,` value pair, checks if the field matches the regular expression `pattern` and if so, returns that `value`. If no `pattern` matches, then `else_value` is returned. You can have as many `pattern, value` pairs as you want.

- `test(text if not empty, text if empty)` – return *text if not empty* if the field is not empty, otherwise return *text if empty*.

- `transliterate()` – Returns a string in a latin alphabet formed by approximating the sound of the words in the source field. For example, if the source field is Фёдор Михайлович Достоевский the function returns `Fiodor Mikhailovich Dostoievskii.'`

Now, what about using functions and formatting in the same field. Suppose you have an integer custom column called `#myint` that you want to see with leading zeros, as in `003`. To do this, you would use a format of `0>3s`. However, by default, if a number (integer or float) equals zero then the field produces the empty value, so zero values will produce nothing, not `000`. If you really want to see `000` values, then you use both the format string and the `ifempty` function to change the empty value back to a zero. The field reference would be:

```
{#myint:0>3s:ifempty(0)}
```

Note that you can use the prefix and suffix as well. If you want the number to appear as `[003]` or `[000]`, then use the field:

```
{#myint:0>3s:ifempty(0)|[|]}
```

Using functions in templates - template program mode

The template language program mode differs from single-function mode in that it permits you to write template expressions that refer to other metadata fields, modify values, and do arithmetic. It is a reasonably complete programming language.

You can use the functions documented above in template program mode. See below for details.

Beginning with an example, assume that you want your template to show the series for a book if it has one, otherwise show the value of a custom field #genre. You cannot do this in the basic language because you cannot make reference to another metadata field within a template expression. In program mode, you can. The following expression works:

```
{#series:'ifempty($, field('#genre'))'}
```

The example shows several things:

- program mode is used if the expression begins with `:'` and ends with `'`. Anything else is assumed to be single-function.

- the variable `$` stands for the field the expression is operating upon, `#series` in this case.

- functions must be given all their arguments. There is no default value. For example, the standard built-in functions must be given an additional initial parameter indicating the source field, which is a significant difference from single-function mode.

- white space is ignored and can be used anywhere within the expression.

- constant strings are enclosed in matching quotes, either `'` or `"`.

The language is similar to `functional` languages in that it is built almost entirely from functions. A statement is a function. An expression is a function. Constants and identifiers can be thought of as functions returning the value indicated by the constant or stored in the identifier.

The syntax of the language is shown by the following grammar:

```
constant    ::= " string " | ' string ' | number
identifier ::= sequence of letters or ``_`` characters
function    ::= identifier ( statement [ , statement ]* )
expression ::= identifier | constant | function | assignment
assignment ::= identifier '=' expression
statement   ::= expression [ ; expression ]*
program     ::= statement
```

Comments are lines with a '#' character at the beginning of the line.

An expression always has a value, either the value of the constant, the value contained in the identifier, or the value returned by a function. The value of a statement is the value of the last expression in the sequence of statements. As such, the value of the program (statement):

```
1; 2; 'foobar'; 3
```

is 3.

Another example of a complex but rather silly program might help make things clearer:

```
{series_index:'
    substr(
        strcat($, '->',
            cmp(divide($, 2), 1,
                assign(c, 1); substr('lt123', c, 0),
                'eq', 'gt')),
        0, 6)
    '| prefix | suffix}
```

This program does the following:

- specify that the field being looked at is series_index. This sets the value of the variable $.

- calls the substr function, which takes 3 parameters (str, start, end). It returns a string formed by extracting the start through end characters from string, zero-based (the first character is character zero). In this case the string will be computed by the strcat function, the start is 0, and the end is 6. In this case it will return the first 6 characters of the string returned by strcat, which must be evaluated before substr can return.

- calls the strcat (string concatenation) function. Strcat accepts 1 or more arguments, and returns a string formed by concatenating all the values. In this case there are three arguments. The first parameter is the value in $, which here is the value of series_index. The second paremeter is the constant string '->'. The third parameter is the value returned by the cmp function, which must be fully evaluated before strcat can return.

- The cmp function takes 5 arguments (x, y, lt, eq, gt). It compares x and y and returns the third argument lt if x < y, the fourth argument eq if x == y, and the fifth argument gt if x > y. As with all functions, all of the parameters can be statements. In this case the first parameter (the value for x) is the result of dividing the series_index by 2. The second parameter y is the constant 1. The third parameter lt is a statement (more later). The fourth parameter eq is the constant string 'eq'. The fifth parameter is the constant string 'gt'.

- The third parameter (the one for lt) is a statement, or a sequence of expressions. Remember that a statement (a sequence of semicolon-separated expressions) is also an expression, returning the value of the last expression in the list. In this case, the program first assigns the value 1 to a local variable c, then returns a substring made by extracting the c'th character to the end. Since c always contains the constant 1, the substring will return the second through end'th characters, or 't123'.

- Once the statement providing the value to the third parameter is executed, cmp can return a value. At that point, strcat` can return a value, then ``substr can return a value. The program then terminates.

For various values of series_index, the program returns:

- series_index == undefined, result = prefix ->t123 suffix

- series_index == 0.5, result = `prefix 0.50-> suffix`

- series_index == 1, result = `prefix 1->t12 suffix`

- series_index == 2, result = `prefix 2->eq suffix`

- series_index == 3, result = `prefix 3->gt suffix`

All the functions listed under single-function mode can be used in program mode. To do so, you must supply the value that the function is to act upon as the first parameter, in addition to the parameters documented above. For example, in program mode the parameters of the *test* function are `test(x, text_if_not_empty, text_if_empty)`. The *x* parameter, which is the value to be tested, will almost always be a variable or a function call, often *field()*.

The following functions are available in addition to those described in single-function mode. Remember from the example above that the single-function mode functions require an additional first parameter specifying the field to operate on. With the exception of the `id` parameter of assign, all parameters can be statements (sequences of expressions). Note that the definitive documentation for functions is available in the section *Function classification* (page 172):

- `and(value, value, ...)` – returns the string "1" if all values are not empty, otherwise returns the empty string. This function works well with test or first_non_empty. You can have as many values as you want.

- `add(x, y)` – returns x + y. Throws an exception if either x or y are not numbers.

- `assign(id, val)` – assigns val to id, then returns val. id must be an identifier, not an expression

- `approximate_formats()` – return a comma-separated list of formats that at one point were associated with the book. There is no guarantee that the list is correct, although it probably is. This function can be called in template program mode using the template `{:'approximate_formats()'}`. Note that format names are always uppercase, as in EPUB.

- `author_links(val_separator, pair_separator)` – returns a string containing a list of authors and that author's link values in the form `author1 val_separator author1link pair_separator author2 val_separator author2link` etc. An author is separated from its link value by the `val_separator` string with no added spaces. `author:linkvalue` pairs are separated by the `pair_separator` string argument with no added spaces. It is up to you to choose separator strings that do not occur in author names or links. An author is included even if the author link is empty.

- `author_sorts(val_separator)` – returns a string containing a list of author's sort values for the authors of the book. The sort is the one in the author metadata (different from the author_sort in books). The returned list has the form author sort 1 `val_separator` author sort 2 etc. The author sort values in this list are in the same order as the authors of the book. If you want spaces around `val_separator` then include them in the separator string

- `booksize()` – returns the value of the calibre 'size' field. Returns '' if there are no formats.

- `cmp(x, y, lt, eq, gt)` – compares x and y after converting both to numbers. Returns `lt` if x < y. Returns `eq` if x == y. Otherwise returns `gt`.

- `current_library_name() -- `` return the last name on the path to the current calibre library. This function can be called in template program mode using the template ``{:'current_library_name()'}`.

- `current_library_path() -- `` return the path to the current calibre library. This function can be called in template program mode using the template ``{:'current_library_path()'}`..

- days_between(date1, date2) – return the number of days between date1 and date2. The number is positive if date1 is greater than date2, otherwise negative. If either date1 or date2 are not dates, the function returns the empty string.

- divide(x, y) – returns x / y. Throws an exception if either x or y are not numbers.

- eval(string) – evaluates the string as a program, passing the local variables (those assigned ed to). This permits using the template processor to construct complex results from local variables. Because the { and } characters are special, you must use [[for the { character and]] for the '}' character; they are converted automatically. Note also that prefixes and suffixes (the |prefix|suffix syntax) cannot be used in the argument to this function when using template program mode.

- field(name) – returns the metadata field named by name.

- first_matching_cmp(val, cmp1, result1, cmp2, r2, ..., else_result) – compares "val < cmpN" in sequence, returning resultN for the first comparison that succeeds. Returns else_result if no comparison succeeds. Example:

```
``first_matching_cmp(10,5,"small",10,"middle",15,"large","giant")``
```

returns "large". The same example with a first value of 16 returns "giant". * first_non_empty(value, value, ...) – returns the first value that is not empty. If all values are empty, then the empty value is returned. You can have as many values as you want. * format_date(x, date_format) – format_date(val, format_string) – format the value, which must be a date field, using the format_string, returning a string. The formatting codes are:

```
d    : the day as number without a leading zero (1 to 31)
dd   : the day as number with a leading zero (01 to 31)
ddd  : the abbreviated localized day name (e.g. "Mon" to "Sun").
dddd : the long localized day name (e.g. "Monday" to "Sunday").
M    : the month as number without a leading zero (1 to 12).
MM   : the month as number with a leading zero (01 to 12)
MMM  : the abbreviated localized month name (e.g. "Jan" to "Dec").
MMMM : the long localized month name (e.g. "January" to "December").
yy   : the year as two digit number (00 to 99).
yyyy : the year as four digit number.
h    : the hours without a leading 0 (0 to 11 or 0 to 23, depending on am/pm)
hh   : the hours with a leading 0 (00 to 11 or 00 to 23, depending on am/pm)
m    : the minutes without a leading 0 (0 to 59)
mm   : the minutes with a leading 0 (00 to 59)
s    : the seconds without a leading 0 (0 to 59)
ss   : the seconds with a leading 0 (00 to 59)
ap   : use a 12-hour clock instead of a 24-hour clock, with 'ap' replaced by the localize
AP   : use a 12-hour clock instead of a 24-hour clock, with 'AP' replaced by the localize
iso  : the date with time and timezone. Must be the only format present.
```

You might get unexpected results if the date you are formatting contains localized month names, which can happen if you changed the format tweaks to contain MMMM. In this case, instead of using something like {pubdate:format_date(yyyy)}, write the template using template program mode as in {:'format_date(raw_field('pubdate'),'yyyy')'}.

- finish_formatting(val, fmt, prefix, suffix) – apply the format, prefix, and suffix to a value in the same way as done in a template like {series_index:05.2f| - |- }. This function is provided to ease conversion of complex single-function- or template-program-mode templates to *general program mode* (page 187) (see below) to take advantage of GPM template compilation. For example, the following program produces the same output as the above template:

```
program: finish_formatting(field("series_index"), "05.2f", " - ", " - ")
```

Another example: for the template `{series:re(([^\s])[^\s]+(\s|$),\1)}{series_index:0>2s|` `- | - }{title}` use:

```
program:
    strcat(
        re(field('series'), '([^\s])[^\s]+(\s|$)', '\1'),
        finish_formatting(field('series_index'), '0>2s', ' - ', ' - '),
        field('title')
    )
```

- `formats_modtimes(date_format)` – return a comma-separated list of colon-separated items representing modification times for the formats of a book. The date_format parameter specifies how the date is to be formatted. See the date_format function for details. You can use the select function to get the mod time for a specific format. Note that format names are always uppercase, as in EPUB.

- `formats_paths()` – return a comma-separated list of colon-separated items representing full path to the formats of a book. You can use the select function to get the path for a specific format. Note that format names are always uppercase, as in EPUB.

- `formats_sizes()` – return a comma-separated list of colon-separated items representing sizes in bytes of the formats of a book. You can use the select function to get the size for a specific format. Note that format names are always uppercase, as in EPUB.

- `has_cover()` – return `Yes` if the book has a cover, otherwise return the empty string

- `not(value)` – returns the string "1" if the value is empty, otherwise returns the empty string. This function works well with test or first_non_empty. You can have as many values as you want.

- `list_difference(list1, list2, separator)` – return a list made by removing from *list1* any item found in *list2*, using a case-insensitive compare. The items in *list1* and *list2* are separated by separator, as are the items in the returned list.

- `list_equals(list1, sep1, list2, sep2, yes_val, no_val)` – return *yes_val* if *list1* and *list2* contain the same items, otherwise return *no_val*. The items are determined by splitting each list using the appropriate separator character (*sep1* or *sep2*). The order of items in the lists is not relevant. The compare is case insensitive.

- `list_intersection(list1, list2, separator)` – return a list made by removing from *list1* any item not found in *list2*, using a case-insensitive compare. The items in *list1* and *list2* are separated by separator, as are the items in the returned list.

- `list_re(src_list, separator, include_re, opt_replace)` – Construct a list by first separating *src_list* into items using the *separator* character. For each item in the list, check if it matches *include_re*. If it does, then add it to the list to be returned. If *opt_replace* is not the empty string, then apply the replacement before adding the item to the returned list.

- `list_re_group(src_list, separator, include_re, search_re, template_for_group_1, for_group_2, ...)` – Like list_re except replacements are not optional. It uses re_group(item, search_re, template ...) when doing the replacements.

- `list_sort(list, direction, separator)` – return list sorted using a case-insensitive sort. If *direction* is zero, the list is sorted ascending, otherwise descending. The list items are separated by separator, as are the items in the returned list.

- `list_union(list1, list2, separator)` – return a list made by merging the items in list1 and list2, removing duplicate items using a case-insensitive compare. If items differ in case, the one in list1 is used. The items in list1 and list2 are separated by separator, as are the items in the returned list.

- `multiply(x, y)` – returns x * y. Throws an exception if either x or y are not numbers.

- `ondevice()` – return the string "Yes" if ondevice is set, otherwise return the empty string

- `or(value, value, ...)` – returns the string "1" if any value is not empty, otherwise returns the empty string. This function works well with test or first_non_empty. You can have as many values as you want.

- `print(a, b, ...)` – prints the arguments to standard output. Unless you start calibre from the command line (`calibre-debug -g`), the output will go to a black hole.

- `raw_field(name)` – returns the metadata field named by name without applying any formatting.

- `raw_list(name, separator)` – returns the metadata list named by name without applying any formatting or sorting and with items separated by separator.

- `re_group(val, pattern, template_for_group_1, for_group_2, ...)` – return a string made by applying the regular expression pattern to the val and replacing each matched instance with the string computed by replacing each matched group by the value returned by the corresponding template. The original matched value for the group is available as $. In template program mode, like for the template and the eval functions, you use [[for { and]] for }. The following example in template program mode looks for series with more than one word and uppercases the first word:

```
{series:'re_group($, "(\S* )(.*)", "[[$:uppercase()]]", "[[$]]")'}
```

- `series_sort()` – returns the series sort value.

- `strcat(a, b, ...)` – can take any number of arguments. Returns a string formed by concatenating all the arguments.

- `strcat_max(max, string1, prefix2, string2, ...)` – Returns a string formed by concatenating the arguments. The returned value is initialized to string1. *Prefix, string* pairs are added to the end of the value as long as the resulting string length is less than *max*. String1 is returned even if string1 is longer than max. You can pass as many *prefix, string* pairs as you wish.

- `strcmp(x, y, lt, eq, gt)` – does a case-insensitive comparison x and y as strings. Returns lt if x < y. Returns eq if x == y. Otherwise returns gt.

- `strlen(a)` – Returns the length of the string passed as the argument.

- `substr(str, start, end)` – returns the start'th through the end'th characters of str. The first character in str is the zero'th character. If end is negative, then it indicates that many characters counting from the right. If end is zero, then it indicates the last character. For example, substr('12345', 1, 0) returns '2345', and substr('12345', 1, -1) returns '234'.

- `subtract(x, y)` – returns x - y. Throws an exception if either x or y are not numbers.

- `today()` – return a date string for today. This value is designed for use in format_date or days_between, but can be manipulated like any other string. The date is in ISO format.

- `template(x)` – evaluates x as a template. The evaluation is done in its own context, meaning that variables are not shared between the caller and the template evaluation. Because the { and } characters are special, you must use [[for the { character and]] for the '}' character; they are converted automatically. For example, template('[[title_sort]]') will evaluate the template ``{title_sort} and return its value. Note also that prefixes and suffixes (the |prefix|suffix syntax) cannot be used in the argument to this function when using template program mode.

Function classification

Reference for all built-in template language functions

Here, we document all the built-in functions available in the calibre template language. Every function is implemented as a class in python and you can click the source links to see the source code, in case the documentation is insufficient. The functions are arranged in logical groups by type.

Arithmetic

add(x, y)
class calibre.utils.formatter_functions.**BuiltinAdd**
>   add(x, y) – returns x + y. Throws an exception if either x or y are not numbers.

divide(x, y)
class calibre.utils.formatter_functions.**BuiltinDivide**
>   divide(x, y) – returns x / y. Throws an exception if either x or y are not numbers.

multiply(x, y)
class calibre.utils.formatter_functions.**BuiltinMultiply**
>   multiply(x, y) – returns x * y. Throws an exception if either x or y are not numbers.

subtract(x, y)
class calibre.utils.formatter_functions.**BuiltinSubtract**
>   subtract(x, y) – returns x - y. Throws an exception if either x or y are not numbers.

Boolean

and(value, value, ...)
class calibre.utils.formatter_functions.**BuiltinAnd**
>   and(value, value, ...) – returns the string "1" if all values are not empty, otherwise returns the empty string. This function works well with test or first_non_empty. You can have as many values as you want.

not(value)
class calibre.utils.formatter_functions.**BuiltinNot**
>   not(value) – returns the string "1" if the value is empty, otherwise returns the empty string. This function works well with test or first_non_empty. You can have as many values as you want.

or(value, value, ...)
class calibre.utils.formatter_functions.**BuiltinOr**
>   or(value, value, ...) – returns the string "1" if any value is not empty, otherwise returns the empty string. This function works well with test or first_non_empty. You can have as many values as you want.

Date functions

days_between(date1, date2)
class calibre.utils.formatter_functions.**BuiltinDaysBetween**
>   days_between(date1, date2) – return the number of days between date1 and date2. The number is positive if date1 is greater than date2, otherwise negative. If either date1 or date2 are not dates, the function returns the empty string.

today()
class calibre.utils.formatter_functions.**BuiltinToday**
>   today() – return a date string for today. This value is designed for use in format_date or days_between, but can be manipulated like any other string. The date is in ISO format.

Formatting values

finish_formatting(val, fmt, prefix, suffix)

class `calibre.utils.formatter_functions`.**BuiltinFinishFormatting**

finish_formatting(val, fmt, prefix, suffix) – apply the format, prefix, and suffix to a value in the same way as done in a template like *[series_index:05.2f| - |- }*. For example, the following program produces the same output as the above template: program: finish_formatting(field("series_index"), "05.2f", " - ", " - ")

format_date(val, format_string)

class `calibre.utils.formatter_functions`.**BuiltinFormatDate**

format_date(val, format_string) – format the value, which must be a date, using the format_string, returning a string. The formatting codes are: d : the day as number without a leading zero (1 to 31) dd : the day as number with a leading zero (01 to 31) ddd : the abbreviated localized day name (e.g. "Mon" to "Sun"). dddd : the long localized day name (e.g. "Monday" to "Sunday"). M : the month as number without a leading zero (1 to 12). MM : the month as number with a leading zero (01 to 12) MMM : the abbreviated localized month name (e.g. "Jan" to "Dec"). MMMM : the long localized month name (e.g. "January" to "December"). yy : the year as two digit number (00 to 99). yyyy : the year as four digit number. h : the hours without a leading 0 (0 to 11 or 0 to 23, depending on am/pm) hh : the hours with a leading 0 (00 to 11 or 00 to 23, depending on am/pm) m : the minutes without a leading 0 (0 to 59) mm : the minutes with a leading 0 (00 to 59) s : the seconds without a leading 0 (0 to 59) ss : the seconds with a leading 0 (00 to 59) ap : use a 12-hour clock instead of a 24-hour clock, with "ap" replaced by the localized string for am or pm AP : use a 12-hour clock instead of a 24-hour clock, with "AP" replaced by the localized string for AM or PM iso : the date with time and timezone. Must be the only format present

format_number(v, template)

class `calibre.utils.formatter_functions`.**BuiltinFormatNumber**

format_number(v, template) – format the number v using a python formatting template such as "{0:5.2f}" or "{0:,d}" or "${0:5,.2f}". The field_name part of the template must be a 0 (zero) (the "{0:" in the above examples). See the template language and python documentation for more examples. Returns the empty string if formatting fails.

human_readable(v)

class `calibre.utils.formatter_functions`.**BuiltinHumanReadable**

human_readable(v) – return a string representing the number v in KB, MB, GB, etc.

Get values from metadata

approximate_formats()

class `calibre.utils.formatter_functions`.**BuiltinApproximateFormats**

approximate_formats() – return a comma-separated list of formats that at one point were associated with the book. There is no guarantee that this list is correct, although it probably is. This function can be called in template program mode using the template "{:'approximate_formats()'}". Note that format names are always uppercase, as in EPUB. This function works only in the GUI. If you want to use these values in save-to-disk or send-to-device templates then you must make a custom "Column built from other columns", use the function in that column's template, and use that column's value in your save/send templates

author_links(val_separator, pair_separator)

class `calibre.utils.formatter_functions.`**BuiltinAuthorLinks**

> author_links(val_separator, pair_separator) – returns a string containing a list of authors and that author's link values in the form author1 val_separator author1link pair_separator author2 val_separator author2link etc. An author is separated from its link value by the val_separator string with no added spaces. author:linkvalue pairs are separated by the pair_separator string argument with no added spaces. It is up to you to choose separator strings that do not occur in author names or links. An author is included even if the author link is empty.

author_sorts(val_separator)

class `calibre.utils.formatter_functions.`**BuiltinAuthorSorts**

> author_sorts(val_separator) – returns a string containing a list of author's sort values for the authors of the book. The sort is the one in the author metadata (different from the author_sort in books). The returned list has the form author sort 1 val_separator author sort 2 etc. The author sort values in this list are in the same order as the authors of the book. If you want spaces around val_separator then include them in the separator string

booksize()

class `calibre.utils.formatter_functions.`**BuiltinBooksize**

> booksize() – return value of the size field. This function works only in the GUI. If you want to use this value in save-to-disk or send-to-device templates then you must make a custom "Column built from other columns", use the function in that column's template, and use that column's value in your save/send templates

current_library_name()

class `calibre.utils.formatter_functions.`**BuiltinCurrentLibraryName**

> current_library_name() – return the last name on the path to the current calibre library. This function can be called in template program mode using the template "{:'current_library_name()'}".

current_library_path()

class `calibre.utils.formatter_functions.`**BuiltinCurrentLibraryPath**

> current_library_path() – return the path to the current calibre library. This function can be called in template program mode using the template "{:'current_library_path()'}".

field(name)

class `calibre.utils.formatter_functions.`**BuiltinField**

> field(name) – returns the metadata field named by name

formats_modtimes(date_format)

class `calibre.utils.formatter_functions.`**BuiltinFormatsModtimes**

> formats_modtimes(date_format) – return a comma-separated list of colon_separated items representing modification times for the formats of a book. The date_format parameter specifies how the date is to be formatted. See the date_format function for details. You can use the select function to get the mod time for a specific format. Note that format names are always uppercase, as in EPUB.

formats_paths()

class `calibre.utils.formatter_functions.`**BuiltinFormatsPaths**

> formats_paths() – return a comma-separated list of colon_separated items representing full path to the formats of a book. You can use the select function to get the path for a specific format. Note that format names are always uppercase, as in EPUB.

formats_sizes()

class calibre.utils.formatter_functions.**BuiltinFormatsSizes**

formats_sizes() – return a comma-separated list of colon_separated items representing sizes in bytes of the formats of a book. You can use the select function to get the size for a specific format. Note that format names are always uppercase, as in EPUB.

has_cover()

class calibre.utils.formatter_functions.**BuiltinHasCover**

has_cover() – return Yes if the book has a cover, otherwise return the empty string

language_codes(lang_strings)

class calibre.utils.formatter_functions.**BuiltinLanguageCodes**

language_codes(lang_strings) – return the language codes for the strings passed in lang_strings. The strings must be in the language of the current locale. Lang_strings is a comma-separated list.

language_strings(lang_codes, localize)

class calibre.utils.formatter_functions.**BuiltinLanguageStrings**

language_strings(lang_codes, localize) – return the strings for the language codes passed in lang_codes. If localize is zero, return the strings in English. If localize is not zero, return the strings in the language of the current locale. Lang_codes is a comma-separated list.

ondevice()

class calibre.utils.formatter_functions.**BuiltinOndevice**

ondevice() – return Yes if ondevice is set, otherwise return the empty string. This function works only in the GUI. If you want to use this value in save-to-disk or send-to-device templates then you must make a custom "Column built from other columns", use the function in that column's template, and use that column's value in your save/send templates

raw_field(name)

class calibre.utils.formatter_functions.**BuiltinRawField**

raw_field(name) – returns the metadata field named by name without applying any formatting.

raw_list(name, separator)

class calibre.utils.formatter_functions.**BuiltinRawList**

raw_list(name, separator) – returns the metadata list named by name without applying any formatting or sorting and with items separated by separator.

series_sort()

class calibre.utils.formatter_functions.**BuiltinSeriesSort**

series_sort() – return the series sort value

user_categories()

class calibre.utils.formatter_functions.**BuiltinUserCategories**

user_categories() – return a comma-separated list of the user categories that contain this book. This function works only in the GUI. If you want to use these values in save-to-disk or send-to-device templates then you must make a custom "Column built from other columns", use the function in that column's template, and use that column's value in your save/send templates

---

virtual_libraries()

class calibre.utils.formatter_functions.**BuiltinVirtualLibraries**

> virtual_libraries() – return a comma-separated list of virtual libraries that contain this book. This function works only in the GUI. If you want to use these values in save-to-disk or send-to-device templates then you must make a custom "Column built from other columns", use the function in that column's template, and use that column's value in your save/send templates

If-then-else

contains(val, pattern, text if match, text if not match)

class calibre.utils.formatter_functions.**BuiltinContains**

> contains(val, pattern, text if match, text if not match) – checks if field contains matches for the regular expression *pattern*. Returns *text if match* if matches are found, otherwise it returns *text if no match*

ifempty(val, text if empty)

class calibre.utils.formatter_functions.**BuiltinIfempty**

> ifempty(val, text if empty) – return val if val is not empty, otherwise return *text if empty*

test(val, text if not empty, text if empty)

class calibre.utils.formatter_functions.**BuiltinTest**

> test(val, text if not empty, text if empty) – return *text if not empty* if the field is not empty, otherwise return *text if empty*

Iterating over values

first_non_empty(value, value, ...)

class calibre.utils.formatter_functions.**BuiltinFirstNonEmpty**

> first_non_empty(value, value, ...) – returns the first value that is not empty. If all values are empty, then the empty value is returned. You can have as many values as you want.

lookup(val, pattern, field, pattern, field, ..., else_field)

class calibre.utils.formatter_functions.**BuiltinLookup**

> lookup(val, pattern, field, pattern, field, ..., else_field) – like switch, except the arguments are field (metadata) names, not text. The value of the appropriate field will be fetched and used. Note that because composite columns are fields, you can use this function in one composite field to use the value of some other composite field. This is extremely useful when constructing variable save paths

switch(val, pattern, value, pattern, value, ..., else_value)

class calibre.utils.formatter_functions.**BuiltinSwitch**

> switch(val, pattern, value, pattern, value, ..., else_value) – for each *pattern, value* pair, checks if the field matches the regular expression *pattern* and if so, returns that *value*. If no pattern matches, then else_value is returned. You can have as many *pattern, value* pairs as you want

List lookup

identifier_in_list(val, id, found_val, not_found_val)

class calibre.utils.formatter_functions.**BuiltinIdentifierInList**

identifier_in_list(val, id, found_val, not_found_val) – treat val as a list of identifiers separated by commas, comparing the string against each value in the list. An identifier has the format "identifier:value". The id parameter should be either "id" or "id:regexp". The first case matches if there is any identifier with that id. The second case matches if the regexp matches the identifier's value. If there is a match, return found_val, otherwise return not_found_val.

in_list(val, separator, pattern, found_val, not_found_val)

class calibre.utils.formatter_functions.**BuiltinInList**

in_list(val, separator, pattern, found_val, not_found_val) – treat val as a list of items separated by separator, comparing the pattern against each value in the list. If the pattern matches a value, return found_val, otherwise return not_found_val.

list_item(val, index, separator)

class calibre.utils.formatter_functions.**BuiltinListitem**

list_item(val, index, separator) – interpret the value as a list of items separated by *separator*, returning the *index'th item. The first item is number zero. The last item can be returned using 'list_item(-1,separator). If* the item is not in the list, then the empty value is returned. The separator has the same meaning as in the count function.

select(val, key)

class calibre.utils.formatter_functions.**BuiltinSelect**

select(val, key) – interpret the value as a comma-separated list of items, with the items being "id:value". Find the pair with the id equal to key, and return the corresponding value.

str_in_list(val, separator, string, found_val, not_found_val)

class calibre.utils.formatter_functions.**BuiltinStrInList**

str_in_list(val, separator, string, found_val, not_found_val) – treat val as a list of items separated by separator, comparing the string against each value in the list. If the string matches a value, return found_val, otherwise return not_found_val. If the string contains separators, then it is also treated as a list and each value is checked.

List manipulation

count(val, separator)

class calibre.utils.formatter_functions.**BuiltinCount**

count(val, separator) – interprets the value as a list of items separated by *separator*, returning the number of items in the list. Most lists use a comma as the separator, but authors uses an ampersand. Examples: {tags:count(,)}, {authors:count(&)}

list_difference(list1, list2, separator)

class calibre.utils.formatter_functions.**BuiltinListDifference**

list_difference(list1, list2, separator) – return a list made by removing from list1 any item found in list2, using a case-insensitive compare. The items in list1 and list2 are separated by separator, as are the items in the returned list.

list_equals(list1, sep1, list2, sep2, yes_val, no_val)

class `calibre.utils.formatter_functions.`**BuiltinListEquals**

list_equals(list1, sep1, list2, sep2, yes_val, no_val) – return yes_val if list1 and list2 contain the same items, otherwise return no_val. The items are determined by splitting each list using the appropriate separator character (sep1 or sep2). The order of items in the lists is not relevant. The compare is case insensitive.

list_intersection(list1, list2, separator)

class `calibre.utils.formatter_functions.`**BuiltinListIntersection**

list_intersection(list1, list2, separator) – return a list made by removing from list1 any item not found in list2, using a case-insensitive compare. The items in list1 and list2 are separated by separator, as are the items in the returned list.

list_re(src_list, separator, include_re, opt_replace)

class `calibre.utils.formatter_functions.`**BuiltinListRe**

list_re(src_list, separator, include_re, opt_replace) – Construct a list by first separating src_list into items using the separator character. For each item in the list, check if it matches include_re. If it does, then add it to the list to be returned. If opt_replace is not the empty string, then apply the replacement before adding the item to the returned list.

list_re_group(src_list, separator, include_re, search_re, group_1_template, ...)

class `calibre.utils.formatter_functions.`**BuiltinListReGroup**

list_re_group(src_list, separator, include_re, search_re, group_1_template, ...) – Like list_re except replacements are not optional. It uses re_group(list_item, search_re, group_1_template, ...) when doing the replacements on the resulting list.

list_sort(list, direction, separator)

class `calibre.utils.formatter_functions.`**BuiltinListSort**

list_sort(list, direction, separator) – return list sorted using a case-insensitive sort. If direction is zero, the list is sorted ascending, otherwise descending. The list items are separated by separator, as are the items in the returned list.

list_union(list1, list2, separator)

class `calibre.utils.formatter_functions.`**BuiltinListUnion**

list_union(list1, list2, separator) – return a list made by merging the items in list1 and list2, removing duplicate items using a case-insensitive compare. If items differ in case, the one in list1 is used. The items in list1 and list2 are separated by separator, as are the items in the returned list.

subitems(val, start_index, end_index)

class `calibre.utils.formatter_functions.`**BuiltinSubitems**

subitems(val, start_index, end_index) – This function is used to break apart lists of items such as genres. It interprets the value as a comma-separated list of items, where each item is a period-separated list. Returns a new list made by first finding all the period-separated items, then for each such item extracting the *start_index* to the *end_index* components, then combining the results back together. The first component in a period-separated list has an index of zero. If an index is negative, then it counts from the end of the list. As a special case, an end_index of zero is assumed to be the length of the list. Example using basic template mode and assuming a #genre value of "A.B.C": {#genre:subitems(0,1)} returns "A". {#genre:subitems(0,2)} returns "A.B". {#genre:subitems(1,0)} returns "B.C". Assuming a #genre value of "A.B.C, D.E.F", {#genre:subitems(0,1)} returns "A, D". {#genre:subitems(0,2)} returns "A.B, D.E"

sublist(val, start_index, end_index, separator)

class `calibre.utils.formatter_functions.`**BuiltinSublist**

> sublist(val, start_index, end_index, separator) – interpret the value as a list of items separated by *separator*, returning a new list made from the *start_index* to the *end_index* item. The first item is number zero. If an index is negative, then it counts from the end of the list. As a special case, an end_index of zero is assumed to be the length of the list. Examples using basic template mode and assuming that the tags column (which is comma-separated) contains "A, B, C": {tags:sublist(0,1,,)} returns "A". {tags:sublist(-1,0,,)} returns "C". {tags:sublist(0,-1,,)} returns "A, B".

Other

assign(id, val)

class `calibre.utils.formatter_functions.`**BuiltinAssign**

> assign(id, val) – assigns val to id, then returns val. id must be an identifier, not an expression

print(a, b, ...)

class `calibre.utils.formatter_functions.`**BuiltinPrint**

> print(a, b, ...) – prints the arguments to standard output. Unless you start calibre from the command line (calibre-debug -g), the output will go to a black hole.

Recursion

eval(template)

class `calibre.utils.formatter_functions.`**BuiltinEval**

> eval(template) – evaluates the template, passing the local variables (those 'assign'ed to) instead of the book metadata. This permits using the template processor to construct complex results from local variables. Because the { and } characters are special, you must use [[for the { character and]] for the } character; they are converted automatically. Note also that prefixes and suffixes (the |*prefix*|*suffix* syntax) cannot be used in the argument to this function when using template program mode.

template(x)

class `calibre.utils.formatter_functions.`**BuiltinTemplate**

> template(x) – evaluates x as a template. The evaluation is done in its own context, meaning that variables are not shared between the caller and the template evaluation. Because the { and } characters are special, you must use [[for the { character and]] for the } character; they are converted automatically. For example, template('[[title_sort]]') will evaluate the template {title_sort} and return its value. Note also that prefixes and suffixes (the |*prefix*|*suffix* syntax) cannot be used in the argument to this function when using template program mode.

Relational

cmp(x, y, lt, eq, gt)

class `calibre.utils.formatter_functions.`**BuiltinCmp**

> cmp(x, y, lt, eq, gt) – compares x and y after converting both to numbers. Returns lt if x < y. Returns eq if x == y. Otherwise returns gt.

first_matching_cmp(val, cmp1, result1, cmp2, r2, ..., else_result)

class calibre.utils.formatter_functions.**BuiltinFirstMatchingCmp**

first_matching_cmp(val, cmp1, result1, cmp2, r2, ..., else_result) – compares "val < cmpN" in sequence, returning resultN for the first comparison that succeeds. Returns else_result if no comparison succeeds. Example: first_matching_cmp(10,5,"small",10,"middle",15,"large","giant") returns "large". The same example with a first value of 16 returns "giant".

strcmp(x, y, lt, eq, gt)

class calibre.utils.formatter_functions.**BuiltinStrcmp**

strcmp(x, y, lt, eq, gt) – does a case-insensitive comparison of x and y as strings. Returns lt if x < y. Returns eq if x == y. Otherwise returns gt.

String case changes

capitalize(val)

class calibre.utils.formatter_functions.**BuiltinCapitalize**

capitalize(val) – return value of the field capitalized

lowercase(val)

class calibre.utils.formatter_functions.**BuiltinLowercase**

lowercase(val) – return value of the field in lower case

titlecase(val)

class calibre.utils.formatter_functions.**BuiltinTitlecase**

titlecase(val) – return value of the field in title case

uppercase(val)

class calibre.utils.formatter_functions.**BuiltinUppercase**

uppercase(val) – return value of the field in upper case

String manipulation

re(val, pattern, replacement)

class calibre.utils.formatter_functions.**BuiltinRe**

re(val, pattern, replacement) – return the field after applying the regular expression. All instances of *pattern* are replaced with *replacement*. As in all of calibre, these are python-compatible regular expressions

re_group(val, pattern, template_for_group_1, for_group_2, ...)

class calibre.utils.formatter_functions.**BuiltinReGroup**

re_group(val, pattern, template_for_group_1, for_group_2, ...) – return a string made by applying the reqular expression pattern to the val and replacing each matched instance with the string computed by replacing each matched group by the value returned by the corresponding template. The original matched value for the group is available as $. In template program mode, like for the template and the eval functions, you use [[for { and]] for }. The following example in template program mode looks for series with more than one word and uppercases the first word: {series:'re_group($, "(S*)(.*)", "[[$:uppercase()]]", "[[$]]")'}

shorten(val, left chars, middle text, right chars)

class `calibre.utils.formatter_functions.`**`BuiltinShorten`**

> shorten(val, left chars, middle text, right chars) – Return a shortened version of the field, consisting of *left chars* characters from the beginning of the field, followed by *middle text*, followed by *right chars* characters from the end of the string. *Left chars* and *right chars* must be integers. For example, assume the title of the book is *Ancient English Laws in the Times of Ivanhoe*, and you want it to fit in a space of at most 15 characters. If you use {title:shorten(9,-,5)}, the result will be *Ancient E-nhoe*. If the field's length is less than left chars + right chars + the length of *middle text*, then the field will be used intact. For example, the title *The Dome* would not be changed.

strcat(a, b, ...)

class `calibre.utils.formatter_functions.`**`BuiltinStrcat`**

> strcat(a, b, ...) – can take any number of arguments. Returns a string formed by concatenating all the arguments

strcat_max(max, string1, prefix2, string2, ...)

class `calibre.utils.formatter_functions.`**`BuiltinStrcatMax`**

> strcat_max(max, string1, prefix2, string2, ...) – Returns a string formed by concatenating the arguments. The returned value is initialized to string1. *Prefix, string* pairs are added to the end of the value as long as the resulting string length is less than *max*. String1 is returned even if string1 is longer than max. You can pass as many *prefix, string* pairs as you wish.

strlen(a)

class `calibre.utils.formatter_functions.`**`BuiltinStrlen`**

> strlen(a) – Returns the length of the string passed as the argument

substr(str, start, end)

class `calibre.utils.formatter_functions.`**`BuiltinSubstr`**

> substr(str, start, end) – returns the start'th through the end'th characters of str. The first character in str is the zero'th character. If end is negative, then it indicates that many characters counting from the right. If end is zero, then it indicates the last character. For example, substr('12345', 1, 0) returns '2345', and substr('12345', 1, -1) returns '234'.

swap_around_comma(val)

class `calibre.utils.formatter_functions.`**`BuiltinSwapAroundComma`**

> swap_around_comma(val) – given a value of the form "B, A", return "A B". This is most useful for converting names in LN, FN format to FN LN. If there is no comma, the function returns val unchanged

transliterate(a)

class `calibre.utils.formatter_functions.`**`BuiltinTransliterate`**

> transliterate(a) – Returns a string in a latin alphabet formed by approximating the sound of the words in the source string. For example, if the source is "Фёдор Михайлович Достоевский" the function returns "Fiodor Mikhailovich Dostoievskii".

API of the Metadata objects   The python implementation of the template functions is passed in a Metadata object. Knowing it's API is useful if you want to define your own template functions.

class `calibre.ebooks.metadata.book.base.`**`Metadata`**(*title,*   *authors=(u'Unknown',*   *),*
                                                              other=None,   *template_cache=None,*
                                                              formatter=None)

> A class representing all the metadata for a book. The various standard metadata fields are available as attributes

of this object. You can also stick arbitrary attributes onto this object.

Metadata from custom columns should be accessed via the get() method, passing in the lookup name for the column, for example: "#mytags".

Use the *is_null ()* (page 202) method to test if a field is null.

This object also has functions to format fields into strings.

The list of standard metadata fields grows with time is in *STANDARD_METADATA_FIELDS* (page 203).

Please keep the method based API of this class to a minimum. Every method becomes a reserved field name.

is_null (*field*)
> Return True if the value of field is null in this object. 'null' means it is unknown or evaluates to False. So a title of _('Unknown') is null or a language of 'und' is null.
>
> Be careful with numeric fields since this will return True for zero as well as None.
>
> Also returns True if the field does not exist.

deepcopy (*class_generator=<function <lambda>>*)
> Do not use this method unless you know what you are doing, if you want to create a simple clone of this object, use deepcopy_metadata() instead. Class_generator must be a function that returns an instance of Metadata or a subclass of it.

get_identifiers ()
> Return a copy of the identifiers dictionary. The dict is small, and the penalty for using a reference where a copy is needed is large. Also, we don't want any manipulations of the returned dict to show up in the book.

set_identifiers (*identifiers*)
> Set all identifiers. Note that if you previously set ISBN, calling this method will delete it.

set_identifier (*typ, val*)
> If val is empty, deletes identifier of type typ

standard_field_keys ()
> return a list of all possible keys, even if this book doesn't have them

custom_field_keys ()
> return a list of the custom fields in this book

all_field_keys ()
> All field keys known by this instance, even if their value is None

metadata_for_field (*key*)
> return metadata describing a standard or custom field.

all_non_none_fields ()
> Return a dictionary containing all non-None metadata fields, including the custom ones.

get_standard_metadata (*field, make_copy*)
> return field metadata from the field if it is there. Otherwise return None. field is the key name, not the label. Return a copy if requested, just in case the user wants to change values in the dict.

get_all_standard_metadata (*make_copy*)
> return a dict containing all the standard field metadata associated with the book.

get_all_user_metadata (*make_copy*)
> return a dict containing all the custom field metadata associated with the book.

get_user_metadata (*field*, *make_copy*)

return field metadata from the object if it is there. Otherwise return None. field is the key name, not the label. Return a copy if requested, just in case the user wants to change values in the dict.

set_all_user_metadata (*metadata*)

store custom field metadata into the object. Field is the key name not the label

set_user_metadata (*field*, *metadata*)

store custom field metadata for one column into the object. Field is the key name not the label

template_to_attribute (*other*, *ops*)

Takes a list [(src,dest), (src,dest)], evaluates the template in the context of other, then copies the result to self[dest]. This is on a best-efforts basis. Some assignments can make no sense.

smart_update (*other*, *replace_metadata=False*)

Merge the information in *other* into self. In case of conflicts, the information in *other* takes precedence, unless the information in *other* is NULL.

format_field (*key*, *series_with_index=True*)

Returns the tuple (display_name, formatted_value)

to_html ()

A HTML representation of this object.

calibre.ebooks.metadata.book.base.**STANDARD_METADATA_FIELDS**

The set of standard metadata fields.

```
'''
All fields must have a NULL value represented as None for simple types,
an empty list/dictionary for complex types and (None, None) for cover_data
'''

SOCIAL_METADATA_FIELDS = frozenset([
    'tags',                 # Ordered list
    'rating',               # A floating point number between 0 and 10
    'comments',             # A simple HTML enabled string
    'series',               # A simple string
    'series_index',         # A floating point number
    # Of the form { scheme1:value1, scheme2:value2}
    # For example: {'isbn':'123456789', 'doi':'xxxx', ... }
    'identifiers',
])


'''
The list of names that convert to identifiers when in get and set.
'''


TOP_LEVEL_IDENTIFIERS = frozenset([
    'isbn',
])

PUBLICATION_METADATA_FIELDS = frozenset([
    'title',                # title must never be None. Should be _('Unknown')
    # Pseudo field that can be set, but if not set is auto generated
    # from title and languages
    'title_sort',
    'authors',              # Ordered list. Must never be None, can be [_('Unknown')]
    'author_sort_map',      # Map of sort strings for each author
    # Pseudo field that can be set, but if not set is auto generated
    # from authors and languages
```

```
        'author_sort',
        'book_producer',
        'timestamp',          # Dates and times must be timezone aware
        'pubdate',
        'last_modified',
        'rights',
        # So far only known publication type is periodical:calibre
        # If None, means book
        'publication_type',
        'uuid',               # A UUID usually of type 4
        'languages',          # ordered list of languages in this publication
        'publisher',          # Simple string, no special semantics
        # Absolute path to image file encoded in filesystem_encoding
        'cover',
        # Of the form (format, data) where format is, for e.g. 'jpeg', 'png', 'gif'...
        'cover_data',
        # Either thumbnail data, or an object with the attribute
        # image_path which is the path to an image file, encoded
        # in filesystem_encoding
        'thumbnail',
        ])

BOOK_STRUCTURE_FIELDS = frozenset([
        # These are used by code, Null values are None.
        'toc', 'spine', 'guide', 'manifest',
        ])

USER_METADATA_FIELDS = frozenset([
        # A dict of dicts similar to field_metadata. Each field description dict
        # also contains a value field with the key #value#.
        'user_metadata',
])

DEVICE_METADATA_FIELDS = frozenset([
    'device_collections',    # Ordered list of strings
    'lpath',                 # Unicode, / separated
    'size',                  # In bytes
    'mime',                  # Mimetype of the book file being represented

])

CALIBRE_METADATA_FIELDS = frozenset([
    'application_id',    # An application id, currently set to the db_id.
    'db_id',             # the calibre primary key of the item.
    'formats',           # list of formats (extensions) for this book
    # a dict of user category names, where the value is a list of item names
    # from the book that are in that category
    'user_categories',
    # a dict of author to an associated hyperlink
    'author_link_map',

    ]
)

ALL_METADATA_FIELDS =      SOCIAL_METADATA_FIELDS.union(
                           PUBLICATION_METADATA_FIELDS).union(
                           BOOK_STRUCTURE_FIELDS).union(
                           USER_METADATA_FIELDS).union(
```

```
                              DEVICE_METADATA_FIELDS).union(
                              CALIBRE_METADATA_FIELDS)

# All fields except custom fields
STANDARD_METADATA_FIELDS = SOCIAL_METADATA_FIELDS.union(
                              PUBLICATION_METADATA_FIELDS).union(
                              BOOK_STRUCTURE_FIELDS).union(
                              DEVICE_METADATA_FIELDS).union(
                              CALIBRE_METADATA_FIELDS)

# Metadata fields that smart update must do special processing to copy.
SC_FIELDS_NOT_COPIED =     frozenset(['title', 'title_sort', 'authors',
                                      'author_sort', 'author_sort_map',
                                      'cover_data', 'tags', 'languages',
                                      'identifiers'])

# Metadata fields that smart update should copy only if the source is not None
SC_FIELDS_COPY_NOT_NULL = frozenset(['lpath', 'size', 'comments', 'thumbnail'])

# Metadata fields that smart update should copy without special handling
SC_COPYABLE_FIELDS =       SOCIAL_METADATA_FIELDS.union(
                              PUBLICATION_METADATA_FIELDS).union(
                              BOOK_STRUCTURE_FIELDS).union(
                              DEVICE_METADATA_FIELDS).union(
                              CALIBRE_METADATA_FIELDS) - \
                              SC_FIELDS_NOT_COPIED.union(
                              SC_FIELDS_COPY_NOT_NULL)

SERIALIZABLE_FIELDS =      SOCIAL_METADATA_FIELDS.union(
                              USER_METADATA_FIELDS).union(
                              PUBLICATION_METADATA_FIELDS).union(
                              CALIBRE_METADATA_FIELDS).union(
                              DEVICE_METADATA_FIELDS) - \
                              frozenset(['device_collections', 'formats',
                                  'cover_data'])
                              # these are rebuilt when needed
```

Using general program mode

For more complicated template programs, it is sometimes easier to avoid template syntax (all the *{* and *}* characters), instead writing a more classical-looking program. You can do this in calibre by beginning the template with *program:*. In this case, no template processing is done. The special variable *$* is not set. It is up to your program to produce the correct results.

One advantage of *program:* mode is that the brackets are no longer special. For example, it is not necessary to use *[[* and *]]* when using the *template()* function. Another advantage is that program mode templates are compiled to Python and can run much faster than templates in the other two modes. Speed improvement depends on the complexity of the templates; the more complicated the template the more the improvement. Compilation is turned off or on using the tweak `compile_gpm_templates` (Compile General Program Mode templates to Python). The main reason to turn off compilation is if a compiled template does not work, in which case please file a bug report.

The following example is a *program:* mode implementation of a recipe on the MobileRead forum: "Put series into the title, using either initials or a shortened form. Strip leading articles from the series name (any)." For example, for the book The Two Towers in the Lord of the Rings series, the recipe gives *LotR [02] The Two Towers*. Using standard templates, the recipe requires three custom columns and a plugboard, as explained in the following:

The solution requires creating three composite columns. The first column is used to remove the leading articles. The

---

second is used to compute the 'shorten' form. The third is to compute the 'initials' form. Once you have these columns, the plugboard selects between them. You can hide any or all of the three columns on the library view.

First column: Name: #stripped_series. Template: {series:re(^(A|The|An)s+,)||}

Second column (the shortened form): Name: #shortened. Template: {#stripped_series:shorten(4,-,4)}

Third column (the initials form): Name: #initials. Template: {#stripped_series:re(((^s])[^s]+(s|$),1)}

Plugboard expression: Template:{#stripped_series:lookup(.s,#initials,.,#shortened,series)}{series_index:0>2.0f| [|] }{title} Destination field: title

This set of fields and plugboard produces: Series: The Lord of the Rings Series index: 2 Title: The Two Towers Output: LotR [02] The Two Towers

Series: Dahak Series index: 1 Title: Mutineers Moon Output: Dahak [01] Mutineers Moon

Series: Berserkers Series Index: 4 Title: Berserker Throne Output: Bers-kers [04] Berserker Throne

Series: Meg Langslow Mysteries Series Index: 3 Title: Revenge of the Wrought-Iron Flamingos Output: MLM [03] Revenge of the Wrought-Iron Flamingos

The following program produces the same results as the original recipe, using only one custom column to hold the results of a program that computes the special title value:

```
Custom column:
Name: #special_title
Template: (the following with all leading spaces removed)
    program:
    #       compute the equivalent of the composite fields and store them in local variables
        stripped = re(field('series'), '^(A|The|An)\s+', '');
        shortened = shorten(stripped, 4, '-' ,4);
        initials = re(stripped, '[^\w]*(\w?)[^\s]+(\s|$)', '\1');

    #       Format the series index. Ends up as empty if there is no series index.
    #       Note that leading and trailing spaces will be removed by the formatter,
    #       so we cannot add them here. We will do that in the strcat below.
    #       Also note that because we are in 'program' mode, we can freely use
    #       curly brackets in strings, something we cannot do in template mode.
        s_index = template('{series_index:0>2.0f}');

    #       print(stripped, shortened, initials, s_index);

    #       Now concatenate all the bits together. The switch picks between
    #       initials and shortened, depending on whether there is a space
    #       in stripped. We then add the brackets around s_index if it is
    #       not empty. Finally, add the title. As this is the last function in
    #       the program, its value will be returned.
        strcat(
            switch( stripped,
                    '.\s', initials,
                    '.', shortened,
                    field('series')),
            test(s_index, strcat(' [', s_index, '] '), ''),
            field('title'));

Plugboard expression:
Template:{#special_title}
Destination field: title
```

It would be possible to do the above with no custom columns by putting the program into the template box of the plugboard. However, to do so, all comments must be removed because the plugboard text box does not support multi-line editing. It is debatable whether the gain of not having the custom column is worth the vast increase in difficulty caused by the program being one giant line.

User-defined Template Functions

You can add your own functions to the template processor. Such functions are written in python, and can be used in any of the three template programming modes. The functions are added by going to Preferences -> Advanced -> Template Functions. Instructions are shown in that dialog.

Special notes for save/send templates

Special processing is applied when a template is used in a *save to disk* or *send to device* template. The values of the fields are cleaned, replacing characters that are special to file systems with underscores, including slashes. This means that field text cannot be used to create folders. However, slashes are not changed in prefix or suffix strings, so slashes in these strings will cause folders to be created. Because of this, you can create variable-depth folder structure.

For example, assume we want the folder structure *series/series_index - title*, with the caveat that if series does not exist, then the title should be in the top folder. The template to do this is:

```
{series:||/}{series_index:|| - }{title}
```

The slash and the hyphen appear only if series is not empty.

The lookup function lets us do even fancier processing. For example, assume that if a book has a series, then we want the folder structure *series/series index - title.fmt*. If the book does not have a series, then we want the folder structure *genre/author_sort/title.fmt*. If the book has no genre, we want to use 'Unknown'. We want two completely different paths, depending on the value of series.

To accomplish this, we:

1. Create a composite field (call it AA) containing `{series}/{series_index} - {title'}`. If the series is not empty, then this template will produce *series/series_index - title*.

2. Create a composite field (call it BB) containing `{#genre:ifempty(Unknown)}/{author_sort}/{titl` This template produces *genre/author_sort/title*, where an empty genre is replaced with *Unknown*.

3. Set the save template to `{series:lookup(.,AA,BB)}`. This template chooses composite field AA if series is not empty, and composite field BB if series is empty. We therefore have two completely different save paths, depending on whether or not *series* is empty.

Templates and Plugboards

Plugboards are used for changing the metadata written into books during send-to-device and save-to-disk operations. A plugboard permits you to specify a template to provide the data to write into the book's metadata. You can use plugboards to modify the following fields: authors, author_sort, language, publisher, tags, title, title_sort. This feature helps people who want to use different metadata in books on devices to solve sorting or display issues.

When you create a plugboard, you specify the format and device for which the plugboard is to be used. A special device is provided, save_to_disk, that is used when saving formats (as opposed to sending them to a device). Once you have chosen the format and device, you choose the metadata fields to change, providing templates to supply the new values. These templates are *connected* to their destination fields, hence the name *plugboards*. You can, of course, use composite columns in these templates.

When a plugboard might apply (content server, save to disk, or send to device), calibre searches the defined plugboards to choose the correct one for the given format and device. For example, to find the appropriate plugboard for an EPUB book being sent to an ANDROID device, calibre searches the plugboards using the following search order:

- a plugboard with an exact match on format and device, e.g., EPUB and ANDROID

- a plugboard with an exact match on format and the special any device choice, e.g., EPUB and any device

- a plugboard with the special any format choice and an exact match on device, e.g., any format and ANDROID

- a plugboard with any format and any device

The tags and authors fields have special treatment, because both of these fields can hold more than one item. A book can have many tags and many authors. When you specify that one of these two fields is to be changed, the template's result is examined to see if more than one item is there. For tags, the result is cut apart wherever calibre finds a comma. For example, if the template produces the value Thriller, Horror, then the result will be two tags, Thriller and Horror. There is no way to put a comma in the middle of a tag.

The same thing happens for authors, but using a different character for the cut, a & (ampersand) instead of a comma. For example, if the template produces the value Blogs, Joe&Posts, Susan, then the book will end up with two authors, Blogs, Joe and Posts, Susan. If the template produces the value Blogs, Joe;Posts, Susan, then the book will have one author with a rather strange name.

Plugboards affect the metadata written into the book when it is saved to disk or written to the device. Plugboards do not affect the metadata used by save to disk and send to device to create the file names. Instead, file names are constructed using the templates entered on the appropriate preferences window.

Helpful Tips

You might find the following tips useful.

- Create a custom composite column to test templates. Once you have the column, you can change its template simply by double-clicking on the column. Hide the column when you are not testing.

- Templates can use other templates by referencing a composite custom column.

- In a plugboard, you can set a field to empty (or whatever is equivalent to empty) by using the special template { }. This template will always evaluate to an empty string.

- The technique described above to show numbers even if they have a zero value works with the standard field series_index.

Reference for all built-in template language functions

Here, we document all the built-in functions available in the calibre template language. Every function is implemented as a class in python and you can click the source links to see the source code, in case the documentation is insufficient. The functions are arranged in logical groups by type.

Arithmetic

add(x, y)
class calibre.utils.formatter_functions.**BuiltinAdd**
> add(x, y) – returns x + y. Throws an exception if either x or y are not numbers.

divide(x, y)
class calibre.utils.formatter_functions.**BuiltinDivide**
> divide(x, y) – returns x / y. Throws an exception if either x or y are not numbers.

multiply(x, y)
class calibre.utils.formatter_functions.**BuiltinMultiply**
> multiply(x, y) – returns x * y. Throws an exception if either x or y are not numbers.

subtract(x, y)
class calibre.utils.formatter_functions.**BuiltinSubtract**
> subtract(x, y) – returns x - y. Throws an exception if either x or y are not numbers.

Boolean

and(value, value, ...)
class calibre.utils.formatter_functions.**BuiltinAnd**
> and(value, value, ...) – returns the string "1" if all values are not empty, otherwise returns the empty string. This function works well with test or first_non_empty. You can have as many values as you want.

not(value)
class calibre.utils.formatter_functions.**BuiltinNot**
> not(value) – returns the string "1" if the value is empty, otherwise returns the empty string. This function works well with test or first_non_empty. You can have as many values as you want.

or(value, value, ...)
class calibre.utils.formatter_functions.**BuiltinOr**
> or(value, value, ...) – returns the string "1" if any value is not empty, otherwise returns the empty string. This function works well with test or first_non_empty. You can have as many values as you want.

Date functions

days_between(date1, date2)
class calibre.utils.formatter_functions.**BuiltinDaysBetween**
> days_between(date1, date2) – return the number of days between date1 and date2. The number is positive if date1 is greater than date2, otherwise negative. If either date1 or date2 are not dates, the function returns the empty string.

today()
class calibre.utils.formatter_functions.**BuiltinToday**
> today() – return a date string for today. This value is designed for use in format_date or days_between, but can be manipulated like any other string. The date is in ISO format.

Formatting values

finish_formatting(val, fmt, prefix, suffix)

class calibre.utils.formatter_functions.**BuiltinFinishFormatting**

> finish_formatting(val, fmt, prefix, suffix) – apply the format, prefix, and suffix to a value in the same way as done in a template like *{series_index:05.2f| - |- }*. For example, the following program produces the same output as the above template: program: finish_formatting(field("series_index"), "05.2f", " - ", " - ")

format_date(val, format_string)

class calibre.utils.formatter_functions.**BuiltinFormatDate**

> format_date(val, format_string) – format the value, which must be a date, using the format_string, returning a string. The formatting codes are: d : the day as number without a leading zero (1 to 31) dd : the day as number with a leading zero (01 to 31) ddd : the abbreviated localized day name (e.g. "Mon" to "Sun"). dddd : the long localized day name (e.g. "Monday" to "Sunday"). M : the month as number without a leading zero (1 to 12). MM : the month as number with a leading zero (01 to 12) MMM : the abbreviated localized month name (e.g. "Jan" to "Dec"). MMMM : the long localized month name (e.g. "January" to "December"). yy : the year as two digit number (00 to 99). yyyy : the year as four digit number. h : the hours without a leading 0 (0 to 11 or 0 to 23, depending on am/pm) hh : the hours with a leading 0 (00 to 11 or 00 to 23, depending on am/pm) m : the minutes without a leading 0 (0 to 59) mm : the minutes with a leading 0 (00 to 59) s : the seconds without a leading 0 (0 to 59) ss : the seconds with a leading 0 (00 to 59) ap : use a 12-hour clock instead of a 24-hour clock, with "ap" replaced by the localized string for am or pm AP : use a 12-hour clock instead of a 24-hour clock, with "AP" replaced by the localized string for AM or PM iso : the date with time and timezone. Must be the only format present

format_number(v, template)

class calibre.utils.formatter_functions.**BuiltinFormatNumber**

> format_number(v, template) – format the number v using a python formatting template such as "{0:5.2f}" or "{0:,d}" or "${0:5,.2f}". The field_name part of the template must be a 0 (zero) (the "{0:" in the above examples). See the template language and python documentation for more examples. Returns the empty string if formatting fails.

human_readable(v)

class calibre.utils.formatter_functions.**BuiltinHumanReadable**

> human_readable(v) – return a string representing the number v in KB, MB, GB, etc.

Get values from metadata

approximate_formats()

class calibre.utils.formatter_functions.**BuiltinApproximateFormats**

> approximate_formats() – return a comma-separated list of formats that at one point were associated with the book. There is no guarantee that this list is correct, although it probably is. This function can be called in template program mode using the template "{:'approximate_formats()'}". Note that format names are always uppercase, as in EPUB. This function works only in the GUI. If you want to use these values in save-to-disk or send-to-device templates then you must make a custom "Column built from other columns", use the function in that column's template, and use that column's value in your save/send templates

author_links(val_separator, pair_separator)

class `calibre.utils.formatter_functions.`**BuiltinAuthorLinks**

author_links(val_separator, pair_separator) – returns a string containing a list of authors and that author's link values in the form author1 val_separator author1link pair_separator author2 val_separator author2link etc. An author is separated from its link value by the val_separator string with no added spaces. author:linkvalue pairs are separated by the pair_separator string argument with no added spaces. It is up to you to choose separator strings that do not occur in author names or links. An author is included even if the author link is empty.

author_sorts(val_separator)

class `calibre.utils.formatter_functions.`**BuiltinAuthorSorts**

author_sorts(val_separator) – returns a string containing a list of author's sort values for the authors of the book. The sort is the one in the author metadata (different from the author_sort in books). The returned list has the form author sort 1 val_separator author sort 2 etc. The author sort values in this list are in the same order as the authors of the book. If you want spaces around val_separator then include them in the separator string

booksize()

class `calibre.utils.formatter_functions.`**BuiltinBooksize**

booksize() – return value of the size field. This function works only in the GUI. If you want to use this value in save-to-disk or send-to-device templates then you must make a custom "Column built from other columns", use the function in that column's template, and use that column's value in your save/send templates

current_library_name()

class `calibre.utils.formatter_functions.`**BuiltinCurrentLibraryName**

current_library_name() – return the last name on the path to the current calibre library. This function can be called in template program mode using the template "{:'current_library_name()'}".

current_library_path()

class `calibre.utils.formatter_functions.`**BuiltinCurrentLibraryPath**

current_library_path() – return the path to the current calibre library. This function can be called in template program mode using the template "{:'current_library_path()'}".

field(name)

class `calibre.utils.formatter_functions.`**BuiltinField**

field(name) – returns the metadata field named by name

formats_modtimes(date_format)

class `calibre.utils.formatter_functions.`**BuiltinFormatsModtimes**

formats_modtimes(date_format) – return a comma-separated list of colon_separated items representing modification times for the formats of a book. The date_format parameter specifies how the date is to be formatted. See the date_format function for details. You can use the select function to get the mod time for a specific format. Note that format names are always uppercase, as in EPUB.

formats_paths()

class `calibre.utils.formatter_functions.`**BuiltinFormatsPaths**

formats_paths() – return a comma-separated list of colon_separated items representing full path to the formats of a book. You can use the select function to get the path for a specific format. Note that format names are always uppercase, as in EPUB.

formats_sizes()

class calibre.utils.formatter_functions.**BuiltinFormatsSizes**

> formats_sizes() – return a comma-separated list of colon_separated items representing sizes in bytes of the formats of a book. You can use the select function to get the size for a specific format. Note that format names are always uppercase, as in EPUB.

has_cover()

class calibre.utils.formatter_functions.**BuiltinHasCover**

> has_cover() – return Yes if the book has a cover, otherwise return the empty string

language_codes(lang_strings)

class calibre.utils.formatter_functions.**BuiltinLanguageCodes**

> language_codes(lang_strings) – return the language codes for the strings passed in lang_strings. The strings must be in the language of the current locale. Lang_strings is a comma-separated list.

language_strings(lang_codes, localize)

class calibre.utils.formatter_functions.**BuiltinLanguageStrings**

> language_strings(lang_codes, localize) – return the strings for the language codes passed in lang_codes. If localize is zero, return the strings in English. If localize is not zero, return the strings in the language of the current locale. Lang_codes is a comma-separated list.

ondevice()

class calibre.utils.formatter_functions.**BuiltinOndevice**

> ondevice() – return Yes if ondevice is set, otherwise return the empty string. This function works only in the GUI. If you want to use this value in save-to-disk or send-to-device templates then you must make a custom "Column built from other columns", use the function in that column's template, and use that column's value in your save/send templates

raw_field(name)

class calibre.utils.formatter_functions.**BuiltinRawField**

> raw_field(name) – returns the metadata field named by name without applying any formatting.

raw_list(name, separator)

class calibre.utils.formatter_functions.**BuiltinRawList**

> raw_list(name, separator) – returns the metadata list named by name without applying any formatting or sorting and with items separated by separator.

series_sort()

class calibre.utils.formatter_functions.**BuiltinSeriesSort**

> series_sort() – return the series sort value

user_categories()

class calibre.utils.formatter_functions.**BuiltinUserCategories**

> user_categories() – return a comma-separated list of the user categories that contain this book. This function works only in the GUI. If you want to use these values in save-to-disk or send-to-device templates then you must make a custom "Column built from other columns", use the function in that column's template, and use that column's value in your save/send templates

virtual_libraries()

class calibre.utils.formatter_functions.**BuiltinVirtualLibraries**

> virtual_libraries() – return a comma-separated list of virtual libraries that contain this book. This function works only in the GUI. If you want to use these values in save-to-disk or send-to-device templates then you must make a custom "Column built from other columns", use the function in that column's template, and use that column's value in your save/send templates

If-then-else

contains(val, pattern, text if match, text if not match)

class calibre.utils.formatter_functions.**BuiltinContains**

> contains(val, pattern, text if match, text if not match) – checks if field contains matches for the regular expression *pattern*. Returns *text if match* if matches are found, otherwise it returns *text if no match*

ifempty(val, text if empty)

class calibre.utils.formatter_functions.**BuiltinIfempty**

> ifempty(val, text if empty) – return val if val is not empty, otherwise return *text if empty*

test(val, text if not empty, text if empty)

class calibre.utils.formatter_functions.**BuiltinTest**

> test(val, text if not empty, text if empty) – return *text if not empty* if the field is not empty, otherwise return *text if empty*

Iterating over values

first_non_empty(value, value, ...)

class calibre.utils.formatter_functions.**BuiltinFirstNonEmpty**

> first_non_empty(value, value, ...) – returns the first value that is not empty. If all values are empty, then the empty value is returned. You can have as many values as you want.

lookup(val, pattern, field, pattern, field, ..., else_field)

class calibre.utils.formatter_functions.**BuiltinLookup**

> lookup(val, pattern, field, pattern, field, ..., else_field) – like switch, except the arguments are field (metadata) names, not text. The value of the appropriate field will be fetched and used. Note that because composite columns are fields, you can use this function in one composite field to use the value of some other composite field. This is extremely useful when constructing variable save paths

switch(val, pattern, value, pattern, value, ..., else_value)

class calibre.utils.formatter_functions.**BuiltinSwitch**

> switch(val, pattern, value, pattern, value, ..., else_value) – for each *pattern, value* pair, checks if the field matches the regular expression *pattern* and if so, returns that *value*. If no pattern matches, then else_value is returned. You can have as many *pattern, value* pairs as you want

List lookup

identifier_in_list(val, id, found_val, not_found_val)

class `calibre.utils.formatter_functions.`**`BuiltinIdentifierInList`**

identifier_in_list(val, id, found_val, not_found_val) – treat val as a list of identifiers separated by commas, comparing the string against each value in the list. An identifier has the format "identifier:value". The id parameter should be either "id" or "id:regexp". The first case matches if there is any identifier with that id. The second case matches if the regexp matches the identifier's value. If there is a match, return found_val, otherwise return not_found_val.

in_list(val, separator, pattern, found_val, not_found_val)

class `calibre.utils.formatter_functions.`**`BuiltinInList`**

in_list(val, separator, pattern, found_val, not_found_val) – treat val as a list of items separated by separator, comparing the pattern against each value in the list. If the pattern matches a value, return found_val, otherwise return not_found_val.

list_item(val, index, separator)

class `calibre.utils.formatter_functions.`**`BuiltinListitem`**

list_item(val, index, separator) – interpret the value as a list of items separated by *separator*, returning the *index'th item. The first item is number zero. The last item can be returned using 'list_item(-1,separator). If* the item is not in the list, then the empty value is returned. The separator has the same meaning as in the count function.

select(val, key)

class `calibre.utils.formatter_functions.`**`BuiltinSelect`**

select(val, key) – interpret the value as a comma-separated list of items, with the items being "id:value". Find the pair with the id equal to key, and return the corresponding value.

str_in_list(val, separator, string, found_val, not_found_val)

class `calibre.utils.formatter_functions.`**`BuiltinStrInList`**

str_in_list(val, separator, string, found_val, not_found_val) – treat val as a list of items separated by separator, comparing the string against each value in the list. If the string matches a value, return found_val, otherwise return not_found_val. If the string contains separators, then it is also treated as a list and each value is checked.

List manipulation

count(val, separator)

class `calibre.utils.formatter_functions.`**`BuiltinCount`**

count(val, separator) – interprets the value as a list of items separated by *separator*, returning the number of items in the list. Most lists use a comma as the separator, but authors uses an ampersand. Examples: {tags:count(,)}, {authors:count(&)}

list_difference(list1, list2, separator)

class `calibre.utils.formatter_functions.`**`BuiltinListDifference`**

list_difference(list1, list2, separator) – return a list made by removing from list1 any item found in list2, using a case-insensitive compare. The items in list1 and list2 are separated by separator, as are the items in the returned list.

list_equals(list1, sep1, list2, sep2, yes_val, no_val)

class `calibre.utils.formatter_functions.`**`BuiltinListEquals`**

> list_equals(list1, sep1, list2, sep2, yes_val, no_val) – return yes_val if list1 and list2 contain the same items, otherwise return no_val. The items are determined by splitting each list using the appropriate separator character (sep1 or sep2). The order of items in the lists is not relevant. The compare is case insensitive.

list_intersection(list1, list2, separator)

class `calibre.utils.formatter_functions.`**`BuiltinListIntersection`**

> list_intersection(list1, list2, separator) – return a list made by removing from list1 any item not found in list2, using a case-insensitive compare. The items in list1 and list2 are separated by separator, as are the items in the returned list.

list_re(src_list, separator, include_re, opt_replace)

class `calibre.utils.formatter_functions.`**`BuiltinListRe`**

> list_re(src_list, separator, include_re, opt_replace) – Construct a list by first separating src_list into items using the separator character. For each item in the list, check if it matches include_re. If it does, then add it to the list to be returned. If opt_replace is not the empty string, then apply the replacement before adding the item to the returned list.

list_re_group(src_list, separator, include_re, search_re, group_1_template, ...)

class `calibre.utils.formatter_functions.`**`BuiltinListReGroup`**

> list_re_group(src_list, separator, include_re, search_re, group_1_template, ...) – Like list_re except replacements are not optional. It uses re_group(list_item, search_re, group_1_template, ...) when doing the replacements on the resulting list.

list_sort(list, direction, separator)

class `calibre.utils.formatter_functions.`**`BuiltinListSort`**

> list_sort(list, direction, separator) – return list sorted using a case-insensitive sort. If direction is zero, the list is sorted ascending, otherwise descending. The list items are separated by separator, as are the items in the returned list.

list_union(list1, list2, separator)

class `calibre.utils.formatter_functions.`**`BuiltinListUnion`**

> list_union(list1, list2, separator) – return a list made by merging the items in list1 and list2, removing duplicate items using a case-insensitive compare. If items differ in case, the one in list1 is used. The items in list1 and list2 are separated by separator, as are the items in the returned list.

subitems(val, start_index, end_index)

class `calibre.utils.formatter_functions.`**`BuiltinSubitems`**

> subitems(val, start_index, end_index) – This function is used to break apart lists of items such as genres. It interprets the value as a comma-separated list of items, where each item is a period-separated list. Returns a new list made by first finding all the period-separated items, then for each such item extracting the *start_index* to the *end_index* components, then combining the results back together. The first component in a period-separated list has an index of zero. If an index is negative, then it counts from the end of the list. As a special case, an end_index of zero is assumed to be the length of the list. Example using basic template mode and assuming a #genre value of "A.B.C": {#genre:subitems(0,1)} returns "A". {#genre:subitems(0,2)} returns "A.B". {#genre:subitems(1,0)} returns "B.C". Assuming a #genre value of "A.B.C, D.E.F", {#genre:subitems(0,1)} returns "A, D". {#genre:subitems(0,2)} returns "A.B, D.E"

sublist(val, start_index, end_index, separator)

class `calibre.utils.formatter_functions.`**`BuiltinSublist`**

> sublist(val, start_index, end_index, separator) – interpret the value as a list of items separated by *separator*, returning a new list made from the *start_index* to the *end_index* item. The first item is number zero. If an index is negative, then it counts from the end of the list. As a special case, an end_index of zero is assumed to be the length of the list. Examples using basic template mode and assuming that the tags column (which is comma-separated) contains "A, B, C": {tags:sublist(0,1,,)} returns "A". {tags:sublist(-1,0,,)} returns "C". {tags:sublist(0,-1,,)} returns "A, B".

Other

assign(id, val)

class `calibre.utils.formatter_functions.`**`BuiltinAssign`**

> assign(id, val) – assigns val to id, then returns val. id must be an identifier, not an expression

print(a, b, ...)

class `calibre.utils.formatter_functions.`**`BuiltinPrint`**

> print(a, b, ...) – prints the arguments to standard output. Unless you start calibre from the command line (calibre-debug -g), the output will go to a black hole.

Recursion

eval(template)

class `calibre.utils.formatter_functions.`**`BuiltinEval`**

> eval(template) – evaluates the template, passing the local variables (those 'assign'ed to) instead of the book metadata. This permits using the template processor to construct complex results from local variables. Because the { and } characters are special, you must use [[for the { character and]] for the } character; they are converted automatically. Note also that prefixes and suffixes (the *prefix|suffix* syntax) cannot be used in the argument to this function when using template program mode.

template(x)

class `calibre.utils.formatter_functions.`**`BuiltinTemplate`**

> template(x) – evaluates x as a template. The evaluation is done in its own context, meaning that variables are not shared between the caller and the template evaluation. Because the { and } characters are special, you must use [[for the { character and]] for the } character; they are converted automatically. For example, template('[[title_sort]]') will evaluate the template {title_sort} and return its value. Note also that prefixes and suffixes (the *prefix|suffix* syntax) cannot be used in the argument to this function when using template program mode.

Relational

cmp(x, y, lt, eq, gt)

class `calibre.utils.formatter_functions.`**`BuiltinCmp`**

> cmp(x, y, lt, eq, gt) – compares x and y after converting both to numbers. Returns lt if x < y. Returns eq if x == y. Otherwise returns gt.

first_matching_cmp(val, cmp1, result1, cmp2, r2, ..., else_result)

class calibre.utils.formatter_functions.**BuiltinFirstMatchingCmp**

> first_matching_cmp(val, cmp1, result1, cmp2, r2, ..., else_result) – compares "val < cmpN" in sequence, returning resultN for the first comparison that succeeds. Returns else_result if no comparison succeeds. Example: first_matching_cmp(10,5,"small",10,"middle",15,"large","giant") returns "large". The same example with a first value of 16 returns "giant".

strcmp(x, y, lt, eq, gt)

class calibre.utils.formatter_functions.**BuiltinStrcmp**

> strcmp(x, y, lt, eq, gt) – does a case-insensitive comparison of x and y as strings. Returns lt if x < y. Returns eq if x == y. Otherwise returns gt.

String case changes

capitalize(val)

class calibre.utils.formatter_functions.**BuiltinCapitalize**

> capitalize(val) – return value of the field capitalized

lowercase(val)

class calibre.utils.formatter_functions.**BuiltinLowercase**

> lowercase(val) – return value of the field in lower case

titlecase(val)

class calibre.utils.formatter_functions.**BuiltinTitlecase**

> titlecase(val) – return value of the field in title case

uppercase(val)

class calibre.utils.formatter_functions.**BuiltinUppercase**

> uppercase(val) – return value of the field in upper case

String manipulation

re(val, pattern, replacement)

class calibre.utils.formatter_functions.**BuiltinRe**

> re(val, pattern, replacement) – return the field after applying the regular expression. All instances of *pattern* are replaced with *replacement*. As in all of calibre, these are python-compatible regular expressions

re_group(val, pattern, template_for_group_1, for_group_2, ...)

class calibre.utils.formatter_functions.**BuiltinReGroup**

> re_group(val, pattern, template_for_group_1, for_group_2, ...) – return a string made by applying the regular expression pattern to the val and replacing each matched instance with the string computed by replacing each matched group by the value returned by the corresponding template. The original matched value for the group is available as $. In template program mode, like for the template and the eval functions, you use [[for { and]] for }. The following example in template program mode looks for series with more than one word and uppercases the first word: {series:'re_group($, "(S*)(.*)", "[[$:uppercase()]]", "[[$]]")'}

shorten(val, left chars, middle text, right chars)

class `calibre.utils.formatter_functions.`**`BuiltinShorten`**

> shorten(val, left chars, middle text, right chars) – Return a shortened version of the field, consisting of *left chars* characters from the beginning of the field, followed by *middle text*, followed by *right chars* characters from the end of the string. *Left chars* and *right chars* must be integers. For example, assume the title of the book is *Ancient English Laws in the Times of Ivanhoe*, and you want it to fit in a space of at most 15 characters. If you use {title:shorten(9,-,5)}, the result will be *Ancient E-nhoe*. If the field's length is less than left chars + right chars + the length of *middle text*, then the field will be used intact. For example, the title *The Dome* would not be changed.

strcat(a, b, ...)

class `calibre.utils.formatter_functions.`**`BuiltinStrcat`**

> strcat(a, b, ...) – can take any number of arguments. Returns a string formed by concatenating all the arguments

strcat_max(max, string1, prefix2, string2, ...)

class `calibre.utils.formatter_functions.`**`BuiltinStrcatMax`**

> strcat_max(max, string1, prefix2, string2, ...) – Returns a string formed by concatenating the arguments. The returned value is initialized to string1. *Prefix, string* pairs are added to the end of the value as long as the resulting string length is less than *max*. String1 is returned even if string1 is longer than max. You can pass as many *prefix, string* pairs as you wish.

strlen(a)

class `calibre.utils.formatter_functions.`**`BuiltinStrlen`**

> strlen(a) – Returns the length of the string passed as the argument

substr(str, start, end)

class `calibre.utils.formatter_functions.`**`BuiltinSubstr`**

> substr(str, start, end) – returns the start'th through the end'th characters of str. The first character in str is the zero'th character. If end is negative, then it indicates that many characters counting from the right. If end is zero, then it indicates the last character. For example, substr('12345', 1, 0) returns '2345', and substr('12345', 1, -1) returns '234'.

swap_around_comma(val)

class `calibre.utils.formatter_functions.`**`BuiltinSwapAroundComma`**

> swap_around_comma(val) – given a value of the form "B, A", return "A B". This is most useful for converting names in LN, FN format to FN LN. If there is no comma, the function returns val unchanged

transliterate(a)

class `calibre.utils.formatter_functions.`**`BuiltinTransliterate`**

> transliterate(a) – Returns a string in a latin alphabet formed by approximating the sound of the words in the source string. For example, if the source is "Фёдор Михайлович Достоевский" the function returns "Fiodor Mikhailovich Dostoievskii".

API of the Metadata objects The python implementation of the template functions is passed in a Metadata object. Knowing it's API is useful if you want to define your own template functions.

class `calibre.ebooks.metadata.book.base.`**`Metadata`** (*title*, *authors=(u'Unknown'*, *)*, *other=None*, *template_cache=None*, *formatter=None*)

> A class representing all the metadata for a book. The various standard metadata fields are available as attributes

of this object. You can also stick arbitrary attributes onto this object.

Metadata from custom columns should be accessed via the get() method, passing in the lookup name for the column, for example: "#mytags".

Use the `is_null()` (page 202) method to test if a field is null.

This object also has functions to format fields into strings.

The list of standard metadata fields grows with time is in `STANDARD_METADATA_FIELDS` (page 203).

Please keep the method based API of this class to a minimum. Every method becomes a reserved field name.

is_null (*field*)
> Return True if the value of field is null in this object. 'null' means it is unknown or evaluates to False. So a title of _('Unknown') is null or a language of 'und' is null.

> Be careful with numeric fields since this will return True for zero as well as None.

> Also returns True if the field does not exist.

deepcopy (*class_generator=<function <lambda>>*)
> Do not use this method unless you know what you are doing, if you want to create a simple clone of this object, use `deepcopy_metadata()` instead. Class_generator must be a function that returns an instance of Metadata or a subclass of it.

get_identifiers ()
> Return a copy of the identifiers dictionary. The dict is small, and the penalty for using a reference where a copy is needed is large. Also, we don't want any manipulations of the returned dict to show up in the book.

set_identifiers (*identifiers*)
> Set all identifiers. Note that if you previously set ISBN, calling this method will delete it.

set_identifier (*typ*, *val*)
> If val is empty, deletes identifier of type typ

standard_field_keys ()
> return a list of all possible keys, even if this book doesn't have them

custom_field_keys ()
> return a list of the custom fields in this book

all_field_keys ()
> All field keys known by this instance, even if their value is None

metadata_for_field (*key*)
> return metadata describing a standard or custom field.

all_non_none_fields ()
> Return a dictionary containing all non-None metadata fields, including the custom ones.

get_standard_metadata (*field*, *make_copy*)
> return field metadata from the field if it is there. Otherwise return None. field is the key name, not the label. Return a copy if requested, just in case the user wants to change values in the dict.

get_all_standard_metadata (*make_copy*)
> return a dict containing all the standard field metadata associated with the book.

get_all_user_metadata (*make_copy*)
> return a dict containing all the custom field metadata associated with the book.

get_user_metadata (*field*, *make_copy*)

> return field metadata from the object if it is there. Otherwise return None. field is the key name, not the label. Return a copy if requested, just in case the user wants to change values in the dict.

set_all_user_metadata (*metadata*)

> store custom field metadata into the object. Field is the key name not the label

set_user_metadata (*field*, *metadata*)

> store custom field metadata for one column into the object. Field is the key name not the label

template_to_attribute (*other*, *ops*)

> Takes a list [(src,dest), (src,dest)], evaluates the template in the context of other, then copies the result to self[dest]. This is on a best-efforts basis. Some assignments can make no sense.

smart_update (*other*, *replace_metadata=False*)

> Merge the information in *other* into self. In case of conflicts, the information in *other* takes precedence, unless the information in *other* is NULL.

format_field (*key*, *series_with_index=True*)

> Returns the tuple (display_name, formatted_value)

to_html ()

> A HTML representation of this object.

calibre.ebooks.metadata.book.base.**STANDARD_METADATA_FIELDS**

> The set of standard metadata fields.

```
'''
All fields must have a NULL value represented as None for simple types,
an empty list/dictionary for complex types and (None, None) for cover_data
'''

SOCIAL_METADATA_FIELDS = frozenset([
    'tags',              # Ordered list
    'rating',            # A floating point number between 0 and 10
    'comments',          # A simple HTML enabled string
    'series',            # A simple string
    'series_index',      # A floating point number
    # Of the form { scheme1:value1, scheme2:value2}
    # For example: {'isbn':'123456789', 'doi':'xxxx', ... }
    'identifiers',
])


'''
The list of names that convert to identifiers when in get and set.
'''


TOP_LEVEL_IDENTIFIERS = frozenset([
    'isbn',
])

PUBLICATION_METADATA_FIELDS = frozenset([
    'title',             # title must never be None. Should be _('Unknown')
    # Pseudo field that can be set, but if not set is auto generated
    # from title and languages
    'title_sort',
    'authors',           # Ordered list. Must never be None, can be [_('Unknown')]
    'author_sort_map',   # Map of sort strings for each author
    # Pseudo field that can be set, but if not set is auto generated
    # from authors and languages
```

```
            'author_sort',
            'book_producer',
            'timestamp',          # Dates and times must be timezone aware
            'pubdate',
            'last_modified',
            'rights',
            # So far only known publication type is periodical:calibre
            # If None, means book
            'publication_type',
            'uuid',               # A UUID usually of type 4
            'languages',          # ordered list of languages in this publication
            'publisher',          # Simple string, no special semantics
            # Absolute path to image file encoded in filesystem_encoding
            'cover',
            # Of the form (format, data) where format is, for e.g. 'jpeg', 'png', 'gif'...
            'cover_data',
            # Either thumbnail data, or an object with the attribute
            # image_path which is the path to an image file, encoded
            # in filesystem_encoding
            'thumbnail',
            ])

BOOK_STRUCTURE_FIELDS = frozenset([
            # These are used by code, Null values are None.
            'toc', 'spine', 'guide', 'manifest',
            ])

USER_METADATA_FIELDS = frozenset([
            # A dict of dicts similar to field_metadata. Each field description dict
            # also contains a value field with the key #value#.
            'user_metadata',
])

DEVICE_METADATA_FIELDS = frozenset([
            'device_collections',    # Ordered list of strings
            'lpath',                 # Unicode, / separated
            'size',                  # In bytes
            'mime',                  # Mimetype of the book file being represented

])

CALIBRE_METADATA_FIELDS = frozenset([
            'application_id',    # An application id, currently set to the db_id.
            'db_id',             # the calibre primary key of the item.
            'formats',           # list of formats (extensions) for this book
            # a dict of user category names, where the value is a list of item names
            # from the book that are in that category
            'user_categories',
            # a dict of author to an associated hyperlink
            'author_link_map',


            ]
)


ALL_METADATA_FIELDS =        SOCIAL_METADATA_FIELDS.union(
                             PUBLICATION_METADATA_FIELDS).union(
                             BOOK_STRUCTURE_FIELDS).union(
                             USER_METADATA_FIELDS).union(
```

```
                               DEVICE_METADATA_FIELDS).union(
                               CALIBRE_METADATA_FIELDS)

# All fields except custom fields
STANDARD_METADATA_FIELDS = SOCIAL_METADATA_FIELDS.union(
                               PUBLICATION_METADATA_FIELDS).union(
                               BOOK_STRUCTURE_FIELDS).union(
                               DEVICE_METADATA_FIELDS).union(
                               CALIBRE_METADATA_FIELDS)

# Metadata fields that smart update must do special processing to copy.
SC_FIELDS_NOT_COPIED =     frozenset(['title', 'title_sort', 'authors',
                                   'author_sort', 'author_sort_map',
                                   'cover_data', 'tags', 'languages',
                                   'identifiers'])

# Metadata fields that smart update should copy only if the source is not None
SC_FIELDS_COPY_NOT_NULL =  frozenset(['lpath', 'size', 'comments', 'thumbnail'])

# Metadata fields that smart update should copy without special handling
SC_COPYABLE_FIELDS =       SOCIAL_METADATA_FIELDS.union(
                               PUBLICATION_METADATA_FIELDS).union(
                               BOOK_STRUCTURE_FIELDS).union(
                               DEVICE_METADATA_FIELDS).union(
                               CALIBRE_METADATA_FIELDS) - \
                               SC_FIELDS_NOT_COPIED.union(
                               SC_FIELDS_COPY_NOT_NULL)

SERIALIZABLE_FIELDS =      SOCIAL_METADATA_FIELDS.union(
                               USER_METADATA_FIELDS).union(
                               PUBLICATION_METADATA_FIELDS).union(
                               CALIBRE_METADATA_FIELDS).union(
                               DEVICE_METADATA_FIELDS) - \
                               frozenset(['device_collections', 'formats',
                                   'cover_data'])
                               # these are rebuilt when needed
```

1.9.5 All about using regular expressions in calibre

Regular expressions are features used in many places in calibre to perform sophisticated manipulation of ebook content and metadata. This tutorial is a gentle introduction to getting you started with using regular expressions in calibre.

Contents

First, a word of warning and a word of courage

This is, inevitably, going to be somewhat technical- after all, regular expressions are a technical tool for doing technical stuff. I'm going to have to use some jargon and concepts that may seem complicated or convoluted. I'm going to try to explain those concepts as clearly as I can, but really can't do without using them at all. That being said, don't be discouraged by any jargon, as I've tried to explain everything new. And while regular expressions themselves may seem like an arcane, black magic (or, to be more prosaic, a random string of mumbo-jumbo letters and signs), I promise that they are not all that complicated. Even those who understand regular expressions really well have trouble reading the more complex ones, but writing them isn't as difficult- you construct the expression step by step. So, take a step and follow me into the rabbit hole.

Where in calibre can you use regular expressions?

There are a few places calibre uses regular expressions. There's the Search & Replace in conversion options, metadata detection from filenames in the import settings and Search & Replace when editing the metadata of books in bulk. The calibre book editor can also use regular expressions in its search and replace feature.

What on earth *is* a regular expression?

A regular expression is a way to describe sets of strings. A single regular expression can *match* a number of different strings. This is what makes regular expression so powerful – they are a concise way of describing a potentially large number of variations.

Note: I'm using string here in the sense it is used in programming languages: a string of one or more characters, characters including actual characters, numbers, punctuation and so-called whitespace (linebreaks, tabulators etc.). Please note that generally, uppercase and lowercase characters are not considered the same, thus "a" being a different character from "A" and so forth. In calibre, regular expressions are case insensitive in the search bar, but not in the conversion options. There's a way to make every regular expression case insensitive, but we'll discuss that later. It gets complicated because regular expressions allow for variations in the strings it matches, so one expression can match multiple strings, which is why people bother using them at all. More on that in a bit.

Care to explain?

Well, that's why we're here. First, this is the most important concept in regular expressions: *A string by itself is a regular expression that matches itself.* That is to say, if I wanted to match the string `"Hello, World!"` using a regular expression, the regular expression to use would be `Hello, World!`. And yes, it really is that simple. You'll notice, though, that this *only* matches the exact string `"Hello, World!"`, not e.g. `"Hello, wOrld!"` or `"hello, world!"` or any other such variation.

That doesn't sound too bad. What's next?

Next is the beginning of the really good stuff. Remember where I said that regular expressions can match multiple strings? This is were it gets a little more complicated. Say, as a somewhat more practical exercise, the ebook you wanted to convert had a nasty footer counting the pages, like "Page 5 of 423". Obviously the page number would rise from 1 to 423, thus you'd have to match 423 different strings, right? Wrong, actually: regular expressions allow you to define sets of characters that are matched: To define a set, you put all the characters you want to be in the set into square brackets. So, for example, the set `[abc]` would match either the character "a", "b" or "c". *Sets will always only match one of the characters in the set.* They "understand" character ranges, that is, if you wanted to match all the lower case characters, you'd use the set `[a-z]` for lower- and uppercase characters you'd use `[a-zA-Z]` and so on. Got the idea? So, obviously, using the expression `Page [0-9] of 423` you'd be able to match the first 9 pages, thus reducing the expressions needed to three: The second expression `Page [0-9][0-9] of 423` would match all two-digit page numbers, and I'm sure you can guess what the third expression would look like. Yes, go ahead. Write it down.

Hey, neat! This is starting to make sense!

I was hoping you'd say that. But brace yourself, now it gets even better! We just saw that using sets, we could match one of several characters at once. But you can even repeat a character or set, reducing the number of expressions needed to handle the above page number example to one. Yes, ONE! Excited? You should be! It works like this: Some so-called special characters, "+", "?" and "*", *repeat the single element preceding them.* (Element means either a single character, a character set, an escape sequence or a group (we'll learn about those last two later)- in short, any single entity in a regular expression.) These characters are called wildcards or quantifiers. To be more precise, "?" matches *0 or 1* of the preceding element, "*" matches *0 or more* of the preceding element and "+" matches *1 or more* of the preceding element. A few examples: The expression `a?` would match either "" (which is the empty string, not strictly useful in this case) or "a", the expression `a*` would match "", "a", "aa" or any number of a's in a row, and, finally, the expression `a+` would match "a", "aa" or any number of a's in a row (Note: it wouldn't match the empty string!). Same deal for sets: The expression `[0-9]+` would match *every integer number there is*! I know what you're thinking, and you're right: If you use that in the above case of matching page numbers, wouldn't that be the single one expression to match all the page numbers? Yes, the expression `Page [0-9]+ of 423` would match every page number in that book!

Note: A note on these quantifiers: They generally try to match as much text as possible, so be careful when using them. This is called "greedy behaviour"- I'm sure you get why. It gets problematic when you, say, try to match a tag. Consider, for example, the string `"<p class="calibre2">Title here</p>"` and let's say you'd want to match the opening tag (the part between the first pair of angle brackets, a little more on tags later). You'd think that the expression `<p.*>` would match that tag, but actually, it matches the whole string! (The character "." is another special character. It matches anything *except* linebreaks, so, basically, the expression `.*` would match any single line you can think of.) Instead, try using `<p.*?>` which makes the quantifier "*" non-greedy. That expression would only match the first opening tag, as intended. There's actually another way to accomplish this: The expression `<p[^>]*>` will match that same opening tag- you'll see why after the next section. Just note that there quite frequently is more than one way to write a regular expression.

Well, these special characters are very neat and all, but what if I wanted to match a dot or a question mark?

You can of course do that: Just put a backslash in front of any special character and it is interpreted as the literal character, without any special meaning. This pair of a backslash followed by a single character is called an escape sequence, and the act of putting a backslash in front of a special character is called escaping that character. An escape sequence is interpreted as a single element. There are of course escape sequences that do more than just escaping special characters, for example "\t" means a tabulator. We'll get to some of the escape sequences later. Oh, and by the way, concerning those special characters: Consider any character we discuss in this introduction as having some function to be special and thus needing to be escaped if you want the literal character.

So, what are the most useful sets?

Knew you'd ask. Some useful sets are [0-9] matching a single number, [a-z] matching a single lowercase letter, [A-Z] matching a single uppercase letter, [a-zA-Z] matching a single letter and [a-zA-Z0-9] matching a single letter or number. You can also use an escape sequence as shorthand:

```
\d is equivalent to [0-9]
\w is equivalent to [a-zA-Z0-9_]
\s is equivalent to any whitespace
```

Note: "Whitespace" is a term for anything that won't be printed. These characters include space, tabulator, line feed, form feed and carriage return.

As a last note on sets, you can also define a set as any character *but* those in the set. You do that by including the character "^" as the *very first character in the set*. Thus, [^a] would match any character excluding "a". That's called complementing the set. Those escape sequence shorthands we saw earlier can also be complemented: "\D" means any non-number character, thus being equivalent to [^0-9]. The other shorthands can be complemented by, you guessed it, using the respective uppercase letter instead of the lowercase one. So, going back to the example <p[^>]*> from the previous section, now you can see that the character set it's using tries to match any character except for a closing angle bracket.

But if I had a few varying strings I wanted to match, things get complicated?

Fear not, life still is good and easy. Consider this example: The book you're converting has "Title" written on every odd page and "Author" written on every even page. Looks great in print, right? But in ebooks, it's annoying. You can group whole expressions in normal parentheses, and the character "|" will let you match *either* the expression to its right *or* the one to its left. Combine those and you're done. Too fast for you? Okay, first off, we group the expressions for odd and even pages, thus getting (Title) (Author) as our two needed expressions. Now we make things simpler by using the vertical bar ("|" is called the vertical bar character): If you use the expression (Title|Author) you'll either get a match for "Title" (on the odd pages) or you'd match "Author" (on the even pages). Well, wasn't that easy?

You can, of course, use the vertical bar without using grouping parentheses, as well. Remember when I said that quantifiers repeat the element preceding them? Well, the vertical bar works a little differently: The expression "Title|Author" will also match either the string "Title" or the string "Author", just as the above example using grouping. *The vertical bar selects between the entire expression preceding and following it.* So, if you wanted to match the strings "Calibre" and "calibre" and wanted to select only between the upper- and lowercase "c", you'd have to use the expression (c|C)alibre, where the grouping ensures that only the "c" will be selected. If you were to use c|Calibre, you'd get a match on the string "c" or on the string "Calibre", which isn't what we wanted. In short: If in doubt, use grouping together with the vertical bar.

You missed...

... wait just a minute, there's one last, really neat thing you can do with groups. If you have a group that you previously matched, you can use references to that group later in the expression: Groups are numbered starting with 1, and you reference them by escaping the number of the group you want to reference, thus, the fifth group would be referenced as \5. So, if you searched for ([^]+) \1 in the string "Test Test", you'd match the whole string!

In the beginning, you said there was a way to make a regular expression case insensitive?

Yes, I did, thanks for paying attention and reminding me. You can tell calibre how you want certain things handled by using something called flags. You include flags in your expression by using the special construct (?flags go here) where, obviously, you'd replace "flags go here" with the specific flags you want. For ignoring case, the flag is i, thus you include (?i) in your expression. Thus, test(?i) would match "Test", "tEst", "TEst" and any case variation you could think of.

Another useful flag lets the dot match any character at all, *including* the newline, the flag s. If you want to use multiple flags in an expression, just put them in the same statement: (?is) would ignore case and make the dot match all. It doesn't matter which flag you state first, (?si) would be equivalent to the above. By the way, good places for putting flags in your expression would be either the very beginning or the very end. That way, they don't get mixed up with anything else.

I think I'm beginning to understand these regular expressions now... how do I use them in calibre?

Conversions

Let's begin with the conversion settings, which is really neat. In the Search and Replace part, you can input a regexp (short for regular expression) that describes the string that will be replaced during the conversion. The neat part is the wizard. Click on the wizard staff and you get a preview of what calibre "sees" during the conversion process. Scroll down to the string you want to remove, select and copy it, paste it into the regexp field on top of the window. If there are variable parts, like page numbers or so, use sets and quantifiers to cover those, and while you're at it, remember to escape special characters, if there are some. Hit the button labeled *Test* and calibre highlights the parts it would replace were you to use the regexp. Once you're satisfied, hit OK and convert. Be careful if your conversion source has tags like this example:

```
Maybe, but the cops feel like you do, Anita. What's one more dead vampire?
New laws don't change that. </p>
<p class="calibre4"> <b class="calibre2">Generated by ABC Amber LIT Conv
<a href="http://www.processtext.com/abclit.html" class="calibre3">erter,
http://www.processtext.com/abclit.html</a></b></p>
<p class="calibre4"> It had only been two years since Addison v. Clark.
The court case gave us a revised version of what life was
```

(shamelessly ripped out of this thread[97]). You'd have to remove some of the tags as well. In this example, I'd recommend beginning with the tag <b class="calibre2">, now you have to end with the corresponding closing tag (opening tags are <tag>, closing tags are </tag>), which is simply the next </b> in this case. (Refer to a good HTML manual or ask in the forum if you are unclear on this point.) The opening tag can be described using <b.*?>, the closing tag using </b>, thus we could remove everything between those tags using <b.*?>.*?</b>. But using this expression would be a bad idea, because it removes everything enclosed by <b>-tags (which, by the way, render the enclosed text in bold print), and it's a fair bet that we'll remove portions of the book in this way. Instead, include the beginning of the enclosed string as well, making the regular expression <b.*?>\s*Generated\s+by\s+ABC\s+Amber\s+LIT.*?</b> The \s with quantifiers are included here

---

[97] http://www.mobileread.com/forums/showthread.php?t=75594"

instead of explicitly using the spaces as seen in the string to catch any variations of the string that might occur. Remember to check what calibre will remove to make sure you don't remove any portions you want to keep if you test a new expression. If you only check one occurrence, you might miss a mismatch somewhere else in the text. Also note that should you accidentally remove more or fewer tags than you actually wanted to, calibre tries to repair the damaged code after doing the removal.

Adding books

Another thing you can use regular expressions for is to extract metadata from filenames. You can find this feature in the "Adding books" part of the settings. There's a special feature here: You can use field names for metadata fields, for example (?P<title>) would indicate that calibre uses this part of the string as book title. The allowed field names are listed in the windows, together with another nice test field. An example: Say you want to import a whole bunch of files named like Classical Texts: The Divine Comedy by Dante Alighieri.mobi. (Obviously, this is already in your library, since we all love classical italian poetry) or Science Fiction epics: The Foundation Trilogy by Isaac Asimov.epub. This is obviously a naming scheme that calibre won't extract any meaningful data out of - its standard expression for extracting metadata is (?P<title>.+) - (?P<author>[^_]+). A regular expression that works here would be [a-zA-Z]+: (?P<title>.+) by (?P<author>.+). Please note that, inside the group for the metadata field, you need to use expressions to describe what the field actually matches. And also note that, when using the test field calibre provides, you need to add the file extension to your testing filename, otherwise you won't get any matches at all, despite using a working expression.

Bulk editing metadata

The last part is regular expression search and replace in metadata fields. You can access this by selecting multiple books in the library and using bulk metadata edit. Be very careful when using this last feature, as it can do **Very Bad Things** to your library! Doublecheck that your expressions do what you want them to using the test fields, and only mark the books you really want to change! In the regular expression search mode, you can search in one field, replace the text with something and even write the result into another field. A practical example: Say your library contained the books of Frank Herbert's Dune series, named after the fashion Dune 1 - Dune, Dune 2 - Dune Messiah and so on. Now you want to get Dune into the series field. You can do that by searching for (.*?) \d+ - .* in the title field and replacing it with \1 in the series field. See what I did there? That's a reference to the first group you're replacing the series field with. Now that you have the series all set, you only need to do another search for .*? - in the title field and replace it with " " (an empty string), again in the title field, and your metadata is all neat and tidy. Isn't that great? By the way, instead of replacing the entire field, you can also append or prepend to the field, so, if you *wanted* the book title to be prepended with series info, you could do that as well. As you by now have undoubtedly noticed, there's a checkbox labeled *Case sensitive*, so you won't have to use flags to select behaviour here.

Well, that just about concludes the very short introduction to regular expressions. Hopefully I'll have shown you enough to at least get you started and to enable you to continue learning by yourself- a good starting point would be the Python documentation for regexps[98].

One last word of warning, though: Regexps are powerful, but also really easy to get wrong. calibre provides really great testing possibilities to see if your expressions behave as you expect them to. Use them. Try not to shoot yourself in the foot. (God, I love that expression...) But should you, despite the warning, injure your foot (or any other body parts), try to learn from it.

Credits

Thanks for helping with tips, corrections and such:

---

[98] https://docs.python.org/2/library/re.html

- ldolse

- kovidgoyal

- chaley

- dwanthny

- kacir

- Starson17

For more about regexps see The Python User Manual[99].

1.9.6 Integrating the calibre content server into other servers

Here, we will show you how to integrate the calibre content server into another server. The most common reason for this is to make use of SSL or more sophisticated authentication. There are two main techniques: Running the calibre content server as a standalone process and using a reverse proxy to connect it with your main server or running the content server in process in your main server with WSGI. The examples below are all for Apache 2.x on linux, but should be easily adaptable to other platforms.

> **Contents**
> - *Using a reverse proxy* (page 211)
> - *In process* (page 212)

Note: This only applies to calibre releases >= 0.7.25

Using a reverse proxy

A reverse proxy is when your normal server accepts incoming requests and passes them onto the calibre server. It then reads the response from the calibre server and forwards it to the client. This means that you can simply run the calibre server as normal without trying to integrate it closely with your main server, and you can take advantage of whatever authentication systems your main server has in place. This is the simplest approach as it allows you to use the binary calibre install with no external dependencies/system integration requirements. Below, is an example of how to achieve this with Apache as your main server, but it will work with any server that supports Reverse Proxies.

First start the calibre content server as shown below:

```
calibre-server --url-prefix /calibre --port 8080
```

The key parameter here is `--url-prefix /calibre`. This causes the content server to serve all URLs prefixed by calibre. To see this in action, visit `http://localhost:8080/calibre` in your browser. You should see the normal content server website, but now it will run under /calibre.

Now suppose you are using Apache as your main server. First enable the proxy modules in apache, by adding the following to `httpd.conf`:

```
LoadModule proxy_module modules/mod_proxy.so
LoadModule proxy_http_module modules/mod_proxy_http.so
```

The exact technique for enabling the proxy modules will vary depending on your Apache installation. Once you have the proxy modules enabled, add the following rules to httpd.conf (or if you are using virtual hosts to the conf file for the virtual host in question):

---

[99] https://docs.python.org/2/library/re.html

```
RewriteEngine on
RewriteRule ^/calibre/(.*) http://localhost:8080/calibre/$1 [proxy]
RewriteRule ^/calibre http://localhost:8080 [proxy]
SetEnv force-proxy-request-1.0 1
SetEnv proxy-nokeepalive 1
```

That's all, you will now be able to access the calibre Content Server under the /calibre URL in your apache server. The above rules pass all requests under /calibre to the calibre server running on port 8080 and thanks to the –url-prefix option above, the calibre server handles them transparently.

Note: If you are willing to devote an entire VirtualHost to the content server, then there is no need to use –url-prefix and RewriteRule, instead just use the ProxyPass directive.

Note: The server engine calibre uses, CherryPy, can have trouble with proxying and KeepAlive requests, so turn them off in Apache, with the SetEnv directives shown above.

In process

The calibre content server can be run directly, in process, inside a host server like Apache using the WSGI framework.

Note: For this to work, all the dependencies needed by calibre must be installed on your system. Doing so is highly non-trivial and you are encouraged not to use in process servers. You will not get any assistance with debugging in process server problems.

First, we have to create a WSGI *adapter* for the calibre content server. Here is a template you can use for the purpose. Replace the paths as directed in the comments

```python
# WSGI script file to run calibre content server as a WSGI app

import sys, os


# You can get the paths referenced here by running
# calibre-debug --paths
# on your server

# The first entry from CALIBRE_PYTHON_PATH
sys.path.insert(0, '/home/kovid/work/calibre/src')

# CALIBRE_RESOURCES_PATH
sys.resources_location = '/home/kovid/work/calibre/resources'

# CALIBRE_EXTENSIONS_PATH
sys.extensions_location = '/home/kovid/work/calibre/src/calibre/plugins'

# Path to directory containing calibre executables
sys.executables_location = '/usr/bin'

# Path to a directory for which the server has read/write permissions
# calibre config will be stored here
os.environ['CALIBRE_CONFIG_DIRECTORY'] = '/var/www/localhost/calibre-config'

del sys
del os
```

```
from calibre.library.server.main import create_wsgi_app
application = create_wsgi_app(
        # The mount point of this WSGI application (i.e. the first argument to
        # the WSGIScriptAlias directive). Set to empty string is mounted at /
        prefix='/calibre',

        # Path to the calibre library to be served
        # The server process must have write permission for all files/dirs
        # in this directory or BAD things will happen
        path_to_library='/home/kovid/documents/demo library',

        # The virtual library (restriction) to be used when serving this
        # library.
        virtual_library=None
)

del create_wsgi_app
```

Save this adapter as `calibre-wsgi-adpater.py` somewhere your server will have access to it.

Let's suppose that we want to use WSGI in Apache. First enable WSGI in Apache by adding the following to `httpd.conf`:

```
LoadModule wsgi_module modules/mod_wsgi.so
```

The exact technique for enabling the wsgi module will vary depending on your Apache installation. Once you have the proxy modules enabled, add the following rules to httpd.conf (or if you are using virtual hosts to the conf file for the virtual host in question:

```
WSGIScriptAlias /calibre /var/www/localhost/cgi-bin/calibre-wsgi-adapter.py
```

Change the path to `calibre-wsgi-adapter.py` to wherever you saved it previously (make sure Apache has access to it).

That's all, you will now be able to access the calibre Content Server under the /calibre URL in your apache server.

Note: For more help with using mod_wsgi in Apache, see mod_wsgi[100].

1.9.7 Writing your own plugins to extend calibre's functionality

calibre has a very modular design. Almost all functionality in calibre comes in the form of plugins. Plugins are used for conversion, for downloading news (though these are called recipes), for various components of the user interface, to connect to different devices, to process files when adding them to calibre and so on. You can get a complete list of all the built-in plugins in calibre by going to *Preferences->Plugins*.

Here, we will teach you how to create your own plugins to add new features to calibre.

---

[100] http://code.google.com/p/modwsgi/wiki/WhereToGetHelp

Contents

Note: This only applies to calibre releases >= 0.8.60

Anatomy of a calibre plugin

A calibre plugin is very simple, it's just a zip file that contains some python code and any other resources like image files needed by the plugin. Without further ado, let's see a basic example.

Suppose you have an installation of calibre that you are using to self publish various e-documents in EPUB and MOBI formats. You would like all files generated by calibre to have their publisher set as "Hello world", here's how to do it. Create a file named __init__.py (this is a special name and must always be used for the main file of your plugin) and enter the following Python code into it:

```python
import os
from calibre.customize import FileTypePlugin

class HelloWorld(FileTypePlugin):

    name                = 'Hello World Plugin' # Name of the plugin
    description         = 'Set the publisher to Hello World for all new conversions'
    supported_platforms = ['windows', 'osx', 'linux'] # Platforms this plugin will run on
    author              = 'Acme Inc.' # The author of this plugin
    version             = (1, 0, 0)   # The version number of this plugin
    file_types          = set(['epub', 'mobi']) # The file types that this plugin will be app.
    on_postprocess      = True # Run this plugin after conversion is complete
    minimum_calibre_version = (0, 7, 53)

    def run(self, path_to_ebook):
        from calibre.ebooks.metadata.meta import get_metadata, set_metadata
        file = open(path_to_ebook, 'r+b')
        ext  = os.path.splitext(path_to_ebook)[-1][1:].lower()
        mi = get_metadata(file, ext)
        mi.publisher = 'Hello World'
        set_metadata(file, mi, ext)
        return path_to_ebook
```

That's all. To add this code to calibre as a plugin, simply run the following in the directory in which you created __init__.py:

```
calibre-customize -b .
```

Note: On OS X, the command line tools are inside the calibre bundle, for example, if you installed calibre in `/Applications` the command line tools are in
`/Applications/calibre.app/Contents/console.app/Contents/MacOS/`.

You can download the Hello World plugin from helloworld_plugin.zip[101].

Every time you use calibre to convert a book, the plugin's `run()` method will be called and the converted book will
have its publisher set to "Hello World". This is a trivial plugin, lets move on to a more complex example that actually
adds a component to the user interface.

A User Interface plugin

This plugin will be spread over a few files (to keep the code clean). It will show you how to get resources (images
or data files) from the plugin zip file, allow users to configure your plugin, how to create elements in the calibre user
interface and how to access and query the books database in calibre.

You can download this plugin from interface_demo_plugin.zip[102] The first thing to note is that this zip file has a lot
more files in it, explained below, pay particular attention to `plugin-import-name-interface_demo.txt`.

plugin-import-name-interface_demo.txt An empty text file used to enable the multi-file plugin magic.
This file must be present in all plugins that use more than one .py file. It should be empty and its
filename must be of the form: plugin-import-name-**some_name**.txt The presence of this file allows
you to import code from the .py files present inside the zip file, using a statement like:

```
from calibre_plugins.some_name.some_module import some_object
```

The prefix `calibre_plugins` must always be present. `some_name` comes from the filename
of the empty text file. `some_module` refers to `some_module.py` file inside the zip file. Note
that this importing is just as powerful as regular python imports. You can create packages and
subpackages of .py modules inside the zip file, just like you would normally (by defining __init__.py
in each sub-directory), and everything should Just Work.

The name you use for `some_name` enters a global namespace shared by all plugins, **so make it as
unique as possible**. But remember that it must be a valid python identifier (only alphabets, numbers
and the underscore).

__init__.py As before, the file that defines the plugin class

main.py This file contains the actual code that does something useful

ui.py This file defines the interface part of the plugin

images/icon.png The icon for this plugin

about.txt A text file with information about the plugin

translations A folder containing .mo files with the translations of the user interface of your plugin into
different languages. See below for details.

Now let's look at the code.

---
[101]http://calibre-ebook.com/downloads/helloworld_plugin.zip
[102]http://calibre-ebook.com/downloads/interface_demo_plugin.zip

__init__.py

First, the obligatory __init__.py to define the plugin metadata:

```python
# The class that all Interface Action plugin wrappers must inherit from
from calibre.customize import InterfaceActionBase

class InterfacePluginDemo(InterfaceActionBase):
    '''
    This class is a simple wrapper that provides information about the actual
    plugin class. The actual interface plugin class is called InterfacePlugin
    and is defined in the ui.py file, as specified in the actual_plugin field
    below.

    The reason for having two classes is that it allows the command line
    calibre utilities to run without needing to load the GUI libraries.
    '''
    name                = 'Interface Plugin Demo'
    description         = 'An advanced plugin demo'
    supported_platforms = ['windows', 'osx', 'linux']
    author              = 'Kovid Goyal'
    version             = (1, 0, 0)
    minimum_calibre_version = (0, 7, 53)

    #: This field defines the GUI plugin class that contains all the code
    #: that actually does something. Its format is module_path:class_name
    #: The specified class must be defined in the specified module.
    actual_plugin       = 'calibre_plugins.interface_demo.ui:InterfacePlugin'

    def is_customizable(self):
        '''
        This method must return True to enable customization via
        Preferences->Plugins
        '''
        return True

    def config_widget(self):
        '''
        Implement this method and :meth:`save_settings` in your plugin to
        use a custom configuration dialog.

        This method, if implemented, must return a QWidget. The widget can have
        an optional method validate() that takes no arguments and is called
        immediately after the user clicks OK. Changes are applied if and only
        if the method returns True.

        If for some reason you cannot perform the configuration at this time,
        return a tuple of two strings (message, details), these will be
        displayed as a warning dialog to the user and the process will be
        aborted.

        The base class implementation of this method raises NotImplementedError
        so by default no user configuration is possible.
        '''
        # It is important to put this import statement here rather than at the
        # top of the module as importing the config class will also cause the
        # GUI libraries to be loaded, which we do not want when using calibre
        # from the command line
```

```
        from calibre_plugins.interface_demo.config import ConfigWidget
        return ConfigWidget()

    def save_settings(self, config_widget):
        '''
        Save the settings specified by the user with config_widget.

        :param config_widget: The widget returned by :meth:`config_widget`.
        '''
        config_widget.save_settings()

        # Apply the changes
        ac = self.actual_plugin_
        if ac is not None:
            ac.apply_settings()
```

The only noteworthy feature is the field `actual_plugin`. Since calibre has both command line and GUI interfaces, GUI plugins like this one should not load any GUI libraries in __init__.py. The actual_plugin field does this for you, by telling calibre that the actual plugin is to be found in another file inside your zip archive, which will only be loaded in a GUI context.

Remember that for this to work, you must have a plugin-import-name-some_name.txt file in your plugin zip file, as discussed above.

Also there are a couple of methods for enabling user configuration of the plugin. These are discussed below.

ui.py

Now let's look at ui.py which defines the actual GUI plugin. The source code is heavily commented and should be self explanatory:

```
# The class that all interface action plugins must inherit from
from calibre.gui2.actions import InterfaceAction
from calibre_plugins.interface_demo.main import DemoDialog

class InterfacePlugin(InterfaceAction):

    name = 'Interface Plugin Demo'

    # Declare the main action associated with this plugin
    # The keyboard shortcut can be None if you dont want to use a keyboard
    # shortcut. Remember that currently calibre has no central management for
    # keyboard shortcuts, so try to use an unusual/unused shortcut.
    action_spec = ('Interface Plugin Demo', None,
            'Run the Interface Plugin Demo', 'Ctrl+Shift+F1')

    def genesis(self):
        # This method is called once per plugin, do initial setup here

        # Set the icon for this interface action
        # The get_icons function is a builtin function defined for all your
        # plugin code. It loads icons from the plugin zip file. It returns
        # QIcon objects, if you want the actual data, use the analogous
        # get_resources builtin function.
        #
        # Note that if you are loading more than one icon, for performance, you
        # should pass a list of names to get_icons. In this case, get_icons
```

```
        # will return a dictionary mapping names to QIcons. Names that
        # are not found in the zip file will result in null QIcons.
        icon = get_icons('images/icon.png')

        # The qaction is automatically created from the action_spec defined
        # above
        self.qaction.setIcon(icon)
        self.qaction.triggered.connect(self.show_dialog)

    def show_dialog(self):
        # The base plugin object defined in __init__.py
        base_plugin_object = self.interface_action_base_plugin
        # Show the config dialog
        # The config dialog can also be shown from within
        # Preferences->Plugins, which is why the do_user_config
        # method is defined on the base plugin class
        do_user_config = base_plugin_object.do_user_config

        # self.gui is the main calibre GUI. It acts as the gateway to access
        # all the elements of the calibre user interface, it should also be the
        # parent of the dialog
        d = DemoDialog(self.gui, self.qaction.icon(), do_user_config)
        d.show()

    def apply_settings(self):
        from calibre_plugins.interface_demo.config import prefs
        # In an actual non trivial plugin, you would probably need to
        # do something based on the settings in prefs
        prefs
```

main.py

The actual logic to implement the Interface Plugin Demo dialog.

```
from PyQt5.Qt import QDialog, QVBoxLayout, QPushButton, QMessageBox, QLabel

from calibre_plugins.interface_demo.config import prefs

class DemoDialog(QDialog):

    def __init__(self, gui, icon, do_user_config):
        QDialog.__init__(self, gui)
        self.gui = gui
        self.do_user_config = do_user_config

        # The current database shown in the GUI
        # db is an instance of the class LibraryDatabase from db/legacy.py
        # This class has many, many methods that allow you to do a lot of
        # things. For most purposes you should use db.new_api, which has
        # a much nicer interface from db/cache.py
        self.db = gui.current_db

        self.l = QVBoxLayout()
        self.setLayout(self.l)

        self.label = QLabel(prefs['hello_world_msg'])
        self.l.addWidget(self.label)
```

```
        self.setWindowTitle('Interface Plugin Demo')
        self.setWindowIcon(icon)

        self.about_button = QPushButton('About', self)
        self.about_button.clicked.connect(self.about)
        self.l.addWidget(self.about_button)

        self.marked_button = QPushButton(
            'Show books with only one format in the calibre GUI', self)
        self.marked_button.clicked.connect(self.marked)
        self.l.addWidget(self.marked_button)

        self.view_button = QPushButton(
            'View the most recently added book', self)
        self.view_button.clicked.connect(self.view)
        self.l.addWidget(self.view_button)

        self.update_metadata_button = QPushButton(
            'Update metadata in a book\'s files', self)
        self.update_metadata_button.clicked.connect(self.update_metadata)
        self.l.addWidget(self.update_metadata_button)

        self.conf_button = QPushButton(
                'Configure this plugin', self)
        self.conf_button.clicked.connect(self.config)
        self.l.addWidget(self.conf_button)

        self.resize(self.sizeHint())

    def about(self):
        # Get the about text from a file inside the plugin zip file
        # The get_resources function is a builtin function defined for all your
        # plugin code. It loads files from the plugin zip file. It returns
        # the bytes from the specified file.
        #
        # Note that if you are loading more than one file, for performance, you
        # should pass a list of names to get_resources. In this case,
        # get_resources will return a dictionary mapping names to bytes. Names that
        # are not found in the zip file will not be in the returned dictionary.
        text = get_resources('about.txt')
        QMessageBox.about(self, 'About the Interface Plugin Demo',
                text.decode('utf-8'))

    def marked(self):
        ''' Show books with only one format '''
        db = self.db.new_api
        matched_ids = {book_id for book_id in db.all_book_ids() if len(db.formats(book_id)) ==
        # Mark the records with the matching ids
        # new_api does not know anything about marked books, so we use the full
        # db object
        self.db.set_marked_ids(matched_ids)

        # Tell the GUI to search for all marked records
        self.gui.search.setEditText('marked:true')
        self.gui.search.do_search()

    def view(self):
        ''' View the most recently added book '''
```

```python
        most_recent = most_recent_id = None
        db = self.db.new_api
        for book_id, timestamp in db.all_field_for('timestamp', db.all_book_ids()).iteritems()
            if most_recent is None or timestamp > most_recent:
                most_recent = timestamp
                most_recent_id = book_id

        if most_recent_id is not None:
            # Get a reference to the View plugin
            view_plugin = self.gui.iactions['View']
            # Ask the view plugin to launch the viewer for row_number
            view_plugin._view_calibre_books([most_recent_id])

    def update_metadata(self):
        '''
        Set the metadata in the files in the selected book's record to
        match the current metadata in the database.
        '''
        from calibre.ebooks.metadata.meta import set_metadata
        from calibre.gui2 import error_dialog, info_dialog

        # Get currently selected books
        rows = self.gui.library_view.selectionModel().selectedRows()
        if not rows or len(rows) == 0:
            return error_dialog(self.gui, 'Cannot update metadata',
                                'No books selected', show=True)
        # Map the rows to book ids
        ids = list(map(self.gui.library_view.model().id, rows))
        db = self.db.new_api
        for book_id in ids:
            # Get the current metadata for this book from the db
            mi = db.get_metadata(book_id, get_cover=True, cover_as_data=True)
            fmts = db.formats(book_id)
            if not fmts:
                continue
            for fmt in fmts:
                fmt = fmt.lower()
                # Get a python file object for the format. This will be either
                # an in memory file or a temporary on disk file
                ffile = db.format(book_id, fmt, as_file=True)
                ffile.seek(0)
                # Set metadata in the format
                set_metadata(ffile, mi, fmt)
                ffile.seek(0)
                # Now replace the file in the calibre library with the updated
                # file. We dont use add_format_with_hooks as the hooks were
                # already run when the file was first added to calibre.
                db.add_format(book_id, fmt, ffile, run_hooks=False)

        info_dialog(self, 'Updated files',
                    'Updated the metadata in the files of %d book(s)'%len(ids),
                    show=True)

    def config(self):
        self.do_user_config(parent=self)
        # Apply the changes
        self.label.setText(prefs['hello_world_msg'])
```

calibre User Manual, Release 2.41.0

Getting resources from the plugin zip file

calibre's plugin loading system defines a couple of built-in functions that allow you to conveniently get files from the plugin zip file.

get_resources(name_or_list_of_names) This function should be called with a list of paths to files inside the zip file. For example to access the file icon.png in the directory images in the zip file, you would use: `images/icon.png`. Always use a forward slash as the path separator, even on windows. When you pass in a single name, the function will return the raw bytes of that file or None if the name was not found in the zip file. If you pass in more than one name then it returns a dict mapping the names to bytes. If a name is not found, it will not be present in the returned dict.

get_icons(name_or_list_of_names) A convenience wrapper for get_resources() that creates QIcon objects from the raw bytes returned by get_resources. If a name is not found in the zip file the corresponding QIcon will be null.

Enabling user configuration of your plugin

To allow users to configure your plugin, you must define three methods in your base plugin class, '**is_customizable**, **config_widget** and **save_settings** as shown below:

```
def is_customizable(self):
    '''
    This method must return True to enable customization via
    Preferences->Plugins
    '''
    return True
```

```
def config_widget(self):
    '''
    Implement this method and :meth:`save_settings` in your plugin to
    use a custom configuration dialog.

    This method, if implemented, must return a QWidget. The widget can have
    an optional method validate() that takes no arguments and is called
    immediately after the user clicks OK. Changes are applied if and only
    if the method returns True.

    If for some reason you cannot perform the configuration at this time,
    return a tuple of two strings (message, details), these will be
    displayed as a warning dialog to the user and the process will be
    aborted.

    The base class implementation of this method raises NotImplementedError
    so by default no user configuration is possible.
    '''
    # It is important to put this import statement here rather than at the
    # top of the module as importing the config class will also cause the
    # GUI libraries to be loaded, which we do not want when using calibre
    # from the command line
    from calibre_plugins.interface_demo.config import ConfigWidget
    return ConfigWidget()
```

```
def save_settings(self, config_widget):
    '''
    Save the settings specified by the user with config_widget.
```

1.9. Tutorials   **221**

```
        :param config_widget: The widget returned by :meth:`config_widget`.
        '''
        config_widget.save_settings()

        # Apply the changes
        ac = self.actual_plugin_
        if ac is not None:
            ac.apply_settings()
```

calibre has many different ways to store configuration data (a legacy of its long history). The recommended way is to use the **JSONConfig** class, which stores your configuration information in a .json file.

The code to manage configuration data in the demo plugin is in config.py:

```
from PyQt5.Qt import QWidget, QHBoxLayout, QLabel, QLineEdit

from calibre.utils.config import JSONConfig

# This is where all preferences for this plugin will be stored
# Remember that this name (i.e. plugins/interface_demo) is also
# in a global namespace, so make it as unique as possible.
# You should always prefix your config file name with plugins/,
# so as to ensure you dont accidentally clobber a calibre config file
prefs = JSONConfig('plugins/interface_demo')

# Set defaults
prefs.defaults['hello_world_msg'] = 'Hello, World!'

class ConfigWidget(QWidget):

    def __init__(self):
        QWidget.__init__(self)
        self.l = QHBoxLayout()
        self.setLayout(self.l)

        self.label = QLabel('Hello world &message:')
        self.l.addWidget(self.label)

        self.msg = QLineEdit(self)
        self.msg.setText(prefs['hello_world_msg'])
        self.l.addWidget(self.msg)
        self.label.setBuddy(self.msg)

    def save_settings(self):
        prefs['hello_world_msg'] = unicode(self.msg.text())
```

The prefs object is now available throughout the plugin code by a simple:

```
from calibre_plugins.interface_demo.config import prefs
```

You can see the prefs object being used in main.py:

```
    def config(self):
        self.do_user_config(parent=self)
        # Apply the changes
        self.label.setText(prefs['hello_world_msg'])
```

Edit Book plugins

Now let's change gears for a bit and look at creating a plugin to add tools to the calibre book editor. The plugin is available here: editor_demo_plugin.zip[103].

The first step, as for all plugins is to create the import name empty txt file, as described *above* (page 215). We shall name the file `plugin-import-name-editor_plugin_demo.txt`.

Now we create the mandatory `__init__.py` file that contains metadata about the plugin – its name, author, version, etc.

```
from calibre.customize import EditBookToolPlugin


class DemoPlugin(EditBookToolPlugin):

    name = 'Edit Book plugin demo'
    version = (1, 0, 0)
    author = 'Kovid Goyal'
    supported_platforms = ['windows', 'osx', 'linux']
    description = 'A demonstration of the plugin interface for the ebook editor'
    minimum_calibre_version = (1, 46, 0)
```

A single editor plugin can provide multiple tools each tool corresponds to a single button in the toolbar and entry in the *Plugins* menu in the editor. These can have sub-menus in case the tool has multiple related actions.

The tools must all be defined in the file `main.py` in your plugin. Every tool is a class that inherits from the *calibre.gui2.tweak_book.plugin.Tool* (page 369) class. Let's look at `main.py` from the demo plugin, the source code is heavily commented and should be self-explanatory. Read the API documents of the *calibre.gui2.tweak_book.plugin.Tool* (page 369) class for more details.

main.py

Here we will see the definition of a single tool that will multiply all font sizes in the book by a number provided by the user. This tool demonstrates various important concepts that you will need in developing your own plugins, so you should read the (heavily commented) source code carefully.

```
import re
from PyQt5.Qt import QAction, QInputDialog
from cssutils.css import CSSRule

# The base class that all tools must inherit from
from calibre.gui2.tweak_book.plugin import Tool

from calibre import force_unicode
from calibre.gui2 import error_dialog
from calibre.ebooks.oeb.polish.container import OEB_DOCS, OEB_STYLES, serialize

class DemoTool(Tool):

    #: Set this to a unique name it will be used as a key
    name = 'demo-tool'

    #: If True the user can choose to place this tool in the plugins toolbar
    allowed_in_toolbar = True
```

---

[103]http://calibre-ebook.com/downloads/editor_demo_plugin.zip

```
    #: If True the user can choose to place this tool in the plugins menu
    allowed_in_menu = True

    def create_action(self, for_toolbar=True):
        # Create an action, this will be added to the plugins toolbar and
        # the plugins menu
        ac = QAction(get_icons('images/icon.png'), 'Magnify fonts', self.gui)  # noqa
        if not for_toolbar:
            # Register a keyboard shortcut for this toolbar action. We only
            # register it for the action created for the menu, not the toolbar,
            # to avoid a double trigger
            self.register_shortcut(ac, 'magnify-fonts-tool', default_keys=('Ctrl+Shift+Alt+D',
        ac.triggered.connect(self.ask_user)
        return ac

    def ask_user(self):
        # Ask the user for a factor by which to multiply all font sizes
        factor, ok = QInputDialog.getDouble(
            self.gui, 'Enter a magnification factor', 'Allow font sizes in the book will be mu
            value=2, min=0.1, max=4
        )
        if ok:
            # Ensure any in progress editing the user is doing is present in the container
            self.boss.commit_all_editors_to_container()
            try:
                self.magnify_fonts(factor)
            except Exception:
                # Something bad happened report the error to the user
                import traceback
                error_dialog(self.gui, _('Failed to magnify fonts'), _(
                    'Failed to magnify fonts, click "Show details" for more info'),
                    det_msg=traceback.format_exc(), show=True)
                # Revert to the saved restore point
                self.boss.revert_requested(self.boss.global_undo.previous_container)
            else:
                # Show the user what changes we have made, allowing her to
                # revert them if necessary
                self.boss.show_current_diff()
                # Update the editor UI to take into account all the changes we
                # have made
                self.boss.apply_container_update_to_gui()

    def magnify_fonts(self, factor):
        # Magnify all font sizes defined in the book by the specified factor
        # First we create a restore point so that the user can undo all changes
        # we make.
        self.boss.add_savepoint('Before: Magnify fonts')

        container = self.current_container  # The book being edited as a container object

        # Iterate over all style declarations in the book, this means css
        # stylesheets, <style> tags and style="" attributes
        for name, media_type in container.mime_map.iteritems():
            if media_type in OEB_STYLES:
                # A stylesheet. Parsed stylesheets are cssutils CSSStylesheet
                # objects.
                self.magnify_stylesheet(container.parsed(name), factor)
                container.dirty(name)  # Tell the container that we have changed the styleshee
```

```
        elif media_type in OEB_DOCS:
            # A HTML file. Parsed HTML files are lxml elements

            for style_tag in container.parsed(name).xpath('//*[local-name="style"]'):
                if style_tag.text and style_tag.get('type', None) in {None, 'text/css'}:
                    # We have an inline CSS <style> tag, parse it into a
                    # stylesheet object
                    sheet = container.parse_css(style_tag.text)
                    self.magnify_stylesheet(sheet, factor)
                    style_tag.text = serialize(sheet, 'text/css', pretty_print=True)
                    container.dirty(name)  # Tell the container that we have changed the :
            for elem in container.parsed(name).xpath('//*[@style]'):
                # Process inline style attributes
                block = container.parse_css(elem.get('style'), is_declaration=True)
                self.magnify_declaration(block, factor)
                elem.set('style', force_unicode(block.getCssText(separator=' '), 'utf-8'))

    def magnify_stylesheet(self, sheet, factor):
        # Magnify all fonts in the specified stylesheet by the specified
        # factor.
        for rule in sheet.cssRules.rulesOfType(CSSRule.STYLE_RULE):
            self.magnify_declaration(rule.style, factor)

    def magnify_declaration(self, style, factor):
        # Magnify all fonts in the specified style declaration by the specified
        # factor
        val = style.getPropertyValue('font-size')
        if not val:
            return
        # see if the font-size contains a number
        num = re.search(r'[0-9.]+', val)
        if num is not None:
            num = num.group()
            val = val.replace(num, '%f' % (float(num) * factor))
            style.setProperty('font-size', val)
        # We should also be dealing with the font shorthand property and
        # font sizes specified as non numbers, but those are left as exercises
        # for the reader
```

Let's break down `main.py`. We see that it defines a single tool, named *Magnify fonts*. This tool will ask the user for a number and multiply all font sizes in the book by that number.

The first important thing is the tool name which you must set to some relatively unique string as it will be used as the key for this tool.

The next important entry point is the `calibre.gui2.tweak_book.plugin.Tool.create_action()` (page 370). This method creates the QAction objects that appear in the plugins toolbar and plugin menu. It also, optionally, assigns a keyboard shortcut that the user can customize. The triggered signal from the QAction is connected to the ask_user() method that asks the user for the font size multiplier, and then runs the magnification code.

The magnification code is well commented and fairly simple. The main things to note are that you get a reference to the editor window as `self.gui` and the editor *Boss* as `self.boss`. The *Boss* is the object that controls the editor user interface. It has many useful methods, that are documented in the `calibre.gui2.tweak_book.boss.Boss` (page 371) class.

Finally, there is `self.current_container` which is a reference to the book being edited as a `calibre.ebooks.oeb.polish.container.Container` (page 363) object. This represents the book as a collection of its constituent HTML/CSS/image files and has convenience methods for doing many useful things. The container object and various useful utility functions that can be reused in your plugin code are documented in *API*

Documentation for the ebook editing tools (page 363).

Adding translations to your plugin

You can have all the user interface strings in your plugin translated and displayed in whatever language is set for the main calibre user interface.

The first step is to go through your plugin's source code and mark all user visible strings as translatable, by surrounding them in _(). For example:

```
action_spec = (_('My plugin'), None, _('My plugin is cool'), None)
```

Then use some program to generate .po files from your plugin source code. There should be one .po file for every language you want to translate into. For example: de.po for German, fr.po for French and so on. You can use the poedit[104] program for this.

Send these .po files to your translators. Once you get them back, compile them into .mo files. You can again use poedit for that, or just do:

```
calibre-debug -c "from calibre.translations.msgfmt import main; main()" filename.po
```

Put the .mo files into the `translations` folder in your plugin.

The last step is to simply call the function *load_translations()* at the top of your plugin's .py files. For performance reasons you should only call this function in those .py files that actually have translatable strings. So in a typical User Interface plugin you would call it at the top of `ui.py` but not `__init__.py`.

You can test the translations of your plugins by changing the user interface language in calibre under Preferences->Look & Feel or by running calibre like this:

```
CALIBRE_OVERRIDE_LANG=de calibre
```

Replace `de` with the language code of the language you want to test.

The plugin API

As you may have noticed above, a plugin in calibre is a class. There are different classes for the different types of plugins in calibre. Details on each class, including the base class of all plugins can be found in *API Documentation for plugins* (page 333).

Your plugin is almost certainly going to use code from calibre. To learn how to find various bits of functionality in the calibre code base, read the section on the calibre *Code layout* (page 318).

Debugging plugins

The first, most important step is to run calibre in debug mode. You can do this from the command line with:

```
calibre-debug -g
```

Or from within calibre by right-clicking the preferences button or using the *Ctrl+Shift+R* keyboard shortcut.

When running from the command line, debug output will be printed to the console, when running from within calibre the output will go to a txt file.

You can insert print statements anywhere in your plugin code, they will be output in debug mode. Remember, this is python, you really shouldn't need anything more than print statements to debug ;) I developed all of calibre using just this debugging technique.

---

[104]http://poedit.net/

You can quickly test changes to your plugin by using the following command line:

```
calibre-debug -s; calibre-customize -b /path/to/your/plugin/directory; calibre
```

This will shutdown a running calibre, wait for the shutdown to complete, then update your plugin in calibre and relaunch calibre.

More plugin examples

You can find a list of many, sophisticated calibre plugins here[105].

Sharing your plugins with others

If you would like to share the plugins you have created with other users of calibre, post your plugin in a new thread in the calibre plugins forum[106].

1.9.8 Typesetting Math in ebooks

The calibre ebook viewer has the ability to display math embedded in ebooks (ePub and HTML files). You can typeset the math directly with TeX or MathML or AsciiMath. The calibre viewer uses the excellent MathJax[107] library to do this. This is a brief tutorial on creating ebooks with math in them that work well with the calibre viewer.

A simple HTML file with mathematics

You can write mathematics inline inside a simple HTML file and the calibre viewer will render it into properly typeset mathematics. In the example below, we use TeX notation for mathematics. You will see that you can use normal TeX commands, with the small caveat that ampersands and less than and greater than signs have to be written as & < and > respectively.

The first step is to tell calibre that this will contains maths. You do this by adding the following snippet of code to the <head> section of the HTML file:

```
<script type="text/x-mathjax-config"></script>
```

That's it, now you can type mathematics just as you would in a .tex file. For example, here are Lorentz's equations:

```
<h2>The Lorenz Equations</h2>

<p>
\begin{align}
\dot{x} &amp; = \sigma(y-x) \\
\dot{y} &amp; = \rho x - y - xz \\
\dot{z} &amp; = -\beta z + xy
\end{align}
</p>
```

This snippet looks like the following screen shot in the calibre viewer.

The complete HTML file, with more equations and inline mathematics is reproduced below. You can convert this HTML file to EPUB in calibre to end up with an ebook you can distribute easily to other people.

---

[105]http://www.mobileread.com/forums/showthread.php?t=118764
[106]http://www.mobileread.com/forums/forumdisplay.php?f=237
[107]http://www.mathjax.org

$$\dot{x} = \sigma\left(y - x\right)$$

$$\dot{y} = \rho x - y - xz$$

$$\dot{z} = -\beta z + xy$$

Fig. 1.2: *The Lorenz Equations*

```
<!DOCTYPE html>
<html>
<!-- Copyright (c) 2012 Design Science, Inc. -->
<head>
<title>Math Test Page</title>
<meta http-equiv="content-type" content="text/html; charset=UTF-8" />

<!-- This script tag is needed to make calibre's ebook-viewer recpgnize that this file needs
<script type="text/x-mathjax-config">
    // This line adds numbers to all equations automatically, unless explicitly suppressed.
    MathJax.Hub.Config({ TeX: { equationNumbers: {autoNumber: "all"} } });
</script>

<style>
h1 {text-align:center}
h2 {
  font-weight: bold;
  background-color: #DDDDDD;
  padding: .2em .5em;
  margin-top: 1.5em;
  border-top: 3px solid #666666;
  border-bottom: 2px solid #999999;
}
</style>
</head>
<body>

<h1>Sample Equations</h1>

<h2>The Lorenz Equations</h2>

<p>
\begin{align}
\dot{x} &amp; = \sigma(y-x) \label{lorenz}\\
\dot{y} &amp; = \rho x - y - xz \\
\dot{z} &amp; = -\beta z + xy
\end{align}
</p>

<h2>The Cauchy-Schwarz Inequality</h2>

<p>\[
\left( \sum_{k=1}^n a_k b_k \right)^{\!\!2} \leq
 \left( \sum_{k=1}^n a_k^2 \right) \left( \sum_{k=1}^n b_k^2 \right)
\]</p>
```

```
<h2>A Cross Product Formula</h2>

<p>\[
  \mathbf{V}_1 \times \mathbf{V}_2 =
   \begin{vmatrix}
    \mathbf{i} &amp; \mathbf{j} &amp; \mathbf{k} \\
    \frac{\partial X}{\partial u} &amp; \frac{\partial Y}{\partial u} &amp; 0 \\
    \frac{\partial X}{\partial v} &amp; \frac{\partial Y}{\partial v} &amp; 0 \\
   \end{vmatrix}
\]</p>

<h2>The probability of getting \(k\) heads when flipping \(n\) coins is:</h2>

<p>\[P(E) = {n \choose k} p^k (1-p)^{ n-k} \]</p>

<h2>An Identity of Ramanujan</h2>

<p>\[
   \frac{1}{(\sqrt{\phi \sqrt{5}}-\phi) e^{\frac25 \pi}} =
     1+\frac{e^{-2\pi}} {1+\frac{e^{-4\pi}} {1+\frac{e^{-6\pi}}
      {1+\frac{e^{-8\pi}} {1+\ldots} } } }
\]</p>

<h2>A Rogers-Ramanujan Identity</h2>

<p>\[
  1 +  \frac{q^2}{(1-q)}+\frac{q^6}{(1-q)(1-q^2)}+\cdots =
    \prod_{j=0}^{\infty}\frac{1}{(1-q^{5j+2})(1-q^{5j+3})},
     \quad\quad \text{for $|q|&lt;1$}.
\]</p>

<h2>Maxwell's Equations</h2>

<p>
\begin{align}
  \nabla \times \vec{\mathbf{B}} -\, \frac1c\, \frac{\partial\vec{\mathbf{E}}}{\partial t} &ar
  \nabla \cdot \vec{\mathbf{E}} &amp; = 4 \pi \rho \\
  \nabla \times \vec{\mathbf{E}}\, +\, \frac1c\, \frac{\partial\vec{\mathbf{B}}}{\partial t} &
  \nabla \cdot \vec{\mathbf{B}} &amp; = 0
\end{align}
</p>

<h2>In-line Mathematics</h2>

<p>While display equations look good for a page of samples, the
ability to mix math and text in a paragraph is also important.  This
expression \(\sqrt{3x-1}+(1+x)^2\) is an example of an inline equation.  As
you see, equations can be used this way as well, without unduly
disturbing the spacing between lines.</p>

<h2>References to equations</h2>

<p>Here is a reference to the Lorenz Equations (\ref{lorenz}). Clicking on the equation number

</body>
</html>
```

More information

Since the calibre viewer uses the MathJax library to render mathematics, the best place to find out more about math in ebooks and get help is the MathJax website[108].

1.9.9 Creating AZW3 • EPUB • MOBI Catalogs

calibre's Create catalog feature enables you to create a catalog of your library in a variety of formats. This help file describes cataloging options when generating a catalog in AZW3, EPUB and MOBI formats.

Selecting books to catalog

If you want *all* of your library cataloged, remove any search or filtering criteria in the main window. With a single book selected, all books in your library will be candidates for inclusion in the generated catalog. Individual books may be excluded by various criteria; see the *Excluded genres* (page 232) section below for more information.

If you want only *some* of your library cataloged, you have two options:

- Create a multiple selection of the books you want cataloged. With more than one book selected in calibre's main window, only the selected books will be cataloged.

- Use the Search field or the Tag Browser to filter the displayed books. Only the displayed books will be cataloged.

To begin catalog generation, select the menu item *Convert books > Create a catalog of the books in your calibre library*. You may also add a *Create Catalog* button to a toolbar in *Preferences > Interface > Toolbars* for easier access to the Generate catalog dialog.

In *Catalog options*, select **AZW3, EPUB or MOBI** as the Catalog format. In the *Catalog title* field, provide a name that will be used for the generated catalog. If a catalog of the same name and format already exists, it will be replaced with the newly-generated catalog.

---

[108] http://www.mathjax.org

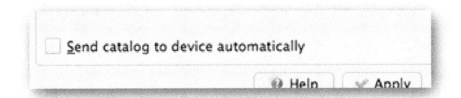

Enabling *Send catalog to device automatically* will download the generated catalog to a connected device upon completion.

Included sections

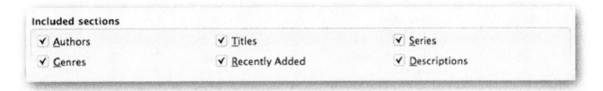

Sections enabled by a checkmark will be included in the generated catalog:

- *Authors* - all books, sorted by author, presented in a list format. Non-series books are listed before series books.

- *Titles* - all books, sorted by title, presented in a list format.

- *Series* - all books that are part of a series, sorted by series, presented in a list format.

- *Genres* - individual genres presented in a list, sorted by Author and Series.

- *Recently Added* - all books, sorted in reverse chronological order. List includes books added in the last 30 days, then a month-by-month listing of added books.

- *Descriptions* - detailed description page for each book, including a cover thumbnail and comments. Sorted by author, with non-series books listed before series books.

Prefixes

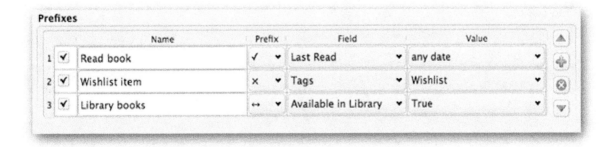

Prefix rules allow you to add a prefix to book listings when certain criteria are met. For example, you might want to mark books you've read with a checkmark, or books on your wishlist with an X.

The checkbox in the first column enables the rule. *Name* is a rule name that you provide. *Field* is either *Tags* or a custom column from your library. *Value* is the content of *Field* to match. When a prefix rule is satisfied, the book will be marked with the selected *Prefix*.

Three prefix rules have been specified in the example above:

1. *Read book* specifies that a book with any date in a custom column named *Last read* will be prefixed with a checkmark symbol.

2. *Wishlist* item specifies that any book with a *Wishlist* tag will be prefixed with an X symbol.

3. *Library* books specifies that any book with a value of True (or Yes) in a custom column *Available in Library* will be prefixed with a double arrow symbol.

The first matching rule supplies the prefix. Disabled or incomplete rules are ignored.

Excluded books

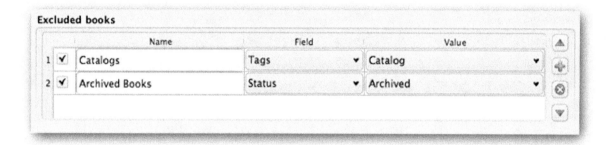

Exclusion rules allow you to specify books that will not be cataloged.

The checkbox in the first column enables the rule. *Name* is a rule name that you provide. *Field* is either *Tags* or a custom column in your library. *Value* is the content of *Field* to match. When an exclusion rule is satisfied, the book will be excluded from the generated catalog.

Two exclusion rules have been specified in the example above:

1. The *Catalogs* rule specifies that any book with a *Catalog* tag will be excluded from the generated catalog.

2. The *Archived* Books rule specifies that any book with a value of *Archived* in the custom column *Status* will be excluded from the generated catalog.

All rules are evaluated for every book. Disabled or incomplete rules are ignored.

Excluded genres

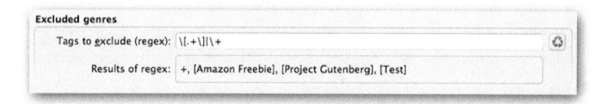

When the catalog is generated, tags in your database are used as genres. For example, you may use the tags `Fiction` and `Nonfiction`. These tags become genres in the generated catalog, with books listed under their respective genre lists based on their assigned tags. A book will be listed in every genre section for which it has a corresponding tag.

You may be using certain tags for other purposes, perhaps a + to indicate a read book, or a bracketed tag like [Amazon Freebie] to indicate a book's source. The *Excluded genres* regex allows you to specify tags that you don't want used as genres in the generated catalog. The default exclusion regex pattern \[.+\]\+ excludes any tags of the form [tag], as well as excluding +, the default tag for read books, from being used as genres in the generated catalog.

You can also use an exact tag name in a regex. For example, [Amazon Freebie] or [Project Gutenberg]. If you want to list multiple exact tags for exclusion, put a pipe (vertical bar) character between them: [Amazon Freebie]|[Project Gutenberg].

Results of regex shows you which tags will be excluded when the catalog is built, based on the tags in your database and the regex pattern you enter. The results are updated as you modify the regex pattern.

Other options

Catalog cover specifies whether to generate a new cover or use an existing cover. It is possible to create a custom cover for your catalogs - see *Custom catalog covers* (page 234) for more information. If you have created a custom cover that you want to reuse, select *Use existing cover*. Otherwise, select *Generate new cover*.

Extra Description note specifies a custom column's contents to be inserted into the Description page, next to the cover thumbnail. For example, you might want to display the date you last read a book using a *Last Read* custom column. For advanced use of the Description note feature, see this post in the calibre forum[109].

Thumb width specifies a width preference for cover thumbnails included with Descriptions pages. Thumbnails are cached to improve performance.To experiment with different widths, try generating a catalog with just a few books until you've determined your preferred width, then generate your full catalog. The first time a catalog is generated with a new thumbnail width, performance will be slower, but subsequent builds of the catalog will take advantage of the thumbnail cache.

Merge with Comments specifies a custom column whose content will be non-destructively merged with the Comments metadata during catalog generation. For example, you might have a custom column *Author Bio* that you'd like to append to the Comments metadata. You can choose to insert the custom column contents *before or after* the Comments section, and optionally separate the appended content with a horizontal rule separator. Eligible custom column types include text, comments, and composite.

---

[109]http://www.mobileread.com/forums/showpost.php?p=1335767&postcount=395

Custom catalog covers

With the Generate Cover plugin[110] installed, you can create custom covers for your catalog. To install the plugin, go to *Preferences > Advanced > Plugins > Get new plugins*.

Additional help resources

For more information on calibre's Catalog feature, see the MobileRead forum sticky Creating Catalogs - Start here[111], where you can find information on how to customize the catalog templates, and how to submit a bug report.

To ask questions or discuss calibre's Catalog feature with other users, visit the MobileRead forum Calibre Catalogs[112].

1.9.10 Virtual Libraries

In calibre, a virtual library is a way to tell calibre to open only a subset of a normal library. For example, you might want to only work with books by a certain author, or books having only a certain tag. Using virtual libraries is the preferred way of partitioning your large book collection into smaller sub collections. It is superior to splitting up your library into multiple smaller libraries as, when you want to search through your entire collection, you can simply go back to the full library. There is no way to search through multiple separate libraries simultaneously in calibre.

A virtual library is different from a simple search. A search will only restrict the list of books shown in the book list. A virtual library does that, and in addition it also restricts the entries shown in the *Tag Browser* to the left. The Tag Browser will only show tags, authors, series, publishers, etc. that come from the books in the virtual library. A virtual library thus behaves as though the actual library contains only the restricted set of books.

---

[110]http://www.mobileread.com/forums/showthread.php?t=124219
[111]http://www.mobileread.com/forums/showthread.php?t=118556
[112]http://www.mobileread.com/forums/forumdisplay.php?f=236

Creating Virtual Libraries

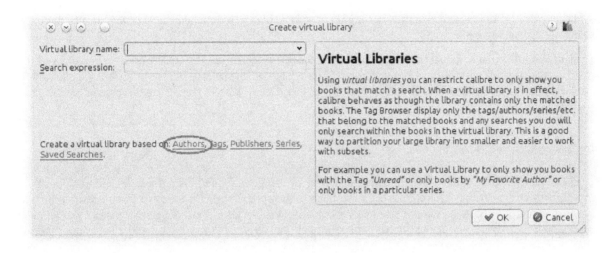 To use a virtual library click the *Virtual Library* button located to the left of the search bar and select the *Create Virtual Library* option. As a first example, let's create a virtual library that shows us only the books by a particular author. Click the *Authors* link as shown in the image below and choose the author you want to use and click OK.

The Create Virtual Library dialog has been filled in for you. Click OK and you will see that a new Virtual Library has been created, and automatically switched to, that displays only the books by the selected author. As far as calibre is concerned, it is as if your library contains only the books by the selected author.

You can switch back to the full library at any time by once again clicking the *Virtual Library* and selecting the entry named *<None>*.

Virtual Libraries are based on *searches*. You can use any search as the basis of a virtual library. The virtual library will contain only the books matched by that search. First, type in the search you want to use in the search bar or build a search using the *Tag Browser*. When you are happy with the returned results, click the Virtual Library button, choose Create Library and enter a name for the new virtual library. The virtual library will then be created based on the search you just typed in. Searches are very powerful, for examples of the kinds of things you can do with them, see *The Search Interface* (page 11).

Examples of useful Virtual Libraries

- **Books added to calibre in the last day::** date:>1daysago
- **Books added to calibre in the last month::** date:>30daysago
- **Books with a rating of 5 stars::** rating:5
- **Books with a rating of at least 4 stars::** rating:>=4
- **Books with no rating::** rating:false
- **Periodicals downloaded by the Fetch News function in calibre::** tags:=News and author:=calibre
- **Books with no tags::** tags:false
- **Books with no covers::** cover:false

Working with Virtual Libraries

You can edit a previously created virtual library or remove it, by clicking the *Virtual Library* and choosing the appropriate action.

You can tell calibre that you always want to apply a particular virtual library when the current library is opened, by going to *Preferences->Behavior*.

If you use the calibre Content Server, you can have it share a virtual library instead of the full library by going to *Preferences->Sharing over the net*.

You can quickly use the current search as a temporary virtual library by clicking the *Virtual Library* button and choosing the **current search* entry.

You can display all available virtual libraries as tabs above the book list. This is particularly handy if you like switching between virtual libraries very often. Click the *Virtual Library* button and select *Show virtual libraries as tabs*. You can re-arrange the tabs by drag and drop and close ones you do not want to see. Closed tabs can be restored by right-clicking on the tab bar.

Using additional restrictions

You can further restrict the books shown in a Virtual Library by using *Additional restrictions*. An additional restriction is saved search you previously created that can be applied to the current Virtual Library to further restrict the books shown in a virtual library. For example, say you have a Virtual Library for books tagged as *Historical Fiction* and a saved search that shows you unread books, you can click the *Virtual Library* button and choose the *Additional restriction* option to show only unread Historical Fiction books. To learn about saved searches, see *Saving searches* (page 13).

1.10 Customizing calibre

calibre has a highly modular design. Various parts of it can be customized. You can learn how to create *recipes* to add new sources of online content to calibre in the Section *Adding your favorite news website* (page 125). Here, you will learn, first, how to use environment variables and *tweaks* to customize calibre's behavior, and then how to specify your own static resources like icons and templates to override the defaults and finally how to use *plugins* to add functionality to calibre.

1.10.1 API Documentation for plugins

Defines various abstract base classes that can be subclassed to create powerful plugins. The useful classes are:

Plugin

class calibre.customize.**Plugin**(*plugin_path*)

> A calibre plugin. Useful members include:

> > • **self.plugin_path: Stores path to the zip file that contains** this plugin or None if it is a builtin plugin

> > • **self.site_customization: Stores a customization string entered** by the user.

> Methods that should be overridden in sub classes:

> > • *initialize()* (page 334)

> > • *customization_help()* (page 335)

> Useful methods:

> > • *temporary_file()* (page 335)

> > • *__enter__()*

> > • *load_resources()* (page 335)

supported_platforms = []

> List of platforms this plugin works on. For example: ['windows', 'osx', 'linux']

name = 'Trivial Plugin'

> The name of this plugin. You must set it something other than Trivial Plugin for it to work.

version = (1, 0, 0)

> The version of this plugin as a 3-tuple (major, minor, revision)

description = u'Does absolutely nothing'

> A short string describing what this plugin does

author = u'Unknown'

> The author of this plugin

priority = 1

> When more than one plugin exists for a filetype, the plugins are run in order of decreasing priority i.e. plugins with higher priority will be run first. The highest possible priority is sys.maxint. Default priority is 1.

minimum_calibre_version = (0, 4, 118)

> The earliest version of calibre this plugin requires

can_be_disabled = True

> If False, the user will not be able to disable this plugin. Use with care.

---

type = u'Base'

> The type of this plugin. Used for categorizing plugins in the GUI

initialize ()

> Called once when calibre plugins are initialized. Plugins are re-initialized every time a new plugin is added. Also note that if the plugin is run in a worker process, such as for adding books, then the plugin will be initialized for every new worker process.
>
> Perform any plugin specific initialization here, such as extracting resources from the plugin zip file. The path to the zip file is available as `self.plugin_path`.
>
> Note that `self.site_customization` is **not** available at this point.

config_widget ()

> Implement this method and `save_settings ()` (page 334) in your plugin to use a custom configuration dialog, rather then relying on the simple string based default customization.
>
> This method, if implemented, must return a QWidget. The widget can have an optional method validate() that takes no arguments and is called immediately after the user clicks OK. Changes are applied if and only if the method returns True.
>
> If for some reason you cannot perform the configuration at this time, return a tuple of two strings (message, details), these will be displayed as a warning dialog to the user and the process will be aborted.

save_settings (*config_widget*)

> Save the settings specified by the user with config_widget.
>
> > **Parameters config_widget** – The widget returned by `config_widget ()` (page 334).

do_user_config (*parent=None*)

> This method shows a configuration dialog for this plugin. It returns True if the user clicks OK, False otherwise. The changes are automatically applied.

load_resources (*names*)

> If this plugin comes in a ZIP file (user added plugin), this method will allow you to load resources from the ZIP file.
>
> For example to load an image:

```
pixmap = QPixmap()
pixmap.loadFromData(self.load_resources(['images/icon.png']).itervalues().next())
icon = QIcon(pixmap)
```

> > **Parameters names** – List of paths to resources in the zip file using / as separator
> >
> > **Returns** A dictionary of the form {name: file_contents}. Any names that were not found in the zip file will not be present in the dictionary.

customization_help (*gui=False*)

> Return a string giving help on how to customize this plugin. By default raise a `NotImplementedError`, which indicates that the plugin does not require customization.
>
> If you re-implement this method in your subclass, the user will be asked to enter a string as customization for this plugin. The customization string will be available as `self.site_customization`.
>
> Site customization could be anything, for example, the path to a needed binary on the user's computer.
>
> > **Parameters gui** – If True return HTML help, otherwise return plain text help.

temporary_file (*suffix*)

> Return a file-like object that is a temporary file on the file system. This file will remain available even after

being closed and will only be removed on interpreter shutdown. Use the `name` member of the returned object to access the full path to the created temporary file.

> **Parameters** `suffix` – The suffix that the temporary file will have.

`cli_main` (*args*)
> This method is the main entry point for your plugins command line interface. It is called when the user does: calibre-debug -r "Plugin Name". Any arguments passed are present in the args variable.

FileTypePlugin

class `calibre.customize.`**`FileTypePlugin`** (*plugin_path*)
> Bases: *calibre.customize.Plugin* (page 333)

A plugin that is associated with a particular set of file types.

`file_types` = set([])
> Set of file types for which this plugin should be run. For example: {'lit', 'mobi', 'prc'}

`on_import` = **False**
> If True, this plugin is run when books are added to the database

`on_postimport` = **False**
> If True, this plugin is run after books are added to the database

`on_preprocess` = **False**
> If True, this plugin is run just before a conversion

`on_postprocess` = **False**
> If True, this plugin is run after conversion on the final file produced by the conversion output plugin.

`run` (*path_to_ebook*)
> Run the plugin. Must be implemented in subclasses. It should perform whatever modifications are required on the ebook and return the absolute path to the modified ebook. If no modifications are needed, it should return the path to the original ebook. If an error is encountered it should raise an Exception. The default implementation simply return the path to the original ebook.

> The modified ebook file should be created with the `temporary_file()` method.

> > **Parameters** `path_to_ebook` – Absolute path to the ebook.

> > **Returns** Absolute path to the modified ebook.

`postimport` (*book_id*, *book_format*, *db*)
> Called post import, i.e., after the book file has been added to the database.

> > **Parameters**

> > > • **`book_id`** – Database id of the added book.

> > > • **`book_format`** – The file type of the book that was added.

> > > • **`db`** – Library database.

Metadata plugins

class `calibre.customize.`**`MetadataReaderPlugin`** (**args*, ***kwargs*)
> Bases: *calibre.customize.Plugin* (page 333)

A plugin that implements reading metadata from a set of file types.

file_types = set([])
> Set of file types for which this plugin should be run For example: `set(['lit', 'mobi', 'prc'])`

get_metadata (*stream*, *type*)
> Return metadata for the file represented by stream (a file like object that supports reading). Raise an exception when there is an error with the input data. :param type: The type of file. Guaranteed to be one of the entries in *file_types* (page 336). :return: A `calibre.ebooks.metadata.book.Metadata` object

class `calibre.customize.`**MetadataWriterPlugin**(**args*, ***kwargs*)
> Bases: `calibre.customize.Plugin` (page 333)

A plugin that implements reading metadata from a set of file types.

file_types = set([])
> Set of file types for which this plugin should be run For example: `set(['lit', 'mobi', 'prc'])`

set_metadata (*stream*, *mi*, *type*)
> Set metadata for the file represented by stream (a file like object that supports reading). Raise an exception when there is an error with the input data. :param type: The type of file. Guaranteed to be one of the entries in *file_types* (page 336). :param mi: A `calibre.ebooks.metadata.book.Metadata` object

Catalog plugins

class `calibre.customize.`**CatalogPlugin**(*plugin_path*)
> Bases: `calibre.customize.Plugin` (page 333)

A plugin that implements a catalog generator.

file_types = set([])
> Output file type for which this plugin should be run For example: 'epub' or 'xml'

cli_options = []
> CLI parser options specific to this plugin, declared as namedtuple Option:

```
from collections import namedtuple
Option = namedtuple('Option', 'option, default, dest, help')
cli_options = [Option('--catalog-title',
                    default = 'My Catalog',
                    dest = 'catalog_title',
                    help = (_('Title of generated catalog. \nDefault:') + " '" +
                    '%default' + "'"))]
cli_options parsed in library.cli:catalog_option_parser()
```

initialize ()
> If plugin is not a built-in, copy the plugin's .ui and .py files from the zip file to $TMPDIR. Tab will be dynamically generated and added to the Catalog Options dialog in calibre.gui2.dialogs.catalog.py:Catalog

run (*path_to_output*, *opts*, *db*, *ids*, *notification=None*)
> Run the plugin. Must be implemented in subclasses. It should generate the catalog in the format specified in file_types, returning the absolute path to the generated catalog file. If an error is encountered it should raise an Exception.

> The generated catalog file should be created with the `temporary_file()` method.

> **Parameters**

> • **path_to_output** – Absolute path to the generated catalog file.

> • **opts** – A dictionary of keyword arguments

- **db** – A LibraryDatabase2 object

Metadata download plugins

class `calibre.ebooks.metadata.sources.base.`**Source** (**args*, ***kwargs*)
　　Bases: *calibre.customize.Plugin* (page 333)

　　capabilities = frozenset([])
　　　　Set of capabilities supported by this plugin. Useful capabilities are: 'identify', 'cover'

　　touched_fields = frozenset([])
　　　　List of metadata fields that can potentially be download by this plugin during the identify phase

　　has_html_comments = False
　　　　Set this to True if your plugin returns HTML formatted comments

　　supports_gzip_transfer_encoding = False
　　　　Setting this to True means that the browser object will add Accept-Encoding: gzip to all requests. This can speedup downloads but make sure that the source actually supports gzip transfer encoding correctly first

　　cached_cover_url_is_reliable = True
　　　　Cached cover URLs can sometimes be unreliable (i.e. the download could fail or the returned image could be bogus. If that is often the case with this source set to False

　　options = ()
　　　　A list of `Option` objects. They will be used to automatically construct the configuration widget for this plugin

　　config_help_message = None
　　　　A string that is displayed at the top of the config widget for this plugin

　　can_get_multiple_covers = False
　　　　If True this source can return multiple covers for a given query

　　auto_trim_covers = False
　　　　If set to True covers downloaded by this plugin are automatically trimmed.

　　prefer_results_with_isbn = True
　　　　If set to True, and this source returns multiple results for a query, some of which have ISBNs and some of which do not, the results without ISBNs will be ignored

　　is_configured ()
　　　　Return False if your plugin needs to be configured before it can be used. For example, it might need a username/password/API key.

　　get_author_tokens (*authors*, *only_first_author=True*)
　　　　Take a list of authors and return a list of tokens useful for an AND search query. This function tries to return tokens in first name middle names last name order, by assuming that if a comma is in the author name, the name is in lastname, other names form.

　　get_title_tokens (*title*, *strip_joiners=True*, *strip_subtitle=False*)
　　　　Take a title and return a list of tokens useful for an AND search query. Excludes connectives(optionally) and punctuation.

　　split_jobs (*jobs*, *num*)
　　　　Split a list of jobs into at most num groups, as evenly as possible

　　test_fields (*mi*)
　　　　Return the first field from self.touched_fields that is null on the mi object

clean_downloaded_metadata (*mi*)

Call this method in your plugin's identify method to normalize metadata before putting the Metadata object into result_queue. You can of course, use a custom algorithm suited to your metadata source.

get_book_url (*identifiers*)

Return a 3-tuple or None. The 3-tuple is of the form: (identifier_type, identifier_value, URL). The URL is the URL for the book identified by identifiers at this source. identifier_type, identifier_value specify the identifier corresponding to the URL. This URL must be browseable to by a human using a browser. It is meant to provide a clickable link for the user to easily visit the books page at this source. If no URL is found, return None. This method must be quick, and consistent, so only implement it if it is possible to construct the URL from a known scheme given identifiers.

get_book_url_name (*idtype*, *idval*, *url*)

Return a human readable name from the return value of get_book_url().

get_book_urls (*identifiers*)

Override this method if you would like to return multiple urls for this book. Return a list of 3-tuples. By default this method simply calls *get_book_url ()* (page 338).

get_cached_cover_url (*identifiers*)

Return cached cover URL for the book identified by the identifiers dict or None if no such URL exists.

Note that this method must only return validated URLs, i.e. not URLS that could result in a generic cover image or a not found error.

identify_results_keygen (*title=None*, *authors=None*, *identifiers={}*)

Return a function that is used to generate a key that can sort Metadata objects by their relevance given a search query (title, authors, identifiers).

These keys are used to sort the results of a call to *identify ()* (page 339).

For details on the default algorithm see *InternalMetadataCompareKeyGen* (page 339). Re-implement this function in your plugin if the default algorithm is not suitable.

identify (*log*, *result_queue*, *abort*, *title=None*, *authors=None*, *identifiers={}*, *timeout=30*)

Identify a book by its title/author/isbn/etc.

If identifiers(s) are specified and no match is found and this metadata source does not store all related identifiers (for example, all ISBNs of a book), this method should retry with just the title and author (assuming they were specified).

If this metadata source also provides covers, the URL to the cover should be cached so that a subsequent call to the get covers API with the same ISBN/special identifier does not need to get the cover URL again. Use the caching API for this.

Every Metadata object put into result_queue by this method must have a *source_relevance* attribute that is an integer indicating the order in which the results were returned by the metadata source for this query. This integer will be used by compare_identify_results(). If the order is unimportant, set it to zero for every result.

Make sure that any cover/isbn mapping information is cached before the Metadata object is put into result_queue.

Parameters

- **log** – A log object, use it to output debugging information/errors

- **result_queue** – A result Queue, results should be put into it. Each result is a Metadata object

- **abort** – If abort.is_set() returns True, abort further processing and return as soon as possible

- **title** – The title of the book, can be None

- **authors** – A list of authors of the book, can be None

- **identifiers** – A dictionary of other identifiers, most commonly { 'isbn':'1234...'}

- **timeout** – Timeout in seconds, no network request should hang for longer than timeout.

> **Returns** None if no errors occurred, otherwise a unicode representation of the error suitable for showing to the user

download_cover (*log, result_queue, abort, title=None, authors=None, identifiers={}, timeout=30, get_best_cover=False*)

Download a cover and put it into result_queue. The parameters all have the same meaning as for *identify()* (page 339). Put (self, cover_data) into result_queue.

This method should use cached cover URLs for efficiency whenever possible. When cached data is not present, most plugins simply call identify and use its results.

If the parameter get_best_cover is True and this plugin can get multiple covers, it should only get the "best" one.

class calibre.ebooks.metadata.sources.base.**InternalMetadataCompareKeyGen** (*mi, source_plugin, title, authors, identifiers*)

Generate a sort key for comparison of the relevance of Metadata objects, given a search query. This is used only to compare results from the same metadata source, not across different sources.

The sort key ensures that an ascending order sort is a sort by order of decreasing relevance.

The algorithm is:

- Prefer results that have at least one identifier the same as for the query

- Prefer results with a cached cover URL

- Prefer results with all available fields filled in

- Prefer results with the same language as the current user interface language

- Prefer results that are an exact title match to the query

- Prefer results with longer comments (greater than 10% longer)

- **Use the relevance of the result as reported by the metadata source's search** engine

Conversion plugins

class calibre.customize.conversion.**InputFormatPlugin** (**args*)

Bases: *calibre.customize.Plugin* (page 333)

InputFormatPlugins are responsible for converting a document into HTML+OPF+CSS+etc. The results of the conversion *must* be encoded in UTF-8. The main action happens in *convert ()* (page 340).

file_types = set([])

Set of file types for which this plugin should be run For example: set (['azw', 'mobi', 'prc'])

---

is_image_collection = False
> If True, this input plugin generates a collection of images, one per HTML file. This can be set dynamically, in the convert method if the input files can be both image collections and non-image collections. If you set this to True, you must implement the get_images() method that returns a list of images.

core_usage = 1
> Number of CPU cores used by this plugin A value of -1 means that it uses all available cores

for_viewer = False
> If set to True, the input plugin will perform special processing to make its output suitable for viewing

output_encoding = 'utf-8'
> The encoding that this input plugin creates files in. A value of None means that the encoding is undefined and must be detected individually

common_options = set([<calibre.customize.conversion.OptionRecommendation object at 0x7f30cae00150>])
> Options shared by all Input format plugins. Do not override in sub-classes. Use *options* (page 340) instead. Every option must be an instance of OptionRecommendation.

options = set([])
> Options to customize the behavior of this plugin. Every option must be an instance of OptionRecommendation.

recommendations = set([])
> A set of 3-tuples of the form (option_name, recommended_value, recommendation_level)

get_images ()
> Return a list of absolute paths to the images, if this input plugin represents an image collection. The list of images is in the same order as the spine and the TOC.

convert (*stream, options, file_ext, log, accelerators*)
> This method must be implemented in sub-classes. It must return the path to the created OPF file or an OEBBook instance. All output should be contained in the current directory. If this plugin creates files outside the current directory they must be deleted/marked for deletion before this method returns.
>
> **Parameters**
>
> - **stream** – A file like object that contains the input file.
>
> - **options** – Options to customize the conversion process. Guaranteed to have attributes corresponding to all the options declared by this plugin. In addition, it will have a verbose attribute that takes integral values from zero upwards. Higher numbers mean be more verbose. Another useful attribute is input_profile that is an instance of calibre.customize.profiles.InputProfile.
>
> - **file_ext** – The extension (without the .) of the input file. It is guaranteed to be one of the *file_types* supported by this plugin.
>
> - **log** – A calibre.utils.logging.Log object. All output should use this object.
>
> - **accelerators** – A dictionary of various information that the input plugin can get easily that would speed up the subsequent stages of the conversion.

postprocess_book (*oeb, opts, log*)
> Called to allow the input plugin to perform postprocessing after the book has been parsed.

specialize (*oeb, opts, log, output_fmt*)
> Called to allow the input plugin to specialize the parsed book for a particular output format. Called after postprocess_book and before any transforms are performed on the parsed book.

gui_configuration_widget (*parent*, *get_option_by_name*, *get_option_help*, *db*, *book_id=None*)
Called to create the widget used for configuring this plugin in the calibre GUI. The widget must be an instance of the PluginWidget class. See the builtin input plugins for examples.

class calibre.customize.conversion.**OutputFormatPlugin** (**args*)
Bases: *calibre.customize.Plugin* (page 333)

OutputFormatPlugins are responsible for converting an OEB document (OPF+HTML) into an output ebook.

The OEB document can be assumed to be encoded in UTF-8. The main action happens in *convert ()* (page 341).

file_type = **None**
The file type (extension without leading period) that this plugin outputs

common_options = set([<calibre.customize.conversion.OptionRecommendation object at 0x7f30cae002d0>])
Options shared by all Input format plugins. Do not override in sub-classes. Use *options* (page 341) instead. Every option must be an instance of OptionRecommendation.

options = set([])
Options to customize the behavior of this plugin. Every option must be an instance of OptionRecommendation.

recommendations = set([])
A set of 3-tuples of the form (option_name, recommended_value, recommendation_level).

convert (*oeb_book*, *output*, *input_plugin*, *opts*, *log*)
Render the contents of *oeb_book* (which is an instance of calibre.ebooks.oeb.OEBBook to the file specified by output.

> Parameters

  - **output** – Either a file like object or a string. If it is a string it is the path to a directory that may or may not exist. The output plugin should write its output into that directory. If it is a file like object, the output plugin should write its output into the file.

  - **input_plugin** – The input plugin that was used at the beginning of the conversion pipeline.

  - **opts** – Conversion options. Guaranteed to have attributes corresponding to the OptionRecommendations of this plugin.

  - **log** – The logger. Print debug/info messages etc. using this.

specialize_css_for_output (*log*, *opts*, *item*, *stylizer*)
Can be used to make changes to the css during the CSS flattening process.

> Parameters

  - **item** – The item (HTML file) being processed

  - **stylizer** – A Stylizer object containing the flattened styles for item. You can get the style for any element by stylizer.style(element).

gui_configuration_widget (*parent*, *get_option_by_name*, *get_option_help*, *db*, *book_id=None*)
Called to create the widget used for configuring this plugin in the calibre GUI. The widget must be an instance of the PluginWidget class. See the builtin output plugins for examples.

Device Drivers

The base class for all device drivers is *DevicePlugin* (page 342). However, if your device exposes itself as a USBMS drive to the operating system, you should use the USBMS class instead as it implements all the logic needed to support these kinds of devices.

class calibre.devices.interface.**DevicePlugin**(*plugin_path*)

> Bases: *calibre.customize.Plugin* (page 333)

> Defines the interface that should be implemented by backends that communicate with an ebook reader.

> **FORMATS = ['lrf', 'rtf', 'pdf', 'txt']**
> > Ordered list of supported formats

> **VENDOR_ID = 0**
> > VENDOR_ID can be either an integer, a list of integers or a dictionary If it is a dictionary, it must be a dictionary of dictionaries, of the form:
> >
> > ```
> > {
> >  integer_vendor_id : { product_id : [list of BCDs], ... },
> >  ...
> > }
> > ```

> **PRODUCT_ID = 0**
> > An integer or a list of integers

> **BCD = None**
> > BCD can be either None to not distinguish between devices based on BCD, or it can be a list of the BCD numbers of all devices supported by this driver.

> **THUMBNAIL_HEIGHT = 68**
> > Height for thumbnails on the device

> **THUMBNAIL_COMPRESSION_QUALITY = 75**
> > Width for thumbnails on the device. Setting this will force thumbnails to this size, not preserving aspect ratio. If it is not set, then the aspect ratio will be preserved and the thumbnail will be no higher than THUMBNAIL_HEIGHT Compression quality for thumbnails. Set this closer to 100 to have better quality thumbnails with fewer compression artifacts. Of course, the thumbnails get larger as well.

> **WANTS_UPDATED_THUMBNAILS = False**
> > Set this to True if the device supports updating cover thumbnails during sync_booklists. Setting it to true will ask device.py to refresh the cover thumbnails during book matching

> **CAN_SET_METADATA = ['title', 'authors', 'collections']**
> > Whether the metadata on books can be set via the GUI.

> **CAN_DO_DEVICE_DB_PLUGBOARD = False**
> > Whether the device can handle device_db metadata plugboards

> **path_sep = '/'**
> > Path separator for paths to books on device

> **icon = '/home/kovid/work/calibre/resources/images/reader.png'**
> > Icon for this device

> **UserAnnotation**
> > alias of Annotation

> **OPEN_FEEDBACK_MESSAGE = None**
> > GUI displays this as a message if not None. Useful if opening can take a long time

> **VIRTUAL_BOOK_EXTENSIONS = frozenset([])**
> > Set of extensions that are "virtual books" on the device and therefore cannot be viewed/saved/added to library. For example: frozenset(['kobo'])

> **VIRTUAL_BOOK_EXTENSION_MESSAGE = None**
> > Message to display to user for virtual book extensions.

NUKE_COMMENTS = None

> Whether to nuke comments in the copy of the book sent to the device. If not None this should be short string that the comments will be replaced by.

MANAGES_DEVICE_PRESENCE = False

> If True indicates that this driver completely manages device detection, ejecting and so forth. If you set this to True, you *must* implement the detect_managed_devices and debug_managed_device_detection methods. A driver with this set to true is responsible for detection of devices, managing a blacklist of devices, a list of ejected devices and so forth. calibre will periodically call the detect_managed_devices() method and if it returns a detected device, calibre will call open(). open() will be called every time a device is returned even is previous calls to open() failed, therefore the driver must maintain its own blacklist of failed devices. Similarly, when ejecting, calibre will call eject() and then assuming the next call to detect_managed_devices() returns None, it will call post_yank_cleanup().

SLOW_DRIVEINFO = False

> If set the True, calibre will call the *get_driveinfo()* (page 345) method after the books lists have been loaded to get the driveinfo.

ASK_TO_ALLOW_CONNECT = False

> If set to True, calibre will ask the user if they want to manage the device with calibre, the first time it is detected. If you set this to True you must implement *get_device_uid()* (page 347) and *ignore_connected_device()* (page 348) and *get_user_blacklisted_devices()* (page 348) and *set_user_blacklisted_devices()* (page 348)

user_feedback_after_callback = None

> Set this to a dictionary of the form { 'title':title, 'msg':msg, 'det_msg':detailed_msg} to have calibre popup a message to the user after some callbacks are run (currently only upload_books). Be careful to not spam the user with too many messages. This variable is checked after *every* callback, so only set it when you really need to.

is_usb_connected (*devices_on_system, debug=False, only_presence=False*)

> Return True, device_info if a device handled by this plugin is currently connected.
>
> > **Parameters** **devices_on_system** – List of devices currently connected

detect_managed_devices (*devices_on_system, force_refresh=False*)

> Called only if MANAGES_DEVICE_PRESENCE is True.
>
> Scan for devices that this driver can handle. Should return a device object if a device is found. This object will be passed to the open() method as the connected_device. If no device is found, return None. The returned object can be anything, calibre does not use it, it is only passed to open().
>
> This method is called periodically by the GUI, so make sure it is not too resource intensive. Use a cache to avoid repeatedly scanning the system.
>
> > **Parameters**
> >
> > - **devices_on_system** – Set of USB devices found on the system.
> > - **force_refresh** – If True and the driver uses a cache to prevent repeated scanning, the cache must be flushed.

debug_managed_device_detection (*devices_on_system, output*)

> Called only if MANAGES_DEVICE_PRESENCE is True.
>
> Should write information about the devices detected on the system to output, which is a file like object.
>
> Should return True if a device was detected and successfully opened, otherwise False.

reset (*key='-1', log_packets=False, report_progress=None, detected_device=None*)

> > **Parameters**

- **key** – The key to unlock the device

- **log_packets** – If true the packet stream to/from the device is logged

- **report_progress** – Function that is called with a % progress (number between 0 and 100) for various tasks If it is called with -1 that means that the task does not have any progress information

- **detected_device** – Device information from the device scanner

can_handle_windows (*device_id*, *debug=False*)

Optional method to perform further checks on a device to see if this driver is capable of handling it. If it is not it should return False. This method is only called after the vendor, product ids and the bcd have matched, so it can do some relatively time intensive checks. The default implementation returns True. This method is called only on windows. See also *can_handle ()* (page 344).

> **Parameters device_info** – On windows a device ID string. On Unix a tuple of `(vendor_id, product_id, bcd)`.

can_handle (*device_info*, *debug=False*)

Unix version of *can_handle_windows ()* (page 344)

> **Parameters device_info** – Is a tuple of (vid, pid, bcd, manufacturer, product, serial number)

open (*connected_device*, *library_uuid*)

Perform any device specific initialization. Called after the device is detected but before any other functions that communicate with the device. For example: For devices that present themselves as USB Mass storage devices, this method would be responsible for mounting the device or if the device has been automounted, for finding out where it has been mounted. The method `calibre.devices.usbms.device.Device.open()` has an implementation of this function that should serve as a good example for USB Mass storage devices.

This method can raise an OpenFeedback exception to display a message to the user.

> **Parameters**
>
> - **connected_device** – The device that we are trying to open. It is a tuple of (vendor id, product id, bcd, manufacturer name, product name, device serial number). However, some devices have no serial number and on windows only the first three fields are present, the rest are None.
>
> - **library_uuid** – The UUID of the current calibre library. Can be None if there is no library (for example when used from the command line).

eject ()

Un-mount / eject the device from the OS. This does not check if there are pending GUI jobs that need to communicate with the device.

NOTE: That this method may not be called on the same thread as the rest of the device methods.

post_yank_cleanup ()

Called if the user yanks the device without ejecting it first.

set_progress_reporter (*report_progress*)

Set a function to report progress information.

> **Parameters report_progress** – Function that is called with a % progress (number between 0 and 100) for various tasks If it is called with -1 that means that the task does not have any progress information

get_device_information (*end_session=True*)

Ask device for device information. See L{DeviceInfoQuery}.

> **Returns** (device name, device version, software version on device, mime type) The tuple can optionally have a fifth element, which is a drive information dictionary. See usbms.driver for an example.

get_driveinfo ()
> Return the driveinfo dictionary. Usually called from get_device_information(), but if loading the driveinfo is slow for this driver, then it should set SLOW_DRIVEINFO. In this case, this method will be called by calibre after the book lists have been loaded. Note that it is not called on the device thread, so the driver should cache the drive info in the books() method and this function should return the cached data.

card_prefix (*end_session=True*)
> Return a 2 element list of the prefix to paths on the cards. If no card is present None is set for the card's prefix. E.G. ('/place', '/place2') (None, 'place2') ('place', None) (None, None)

total_space (*end_session=True*)

> **Get total space available on the mountpoints:**
>
> 1. Main memory
>
> 2. Memory Card A
>
> 3. Memory Card B
>
> **Returns** A 3 element list with total space in bytes of (1, 2, 3). If a particular device doesn't have any of these locations it should return 0.

free_space (*end_session=True*)

> **Get free space available on the mountpoints:**
>
> 1. Main memory
>
> 2. Card A
>
> 3. Card B
>
> **Returns** A 3 element list with free space in bytes of (1, 2, 3). If a particular device doesn't have any of these locations it should return -1.

books (*oncard=None, end_session=True*)
> Return a list of ebooks on the device.

> **Parameters oncard** – If 'carda' or 'cardb' return a list of ebooks on the specific storage card, otherwise return list of ebooks in main memory of device. If a card is specified and no books are on the card return empty list.

> **Returns** A BookList.

upload_books (*files, names, on_card=None, end_session=True, metadata=None*)
> Upload a list of books to the device. If a file already exists on the device, it should be replaced. This method should raise a `FreeSpaceError` if there is not enough free space on the device. The text of the FreeSpaceError must contain the word "card" if `on_card` is not None otherwise it must contain the word "memory".

> **Parameters**

> * **files** – A list of paths

> * **names** – A list of file names that the books should have once uploaded to the device. len(names) == len(files)

- **metadata** – If not None, it is a list of Metadata objects. The idea is to use the metadata to determine where on the device to put the book. len(metadata) == len(files). Apart from the regular cover (path to cover), there may also be a thumbnail attribute, which should be used in preference. The thumbnail attribute is of the form (width, height, cover_data as jpeg).

> **Returns** A list of 3-element tuples. The list is meant to be passed to *add_books_to_metadata()* (page 346).

classmethod add_books_to_metadata (*locations*, *metadata*, *booklists*)

Add locations to the booklists. This function must not communicate with the device.

Parameters

- **locations** – Result of a call to L{upload_books}

- **metadata** – List of Metadata objects, same as for *upload_books()* (page 346).

- **booklists** – A tuple containing the result of calls to (books(oncard=None)(), books(oncard='carda')(), :meth'books(oncard='cardb')').

delete_books (*paths*, *end_session=True*)

Delete books at paths on device.

classmethod remove_books_from_metadata (*paths*, *booklists*)

Remove books from the metadata list. This function must not communicate with the device.

Parameters

- **paths** – paths to books on the device.

- **booklists** – A tuple containing the result of calls to (books(oncard=None)(), books(oncard='carda')(), :meth'books(oncard='cardb')').

sync_booklists (*booklists*, *end_session=True*)

Update metadata on device.

> **Parameters booklists** – A tuple containing the result of calls to (books(oncard=None)(), books(oncard='carda')(), :meth'books(oncard='cardb')').

get_file (*path*, *outfile*, *end_session=True*)

Read the file at path on the device and write it to outfile.

> **Parameters outfile** – file object like sys.stdout or the result of an *open()* (page 344) call.

classmethod config_widget ()

Should return a QWidget. The QWidget contains the settings for the device interface

classmethod save_settings (*settings_widget*)

Should save settings to disk. Takes the widget created in *config_widget()* (page 347) and saves all settings to disk.

classmethod settings ()

Should return an opts object. The opts object should have at least one attribute *format_map* which is an ordered list of formats for the device.

set_plugboards (*plugboards*, *pb_func*)

provide the driver the current set of plugboards and a function to select a specific plugboard. This method is called immediately before add_books and sync_booklists.

pb_func is a callable with the following signature:: def pb_func(device_name, format, plugboards)

You give it the current device name (either the class name or DEVICE_PLUGBOARD_NAME), the format you are interested in (a 'real' format or 'device_db'), and the plugboards (you were given those by set_plugboards, the same place you got this method).

Returns None or a single plugboard instance.

set_driveinfo_name (*location_code, name*)

Set the device name in the driveinfo file to 'name'. This setting will persist until the file is re-created or the name is changed again.

Non-disk devices should implement this method based on the location codes returned by the get_device_information() method.

prepare_addable_books (*paths*)

Given a list of paths, returns another list of paths. These paths point to addable versions of the books.

If there is an error preparing a book, then instead of a path, the position in the returned list for that book should be a three tuple: (original_path, the exception instance, traceback)

startup ()

Called when calibre is is starting the device. Do any initialization required. Note that multiple instances of the class can be instantiated, and thus __init__ can be called multiple times, but only one instance will have this method called. This method is called on the device thread, not the GUI thread.

shutdown ()

Called when calibre is shutting down, either for good or in preparation to restart. Do any cleanup required. This method is called on the device thread, not the GUI thread.

get_device_uid ()

Must return a unique id for the currently connected device (this is called immediately after a successful call to open()). You must implement this method if you set ASK_TO_ALLOW_CONNECT = True

ignore_connected_device (*uid*)

Should ignore the device identified by uid (the result of a call to get_device_uid()) in the future. You must implement this method if you set ASK_TO_ALLOW_CONNECT = True. Note that this function is called immediately after open(), so if open() caches some state, the driver should reset that state.

get_user_blacklisted_devices ()

Return map of device uid to friendly name for all devices that the user has asked to be ignored.

set_user_blacklisted_devices (*devices*)

Set the list of device uids that should be ignored by this driver.

specialize_global_preferences (*device_prefs*)

Implement this method if your device wants to override a particular preference. You must ensure that all call sites that want a preference that can be overridden use device_prefs['something'] instead of prefs['something']. Your method should call device_prefs.set_overrides(pref=val, pref=val, ...). Currently used for: metadata management (prefs['manage_device_metadata'])

set_library_info (*library_name, library_uuid, field_metadata*)

Implement this method if you want information about the current calibre library. This method is called at startup and when the calibre library changes while connected.

is_dynamically_controllable ()

Called by the device manager when starting plugins. If this method returns a string, then a) it supports the device manager's dynamic control interface, and b) that name is to be used when talking to the plugin.

This method can be called on the GUI thread. A driver that implements this method must be thread safe.

start_plugin ()

This method is called to start the plugin. The plugin should begin to accept device connections however it does that. If the plugin is already accepting connections, then do nothing.

This method can be called on the GUI thread. A driver that implements this method must be thread safe.

stop_plugin ()

This method is called to stop the plugin. The plugin should no longer accept connections, and should cleanup behind itself. It is likely that this method should call shutdown. If the plugin is already not accepting connections, then do nothing.

This method can be called on the GUI thread. A driver that implements this method must be thread safe.

get_option (*opt_string*, *default=None*)

Return the value of the option indicated by opt_string. This method can be called when the plugin is not started. Return None if the option does not exist.

This method can be called on the GUI thread. A driver that implements this method must be thread safe.

set_option (*opt_string*, *opt_value*)

Set the value of the option indicated by opt_string. This method can be called when the plugin is not started.

This method can be called on the GUI thread. A driver that implements this method must be thread safe.

is_running ()

Return True if the plugin is started, otherwise false

This method can be called on the GUI thread. A driver that implements this method must be thread safe.

synchronize_with_db (*db*, *book_id*, *book_metadata*, *first_call*)

Called during book matching when a book on the device is matched with a book in calibre's db. The method is responsible for syncronizing data from the device to calibre's db (if needed).

The method must return a two-value tuple. The first value is a set of calibre book ids changed if calibre's database was changed or None if the database was not changed. If the first value is an empty set then the metadata for the book on the device is updated with calibre's metadata and given back to the device, but no GUI refresh of that book is done. This is useful when the calibre data is correct but must be sent to the device.

The second value is itself a 2-value tuple. The first value in the tuple specifies whether a book format should be sent to the device. The intent is to permit verifying that the book on the device is the same as the book in calibre. This value must be None if no book is to be sent, otherwise return the base file name on the device (a string like foobar.epub). Be sure to include the extension in the name. The device subsystem will construct a send_books job for all books with not- None returned values. Note: other than to later retrieve the extension, the name is ignored in cases where the device uses a template to generate the file name, which most do. The second value in the returned tuple indicated whether the format is future-dated. Return True if it is, otherwise return False. Calibre will display a dialog to the user listing all future dated books.

Extremely important: this method is called on the GUI thread. It must be threadsafe with respect to the device manager's thread.

book_id: the calibre id for the book in the database. book_metadata: the Metadata object for the book coming from the device. first_call: True if this is the first call during a sync, False otherwise

class calibre.devices.interface.**BookList** (*oncard*, *prefix*, *settings*)

Bases: list

A list of books. Each Book object must have the fields

1. title

2. authors

3. size (file size of the book)

4. datetime (a UTC time tuple)

5. path (path on the device to the book)

6. thumbnail (can be None) thumbnail is either a str/bytes object with the image data or it should have an attribute image_path that stores an absolute (platform native) path to the image

7. tags (a list of strings, can be empty).

supports_collections ()
> Return True if the device supports collections for this book list.

add_book (*book, replace_metadata*)
> Add the book to the booklist. Intent is to maintain any device-internal metadata. Return True if booklists must be sync'ed

remove_book (*book*)
> Remove a book from the booklist. Correct any device metadata at the same time

get_collections (*collection_attributes*)
> Return a dictionary of collections created from collection_attributes. Each entry in the dictionary is of the form collection name:[list of books]

> The list of books is sorted by book title, except for collections created from series, in which case series_index is used.

> > **Parameters collection_attributes** – A list of attributes of the Book object

USB Mass Storage based devices

The base class for such devices is *calibre.devices.usbms.driver.USBMS* (page 351). This class in turn inherits some of its functionality from its bases, documented below. A typical basic USBMS based driver looks like this:

```
from calibre.devices.usbms.driver import USBMS

class PDNOVEL(USBMS):
    name = 'Pandigital Novel device interface'
    gui_name = 'PD Novel'
    description = _('Communicate with the Pandigital Novel')
    author = 'Kovid Goyal'
    supported_platforms = ['windows', 'linux', 'osx']
    FORMATS = ['epub', 'pdf']

    VENDOR_ID   = [0x18d1]
    PRODUCT_ID  = [0xb004]
    BCD         = [0x224]

    VENDOR_NAME = 'ANDROID'
    WINDOWS_MAIN_MEM = WINDOWS_CARD_A_MEM = '__UMS_COMPOSITE'
    THUMBNAIL_HEIGHT = 144

    EBOOK_DIR_MAIN = 'eBooks'
    SUPPORTS_SUB_DIRS = False

    def upload_cover(self, path, filename, metadata):
        coverdata = getattr(metadata, 'thumbnail', None)
        if coverdata and coverdata[2]:
            with open('%s.jpg' % os.path.join(path, filename), 'wb') as coverfile:
                coverfile.write(coverdata[2])
```

class `calibre.devices.usbms.device.`**`Device`** (*plugin_path*)

> Bases: `calibre.devices.usbms.deviceconfig.DeviceConfig`, *calibre.devices.interface.DevicePlugin* (page 342)

This class provides logic common to all drivers for devices that export themselves as USB Mass Storage devices. Provides implementations for mounting/ejecting of USBMS devices on all platforms.

> **WINDOWS_MAIN_MEM** = **None**
> > String identifying the main memory of the device in the windows PnP id strings This can be None, string, list of strings or compiled regex

> **WINDOWS_CARD_A_MEM** = **None**
> > String identifying the first card of the device in the windows PnP id strings This can be None, string, list of strings or compiled regex

> **WINDOWS_CARD_B_MEM** = **None**
> > String identifying the second card of the device in the windows PnP id strings This can be None, string, list of strings or compiled regex

> **OSX_MAIN_MEM_VOL_PAT** = **None**
> > Used by the new driver detection to disambiguate main memory from storage cards. Should be a regular expression that matches the main memory mount point assigned by OS X

> **MAX_PATH_LEN** = **250**
> > The maximum length of paths created on the device

> **NEWS_IN_FOLDER** = **True**
> > Put news in its own folder

> **windows_sort_drives** (*drives*)
> > Called to disambiguate main memory and storage card for devices that do not distinguish between them on the basis of *WINDOWS_CARD_NAME*. For e.g.: The EB600

> **sanitize_callback** (*path*)
> > Callback to allow individual device drivers to override the path sanitization used by `create_upload_path()`.

> **filename_callback** (*default*, *mi*)
> > Callback to allow drivers to change the default file name set by `create_upload_path()`.

> **sanitize_path_components** (*components*)
> > Perform any device specific sanitization on the path components for files to be uploaded to the device

> **get_annotations** (*path_map*)
> > Resolve path_map to annotation_map of files found on the device

> **add_annotation_to_library** (*db*, *db_id*, *annotation*)
> > Add an annotation to the calibre library

class `calibre.devices.usbms.cli.`**`CLI`**

class `calibre.devices.usbms.driver.`**`USBMS`** (*plugin_path*)

> Bases: *calibre.devices.usbms.cli.CLI* (page 351), *calibre.devices.usbms.device.Device* (page 350)

The base class for all USBMS devices. Implements the logic for sending/getting/updating metadata/caching metadata/etc.

> **upload_cover** (*path*, *filename*, *metadata*, *filepath*)
> > Upload book cover to the device. Default implementation does nothing.

> > **Parameters**

- **path** – The full path to the directory where the associated book is located.

- **filename** – The name of the book file without the extension.

- **metadata** – metadata belonging to the book. Use metadata.thumbnail for cover

- **filepath** – The full path to the ebook file

classmethod normalize_path (*path*)
> Return path with platform native path separators

User Interface Actions

If you are adding your own plugin in a zip file, you should subclass both InterfaceActionBase and InterfaceAction. The `load_actual_plugin()` method of you InterfaceActionBase subclass must return an instantiated object of your InterfaceBase subclass.

class `calibre.gui2.actions.`**InterfaceAction** (*parent*, *site_customization*)
> Bases: `PyQt5.QtCore.QObject`

> A plugin representing an "action" that can be taken in the graphical user interface. All the items in the toolbar and context menus are implemented by these plugins.

> Note that this class is the base class for these plugins, however, to integrate the plugin with calibre's plugin system, you have to make a wrapper class that references the actual plugin. See the `calibre.customize.builtins` module for examples.

> If two `InterfaceAction` objects have the same name, the one with higher priority takes precedence.

> Sub-classes should implement the `genesis()`, `library_changed()`, `location_selected()` `shutting_down()` and `initialization_complete()` methods.

> Once initialized, this plugin has access to the main calibre GUI via the `gui` member. You can access other plugins by name, for example:

```
self.gui.iactions['Save To Disk']
```

> To access the actual plugin, use the `interface_action_base_plugin` attribute, this attribute only becomes available after the plugin has been initialized. Useful if you want to use methods from the plugin class like do_user_config().

> The QAction specified by `action_spec` is automatically create and made available as `self.qaction`.

> **name = 'Implement me'**
>> The plugin name. If two plugins with the same name are present, the one with higher priority takes precedence.

> **priority = 1**
>> The plugin priority. If two plugins with the same name are present, the one with higher priority takes precedence.

> **popup_type = 1**
>> The menu popup type for when this plugin is added to a toolbar

> **auto_repeat = False**
>> Whether this action should be auto repeated when its shortcut key is held down.

> **action_spec = ('text', 'icon', None, None)**
>> Of the form: (text, icon_path, tooltip, keyboard shortcut) icon, tooltip and keyboard shortcut can be None shortcut must be a string, None or tuple of shortcuts. If None, a keyboard shortcut corresponding to the action is not registered. If you pass an empty tuple, then the shortcut is registered with no default key binding.

action_add_menu = **False**
> If True, a menu is automatically created and added to self.qaction

action_menu_clone_qaction = **False**
> If True, a clone of self.qaction is added to the menu of self.qaction If you want the text of this action to be different from that of self.qaction, set this variable to the new text

dont_add_to = **frozenset([])**
> Set of locations to which this action must not be added. See `all_locations` for a list of possible locations

dont_remove_from = **frozenset([])**
> Set of locations from which this action must not be removed. See `all_locations` for a list of possible locations

action_type = **'global'**
> Type of action 'current' means acts on the current view 'global' means an action that does not act on the current view, but rather on calibre as a whole

accepts_drops = **False**
> If True, then this InterfaceAction will have the opportunity to interact with drag and drop events. See the methods, `accept_enter_event()`, :meth':accept_drag_move_event', `drop_event()` for details.

accept_enter_event (*event*, *mime_data*)
> This method should return True iff this interface action is capable of handling the drag event. Do not call accept/ignore on the event, that will be taken care of by the calibre UI.

accept_drag_move_event (*event*, *mime_data*)
> This method should return True iff this interface action is capable of handling the drag event. Do not call accept/ignore on the event, that will be taken care of by the calibre UI.

drop_event (*event*, *mime_data*)
> This method should perform some useful action and return True iff this interface action is capable of handling the drop event. Do not call accept/ignore on the event, that will be taken care of by the calibre UI. You should not perform blocking/long operations in this function. Instead emit a signal or use QTimer.singleShot and return quickly. See the builtin actions for examples.

create_menu_action (*menu*, *unique_name*, *text*, *icon=None*, *shortcut=None*, *description=None*, *triggered=None*, *shortcut_name=None*)
> Convenience method to easily add actions to a QMenu. Returns the created QAction, This action has one extra attribute calibre_shortcut_unique_name which if not None refers to the unique name under which this action is registered with the keyboard manager.

> > **Parameters**

> > - **menu** – The QMenu the newly created action will be added to

> > - **unique_name** – A unique name for this action, this must be globally unique, so make it as descriptive as possible. If in doubt add a uuid to it.

> > - **text** – The text of the action.

> > - **icon** – Either a QIcon or a file name. The file name is passed to the I() builtin, so you do not need to pass the full path to the images directory.

> > - **shortcut** – A string, a list of strings, None or False. If False, no keyboard shortcut is registered for this action. If None, a keyboard shortcut with no default keybinding is registered. String and list of strings register a shortcut with default keybinding as specified.

> > - **description** – A description for this action. Used to set tooltips.

> > - **triggered** – A callable which is connected to the triggered signal of the created action.

- **shortcut_name** – The test displayed to the user when customizing the keyboard shortcuts for this action. By default it is set to the value of `text`.

load_resources (*names*)

> If this plugin comes in a ZIP file (user added plugin), this method will allow you to load resources from the ZIP file.
>
> For example to load an image:

```
pixmap = QPixmap()
pixmap.loadFromData(self.load_resources(['images/icon.png']).itervalues().next())
icon = QIcon(pixmap)
```

> > **Parameters names** – List of paths to resources in the zip file using / as separator
> >
> > **Returns** A dictionary of the form {name : file_contents}. Any names that were not found in the zip file will not be present in the dictionary.

genesis ()

> Setup this plugin. Only called once during initialization. self.gui is available. The action specified by `action_spec` is available as `self.qaction`.

location_selected (*loc*)

> Called whenever the book list being displayed in calibre changes. Currently values for loc are: `library`, `main`, `card` and `cardb`.
>
> This method should enable/disable this action and its sub actions as appropriate for the location.

library_changed (*db*)

> Called whenever the current library is changed.
>
> > **Parameters db** – The LibraryDatabase corresponding to the current library.

gui_layout_complete ()

> Called once per action when the layout of the main GUI is completed. If your action needs to make changes to the layout, they should be done here, rather than in `initialization_complete()`.

initialization_complete ()

> Called once per action when the initialization of the main GUI is completed.

shutting_down ()

> Called once per plugin when the main GUI is in the process of shutting down. Release any used resources, but try not to block the shutdown for long periods of time.
>
> > **Returns** False to halt the shutdown. You are responsible for telling the user why the shutdown was halted.

class calibre.customize.**InterfaceActionBase** (**args*, ***kwargs*)

> Bases: *calibre.customize.Plugin* (page 333)

load_actual_plugin (*gui*)

> This method must return the actual interface action plugin object.

Preferences Plugins

class calibre.customize.**PreferencesPlugin** (*plugin_path*)

> Bases: *calibre.customize.Plugin* (page 333)

A plugin representing a widget displayed in the Preferences dialog.

This plugin has only one important method `create_widget()`. The various fields of the plugin control how it is categorized in the UI.

config_widget = None

Import path to module that contains a class named ConfigWidget which implements the ConfigWidget-Interface. Used by `create_widget()`.

category_order = 100

Where in the list of categories the `category` of this plugin should be.

name_order = 100

Where in the list of names in a category, the `gui_name` of this plugin should be

category = None

The category this plugin should be in

gui_category = None

The category name displayed to the user for this plugin

gui_name = None

The name displayed to the user for this plugin

icon = None

The icon for this plugin, should be an absolute path

description = None

The description used for tooltips and the like

create_widget (*parent=None*)

Create and return the actual Qt widget used for setting this group of preferences. The widget must implement the *calibre.gui2.preferences.ConfigWidgetInterface* (page 355).

The default implementation uses `config_widget` to instantiate the widget.

class calibre.gui2.preferences.**ConfigWidgetInterface**

This class defines the interface that all widgets displayed in the Preferences dialog must implement. See `ConfigWidgetBase` for a base class that implements this interface and defines various convenience methods as well.

changed_signal = None

This signal must be emitted whenever the user changes a value in this widget

supports_restoring_to_defaults = True

Set to True iff the `restore_to_defaults()` method is implemented.

restore_defaults_desc = u'Restore settings to default values. You have to click Apply to actually save the c

The tooltip for the Restore to defaults button

restart_critical = False

If True the Preferences dialog will not allow the user to set any more preferences. Only has effect if `commit()` returns True.

genesis (*gui*)

Called once before the widget is displayed, should perform any necessary setup.

> **Parameters gui** – The main calibre graphical user interface

initialize ()

Should set all config values to their initial values (the values stored in the config files).

restore_defaults ()

Should set all config values to their defaults.

commit ()
> Save any changed settings. Return True if the changes require a restart, False otherwise. Raise an `AbortCommit` exception to indicate that an error occurred. You are responsible for giving the user feedback about what the error is and how to correct it.

refresh_gui (*gui*)
> Called once after this widget is committed. Responsible for causing the gui to reread any changed settings. Note that by default the GUI re-initializes various elements anyway, so most widgets won't need to use this method.

class `calibre.gui2.preferences.`**ConfigWidgetBase** (*parent=None*)
> Base class that contains code to easily add standard config widgets like checkboxes, combo boxes, text fields and so on. See the `register()` method.
>
> This class automatically handles change notification, resetting to default, translation between gui objects and config objects, etc. for registered settings.
>
> If your config widget inherits from this class but includes setting that are not registered, you should override the `ConfigWidgetInterface` methods and call the base class methods inside the overrides.
>
> **register** (*name, config_obj, gui_name=None, choices=None, restart_required=False, empty_string_is_None=True, setting=<class 'calibre.gui2.preferences.Setting'>*)
> > Register a setting.
> >
> > **Parameters**
> >
> > - **name** – The setting name
> > - **config** – The config object that reads/writes the setting
> > - **gui_name** – The name of the GUI object that presents an interface to change the setting. By default it is assumed to be `'opt_'` + name.
> > - **choices** – If this setting is a multiple choice (combobox) based setting, the list of choices. The list is a list of two element tuples of the form: `[(gui name, value), ...]`
> > - **setting** – The class responsible for managing this setting. The default class handles almost all cases, so this param is rarely used.

Viewer plugins

class `calibre.customize.`**ViewerPlugin** (*plugin_path*)
> Bases: `calibre.customize.Plugin` (page 333)
>
> **type = u'Viewer'**
> > These plugins are used to add functionality to the calibre viewer.
>
> **load_fonts** ()
> > This method is called once at viewer startup. It should load any fonts it wants to make available. For example:

```
def load_fonts():
    from PyQt5.Qt import QFontDatabase
    font_data = get_resources(['myfont1.ttf', 'myfont2.ttf'])
    for raw in font_data.itervalues():
        QFontDatabase.addApplicationFontFromData(raw)
```

> **load_javascript** (*evaljs*)
> > This method is called every time a new HTML document is loaded in the viewer. Use it to load javascript libraries into the viewer. For example:

```
        def load_javascript(self, evaljs):
            js = get_resources('myjavascript.js')
            evaljs(js)
```

run_javascript (*evaljs*)
> This method is called every time a document has finished loading. Use it in the same way as load_javascript().

customize_ui (*ui*)
> This method is called once when the viewer is created. Use it to make any customizations you want to the viewer's user interface. For example, you can modify the toolbars via ui.tool_bar and ui.tool_bar2.

customize_context_menu (*menu*, *event*, *hit_test_result*)
> This method is called every time the context (right-click) menu is shown. You can use it to customize the context menu. event is the context menu event and hit_test_result is the QWebHitTestResult for this event in the currently loaded document.

1.10.2 Environment variables

- CALIBRE_CONFIG_DIRECTORY - sets the directory where configuration files are stored/read.

- CALIBRE_TEMP_DIR - sets the temporary directory used by calibre

- CALIBRE_CACHE_DIRECTORY - sets the directory calibre uses to cache persistent data between sessions

- CALIBRE_OVERRIDE_DATABASE_PATH - allows you to specify the full path to metadata.db. Using this variable you can have metadata.db be in a location other than the library folder. Useful if your library folder is on a networked drive that does not support file locking.

- CALIBRE_DEVELOP_FROM - Used to run from a calibre development environment. See *Setting up a calibre development environment* (page 317).

- CALIBRE_OVERRIDE_LANG - Used to force the language used by the interface (ISO 639 language code)

- CALIBRE_TEST_TRANSLATION - Used to test a translation .po file (should be the path to the .po file)

- CALIBRE_NO_NATIVE_FILEDIALOGS - Causes calibre to not use native file dialogs for selecting files/directories. Set it to 1 to enable.

- CALIBRE_NO_NATIVE_MENUBAR - Causes calibre to not create a native (global) menu on Ubuntu Unity and similar linux desktop environments. The menu is instead placed inside the window, as traditional.

- CALIBRE_IGNORE_SYSTEM_THEME - Causes calibre to ignore any system Qt style plugins and use its builtin style plugin instead. Useful to workaround crashes caused by the system Qt plugin being incompatible with the version of Qt shipped with calibre.

- CALIBRE_SHOW_DEPRECATION_WARNINGS - Causes calibre to print deprecation warnings to stdout. Useful for calibre developers.

- SYSFS_PATH - Use if sysfs is mounted somewhere other than /sys

- http_proxy - Used on linux to specify an HTTP proxy

See How to set environment variables in windows[113] or How to set environment variables in OS X[114].

---

[113] http://www.computerhope.com/issues/ch000549.htm
[114] http://www.dowdandassociates.com/blog/content/howto-set-an-environment-variable-in-mac-os-x-launchd-plist/

1.10.3 Tweaks

Tweaks are small changes that you can specify to control various aspects of calibre's behavior. You can change them by going to Preferences->Advanced->Tweaks. The default values for the tweaks are reproduced below

```
#!/usr/bin/env python2
# vim:fileencoding=UTF-8:ts=4:sw=4:sta:et:sts=4:ai
__license__   = 'GPL v3'
__copyright__ = '2010, Kovid Goyal <kovid@kovidgoyal.net>'
__docformat__ = 'restructuredtext en'

'''
Contains various tweaks that affect calibre behavior. Only edit this file if
you know what you are doing. If you delete this file, it will be recreated from
defaults.
'''


#: Auto increment series index
# The algorithm used to assign a book added to an existing series a series number.
# New series numbers assigned using this tweak are always integer values, except
# if a constant non-integer is specified.
# Possible values are:
# next - First available integer larger than the largest existing number
# first_free - First available integer larger than 0
# next_free - First available integer larger than the smallest existing number
# last_free - First available integer smaller than the largest existing number
#             Return largest existing + 1 if no free number is found
# const - Assign the number 1 always
# no_change - Do not change the series index
# a number - Assign that number always. The number is not in quotes. Note that
#            0.0 can be used here.
# Examples:
# series_index_auto_increment = 'next'
# series_index_auto_increment = 'next_free'
# series_index_auto_increment = 16.5
#
# Set the use_series_auto_increment_tweak_when_importing tweak to True to
# use the above values when importing/adding books. If this tweak is set to
# False (the default) then the series number will be set to 1 if it is not
# explicitly set during the import. If set to True, then the
# series index will be set according to the series_index_auto_increment setting.
# Note that the use_series_auto_increment_tweak_when_importing tweak is used
# only when a value is not provided during import. If the importing regular
# expression produces a value for series_index, or if you are reading metadata
# from books and the import plugin produces a value, than that value will
# be used irrespective of the setting of the tweak.
series_index_auto_increment = 'next'
use_series_auto_increment_tweak_when_importing = False


#: Add separator after completing an author name
# Should the completion separator be append
# to the end of the completed text to
# automatically begin a new completion operation
# for authors.
# Can be either True or False
authors_completer_append_separator = False


#: Author sort name algorithm
# The algorithm used to copy author to author_sort
```

```
# Possible values are:
#  invert: use "fn ln" -> "ln, fn"
#  copy  : copy author to author_sort without modification
#  comma : use 'copy' if there is a ',' in the name, otherwise use 'invert'
#  nocomma : "fn ln" -> "ln fn" (without the comma)
# When this tweak is changed, the author_sort values stored with each author
# must be recomputed by right-clicking on an author in the left-hand tags pane,
# selecting 'manage authors', and pressing 'Recalculate all author sort values'.
# The author name suffixes are words that are ignored when they occur at the
# end of an author name. The case of the suffix is ignored and trailing
# periods are automatically handled. The same is true for prefixes.
# The author name copy words are a set of words which if they occur in an
# author name cause the automatically generated author sort string to be
# identical to the author name. This means that the sort for a string like Acme
# Inc. will be Acme Inc. instead of Inc., Acme
author_sort_copy_method = 'comma'
author_name_suffixes = ('Jr', 'Sr', 'Inc', 'Ph.D', 'Phd',
                        'MD', 'M.D', 'I', 'II', 'III', 'IV',
                        'Junior', 'Senior')
author_name_prefixes = ('Mr', 'Mrs', 'Ms', 'Dr', 'Prof')
author_name_copywords = ('Corporation', 'Company', 'Co.', 'Agency', 'Council',
        'Committee', 'Inc.', 'Institute', 'Society', 'Club', 'Team')

#: Splitting multiple author names
# By default, calibre splits a string containing multiple author names on
# ampersands and the words "and" and "with". You can customize the splitting
# by changing the regular expression below. Strings are split on whatever the
# specified regular expression matches, in addition to ampersands.
# Default: r'(?i),?\s+(and|with)\s+'
authors_split_regex = r'(?i),?\s+(and|with)\s+'

#: Use author sort in Tag Browser
# Set which author field to display in the tags pane (the list of authors,
# series, publishers etc on the left hand side). The choices are author and
# author_sort. This tweak affects only what is displayed under the authors
# category in the tags pane and content server. Please note that if you set this
# to author_sort, it is very possible to see duplicate names in the list because
# although it is guaranteed that author names are unique, there is no such
# guarantee for author_sort values. Showing duplicates won't break anything, but
# it could lead to some confusion. When using 'author_sort', the tooltip will
# show the author's name.
# Examples:
#   categories_use_field_for_author_name = 'author'
#   categories_use_field_for_author_name = 'author_sort'
categories_use_field_for_author_name = 'author'

#: Control partitioning of Tag Browser
# When partitioning the tags browser, the format of the subcategory label is
# controlled by a template: categories_collapsed_name_template if sorting by
# name, categories_collapsed_rating_template if sorting by average rating, and
# categories_collapsed_popularity_template if sorting by popularity. There are
# two variables available to the template: first and last. The variable 'first'
# is the initial item in the subcategory, and the variable 'last' is the final
# item in the subcategory. Both variables are 'objects'; they each have multiple
# values that are obtained by using a suffix. For example, first.name for an
# author category will be the name of the author. The sub-values available are:
#  name: the printable name of the item
#  count: the number of books that references this item
```

```
#   avg_rating: the average rating of all the books referencing this item
#   sort: the sort value. For authors, this is the author_sort for that author
#   category: the category (e.g., authors, series) that the item is in.
# Note that the "r'" in front of the { is necessary if there are backslashes
# (\ characters) in the template. It doesn't hurt anything to leave it there
# even if there aren't any backslashes.
categories_collapsed_name_template = r'{first.sort:shorten(4,,0)} - {last.sort:shorten(4,,0)}
categories_collapsed_rating_template = r'{first.avg_rating:4.2f:ifempty(0)} - {last.avg_rating
categories_collapsed_popularity_template = r'{first.count:d} - {last.count:d}'

#: Control order of categories in the tag browser
# Change the following dict to change the order that categories are displayed in
# the tag browser. Items are named using their lookup name, and will be sorted
# using the number supplied. The lookup name '*' stands for all names that
# otherwise do not appear. Two names with the same value will be sorted
# using the default order; the one used when the dict is empty.
# Example: tag_browser_category_order = {'series':1, 'tags':2, '*':3}
# resulting in the order series, tags, then everything else in default order.
tag_browser_category_order = {'*':1}


#: Specify columns to sort the booklist by on startup
# Provide a set of columns to be sorted on when calibre starts
#   The argument is None if saved sort history is to be used
#   otherwise it is a list of column,order pairs. Column is the
#   lookup/search name, found using the tooltip for the column
#   Order is 0 for ascending, 1 for descending
# For example, set it to [('authors',0),('title',0)] to sort by
# title within authors.
sort_columns_at_startup = None

#: Control how dates are displayed
# Format to be used for publication date and the timestamp (date).
#   A string controlling how the publication date is displayed in the GUI
#   d      the day as number without a leading zero (1 to 31)
#   dd     the day as number with a leading zero (01 to 31)
#   ddd    the abbreviated localized day name (e.g. 'Mon' to 'Sun').
#   dddd   the long localized day name (e.g. 'Monday' to 'Sunday').
#   M      the month as number without a leading zero (1-12)
#   MM     the month as number with a leading zero (01-12)
#   MMM    the abbreviated localized month name (e.g. 'Jan' to 'Dec').
#   MMMM   the long localized month name (e.g. 'January' to 'December').
#   yy     the year as two digit number (00-99)
#   yyyy   the year as four digit number
#   h      the hours without a leading 0 (0 to 11 or 0 to 23, depending on am/pm) '
#   hh     the hours with a leading 0 (00 to 11 or 00 to 23, depending on am/pm) '
#   m      the minutes without a leading 0 (0 to 59) '
#   mm     the minutes with a leading 0 (00 to 59) '
#   s      the seconds without a leading 0 (0 to 59) '
#   ss     the seconds with a leading 0 (00 to 59) '
#   ap     use a 12-hour clock instead of a 24-hour clock, with "ap"
#          replaced by the localized string for am or pm '
#   AP     use a 12-hour clock instead of a 24-hour clock, with "AP"
#          replaced by the localized string for AM or PM '
#   iso    the date with time and timezone. Must be the only format present
# For example, given the date of 9 Jan 2010, the following formats show
# MMM yyyy ==> Jan 2010    yyyy ==> 2010        dd MMM yyyy ==> 09 Jan 2010
# MM/yyyy ==> 01/2010      d/M/yy ==> 9/1/10    yy ==> 10
```

```
# publication default if not set: MMM yyyy
# timestamp default if not set: dd MMM yyyy
# last_modified_display_format if not set: dd MMM yyyy
gui_pubdate_display_format = 'MMM yyyy'
gui_timestamp_display_format = 'dd MMM yyyy'
gui_last_modified_display_format = 'dd MMM yyyy'

#: Control sorting of titles and series in the library display
# Control title and series sorting in the library view. If set to
# 'library_order', the title sort field will be used instead of the title.
# Unless you have manually edited the title sort field, leading articles such as
# The and A will be ignored. If set to 'strictly_alphabetic', the titles will be
# sorted as-is (sort by title instead of title sort). For example, with
# library_order, The Client will sort under 'C'. With strictly_alphabetic, the
# book will sort under 'T'.
# This flag affects Calibre's library display. It has no effect on devices. In
# addition, titles for books added before changing the flag will retain their
# order until the title is edited. Double-clicking on a title and hitting return
# without changing anything is sufficient to change the sort.
title_series_sorting = 'library_order'

#: Control formatting of title and series when used in templates
# Control how title and series names are formatted when saving to disk/sending
# to device. The behavior depends on the field being processed. If processing
# title, then if this tweak is set to 'library_order', the title will be
# replaced with title_sort. If it is set to 'strictly_alphabetic', then the
# title will not be changed. If processing series, then if set to
# 'library_order', articles such as 'The' and 'An' will be moved to the end. If
# set to 'strictly_alphabetic', the series will be sent without change.
# For example, if the tweak is set to library_order, "The Lord of the Rings"
# will become "Lord of the Rings, The". If the tweak is set to
# strictly_alphabetic, it would remain "The Lord of the Rings". Note that the
# formatter function raw_field will return the base value for title and
# series regardless of the setting of this tweak.
save_template_title_series_sorting = 'library_order'

#: Set the list of words considered to be "articles" for sort strings
# Set the list of words that are to be considered 'articles' when computing the
# title sort strings. The articles differ by language. By default, calibre uses
# a combination of articles from English and whatever language the calibre user
# interface is set to. In addition, in some contexts where the book language is
# available, the language of the book is used. You can change the list of
# articles for a given language or add a new language by editing
# per_language_title_sort_articles. To tell calibre to use a language other
# than the user interface language, set, default_language_for_title_sort. For
# example, to use German, set it to 'deu'. A value of None means the user
# interface language is used. The setting title_sort_articles is ignored
# (present only for legacy reasons).
per_language_title_sort_articles = {
        # English
        'eng'  : (r'A\s+', r'The\s+', r'An\s+'),

        # Esperanto
        'epo': (r'La\s+', r"L'", 'L\xb4'),

        # Spanish
        'spa'  : (r'El\s+', r'La\s+', r'Lo\s+', r'Los\s+', r'Las\s+', r'Un\s+',
                r'Una\s+', r'Unos\s+', r'Unas\s+'),
```

```
        # French
        'fra'  : (r'Le\s+', r'La\s+', r"L'", u'L´', u'L′', r'Les\s+', r'Un\s+', r'Une\s+',
                  r'Des\s+', r'De\s+La\s+', r'De\s+', r"D'", u'D´', u'L′'),

        # Italian
        'ita': ('Lo\\s+', 'Il\\s+', "L'", 'L\xb4', 'La\\s+', 'Gli\\s+',
                'I\\s+', 'Le\\s+', 'Uno\\s+', 'Un\\s+', 'Una\\s+', "Un'",
                'Un\xb4', 'Dei\\s+', 'Degli\\s+', 'Delle\\s+', 'Del\\s+',
                'Della\\s+', 'Dello\\s+', "Dell'", 'Dell\xb4'),

        # Portuguese
        'por'  : (r'A\s+', r'O\s+', r'Os\s+', r'As\s+', r'Um\s+', r'Uns\s+',
                  r'Uma\s+', r'Umas\s+', ),
        # Romanian
        'ron'  : (r'Un\s+', r'O\s+', r'Ni\u015fte\s+', ),
        # German
        'deu'  : (r'Der\s+', r'Die\s+', r'Das\s+', r'Den\s+', r'Ein\s+',
                  r'Eine\s+', r'Einen\s+', r'Dem\s+', r'Des\s+', r'Einem\s+',
                  r'Eines\s+'),
        # Dutch
        'nld'  : (r'De\s+', r'Het\s+', r'Een\s+', r"'n\s+", r"'s\s+", r'Ene\s+',
                  r'Ener\s+', r'Enes\s+', r'Den\s+', r'Der\s+', r'Des\s+',
                  r"'t\s+"),
        # Swedish
        'swe'  : (r'En\s+', r'Ett\s+', r'Det\s+', r'Den\s+', r'De\s+', ),
        # Turkish
        'tur'  : (r'Bir\s+', ),
        # Afrikaans
        'afr'  : (r"'n\s+", r'Die\s+', ),
        # Greek
        'ell'  : (r'O\s+', r'I\s+', r'To\s+', r'Ta\s+', r'Tus\s+', r'Tis\s+',
                  r"'Enas\s+", r"'Mia\s+", r"'Ena\s+", r"'Enan\s+", ),
        # Hungarian
        'hun'  : (r'A\s+', 'Az\s+', 'Egy\s+',),
}
default_language_for_title_sort = None
title_sort_articles=r'^(A|The|An)\s+'


#: Specify a folder calibre should connect to at startup
# Specify a folder that calibre should connect to at startup using
# connect_to_folder. This must be a full path to the folder. If the folder does
# not exist when calibre starts, it is ignored. If there are '\' characters in
# the path (such as in Windows paths), you must double them.
# Examples:
#     auto_connect_to_folder = 'C:\\Users\\someone\\Desktop\\testlib'
#     auto_connect_to_folder = '/home/dropbox/My Dropbox/someone/library'
auto_connect_to_folder = ''


#: Specify renaming rules for SONY collections
# Specify renaming rules for sony collections. This tweak is only applicable if
# metadata management is set to automatic. Collections on Sonys are named
# depending upon whether the field is standard or custom. A collection derived
# from a standard field is named for the value in that field. For example, if
# the standard 'series' column contains the value 'Darkover', then the
# collection name is 'Darkover'. A collection derived from a custom field will
# have the name of the field added to the value. For example, if a custom series
# column named 'My Series' contains the name 'Darkover', then the collection
# will by default be named 'Darkover (My Series)'. For purposes of this
```

```
# documentation, 'Darkover' is called the value and 'My Series' is called the
# category. If two books have fields that generate the same collection name,
# then both books will be in that collection.
# This set of tweaks lets you specify for a standard or custom field how
# the collections are to be named. You can use it to add a description to a
# standard field, for example 'Foo (Tag)' instead of the 'Foo'. You can also use
# it to force multiple fields to end up in the same collection. For example, you
# could force the values in 'series', '#my_series_1', and '#my_series_2' to
# appear in collections named 'some_value (Series)', thereby merging all of the
# fields into one set of collections.
# There are two related tweaks. The first determines the category name to use
# for a metadata field.  The second is a template, used to determines how the
# value and category are combined to create the collection name.
# The syntax of the first tweak, sony_collection_renaming_rules, is:
# {'field_lookup_name':'category_name_to_use', 'lookup_name':'name', ...}
# The second tweak, sony_collection_name_template, is a template. It uses the
# same template language as plugboards and save templates. This tweak controls
# how the value and category are combined together to make the collection name.
# The only two fields available are {category} and {value}. The {value} field is
# never empty. The {category} field can be empty. The default is to put the
# value first, then the category enclosed in parentheses, it isn't empty:
# '{value} {category:| (|)}'
# Examples: The first three examples assume that the second tweak
# has not been changed.
# 1: I want three series columns to be merged into one set of collections. The
# column lookup names are 'series', '#series_1' and '#series_2'. I want nothing
# in the parenthesis. The value to use in the tweak value would be:
#    sony_collection_renaming_rules={'series':'', '#series_1':'', '#series_2':''}
# 2: I want the word '(Series)' to appear on collections made from series, and
# the word '(Tag)' to appear on collections made from tags. Use:
#    sony_collection_renaming_rules={'series':'Series', 'tags':'Tag'}
# 3: I want 'series' and '#myseries' to be merged, and for the collection name
# to have '(Series)' appended. The renaming rule is:
#    sony_collection_renaming_rules={'series':'Series', '#myseries':'Series'}
# 4: Same as example 2, but instead of having the category name in parentheses
# and appended to the value, I want it prepended and separated by a colon, such
# as in Series: Darkover. I must change the template used to format the category name
# The resulting two tweaks are:
#    sony_collection_renaming_rules={'series':'Series', 'tags':'Tag'}
#    sony_collection_name_template='{category:|: }{value}'
sony_collection_renaming_rules={}
sony_collection_name_template='{value}{category:| (|)}'


#: Specify how SONY collections are sorted
# Specify how sony collections are sorted. This tweak is only applicable if
# metadata management is set to automatic. You can indicate which metadata is to
# be used to sort on a collection-by-collection basis. The format of the tweak
# is a list of metadata fields from which collections are made, followed by the
# name of the metadata field containing the sort value.
# Example: The following indicates that collections built from pubdate and tags
# are to be sorted by the value in the custom column '#mydate', that collections
# built from 'series' are to be sorted by 'series_index', and that all other
# collections are to be sorted by title. If a collection metadata field is not
# named, then if it is a series- based collection it is sorted by series order,
# otherwise it is sorted by title order.
# [(['pubdate', 'tags'],'#mydate'), (['series'],'series_index'), (['*'], 'title')]
# Note that the bracketing and parentheses are required. The syntax is
# [ ( [list of fields], sort field ) , ( [ list of fields ] , sort field ) ]
```

```
# Default: empty (no rules), so no collection attributes are named.
sony_collection_sorting_rules = []

#: Control how tags are applied when copying books to another library
# Set this to True to ensure that tags in 'Tags to add when adding
# a book' are added when copying books to another library
add_new_book_tags_when_importing_books = False

#: Set the maximum number of tags to show per book in the content server
max_content_server_tags_shown=5

#: Set custom metadata fields that the content server will or will not display.
# content_server_will_display is a list of custom fields to be displayed.
# content_server_wont_display is a list of custom fields not to be displayed.
# wont_display has priority over will_display.
# The special value '*' means all custom fields. The value [] means no entries.
# Defaults:
#     content_server_will_display = ['*']
#     content_server_wont_display = []
# Examples:
# To display only the custom fields #mytags and #genre:
#    content_server_will_display = ['#mytags', '#genre']
#    content_server_wont_display = []
# To display all fields except #mycomments:
#    content_server_will_display = ['*']
#    content_server_wont_display['#mycomments']
content_server_will_display = ['*']
content_server_wont_display = []

#: Set the maximum number of sort 'levels'
# Set the maximum number of sort 'levels' that calibre will use to resort the
# library after certain operations such as searches or device insertion. Each
# sort level adds a performance penalty. If the database is large (thousands of
# books) the penalty might be noticeable. If you are not concerned about multi-
# level sorts, and if you are seeing a slowdown, reduce the value of this tweak.
maximum_resort_levels = 5

#: Choose whether dates are sorted using visible fields
# Date values contain both a date and a time. When sorted, all the fields are
# used, regardless of what is displayed. Set this tweak to True to use only
# the fields that are being displayed.
sort_dates_using_visible_fields = False

#: Fuzz value for trimming covers
# The value used for the fuzz distance when trimming a cover.
# Colors within this distance are considered equal.
# The distance is in absolute intensity units.
cover_trim_fuzz_value = 10

#: Control behavior of the book list
# You can control the behavior of doubleclicks on the books list.
# Choices: open_viewer, do_nothing,
# edit_cell, edit_metadata. Selecting anything other than open_viewer has the
# side effect of disabling editing a field using a single click.
# Default: open_viewer.
# Example: doubleclick_on_library_view = 'do_nothing'
# You can also control whether the book list scrolls horizontal per column or
# per pixel. Default is per column.
```

```
doubleclick_on_library_view = 'open_viewer'
horizontal_scrolling_per_column = True


#: Language to use when sorting.
# Setting this tweak will force sorting to use the
# collating order for the specified language. This might be useful if you run
# calibre in English but want sorting to work in the language where you live.
# Set the tweak to the desired ISO 639-1 language code, in lower case.
# You can find the list of supported locales at
# http://publib.boulder.ibm.com/infocenter/iseries/v5r3/topic/nls/rbagsicusortsequencetables.l
# Default: locale_for_sorting = '' -- use the language calibre displays in
# Example: locale_for_sorting = 'fr' -- sort using French rules.
# Example: locale_for_sorting = 'nb' -- sort using Norwegian rules.
locale_for_sorting = ''


#: Number of columns for custom metadata in the edit metadata dialog
# Set whether to use one or two columns for custom metadata when editing
# metadata  one book at a time. If True, then the fields are laid out using two
# columns. If False, one column is used.
metadata_single_use_2_cols_for_custom_fields = True


#: Order of custom column(s) in edit metadata
# Controls the order that custom columns are listed in edit metadata single
# and bulk. The columns listed in the tweak are displayed first and in the
# order provided. Any columns not listed are dislayed after the listed ones,
# in alphabetical order. Do note that this tweak does not change the size of
# the edit widgets. Putting comments widgets in this list may result in some
# odd widget spacing when using two-column mode.
# Enter a comma-separated list of custom field lookup names, as in
# metadata_edit_custom_column_order = ['#genre', '#mytags', '#etc']
metadata_edit_custom_column_order = []


#: The number of seconds to wait before sending emails
# The number of seconds to wait before sending emails when using a
# public email server like gmx/hotmail/gmail. Default is: 5 minutes
# Setting it to lower may cause the server's SPAM controls to kick in,
# making email sending fail. Changes will take effect only after a restart of
# calibre.
public_smtp_relay_delay = 301


#: The maximum width and height for covers saved in the calibre library
# All covers in the calibre library will be resized, preserving aspect ratio,
# to fit within this size. This is to prevent slowdowns caused by extremely
# large covers
maximum_cover_size = (1650, 2200)


#: Where to send downloaded news
# When automatically sending downloaded news to a connected device, calibre
# will by default send it to the main memory. By changing this tweak, you can
# control where it is sent. Valid values are "main", "carda", "cardb". Note
# that if there isn't enough free space available on the location you choose,
# the files will be sent to the location with the most free space.
send_news_to_device_location = "main"


#: What interfaces should the content server listen on
# By default, the calibre content server listens on '0.0.0.0' which means that it
# accepts IPv4 connections on all interfaces. You can change this to, for
# example, '127.0.0.1' to only listen for connections from the local machine, or
```

```
# to '::' to listen to all incoming IPv6 and IPv4 connections (this may not
# work on all operating systems)
server_listen_on = '0.0.0.0'

#: Unified toolbar on OS X
# If you enable this option and restart calibre, the toolbar will be 'unified'
# with the titlebar as is normal for OS X applications. However, doing this has
# various bugs, for instance the minimum width of the toolbar becomes twice
# what it should be and it causes other random bugs on some systems, so turn it
# on at your own risk!
unified_title_toolbar_on_osx = False

#: Save original file when converting/polishing from same format to same format
# When calibre does a conversion from the same format to the same format, for
# example, from EPUB to EPUB, the original file is saved, so that in case the
# conversion is poor, you can tweak the settings and run it again. By setting
# this to False you can prevent calibre from saving the original file.
# Similarly, by setting save_original_format_when_polishing to False you can
# prevent calibre from saving the original file when polishing.
save_original_format = True
save_original_format_when_polishing = True

#: Number of recently viewed books to show
# Right-clicking the View button shows a list of recently viewed books. Control
# how many should be shown, here.
gui_view_history_size = 15

#: Change the font size of book details in the interface
# Change the font size at which book details are rendered in the side panel and
# comments are rendered in the metadata edit dialog. Set it to a positive or
# negative number to increase or decrease the font size.
change_book_details_font_size_by = 0

#: Compile General Program Mode templates to Python
# Compiled general program mode templates are significantly faster than
# interpreted templates. Setting this tweak to True causes calibre to compile
# (in most cases) general program mode templates. Setting it to False causes
# calibre to use the old behavior -- interpreting the templates. Set the tweak
# to False if some compiled templates produce incorrect values.
# Default:    compile_gpm_templates = True
# No compile: compile_gpm_templates = False
compile_gpm_templates = True

#: What format to default to when using the Tweak feature
# The Tweak feature of calibre allows direct editing of a book format.
# If multiple formats are available, calibre will offer you a choice
# of formats, defaulting to your preferred output format if it is available.
# Set this tweak to a specific value of 'EPUB' or 'AZW3' to always default
# to that format rather than your output format preference.
# Set to a value of 'remember' to use whichever format you chose last time you
# used the Tweak feature.
# Examples:
#   default_tweak_format = None      (Use output format)
#   default_tweak_format = 'EPUB'
#   default_tweak_format = 'remember'
default_tweak_format = None

#: Do not preselect a completion when editing authors/tags/series/etc.
```

```
# This means that you can make changes and press Enter and your changes will
# not be overwritten by a matching completion. However, if you wish to use the
# completions you will now have to press Tab to select one before pressing
# Enter. Which technique you prefer will depend on the state of metadata in
# your library and your personal editing style.
preselect_first_completion = False

#: Completion mode when editing authors/tags/series/etc.
# By default, when completing items, calibre will show you all the candidates
# that start with the text you have already typed. You can instead have it show
# all candidates that contain the text you have already typed. To do this, set
# completion_mode to 'contains'. For example, if you type asi it will match both
# Asimov and Quasimodo, whereas the default behavior would match only Asimov.
completion_mode = 'prefix'

#: Recognize numbers inside text when sorting
# This means that when sorting on text fields like title the text "Book 2"
# will sort before the text "Book 100". If you want this behavior, set
# numeric_collation = True note that doing so will cause problems with text
# that starts with numbers and is a little slower.
numeric_collation = False

#: Sort the list of libraries alphabetically
# The list of libraries in the Copy to Library and Quick Switch menus are
# normally sorted by most used. However, if there are more than a certain
# number of such libraries, the sorting becomes alphabetic. You can set that
# number here. The default is ten libraries.
many_libraries = 10

#: Highlight the virtual library name when using a Virtual Library
# The virtual library name next to the Virtual Library button is highlighted in
# yellow when using a Virtual Library. You can choose the color used for the
# highlight with this tweak. Set it to 'transparent' to disable highlighting.
highlight_virtual_library = 'yellow'

#: Choose available output formats for conversion
# Restrict the list of available output formats in the conversion dialogs.
# For example, if you only want to convert to EPUB and AZW3, change this to
# restrict_output_formats = ['EPUB', 'AZW3']. The default value of None causes
# all available output formats to be present.
restrict_output_formats = None

#: Set the thumbnail image quality used by the content server
# The quality of a thumbnail is largely controlled by the compression quality
# used when creating it. Set this to a larger number to improve the quality.
# Note that the thumbnails get much larger with larger compression quality
# numbers.
# The value can be between 50 and 99
content_server_thumbnail_compression_quality = 75
```

1.10.4 Overriding icons, templates, et cetera

Note: calibre has direct support for icon themes, there are several icon themes available for calibre, that you can use by going to *Preferences->Look & Feel->Change Icon theme*. The icon themes use the same mechanism as described below for overriding static resources.

calibre allows you to override the static resources, like icons, javascript and templates for the metadata jacket, catalogs, etc. with customized versions that you like. All static resources are stored in the resources sub-folder of the calibre install location. On Windows, this is usually `C:\Program Files\Calibre2\resources`. On OS X, `/Applications/calibre.app/Contents/Resources/resources/`. On linux, if you are using the binary installer from the calibre website it will be `/opt/calibre/resources`. These paths can change depending on where you choose to install calibre.

You should not change the files in this resources folder, as your changes will get overwritten the next time you update calibre. Instead, go to *Preferences->Advanced->Miscellaneous* and click *Open calibre configuration directory*. In this configuration directory, create a sub-folder called resources and place the files you want to override in it. Place the files in the appropriate sub folders, for example place images in `resources/images`, etc. calibre will automatically use your custom file in preference to the built-in one the next time it is started.

For example, if you wanted to change the icon for the *Remove books* action, you would first look in the built-in resources folder and see that the relevant file is `resources/images/trash.png`. Assuming you have an alternate icon in PNG format called `mytrash.png` you would save it in the configuration directory as `resources/images/trash.png`. All the icons used by the calibre user interface are in `resources/images` and its sub-folders.

1.10.5 Creating your own icon theme for calibre

If you have created a beautiful set of icons and wish to share them with other calibre users via calibre's builtin icon theme support, you can easily package up your icons into a theme. To do so, go to *Preferences->Miscellaneous->Create icon theme*, select the folder where you have put your icons (usually the `resources/images` folder in the calibre config directory, as described above). Then fill up the theme metadata and click OK. This will result in a zip file containing the theme icons. You can upload that to the calibre forum at Mobileread[115] and then I will make your theme available via calibre's builtin icon theme system.

1.10.6 Customizing calibre with plugins

calibre has a very modular design. Almost all functionality in calibre comes in the form of plugins. Plugins are used for conversion, for downloading news (though these are called recipes), for various components of the user interface, to connect to different devices, to process files when adding them to calibre and so on. You can get a complete list of all the built-in plugins in calibre by going to *Preferences->Plugins*.

You can write your own plugins to customize and extend the behavior of calibre. The plugin architecture in calibre is very simple, see the tutorial *Writing your own plugins to extend calibre's functionality* (page 213).

1.11 Command Line Interface

`kovid giskard ~/work/libprs500/src/libprs500/manual $ []`

Note: On OS X, the command line tools are inside the calibre bundle, for example, if you installed calibre in `/Applications` the command line tools are in `/Applications/calibre.app/Contents/console.app/Contents/MacOS/`.

---

[115]http://www.mobileread.com/forums/forumdisplay.php?f=166

1.11.1 Documented Commands

calibre

```
calibre [opts] [path_to_ebook]
```

Launch the main **calibre** Graphical User Interface and optionally add the ebook at path_to_ebook to the database.

Whenever you pass arguments to **calibre** that have spaces in them, enclose the arguments in quotation marks. For example "C:some path with spaces"

[options]

--detach
> Detach from the controlling terminal, if any (linux only)

--help, -h
> show this help message and exit

--ignore-plugins
> Ignore custom plugins, useful if you installed a plugin that is preventing calibre from starting

--no-update-check
> Do not check for updates

--shutdown-running-calibre, -s
> Cause a running calibre instance, if any, to be shutdown. Note that if there are running jobs, they will be silently aborted, so use with care.

--start-in-tray
> Start minimized to system tray.

--verbose, -v
> Ignored, do not use. Present only for legacy reasons

--version
> show program's version number and exit

--with-library
> Use the library located at the specified path.

calibre-customize

```
calibre-customize options
```

Customize calibre by loading external plugins.

Whenever you pass arguments to **calibre-customize** that have spaces in them, enclose the arguments in quotation marks. For example "C:some path with spaces"

[options]

--add-plugin, -a
> Add a plugin by specifying the path to the zip file containing it.

--build-plugin, -b
> For plugin developers: Path to the directory where you are developing the plugin. This command will automatically zip up the plugin and update it in calibre.

--customize-plugin
> Customize plugin. Specify name of plugin and customization string separated by a comma.

--disable-plugin
> Disable the named plugin

--enable-plugin
> Enable the named plugin

--help, -h
> show this help message and exit

--list-plugins, -l
> List all installed plugins

--remove-plugin, -r
> Remove a custom plugin by name. Has no effect on builtin plugins

--version
> show program's version number and exit

calibre-debug

```
calibre-debug [options]
```

Various command line interfaces useful for debugging calibre. With no options, this command starts an embedded python interpreter. You can also run the main calibre GUI, the calibre viewer and the calibre editor in debug mode.

It also contains interfaces to various bits of calibre that do not have dedicated command line tools, such as font subsetting, the ebook diff tool and so on.

You can also use **calibre-debug** to run standalone scripts. To do that use it like this:

> **calibre-debug** myscript.py -- --option1 --option2 file1 file2 ...

Everything after the -- is passed to the script.

Whenever you pass arguments to **calibre-debug** that have spaces in them, enclose the arguments in quotation marks. For example "C:some path with spaces"

[options]

--add-simple-plugin
> Add a simple plugin (i.e. a plugin that consists of only a .py file), by specifying the path to the py file containing the plugin code.

--command, -c
> Run python code.

--debug-device-driver, -d
> Debug device detection

--default-programs
> (Un)register calibre from Windows Default Programs. --default-programs=(register|unregister)

--diff

 Run the calibre diff tool. For example: calibre-debug *--diff* (page 273) file1 file2

--edit-book, -t

 Launch the calibre Edit Book tool in debug mode.

--exec-file, -e

 Run the python code in file.

--explode-book, -x

 Explode the book (exports the book as a collection of HTML files and metadata, which you can edit using standard HTML editing tools, and then rebuilds the file from the edited HTML. Makes no additional changes to the HTML, unlike a full calibre conversion).

--gui, -g

 Run the GUI with debugging enabled. Debug output is printed to stdout and stderr.

--gui-debug

 Run the GUI with a debug console, logging to the specified path. For internal use only, use the -g option to run the GUI in debug mode

--help, -h

 show this help message and exit

--inspect-mobi, -m

 Inspect the MOBI file(s) at the specified path(s)

--new-server

 Run the new calibre content server. Any options specified after a -- will be passed to the server.

--paths

 Output the paths necessary to setup the calibre environment

--py-console, -p

 Run python console

--reinitialize-db

 Re-initialize the sqlite calibre database at the specified path. Useful to recover from db corruption.

--run-plugin, -r

 Run a plugin that provides a command line interface. For example: calibre-debug -r "Add Books" -- file1 --option1 Everything after the -- will be passed to the plugin as arguments.

--shutdown-running-calibre, -s

 Cause a running calibre instance, if any, to be shutdown. Note that if there are running jobs, they will be silently aborted, so use with care.

--subset-font, -f

 Subset the specified font. Use -- after this option to pass option to the font subsetting program.

--test-build

 Test binary modules in build

--version

 show program's version number and exit

--viewer, -w

 Run the ebook viewer in debug mode

`calibre-server`

```
calibre-server [options]
```

Start the calibre content server. The calibre content server exposes your calibre library over the internet. The default interface allows you to browse you calibre library by categories. You can also access an interface optimized for mobile browsers at /mobile and an OPDS based interface for use with reading applications at /opds.

The OPDS interface is advertised via BonJour automatically.

Whenever you pass arguments to **calibre-server** that have spaces in them, enclose the arguments in quotation marks. For example "C:some path with spaces"

[options]

--auto-reload
> Auto reload server when source code changes. May not work in all environments.

--daemonize
> Run process in background as a daemon. No effect on windows.

--develop
> Development mode. Server automatically restarts on file changes and serves code files (html, css, js) from the file system instead of calibre's resource system.

--help, -h
> show this help message and exit

--max-cover
> The maximum size for displayed covers. Default is '600x800'.

--max-opds-items
> The maximum number of matches to return per OPDS query. This affects Stanza, WordPlayer, etc. integration.

--max-opds-ungrouped-items
> Group items in categories such as author/tags by first letter when there are more than this number of items. Default: 100. Set to a large number to disable grouping.

--password
> Set a password to restrict access. By default access is unrestricted.

--pidfile
> Write process PID to the specified file

--port, -p
> The port on which to listen. Default is 8080

--restriction
> Specifies a virtual library to be used for this invocation. This option overrides any per-library settings specified in the GUI. For compatibility, if the value is not a virtual library but is a saved search, that saved search is used. Also note that if you do not specify a restriction, the value specified in the GUI (if any) will be used.

--thread-pool
> The max number of worker threads to use. Default is 30

--timeout, -t
> The server timeout in seconds. Default is 120

--url-prefix
> Prefix to prepend to all URLs. Useful for reverseproxying to this server from Apache/nginx/etc.

--username

    Username for access. By default, it is: 'calibre'

--version

    show program's version number and exit

--with-library

    Path to the library folder to serve with the content server

calibre-smtp

```
calibre-smtp [options] [from to text]
```

Send mail using the SMTP protocol. **calibre-smtp** has two modes of operation. In the compose mode you specify from to and text and these are used to build and send an email message. In the filter mode, **calibre-smtp** reads a complete email message from STDIN and sends it.

text is the body of the email message. If text is not specified, a complete email message is read from STDIN. from is the email address of the sender and to is the email address of the recipient. When a complete email is read from STDIN, from and to are only used in the SMTP negotiation, the message headers are not modified.

Whenever you pass arguments to **calibre-smtp** that have spaces in them, enclose the arguments in quotation marks. For example "C:some path with spaces"

[options]

--fork, -f

    Fork and deliver message in background. If you use this option, you should also use *--outbox* (page 276) to handle delivery failures.

--help, -h

    show this help message and exit

--localhost, -l

    Host name of localhost. Used when connecting to SMTP server.

--outbox, -o

    Path to maildir folder to store failed email messages in.

--timeout, -t

    Timeout for connection

--verbose, -v

    Be more verbose

--version

    show program's version number and exit

COMPOSE MAIL   Options to compose an email. Ignored if text is not specified

--attachment, -a

    File to attach to the email

--subject, -s

    Subject of the email

SMTP RELAY   Options to use an SMTP relay server to send mail. calibre will try to send the email directly unless –relay is specified.

--encryption-method, -e
> Encryption method to use when connecting to relay. Choices are TLS, SSL and NONE. Default is TLS. WARNING: Choosing NONE is highly insecure

--password, -p
> Password for relay

--port
> Port to connect to on relay server. Default is to use 465 if encryption method is SSL and 25 otherwise.

--relay, -r
> An SMTP relay server to use to send mail.

--username, -u
> Username for relay

calibredb

```
calibredb command [options] [arguments]
```

calibredb is the command line interface to the calibre database. It has several sub-commands, documented below:

Global options

--dont-notify-gui
> Do not notify the running calibre GUI (if any) that the database has changed. Use with care, as it can lead to database corruption!

--library-path
    Path to the calibre library. Default is to use the path stored in the settings.

list

```
calibredb list [options]
```

List the books available in the calibre database.

Whenever you pass arguments to calibredb that have spaces in them, enclose the arguments in quotation marks. For example "C:some path with spaces"

--ascending
    Sort results in ascending order

--fields, -f
    The fields to display when listing books in the database. Should be a comma separated list of fields. Available fields: author_sort, authors, comments, cover, formats, id, identifiers, isbn, languages, last_modified, pubdate, publisher, rating, series, series_index, size, tags, timestamp, title, uuid Default: title,authors. The special field "all" can be used to select all fields.

--for-machine
    Generate output in JSON format, which is more suitable for machine parsing. Causes the line width and separator options to be ignored.

--help, -h
    show this help message and exit

--limit
    The maximum number of results to display. Default: all

--line-width, -w
    The maximum width of a single line in the output. Defaults to detecting screen size.

--prefix
    The prefix for all file paths. Default is the absolute path to the library folder.

--search, -s
    Filter the results by the search query. For the format of the search query, please see the search related documentation in the User Manual. Default is to do no filtering.

--separator
    The string used to separate fields. Default is a space.

--sort-by
    The field by which to sort the results. Available fields: author_sort, authors, comments, cover, formats, identifiers, isbn, languages, last_modified, pubdate, publisher, rating, series, series_index, size, tags, timestamp, title, uuid Default: id

--version
    show program's version number and exit

add

```
calibredb add [options] file1 file2 file3 ...
```

Add the specified files as books to the database. You can also specify directories, see the directory related options below.

Whenever you pass arguments to calibredb that have spaces in them, enclose the arguments in quotation marks. For example "C:some path with spaces"

--authors, -a
> Set the authors of the added book(s)

--cover, -c
> Path to the cover to use for the added book

--duplicates, -d
> Add books to database even if they already exist. Comparison is done based on book titles.

--empty, -e
> Add an empty book (a book with no formats)

--help, -h
> show this help message and exit

--identifier, -I
> Set the identifiers for this book, for e.g. -I asin:XXX -I isbn:YYY

--isbn, -i
> Set the ISBN of the added book(s)

--languages, -l
> A comma separated list of languages (best to use ISO639 language codes, though some language names may also be recognized)

--one-book-per-directory, -1
> Assume that each directory has only a single logical book and that all files in it are different e-book formats of that book

--recurse, -r
> Process directories recursively

--series, -s
> Set the series of the added book(s)

--series-index, -S
> Set the series number of the added book(s)

--tags, -T
> Set the tags of the added book(s)

--title, -t
> Set the title of the added book(s)

--version
> show program's version number and exit

remove

```
calibredb remove ids
```

Remove the books identified by ids from the database. ids should be a comma separated list of id numbers (you can get id numbers by using the search command). For example, 23,34,57-85 (when specifying a range, the last number in the range is not included).

Whenever you pass arguments to calibredb that have spaces in them, enclose the arguments in quotation marks. For example "C:some path with spaces"

--help, -h
> show this help message and exit

--version
> show program's version number and exit

add_format

```
calibredb add_format [options] id ebook_file
```

Add the ebook in ebook_file to the available formats for the logical book identified by id. You can get id by using the search command. If the format already exists, it is replaced, unless the do not replace option is specified.

Whenever you pass arguments to calibredb that have spaces in them, enclose the arguments in quotation marks. For example "C:some path with spaces"

--dont-replace
> Do not replace the format if it already exists

--help, -h
> show this help message and exit

--version
> show program's version number and exit

remove_format

```
calibredb remove_format [options] id fmt
```

Remove the format fmt from the logical book identified by id. You can get id by using the search command. fmt should be a file extension like LRF or TXT or EPUB. If the logical book does not have fmt available, do nothing.

Whenever you pass arguments to calibredb that have spaces in them, enclose the arguments in quotation marks. For example "C:some path with spaces"

--help, -h
> show this help message and exit

--version
> show program's version number and exit

show_metadata

```
calibredb show_metadata [options] id
```

Show the metadata stored in the calibre database for the book identified by id. id is an id number from the search command.

Whenever you pass arguments to calibredb that have spaces in them, enclose the arguments in quotation marks. For example "C:some path with spaces"

--as-opf
> Print metadata in OPF form (XML)

--help, -h
> show this help message and exit

--version
> show program's version number and exit

set_metadata

```
calibredb set_metadata [options] id [/path/to/metadata.opf]
```

Set the metadata stored in the calibre database for the book identified by id from the OPF file metadata.opf. id is an id number from the search command. You can get a quick feel for the OPF format by using the –as-opf switch to the show_metadata command. You can also set the metadata of individual fields with the –field option. If you use the –field option, there is no need to specify an OPF file.

Whenever you pass arguments to calibredb that have spaces in them, enclose the arguments in quotation marks. For example "C:some path with spaces"

--field, -f
> The field to set. Format is field_name:value, for example: `--field` (page 281) tags:tag1,tag2. Use `--list-fields` (page 281) to get a list of all field names. You can specify this option multiple times to set multiple fields. Note: For languages you must use the ISO639 language codes (e.g. en for English, fr for French and so on). For identifiers, the syntax is `--field` (page 281) identifiers:isbn:XXXX,doi:YYYYY. For boolean (yes/no) fields use true and false or yes and no.

--help, -h
> show this help message and exit

--list-fields, -l
> List the metadata field names that can be used with the `--field` (page 281) option

--version
> show program's version number and exit

export

```
calibredb export [options] ids
```

Export the books specified by ids (a comma separated list) to the filesystem. The **export** operation saves all formats of the book, its cover and metadata (in an opf file). You can get id numbers from the search command.

Whenever you pass arguments to calibredb that have spaces in them, enclose the arguments in quotation marks. For example "C:some path with spaces"

--all
> Export all books in database, ignoring the list of ids.

--dont-asciiize
> Normally, calibre will convert all non English characters into English equivalents for the file names. WARNING: If you turn this off, you may experience errors when saving, depending on how well the filesystem you are saving to supports unicode. Specifying this switch will turn this behavior off.

--dont-save-cover
> Normally, calibre will save the cover in a separate file along with the actual e-book file(s). Specifying this switch will turn this behavior off.

--dont-update-metadata
> Normally, calibre will update the metadata in the saved files from what is in the calibre library. Makes saving to disk slower. Specifying this switch will turn this behavior off.

--dont-write-opf

Normally, calibre will write the metadata into a separate OPF file along with the actual e-book files. Specifying this switch will turn this behavior off.

--formats

Comma separated list of formats to save for each book. By default all available formats are saved.

--help, -h

show this help message and exit

--replace-whitespace

Replace whitespace with underscores.

--single-dir

Export all books into a single directory

--template

The template to control the filename and directory structure of the saved files. Default is "{author_sort}/{title}/{title} - {authors}" which will save books into a per-author subdirectory with filenames containing title and author. Available controls are: {author_sort, authors, id, isbn, languages, last_modified, pubdate, publisher, rating, series, series_index, tags, timestamp, title}

--timefmt

The format in which to display dates. %d - day, %b - month, %m - month number, %Y - year. Default is: %b, %Y

--to-dir

Export books to the specified directory. Default is .

--to-lowercase

Convert paths to lowercase.

--version

show program's version number and exit

catalog

```
calibredb catalog /path/to/destination.(CSV|EPUB|MOBI|XML ...) [options]
```

Export a **catalog** in format specified by path/to/destination extension. Options control how entries are displayed in the generated **catalog** output.

Whenever you pass arguments to calibredb that have spaces in them, enclose the arguments in quotation marks. For example "C:some path with spaces"

--fields

The fields to output when cataloging books in the database. Should be a comma-separated list of fields. Available fields: all, title, title_sort, author_sort, authors, comments, cover, formats, id, isbn, library_name, ondevice, pubdate, publisher, rating, series_index, series, size, tags, timestamp, uuid, languages, identifiers, plus user-created custom fields. Example: `--fields=title,authors,tags` Default: 'all' Applies to: CSV, XML output formats

--help, -h

show this help message and exit

--ids, -i

Comma-separated list of database IDs to catalog. If declared, `--search` (page 282) is ignored. Default: all

--search, -s
> Filter the results by the search query. For the format of the search query, please see the search-related documentation in the User Manual. Default: no filtering

--sort-by
> Output field to sort on. Available fields: author_sort, id, rating, size, timestamp, title_sort Default: 'id' Applies to: CSV, XML output formats

--verbose, -v
> Show detailed output information. Useful for debugging

--version
> show program's version number and exit

saved_searches

```
calibredb saved_searches [options] list
```

calibredb **saved_searches** add name search calibredb **saved_searches** remove name

Manage the saved searches stored in this database. If you try to add a query with a name that already exists, it will be replaced.

Whenever you pass arguments to calibredb that have spaces in them, enclose the arguments in quotation marks. For example "C:some path with spaces"

--help, -h
> show this help message and exit

--version
> show program's version number and exit

add_custom_column

```
calibredb add_custom_column [options] label name datatype
```

Create a custom column. label is the machine friendly name of the column. Should not contain spaces or colons. name is the human friendly name of the column. datatype is one of: bool, comments, composite, datetime, enumeration, float, int, rating, series, text

Whenever you pass arguments to calibredb that have spaces in them, enclose the arguments in quotation marks. For example "C:some path with spaces"

--display
> A dictionary of options to customize how the data in this column will be interpreted. This is a JSON string. For enumeration columns, use --display="{"enum_values":["val1", "val2"]}" There are many options that can go into the display variable.The options by column type are: composite: composite_template, composite_sort, make_category,contains_html, use_decorations datetime: date_format enumeration: enum_values, enum_colors, use_decorations int, float: number_format text: is_names, use_decorations The best way to find legal combinations is to create a custom column of the appropriate type in the GUI then look at the backup OPF for a book (ensure that a new OPF has been created since the column was added). You will see the JSON for the "display" for the new column in the OPF.

--help, -h
> show this help message and exit

--is-multiple
> This column stores tag like data (i.e. multiple comma separated values). Only applies if datatype is text.

--version
> show program's version number and exit

custom_columns

```
calibredb custom_columns [options]
```

List available custom columns. Shows column labels and ids.

Whenever you pass arguments to calibredb that have spaces in them, enclose the arguments in quotation marks. For example "C:some path with spaces"

--details, -d
> Show details for each column.

--help, -h
> show this help message and exit

--version
> show program's version number and exit

remove_custom_column

```
calibredb remove_custom_column [options] label
```

Remove the custom column identified by label. You can see available columns with the custom_columns command.

Whenever you pass arguments to calibredb that have spaces in them, enclose the arguments in quotation marks. For example "C:some path with spaces"

--force, -f
> Do not ask for confirmation

--help, -h
> show this help message and exit

--version
> show program's version number and exit

set_custom

```
calibredb set_custom [options] column id value
```

Set the value of a custom column for the book identified by id. You can get a list of ids using the search command. You can get a list of custom column names using the custom_columns command.

Whenever you pass arguments to calibredb that have spaces in them, enclose the arguments in quotation marks. For example "C:some path with spaces"

--append, -a
> If the column stores multiple values, append the specified values to the existing ones, instead of replacing them.

--help, -h
> show this help message and exit

--version
> show program's version number and exit

restore_database

```
calibredb restore_database [options]
```

Restore this database from the metadata stored in OPF files in each directory of the calibre library. This is useful if your metadata.db file has been corrupted.

WARNING: This command completely regenerates your database. You will lose all saved searches, user categories, plugboards, stored per-book conversion settings, and custom recipes. Restored metadata will only be as accurate as what is found in the OPF files.

Whenever you pass arguments to calibredb that have spaces in them, enclose the arguments in quotation marks. For example "C:some path with spaces"

--help, -h
> show this help message and exit

--really-do-it, -r
> Really do the recovery. The command will not run unless this option is specified.

--version
> show program's version number and exit

check_library

```
calibredb check_library [options]
```

Perform some checks on the filesystem representing a library. Reports are invalid_titles, extra_titles, invalid_authors, extra_authors, missing_formats, extra_formats, extra_files, missing_covers, extra_covers, failed_folders

Whenever you pass arguments to calibredb that have spaces in them, enclose the arguments in quotation marks. For example "C:some path with spaces"

--csv, -c
> Output in CSV

--help, -h
> show this help message and exit

--ignore_extensions, -e
> Comma-separated list of extensions to ignore. Default: all

--ignore_names, -n
> Comma-separated list of names to ignore. Default: all

--report, -r
> Comma-separated list of reports. Default: all

--version
> show program's version number and exit

list_categories

```
calibredb list_categories [options]
```

Produce a report of the category information in the database. The information is the equivalent of what is shown in the tags pane.

Whenever you pass arguments to calibredb that have spaces in them, enclose the arguments in quotation marks. For example "C:some path with spaces"

--categories, -r

> Comma-separated list of category lookup names. Default: all

--csv, -c

> Output in CSV

--help, -h

> show this help message and exit

--item_count, -i

> Output only the number of items in a category instead of the counts per item within the category

--quote, -q

> The character to put around the category value in CSV mode. Default is quotes (").

--separator, -s

> The string used to separate fields in CSV mode. Default is a comma.

--version

> show program's version number and exit

--width, -w

> The maximum width of a single line in the output. Defaults to detecting screen size.

backup_metadata

```
calibredb backup_metadata [options]
```

Backup the metadata stored in the database into individual OPF files in each books directory. This normally happens automatically, but you can run this command to force re-generation of the OPF files, with the –all option.

Note that there is normally no need to do this, as the OPF files are backed up automatically, every time metadata is changed.

Whenever you pass arguments to calibredb that have spaces in them, enclose the arguments in quotation marks. For example "C:some path with spaces"

--all

> Normally, this command only operates on books that have out of date OPF files. This option makes it operate on all books.

--help, -h

> show this help message and exit

--version

> show program's version number and exit

clone

```
calibredb clone path/to/new/library
```

Create a **clone** of the current library. This creates a new, empty library that has all the same custom columns, virtual libraries and other settings as the current library.

The cloned library will contain no books. If you want to create a full duplicate, including all books, then simply use your filesystem tools to copy the library folder.

Whenever you pass arguments to calibredb that have spaces in them, enclose the arguments in quotation marks. For example "C:some path with spaces"

--help, -h
> show this help message and exit

--version
> show program's version number and exit

embed_metadata

```
calibredb embed_metadata [options] book_id
```

Update the metadata in the actual book files stored in the calibre library from the metadata in the calibre database. Normally, metadata is updated only when exporting files from calibre, this command is useful if you want the files to be updated in place. Note that different file formats support different amounts of metadata. You can use the special value 'all' for book_id to update metadata in all books. You can also specify many book ids separated by spaces and id ranges separated by hyphens. For example: calibredb **embed_metadata** 1 2 10-15 23

Whenever you pass arguments to calibredb that have spaces in them, enclose the arguments in quotation marks. For example "C:some path with spaces"

--help, -h
> show this help message and exit

--only-formats, -f
> Only update metadata in files of the specified format. Specify it multiple times for multiple formats. By default, all formats are updated.

--version
> show program's version number and exit

search

```
calibredb search [options] search expression
```

Search the library for the specified **search** term, returning a comma separated list of book ids matching the **search** expression. The output format is useful to feed into other commands that accept a list of ids as input.

The **search** expression can be anything from calibre's powerful **search** query language, for example: author:asimov title:robot

Whenever you pass arguments to calibredb that have spaces in them, enclose the arguments in quotation marks. For example "C:some path with spaces"

--help, -h
> show this help message and exit

--limit, -l
> The maximum number of results to return. Default is all results.

--version
> show program's version number and exit

ebook-convert

```
ebook-convert input_file output_file [options]
```

Convert an ebook from one format to another.

input_file is the input and output_file is the output. Both must be specified as the first two arguments to the command.

The output ebook format is guessed from the file extension of output_file. output_file can also be of the special format .EXT where EXT is the output file extension. In this case, the name of the output file is derived from the name of the input file. Note that the filenames must not start with a hyphen. Finally, if output_file has no extension, then it is treated as a directory and an "open ebook" (OEB) consisting of HTML files is written to that directory. These files are the files that would normally have been passed to the output plugin.

After specifying the input and output file you can customize the conversion by specifying various options. The available options depend on the input and output file types. To get help on them specify the input and output file and then use the -h option.

For full documentation of the conversion system see *Ebook Conversion* (page 54)

Whenever you pass arguments to **ebook-convert** that have spaces in them, enclose the arguments in quotation marks. For example "C:some path with spaces"

The options and default values for the options change depending on both the input and output formats, so you should always check with:

```
ebook-convert myfile.input_format myfile.output_format -h
```

Below are the options that are common to all conversion, followed by the options specific to every input and output format.

--help, -h
> show this help message and exit

--input-profile
> Specify the input profile. The input profile gives the conversion system information on how to interpret various

information in the input document. For example resolution dependent lengths (i.e. lengths in pixels). Choices are:cybookg3, cybook_opus, default, hanlinv3, hanlinv5, illiad, irexdr1000, irexdr800, kindle, msreader, mobipocket, nook, sony, sony300, sony900

--list-recipes

List builtin recipe names. You can create an ebook from a builtin recipe like this: ebook-convert "Recipe Name.recipe" output.epub

--output-profile

Specify the output profile. The output profile tells the conversion system how to optimize the created document for the specified device. In some cases, an output profile can be used to optimize the output for a particular device, but this is rarely necessary. Choices are:cybookg3, cybook_opus, default, generic_eink, generic_eink_hd, generic_eink_large, hanlinv3, hanlinv5, illiad, ipad, ipad3, irexdr1000, irexdr800, jetbook5, kindle, kindle_dx, kindle_fire, kindle_pw, kindle_pw3, kindle_voyage, kobo, msreader, mobipocket, nook, nook_color, nook_hd_plus, pocketbook_900, pocketbook_pro_912, galaxy, bambook, sony, sony300, sony900, sony-landscape, sonyt3, tablet

--version

show program's version number and exit

Look And Feel

Options to control the look and feel of the output

--asciiize

Transliterate unicode characters to an ASCII representation. Use with care because this will replace unicode characters with ASCII. For instance it will replace "Михаил Горбачёв" with "Mikhail Gorbachiov". Also, note that in cases where there are multiple representations of a character (characters shared by Chinese and Japanese for instance) the representation based on the current calibre interface language will be used.

--base-font-size

The base font size in pts. All font sizes in the produced book will be rescaled based on this size. By choosing a larger size you can make the fonts in the output bigger and vice versa. By default, the base font size is chosen based on the output profile you chose.

--change-justification

Change text justification. A value of "left" converts all justified text in the source to left aligned (i.e. unjustified) text. A value of "justify" converts all unjustified text to justified. A value of "original" (the default) does not change justification in the source file. Note that only some output formats support justification.

--disable-font-rescaling

Disable all rescaling of font sizes.

--embed-all-fonts

Embed every font that is referenced in the input document but not already embedded. This will search your system for the fonts, and if found, they will be embedded. Embedding will only work if the format you are converting to supports embedded fonts, such as EPUB, AZW3, DOCX or PDF. Please ensure that you have the proper license for embedding the fonts used in this document.

--embed-font-family

Embed the specified font family into the book. This specifies the "base" font used for the book. If the input document specifies its own fonts, they may override this base font. You can use the filter style information option to remove fonts from the input document. Note that font embedding only works with some output formats, principally EPUB, AZW3 and DOCX.

--expand-css

By default, calibre will use the shorthand form for various css properties such as margin, padding, border, etc. This option will cause it to use the full expanded form instead. Note that CSS is always expanded when generating EPUB files with the output profile set to one of the Nook profiles as the Nook cannot handle shorthand CSS.

--extra-css

Either the path to a CSS stylesheet or raw CSS. This CSS will be appended to the style rules from the source file, so it can be used to override those rules.

--filter-css

A comma separated list of CSS properties that will be removed from all CSS style rules. This is useful if the presence of some style information prevents it from being overridden on your device. For example: font-family,color,margin-left,margin-right

--font-size-mapping

Mapping from CSS font names to font sizes in pts. An example setting is 12,12,14,16,18,20,22,24. These are the mappings for the sizes xx-small to xx-large, with the final size being for huge fonts. The font rescaling algorithm uses these sizes to intelligently rescale fonts. The default is to use a mapping based on the output profile you chose.

--insert-blank-line

Insert a blank line between paragraphs. Will not work if the source file does not use paragraphs (<p> or <div> tags).

--insert-blank-line-size

Set the height of the inserted blank lines (in em). The height of the lines between paragraphs will be twice the value set here.

--keep-ligatures

Preserve ligatures present in the input document. A ligature is a special rendering of a pair of characters like ff, fi, fl et cetera. Most readers do not have support for ligatures in their default fonts, so they are unlikely to render correctly. By default, calibre will turn a ligature into the corresponding pair of normal characters. This option will preserve them instead.

--line-height

The line height in pts. Controls spacing between consecutive lines of text. Only applies to elements that do not define their own line height. In most cases, the minimum line height option is more useful. By default no line height manipulation is performed.

--linearize-tables

Some badly designed documents use tables to control the layout of text on the page. When converted these documents often have text that runs off the page and other artifacts. This option will extract the content from the tables and present it in a linear fashion.

--margin-bottom

Set the bottom margin in pts. Default is 5.0. Setting this to less than zero will cause no margin to be set (the margin setting in the original document will be preserved). Note: 72 pts equals 1 inch

--margin-left

Set the left margin in pts. Default is 5.0. Setting this to less than zero will cause no margin to be set (the margin setting in the original document will be preserved). Note: 72 pts equals 1 inch

--margin-right

Set the right margin in pts. Default is 5.0. Setting this to less than zero will cause no margin to be set (the margin setting in the original document will be preserved). Note: 72 pts equals 1 inch

--margin-top

Set the top margin in pts. Default is 5.0. Setting this to less than zero will cause no margin to be set (the margin setting in the original document will be preserved). Note: 72 pts equals 1 inch

--minimum-line-height

The minimum line height, as a percentage of the element's calculated font size. calibre will ensure that every element has a line height of at least this setting, irrespective of what the input document specifies. Set to zero to disable. Default is 120%. Use this setting in preference to the direct line height specification, unless you know what you are doing. For example, you can achieve "double spaced" text by setting this to 240.

--remove-paragraph-spacing

Remove spacing between paragraphs. Also sets an indent on paragraphs of 1.5em. Spacing removal will not work if the source file does not use paragraphs (<p> or <div> tags).

--remove-paragraph-spacing-indent-size

When calibre removes blank lines between paragraphs, it automatically sets a paragraph indent, to ensure that paragraphs can be easily distinguished. This option controls the width of that indent (in em). If you set this value negative, then the indent specified in the input document is used, that is, calibre does not change the indentation.

--smarten-punctuation

Convert plain quotes, dashes and ellipsis to their typographically correct equivalents. For details, see http://daringfireball.net/projects/smartypants

--subset-embedded-fonts

Subset all embedded fonts. Every embedded font is reduced to contain only the glyphs used in this document. This decreases the size of the font files. Useful if you are embedding a particularly large font with lots of unused glyphs.

--unsmarten-punctuation

Convert fancy quotes, dashes and ellipsis to their plain equivalents.

Heuristic Processing

Modify the document text and structure using common patterns. Disabled by default. Use –enable-heuristics to enable. Individual actions can be disabled with the –disable-* options.

--disable-dehyphenate

Analyze hyphenated words throughout the document. The document itself is used as a dictionary to determine whether hyphens should be retained or removed.

--disable-delete-blank-paragraphs

Remove empty paragraphs from the document when they exist between every other paragraph

--disable-fix-indents

Turn indentation created from multiple non-breaking space entities into CSS indents.

--disable-format-scene-breaks

Left aligned scene break markers are center aligned. Replace soft scene breaks that use multiple blank lines with horizontal rules.

--disable-italicize-common-cases

Look for common words and patterns that denote italics and italicize them.

--disable-markup-chapter-headings

Detect unformatted chapter headings and sub headings. Change them to h2 and h3 tags. This setting will not create a TOC, but can be used in conjunction with structure detection to create one.

--disable-renumber-headings

Looks for occurrences of sequential <h1> or <h2> tags. The tags are renumbered to prevent splitting in the middle of chapter headings.

--disable-unwrap-lines

Unwrap lines using punctuation and other formatting clues.

--enable-heuristics

Enable heuristic processing. This option must be set for any heuristic processing to take place.

--html-unwrap-factor

Scale used to determine the length at which a line should be unwrapped. Valid values are a decimal between 0 and 1. The default is 0.4, just below the median line length. If only a few lines in the document require unwrapping this value should be reduced

--replace-scene-breaks

Replace scene breaks with the specified text. By default, the text from the input document is used.

Search And Replace

Modify the document text and structure using user defined patterns.

--search-replace

Path to a file containing search and replace regular expressions. The file must contain alternating lines of regular expression followed by replacement pattern (which can be an empty line). The regular expression must be in the python regex syntax and the file must be UTF-8 encoded.

--sr1-replace

Replacement to replace the text found with sr1-search.

--sr1-search

Search pattern (regular expression) to be replaced with sr1-replace.

--sr2-replace

Replacement to replace the text found with sr2-search.

--sr2-search

Search pattern (regular expression) to be replaced with sr2-replace.

--sr3-replace

Replacement to replace the text found with sr3-search.

--sr3-search

Search pattern (regular expression) to be replaced with sr3-replace.

Structure Detection

Control auto-detection of document structure.

--chapter

An XPath expression to detect chapter titles. The default is to consider <h1> or <h2> tags that contain the words "chapter","book","section", "prologue", "epilogue", or "part" as chapter titles as well as any tags that have class="chapter". The expression used must evaluate to a list of elements. To disable chapter detection, use the expression "/". See the XPath Tutorial in the calibre User Manual for further help on using this feature.

--chapter-mark

Specify how to mark detected chapters. A value of "pagebreak" will insert page breaks before chapters. A value of "rule" will insert a line before chapters. A value of "none" will disable chapter marking and a value of "both" will use both page breaks and lines to mark chapters.

--disable-remove-fake-margins

Some documents specify page margins by specifying a left and right margin on each individual paragraph. calibre will try to detect and remove these margins. Sometimes, this can cause the removal of margins that should not have been removed. In this case you can disable the removal.

--insert-metadata

Insert the book metadata at the start of the book. This is useful if your ebook reader does not support displaying/searching metadata directly.

--page-breaks-before

An XPath expression. Page breaks are inserted before the specified elements. To disable use the expression: /

--prefer-metadata-cover

Use the cover detected from the source file in preference to the specified cover.

--remove-first-image

Remove the first image from the input ebook. Useful if the input document has a cover image that is not identified as a cover. In this case, if you set a cover in calibre, the output document will end up with two cover images if you do not specify this option.

--start-reading-at

An XPath expression to detect the location in the document at which to start reading. Some ebook reading programs (most prominently the Kindle) use this location as the position at which to open the book. See the XPath tutorial in the calibre User Manual for further help using this feature.

Table Of Contents

Control the automatic generation of a Table of Contents. By default, if the source file has a Table of Contents, it will be used in preference to the automatically generated one.

--duplicate-links-in-toc

When creating a TOC from links in the input document, allow duplicate entries, i.e. allow more than one entry with the same text, provided that they point to a different location.

--level1-toc

XPath expression that specifies all tags that should be added to the Table of Contents at level one. If this is specified, it takes precedence over other forms of auto-detection. See the XPath Tutorial in the calibre User Manual for examples.

--level2-toc

XPath expression that specifies all tags that should be added to the Table of Contents at level two. Each entry is added under the previous level one entry. See the XPath Tutorial in the calibre User Manual for examples.

--level3-toc

XPath expression that specifies all tags that should be added to the Table of Contents at level three. Each entry is added under the previous level two entry. See the XPath Tutorial in the calibre User Manual for examples.

--max-toc-links

Maximum number of links to insert into the TOC. Set to 0 to disable. Default is: 50. Links are only added to the TOC if less than the threshold number of chapters were detected.

--no-chapters-in-toc

Don't add auto-detected chapters to the Table of Contents.

--toc-filter

Remove entries from the Table of Contents whose titles match the specified regular expression. Matching entries and all their children are removed.

--toc-threshold

If fewer than this number of chapters is detected, then links are added to the Table of Contents. Default: 6

--use-auto-toc

Normally, if the source file already has a Table of Contents, it is used in preference to the auto-generated one. With this option, the auto-generated one is always used.

Metadata

Options to set metadata in the output

--author-sort
> String to be used when sorting by author.

--authors
> Set the authors. Multiple authors should be separated by ampersands.

--book-producer
> Set the book producer.

--comments
> Set the ebook description.

--cover
> Set the cover to the specified file or URL

--isbn
> Set the ISBN of the book.

--language
> Set the language.

--pubdate
> Set the publication date.

--publisher
> Set the ebook publisher.

--rating
> Set the rating. Should be a number between 1 and 5.

--read-metadata-from-opf, -m
> Read metadata from the specified OPF file. Metadata read from this file will override any metadata in the source file.

--series
> Set the series this ebook belongs to.

--series-index
> Set the index of the book in this series.

--tags
> Set the tags for the book. Should be a comma separated list.

--timestamp
> Set the book timestamp (no longer used anywhere)

--title
> Set the title.

--title-sort
> The version of the title to be used for sorting.

Debug

Options to help with debugging the conversion

--debug-pipeline, -d
Save the output from different stages of the conversion pipeline to the specified directory. Useful if you are unsure at which stage of the conversion process a bug is occurring.

--verbose, -v
Level of verbosity. Specify multiple times for greater verbosity. Specifying it twice will result in full verbosity, once medium verbosity and zero times least verbosity.

AZW4 Input Options

--input-encoding
Specify the character encoding of the input document. If set this option will override any encoding declared by the document itself. Particularly useful for documents that do not declare an encoding or that have erroneous encoding declarations.

CHM Input Options

--input-encoding
Specify the character encoding of the input document. If set this option will override any encoding declared by the document itself. Particularly useful for documents that do not declare an encoding or that have erroneous encoding declarations.

Comic Input Options

--colors
Number of colors for grayscale image conversion. Default: 256. Values of less than 256 may result in blurred text on your device if you are creating your comics in EPUB format.

--comic-image-size
Specify the image size as widthxheight pixels. Normally, an image size is automatically calculated from the output profile, this option overrides it.

--despeckle
Enable Despeckle. Reduces speckle noise. May greatly increase processing time.

--disable-trim
Disable trimming of comic pages. For some comics, trimming might remove content as well as borders.

--dont-add-comic-pages-to-toc
When converting a CBC do not add links to each page to the TOC. Note this only applies if the TOC has more than one section

--dont-grayscale
Do not convert the image to grayscale (black and white)

--dont-normalize
Disable normalize (improve contrast) color range for pictures. Default: False

--dont-sharpen
Disable sharpening.

--input-encoding
Specify the character encoding of the input document. If set this option will override any encoding declared by the document itself. Particularly useful for documents that do not declare an encoding or that have erroneous encoding declarations.

--keep-aspect-ratio

Maintain picture aspect ratio. Default is to fill the screen.

--landscape

Don't split landscape images into two portrait images

--no-process

Apply no processing to the image

--no-sort

Don't sort the files found in the comic alphabetically by name. Instead use the order they were added to the comic.

--output-format

The format that images in the created ebook are converted to. You can experiment to see which format gives you optimal size and look on your device.

--right2left

Used for right-to-left publications like manga. Causes landscape pages to be split into portrait pages from right to left.

--wide

Keep aspect ratio and scale image using screen height as image width for viewing in landscape mode.

DJVU Input Options

--input-encoding

Specify the character encoding of the input document. If set this option will override any encoding declared by the document itself. Particularly useful for documents that do not declare an encoding or that have erroneous encoding declarations.

DOCX Input Options

--docx-no-cover

Normally, if a large image is present at the start of the document that looks like a cover, it will be removed from the document and used as the cover for created ebook. This option turns off that behavior.

--docx-no-pagebreaks-between-notes

Do not insert a page break after every endnote.

--input-encoding

Specify the character encoding of the input document. If set this option will override any encoding declared by the document itself. Particularly useful for documents that do not declare an encoding or that have erroneous encoding declarations.

EPUB Input Options

--input-encoding

Specify the character encoding of the input document. If set this option will override any encoding declared by the document itself. Particularly useful for documents that do not declare an encoding or that have erroneous encoding declarations.

FB2 Input Options

`--input-encoding`
> Specify the character encoding of the input document. If set this option will override any encoding declared by the document itself. Particularly useful for documents that do not declare an encoding or that have erroneous encoding declarations.

`--no-inline-fb2-toc`
> Do not insert a Table of Contents at the beginning of the book.

HTLZ Input Options

`--input-encoding`
> Specify the character encoding of the input document. If set this option will override any encoding declared by the document itself. Particularly useful for documents that do not declare an encoding or that have erroneous encoding declarations.

HTML Input Options

`--breadth-first`
> Traverse links in HTML files breadth first. Normally, they are traversed depth first.

`--dont-package`
> Normally this input plugin re-arranges all the input files into a standard folder hierarchy. Only use this option if you know what you are doing as it can result in various nasty side effects in the rest of the conversion pipeline.

`--input-encoding`
> Specify the character encoding of the input document. If set this option will override any encoding declared by the document itself. Particularly useful for documents that do not declare an encoding or that have erroneous encoding declarations.

`--max-levels`
> Maximum levels of recursion when following links in HTML files. Must be non-negative. 0 implies that no links in the root HTML file are followed. Default is 5.

LIT Input Options

`--input-encoding`
> Specify the character encoding of the input document. If set this option will override any encoding declared by the document itself. Particularly useful for documents that do not declare an encoding or that have erroneous encoding declarations.

LRF Input Options

`--input-encoding`
> Specify the character encoding of the input document. If set this option will override any encoding declared by the document itself. Particularly useful for documents that do not declare an encoding or that have erroneous encoding declarations.

Chapter 1. Sections

MOBI Input Options

--input-encoding
> Specify the character encoding of the input document. If set this option will override any encoding declared by the document itself. Particularly useful for documents that do not declare an encoding or that have erroneous encoding declarations.

ODT Input Options

--input-encoding
> Specify the character encoding of the input document. If set this option will override any encoding declared by the document itself. Particularly useful for documents that do not declare an encoding or that have erroneous encoding declarations.

PDB Input Options

--input-encoding
> Specify the character encoding of the input document. If set this option will override any encoding declared by the document itself. Particularly useful for documents that do not declare an encoding or that have erroneous encoding declarations.

PDF Input Options

--input-encoding
> Specify the character encoding of the input document. If set this option will override any encoding declared by the document itself. Particularly useful for documents that do not declare an encoding or that have erroneous encoding declarations.

--new-pdf-engine
> Use the new PDF conversion engine.

--no-images
> Do not extract images from the document

--unwrap-factor
> Scale used to determine the length at which a line should be unwrapped. Valid values are a decimal between 0 and 1. The default is 0.45, just below the median line length.

PML Input Options

--input-encoding
> Specify the character encoding of the input document. If set this option will override any encoding declared by the document itself. Particularly useful for documents that do not declare an encoding or that have erroneous encoding declarations.

RB Input Options

--input-encoding
> Specify the character encoding of the input document. If set this option will override any encoding declared by the document itself. Particularly useful for documents that do not declare an encoding or that have erroneous encoding declarations.

RTF Input Options

--ignore-wmf

Ignore WMF images instead of replacing them with a placeholder image.

--input-encoding

Specify the character encoding of the input document. If set this option will override any encoding declared by the document itself. Particularly useful for documents that do not declare an encoding or that have erroneous encoding declarations.

Recipe Input Options

--dont-download-recipe

Do not download latest version of builtin recipes from the calibre server

--input-encoding

Specify the character encoding of the input document. If set this option will override any encoding declared by the document itself. Particularly useful for documents that do not declare an encoding or that have erroneous encoding declarations.

--lrf

Optimize fetching for subsequent conversion to LRF.

--password

Password for sites that require a login to access content.

--test

Useful for recipe development. Forces max_articles_per_feed to 2 and downloads at most 2 feeds. You can change the number of feeds and articles by supplying optional arguments. For example: `--test` (page 300) 3 1 will download at most 3 feeds and only 1 article per feed.

--username

Username for sites that require a login to access content.

SNB Input Options

--input-encoding

Specify the character encoding of the input document. If set this option will override any encoding declared by the document itself. Particularly useful for documents that do not declare an encoding or that have erroneous encoding declarations.

TCR Input Options

--input-encoding

Specify the character encoding of the input document. If set this option will override any encoding declared by the document itself. Particularly useful for documents that do not declare an encoding or that have erroneous encoding declarations.

TXT Input Options

--formatting-type

Formatting used within the document.* auto: Automatically decide which formatting processor to use. * plain: Do not process the document formatting. Everything is a paragraph and no styling is applied. * heuristic:

Process using heuristics to determine formatting such as chapter headings and italic text. * textile: Processing using textile formatting. * markdown: Processing using markdown formatting. To learn more about markdown see http://daringfireball.net/projects/markdown/

--input-encoding

Specify the character encoding of the input document. If set this option will override any encoding declared by the document itself. Particularly useful for documents that do not declare an encoding or that have erroneous encoding declarations.

--markdown-extensions

Enable extensions to markdown syntax. Extensions are formatting that is not part of the standard markdown format. The extensions enabled by default: footnotes, tables, toc. To learn more about markdown extensions, see http://pythonhosted.org/Markdown/extensions/index.html This should be a comma separated list of extensions to enable: * abbr: Abbreviations * def_list: Definition lists * fenced_code: Alternative code block syntax * footnotes: Footnotes * headerid: Allow ids as part of a header * meta: Metadata in the document * tables: Support tables * toc: Generate a table of contents * wikilinks: Wiki style links

--paragraph-type

Paragraph structure. choices are ['auto', 'block', 'single', 'print', 'unformatted', 'off'] * auto: Try to auto detect paragraph type. * block: Treat a blank line as a paragraph break. * single: Assume every line is a paragraph. * print: Assume every line starting with 2+ spaces or a tab starts a paragraph. * unformatted: Most lines have hard line breaks, few/no blank lines or indents. Tries to determine structure and reformat the differentiate elements. * off: Don't modify the paragraph structure. This is useful when combined with Markdown or Textile formatting to ensure no formatting is lost.

--preserve-spaces

Normally extra spaces are condensed into a single space. With this option all spaces will be displayed.

--txt-in-remove-indents

Normally extra space at the beginning of lines is retained. With this option they will be removed.

AZW3 Output Options

--dont-compress

Disable compression of the file contents.

--extract-to

Extract the contents of the generated AZW3 file to the specified directory. The contents of the directory are first deleted, so be careful.

--mobi-toc-at-start

When adding the Table of Contents to the book, add it at the start of the book instead of the end. Not recommended.

--no-inline-toc

Don't add Table of Contents to the book. Useful if the book has its own table of contents.

--prefer-author-sort

When present, use author sort field as author.

--pretty-print

If specified, the output plugin will try to create output that is as human readable as possible. May not have any effect for some output plugins.

--share-not-sync

Enable sharing of book content via Facebook etc. on the Kindle. WARNING: Using this feature means that the book will not auto sync its last read position on multiple devices. Complain to Amazon.

`--toc-title`

> Title for any generated in-line table of contents.

DOCX Output Options

`--docx-custom-page-size`

> Custom size of the document. Use the form widthxheight EG. *123x321* to specify the width and height (in pts). This overrides any specified page-size.

`--docx-no-cover`

> Do not insert the book cover as an image at the start of the document. If you use this option, the book cover will be discarded.

`--docx-no-toc`

> Do not insert the table of contents as a page at the start of the document.

`--docx-page-size`

> The size of the page. Default is letter. Choices are [u'a0', u'a1', u'a2', u'a3', u'a4', u'a5', u'a6', u'b0', u'b1', u'b2', u'b3', u'b4', u'b5', u'b6', u'legal', u'letter']

`--extract-to`

> Extract the contents of the generated DOCX file to the specified directory. The contents of the directory are first deleted, so be careful.

`--pretty-print`

> If specified, the output plugin will try to create output that is as human readable as possible. May not have any effect for some output plugins.

EPUB Output Options

`--dont-split-on-page-breaks`

> Turn off splitting at page breaks. Normally, input files are automatically split at every page break into two files. This gives an output ebook that can be parsed faster and with less resources. However, splitting is slow and if your source file contains a very large number of page breaks, you should turn off splitting on page breaks.

`--epub-flatten`

> This option is needed only if you intend to use the EPUB with FBReaderJ. It will flatten the file system inside the EPUB, putting all files into the top level.

`--epub-inline-toc`

> Insert an inline Table of Contents that will appear as part of the main book content.

`--epub-toc-at-end`

> Put the inserted inline Table of Contents at the end of the book instead of the start.

`--extract-to`

> Extract the contents of the generated EPUB file to the specified directory. The contents of the directory are first deleted, so be careful.

`--flow-size`

> Split all HTML files larger than this size (in KB). This is necessary as most EPUB readers cannot handle large file sizes. The default of 260KB is the size required for Adobe Digital Editions.

`--no-default-epub-cover`

> Normally, if the input file has no cover and you don't specify one, a default cover is generated with the title, authors, etc. This option disables the generation of this cover.

--no-svg-cover

Do not use SVG for the book cover. Use this option if your EPUB is going to be used on a device that does not support SVG, like the iPhone or the JetBook Lite. Without this option, such devices will display the cover as a blank page.

--preserve-cover-aspect-ratio

When using an SVG cover, this option will cause the cover to scale to cover the available screen area, but still preserve its aspect ratio (ratio of width to height). That means there may be white borders at the sides or top and bottom of the image, but the image will never be distorted. Without this option the image may be slightly distorted, but there will be no borders.

--pretty-print

If specified, the output plugin will try to create output that is as human readable as possible. May not have any effect for some output plugins.

--toc-title

Title for any generated in-line table of contents.

FB2 Output Options

--fb2-genre

Genre for the book. Choices: sf_history, sf_action, sf_epic, sf_heroic, sf_detective, sf_cyberpunk, sf_space, sf_social, sf_horror, sf_humor, sf_fantasy, sf, det_classic, det_police, det_action, det_irony, det_history, det_espionage, det_crime, det_political, det_maniac, det_hard, thriller, detective, prose_classic, prose_history, prose_contemporary, prose_counter, prose_rus_classic, prose_su_classics, love_contemporary, love_history, love_detective, love_short, love_erotica, adv_western, adv_history, adv_indian, adv_maritime, adv_geo, adv_animal, adventure, child_tale, child_verse, child_prose, child_sf, child_det, child_adv, child_education, children, poetry, dramaturgy, antique_ant, antique_european, antique_russian, antique_east, antique_myths, antique, sci_history, sci_psychology, sci_culture, sci_religion, sci_philosophy, sci_politics, sci_business, sci_juris, sci_linguistic, sci_medicine, sci_phys, sci_math, sci_chem, sci_biology, sci_tech, science, comp_www, comp_programming, comp_hard, comp_soft, comp_db, comp_osnet, computers, ref_encyc, ref_dict, ref_ref, ref_guide, reference, nonf_biography, nonf_publicism, nonf_criticism, design, nonfiction, religion_rel, religion_esoterics, religion_self, religion, humor_anecdote, humor_prose, humor_verse, humor, home_cooking, home_pets, home_crafts, home_entertain, home_health, home_garden, home_diy, home_sport, home_sex, home See: http://www.fictionbook.org/index.php/Eng:FictionBook_2.1_genres for a complete list with descriptions.

--pretty-print

If specified, the output plugin will try to create output that is as human readable as possible. May not have any effect for some output plugins.

--sectionize

Specify the sectionization of elements. A value of "nothing" turns the book into a single section. A value of "files" turns each file into a separate section; use this if your device is having trouble. A value of "Table of Contents" turns the entries in the Table of Contents into titles and creates sections; if it fails, adjust the "Structure Detection" and/or "Table of Contents" settings (turn on "Force use of auto-generated Table of Contents").

HTML Output Options

--extract-to

Extract the contents of the generated ZIP file to the specified directory. WARNING: The contents of the directory will be deleted.

--pretty-print

If specified, the output plugin will try to create output that is as human readable as possible. May not have any effect for some output plugins.

--template-css
> CSS file used for the output instead of the default file

--template-html
> Template used for the generation of the html contents of the book instead of the default file

--template-html-index
> Template used for generation of the html index file instead of the default file

HTMLZ Output Options

--htmlz-class-style
> How to handle the CSS when using css-type = 'class'. Default is external. external: Use an external CSS file that is linked in the document. inline: Place the CSS in the head section of the document.

--htmlz-css-type
> Specify the handling of CSS. Default is class. class: Use CSS classes and have elements reference them. inline: Write the CSS as an inline style attribute. tag: Turn as many CSS styles as possible into HTML tags.

--htmlz-title-filename
> If set this option causes the file name of the html file inside the htmlz archive to be based on the book title.

--pretty-print
> If specified, the output plugin will try to create output that is as human readable as possible. May not have any effect for some output plugins.

LIT Output Options

--pretty-print
> If specified, the output plugin will try to create output that is as human readable as possible. May not have any effect for some output plugins.

LRF Output Options

--enable-autorotation
> Enable autorotation of images that are wider than the screen width.

--header
> Add a header to all the pages with title and author.

--header-format
> Set the format of the header. %a is replaced by the author and %t by the title. Default is %t by %a

--header-separation
> Add extra spacing below the header. Default is 0 pt.

--minimum-indent
> Minimum paragraph indent (the indent of the first line of a paragraph) in pts. Default: 0

--mono-family
> The monospace family of fonts to embed

--pretty-print
> If specified, the output plugin will try to create output that is as human readable as possible. May not have any effect for some output plugins.

--render-tables-as-images

Render tables in the HTML as images (useful if the document has large or complex tables)

--sans-family

The sans-serif family of fonts to embed

--serif-family

The serif family of fonts to embed

--text-size-multiplier-for-rendered-tables

Multiply the size of text in rendered tables by this factor. Default is 1.0

--wordspace

Set the space between words in pts. Default is 2.5

MOBI Output Options

--dont-compress

Disable compression of the file contents.

--extract-to

Extract the contents of the generated MOBI file to the specified directory. The contents of the directory are first deleted, so be careful.

--mobi-file-type

By default calibre generates MOBI files that contain the old MOBI 6 format. This format is compatible with all devices. However, by changing this setting, you can tell calibre to generate MOBI files that contain both MOBI 6 and the new KF8 format, or only the new KF8 format. KF8 has more features than MOBI 6, but only works with newer Kindles.

--mobi-ignore-margins

Ignore margins in the input document. If False, then the MOBI output plugin will try to convert margins specified in the input document, otherwise it will ignore them.

--mobi-keep-original-images

By default calibre converts all images to JPEG format in the output MOBI file. This is for maximum compatibility as some older MOBI viewers have problems with other image formats. This option tells calibre not to do this. Useful if your document contains lots of GIF/PNG images that become very large when converted to JPEG.

--mobi-toc-at-start

When adding the Table of Contents to the book, add it at the start of the book instead of the end. Not recommended.

--no-inline-toc

Don't add Table of Contents to the book. Useful if the book has its own table of contents.

--personal-doc

Tag for MOBI files to be marked as personal documents. This option has no effect on the conversion. It is used only when sending MOBI files to a device. If the file being sent has the specified tag, it will be marked as a personal document when sent to the Kindle.

--prefer-author-sort

When present, use author sort field as author.

--pretty-print

If specified, the output plugin will try to create output that is as human readable as possible. May not have any effect for some output plugins.

`--share-not-sync`

> Enable sharing of book content via Facebook etc. on the Kindle. WARNING: Using this feature means that the book will not auto sync its last read position on multiple devices. Complain to Amazon.

`--toc-title`

> Title for any generated in-line table of contents.

OEB Output Options

`--pretty-print`

> If specified, the output plugin will try to create output that is as human readable as possible. May not have any effect for some output plugins.

PDB Output Options

`--format, -f`

> Format to use inside the pdb container. Choices are: ['doc', 'ereader', 'ztxt']

`--inline-toc`

> Add Table of Contents to beginning of the book.

`--pdb-output-encoding`

> Specify the character encoding of the output document. The default is cp1252. Note: This option is not honored by all formats.

`--pretty-print`

> If specified, the output plugin will try to create output that is as human readable as possible. May not have any effect for some output plugins.

PDF Output Options

`--custom-size`

> Custom size of the document. Use the form widthxheight EG. *123x321* to specify the width and height. This overrides any specified paper-size.

`--old-pdf-engine`

> Use the old, less capable engine to generate the PDF

`--override-profile-size`

> Normally, the PDF page size is set by the output profile chosen under page options. This option will cause the page size settings under PDF Output to override the size specified by the output profile.

`--paper-size`

> The size of the paper. This size will be overridden when a non default output profile is used. Default is letter. Choices are [u'a0', u'a1', u'a2', u'a3', u'a4', u'a5', u'a6', u'b0', u'b1', u'b2', u'b3', u'b4', u'b5', u'b6', u'legal', u'letter']

`--pdf-add-toc`

> Add a Table of Contents at the end of the PDF that lists page numbers. Useful if you want to print out the PDF. If this PDF is intended for electronic use, use the PDF Outline instead.

`--pdf-default-font-size`

> The default font size

--pdf-footer-template
> An HTML template used to generate footers on every page. The strings _PAGENUM_, _TITLE_, _AUTHOR_ and _SECTION_ will be replaced by their current values.

--pdf-header-template
> An HTML template used to generate headers on every page. The strings _PAGENUM_, _TITLE_, _AUTHOR_ and _SECTION_ will be replaced by their current values.

--pdf-mark-links
> Surround all links with a red box, useful for debugging.

--pdf-mono-family
> The font family used to render monospaced fonts

--pdf-mono-font-size
> The default font size for monospaced text

--pdf-page-numbers
> Add page numbers to the bottom of every page in the generated PDF file. If you specify a footer template, it will take precedence over this option.

--pdf-sans-family
> The font family used to render sans-serif fonts

--pdf-serif-family
> The font family used to render serif fonts

--pdf-standard-font
> The font family used to render monospaced fonts

--preserve-cover-aspect-ratio
> Preserve the aspect ratio of the cover, instead of stretching it to fill the full first page of the generated pdf.

--pretty-print
> If specified, the output plugin will try to create output that is as human readable as possible. May not have any effect for some output plugins.

--toc-title
> Title for generated table of contents.

--uncompressed-pdf
> Generate an uncompressed PDF, useful for debugging, only works with the new PDF engine.

--unit, -u
> The unit of measure for page sizes. Default is inch. Choices are ['millimeter', 'centimeter', 'point', 'inch', 'pica', 'didot', 'cicero', 'devicepixel'] Note: This does not override the unit for margins!

PML Output Options

--full-image-depth
> Do not reduce the size or bit depth of images. Images have their size and depth reduced by default to accommodate applications that can not convert images on their own such as Dropbook.

--inline-toc
> Add Table of Contents to beginning of the book.

--pml-output-encoding
> Specify the character encoding of the output document. The default is cp1252.

`--pretty-print`

> If specified, the output plugin will try to create output that is as human readable as possible. May not have any effect for some output plugins.

RB Output Options

`--inline-toc`

> Add Table of Contents to beginning of the book.

`--pretty-print`

> If specified, the output plugin will try to create output that is as human readable as possible. May not have any effect for some output plugins.

RTF Output Options

`--pretty-print`

> If specified, the output plugin will try to create output that is as human readable as possible. May not have any effect for some output plugins.

SNB Output Options

`--pretty-print`

> If specified, the output plugin will try to create output that is as human readable as possible. May not have any effect for some output plugins.

`--snb-dont-indent-first-line`

> Specify whether or not to insert two space characters to indent the first line of each paragraph.

`--snb-full-screen`

> Resize all the images for full screen view.

`--snb-hide-chapter-name`

> Specify whether or not to hide the chapter title for each chapter. Useful for image-only output (eg. comics).

`--snb-insert-empty-line`

> Specify whether or not to insert an empty line between two paragraphs.

`--snb-max-line-length`

> The maximum number of characters per line. This splits on the first space before the specified value. If no space is found the line will be broken at the space after and will exceed the specified value. Also, there is a minimum of 25 characters. Use 0 to disable line splitting.

`--snb-output-encoding`

> Specify the character encoding of the output document. The default is utf-8.

TCR Output Options

`--pretty-print`

> If specified, the output plugin will try to create output that is as human readable as possible. May not have any effect for some output plugins.

`--tcr-output-encoding`

> Specify the character encoding of the output document. The default is utf-8.

TXT Output Options

--force-max-line-length

Force splitting on the max-line-length value when no space is present. Also allows max-line-length to be below the minimum

--inline-toc

Add Table of Contents to beginning of the book.

--keep-color

Do not remove font color from output. This is only useful when txt-output-formatting is set to textile. Textile is the only formatting that supports setting font color. If this option is not specified font color will not be set and default to the color displayed by the reader (generally this is black).

--keep-image-references

Do not remove image references within the document. This is only useful when paired with a txt-output-formatting option that is not none because links are always removed with plain text output.

--keep-links

Do not remove links within the document. This is only useful when paired with a txt-output-formatting option that is not none because links are always removed with plain text output.

--max-line-length

The maximum number of characters per line. This splits on the first space before the specified value. If no space is found the line will be broken at the space after and will exceed the specified value. Also, there is a minimum of 25 characters. Use 0 to disable line splitting.

--newline, -n

Type of newline to use. Options are ['old_mac', 'system', 'unix', 'windows']. Default is 'system'. Use 'old_mac' for compatibility with Mac OS 9 and earlier. For Mac OS X use 'unix'. 'system' will default to the newline type used by this OS.

--pretty-print

If specified, the output plugin will try to create output that is as human readable as possible. May not have any effect for some output plugins.

--txt-output-encoding

Specify the character encoding of the output document. The default is utf-8.

--txt-output-formatting

Formatting used within the document. * plain: Produce plain text. * markdown: Produce Markdown formatted text. * textile: Produce Textile formatted text.

TXTZ Output Options

--force-max-line-length

Force splitting on the max-line-length value when no space is present. Also allows max-line-length to be below the minimum

--inline-toc

Add Table of Contents to beginning of the book.

--keep-color

Do not remove font color from output. This is only useful when txt-output-formatting is set to textile. Textile is the only formatting that supports setting font color. If this option is not specified font color will not be set and default to the color displayed by the reader (generally this is black).

--keep-image-references
> Do not remove image references within the document. This is only useful when paired with a txt-output-formatting option that is not none because links are always removed with plain text output.

--keep-links
> Do not remove links within the document. This is only useful when paired with a txt-output-formatting option that is not none because links are always removed with plain text output.

--max-line-length
> The maximum number of characters per line. This splits on the first space before the specified value. If no space is found the line will be broken at the space after and will exceed the specified value. Also, there is a minimum of 25 characters. Use 0 to disable line splitting.

--newline, -n
> Type of newline to use. Options are ['old_mac', 'system', 'unix', 'windows']. Default is 'system'. Use 'old_mac' for compatibility with Mac OS 9 and earlier. For Mac OS X use 'unix'. 'system' will default to the newline type used by this OS.

--pretty-print
> If specified, the output plugin will try to create output that is as human readable as possible. May not have any effect for some output plugins.

--txt-output-encoding
> Specify the character encoding of the output document. The default is utf-8.

--txt-output-formatting
> Formatting used within the document. * plain: Produce plain text. * markdown: Produce Markdown formatted text. * textile: Produce Textile formatted text.

ebook-edit

```
ebook-edit [opts] [path_to_ebook] [name_of_file_inside_book ...]
```

Launch the calibre edit book tool. You can optionally also specify the names of files inside the book which will be opened for editing automatically.

Whenever you pass arguments to **ebook-edit** that have spaces in them, enclose the arguments in quotation marks. For example "C:some path with spaces"

[options]

--detach
> Detach from the controlling terminal, if any (linux only)

--help, -h
> show this help message and exit

--version
> show program's version number and exit

ebook-meta

```
ebook-meta ebook_file [options]
```

Read/Write metadata from/to ebook files.

Supported formats for reading metadata: azw, azw1, azw3, azw4, cbr, cbz, chm, docx, epub, fb2, html, htmlz, imp, lit, lrf, lrx, mobi, odt, oebzip, opf, pdb, pdf, pml, pmlz, pobi, prc, rar, rb, rtf, snb, tpz, txt, txtz, updb, zip

Supported formats for writing metadata: azw, azw1, azw3, azw4, docx, epub, fb2, htmlz, lrf, mobi, pdb, pdf, prc, rtf, tpz, txtz

Different file types support different kinds of metadata. If you try to set some metadata on a file type that does not support it, the metadata will be silently ignored.

Whenever you pass arguments to **ebook-meta** that have spaces in them, enclose the arguments in quotation marks. For example "C:some path with spaces"

[options]

--author-sort
> String to be used when sorting by author. If unspecified, and the author(s) are specified, it will be auto-generated from the author(s).

--authors, -a
> Set the authors. Multiple authors should be separated by the & character. Author names should be in the order Firstname Lastname.

--book-producer, -k
> Set the book producer.

--category
> Set the book category.

--comments, -c
> Set the ebook description.

--cover
> Set the cover to the specified file.

--date, -d
> Set the published date.

--from-opf
> Read metadata from the specified OPF file and use it to set metadata in the ebook. Metadata specified on the command line will override metadata read from the OPF file

--get-cover
> Get the cover from the ebook and save it at as the specified file.

--help, -h
> show this help message and exit

--identifier
> Set the identifiers for the book, can be specified multiple times. For example: *--identifier* (page 311) uri:http://acme.com *--identifier* (page 311) isbn:12345 To remove an identifier, specify no value, *--identifier* (page 311) isbn: Note that for EPUB files, an identifier marked as the package identifier cannot be removed.

--index, -i
> Set the index of the book in this series.

--isbn
> Set the ISBN of the book.

--language, -l
> Set the language.

--lrf-bookid
> Set the BookID in LRF files

--publisher, -p
> Set the ebook publisher.

--rating, -r
> Set the rating. Should be a number between 1 and 5.

--series, -s
> Set the series this ebook belongs to.

--tags
> Set the tags for the book. Should be a comma separated list.

--title, -t
> Set the title.

--title-sort
> The version of the title to be used for sorting. If unspecified, and the title is specified, it will be auto-generated from the title.

--to-opf
> Specify the name of an OPF file. The metadata will be written to the OPF file.

--version
> show program's version number and exit

ebook-polish

```
ebook-polish [options] input_file [output_file]
```

Polishing books is all about putting the shine of perfection onto your carefully crafted ebooks.

Polishing tries to minimize the changes to the internal code of your ebook. Unlike conversion, it does not flatten CSS, rename files, change font sizes, adjust margins, etc. Every action performs only the minimum set of changes needed for the desired effect.

You should use this tool as the last step in your ebook creation process.

Note that polishing only works on files in the AZW3 or EPUB formats.

Whenever you pass arguments to **ebook-polish** that have spaces in them, enclose the arguments in quotation marks. For example "C:some path with spaces"

[options]

--cover, -c
> Path to a cover image. Changes the cover specified in the ebook. If no cover is present, or the cover is not properly identified, inserts a new cover.

--embed-fonts, -e
> Embed all fonts that are referenced in the document and are not already embedded. This will scan your computer for the fonts, and if they are found, they will be embedded into the document. Please ensure that you have the proper license for embedding the fonts used in this document.

--help, -h
> show this help message and exit

--jacket, -j
> Insert a "book jacket" page at the start of the book that contains all the book metadata such as title, tags, authors, series, comments, etc. Any previous book jacket will be replaced.

--opf, -o
> Path to an OPF file. The metadata in the book is updated from the OPF file.

--remove-jacket
> Remove a previous inserted book jacket page.

--remove-unused-css, -u
> Remove all unused CSS rules from stylesheets and <style> tags. Some books created from production templates can have a large number of extra CSS rules that dont match any actual content. These extra rules can slow down readers that need to parse them all.

--smarten-punctuation, -p
> Convert plain text dashes, ellipsis, quotes, multiple hyphens, etc. into their typographically correct equivalents. Note that the algorithm can sometimes generate incorrect results, especially when single quotes at the start of contractions are involved.

--subset-fonts, -f
> Subsetting fonts means reducing an embedded font to contain only the characters used from that font in the book. This greatly reduces the size of the font files (halving the font file sizes is common). For example, if the book uses a specific font for headers, then subsetting will reduce that font to contain only the characters present in the actual headers in the book. Or if the book embeds the bold and italic versions of a font, but bold and italic text is relatively rare, or absent altogether, then the bold and italic fonts can either be reduced to only a few characters or completely removed. The only downside to subsetting fonts is that if, at a later date you decide to add more text to your books, the newly added text might not be covered by the subset font.

--verbose
> Produce more verbose output, useful for debugging.

--version
> show program's version number and exit

ebook-viewer

```
ebook-viewer [options] file
```

View an ebook.

Whenever you pass arguments to **ebook-viewer** that have spaces in them, enclose the arguments in quotation marks. For example "C:some path with spaces"

[options]

--continue
> Continue reading at the previously opened book

--debug-javascript
> Print javascript alert and console messages to the console

--detach
> Detach from the controlling terminal, if any (linux only)

--full-screen, -f
> If specified, viewer window will try to open full screen when started.

--help, -h
> show this help message and exit

--open-at
> The position at which to open the specified book. The position is a location as displayed in the top left corner of the viewer.

--raise-window
> If specified, viewer window will try to come to the front when started.

--version
> show program's version number and exit

fetch-ebook-metadata

```
fetch-ebook-metadata [options]
```

Fetch book metadata from online sources. You must specify at least one of title, authors or ISBN.

Whenever you pass arguments to **fetch-ebook-metadata** that have spaces in them, enclose the arguments in quotation marks. For example "C:some path with spaces"

[options]

--authors, -a
> Book author(s)

--cover, -c
> Specify a filename. The cover, if available, will be saved to it. Without this option, no cover will be downloaded.

--help, -h
> show this help message and exit

--isbn, -i
> Book ISBN

--opf, -o
> Output the metadata in OPF format instead of human readable text.

--timeout, -d
> Timeout in seconds. Default is 30

--title, -t
> Book title

--verbose, -v
> Print the log to the console (stderr)

--version
> show program's version number and exit

lrf2lrs

```
lrf2lrs book.lrf
```

Convert an LRF file into an LRS (XML UTF-8 encoded) file

Whenever you pass arguments to **lrf2lrs** that have spaces in them, enclose the arguments in quotation marks. For example "C:some path with spaces"

[options]

--dont-output-resources
> Do not save embedded image and font files to disk

--help, -h
> show this help message and exit

--output, -o
> Output LRS file

--verbose
> Be more verbose

--version
> show program's version number and exit

lrfviewer

```
lrfviewer [options] book.lrf
```

Read the LRF ebook book.lrf

Whenever you pass arguments to **lrfviewer** that have spaces in them, enclose the arguments in quotation marks. For example "C:some path with spaces"

[options]

--disable-hyphenation
> Disable hyphenation. Should significantly speed up rendering.

--help, -h
> show this help message and exit

--profile
> Profile the LRF renderer

--verbose
> Print more information about the rendering process

--version
> show program's version number and exit

--visual-debug
> Turn on visual aids to debugging the rendering engine

--white-background
> By default the background is off white as I find this easier on the eyes. Use this option to make the background pure white.

lrs2lrf

```
lrs2lrf [options] file.lrs
```

Compile an LRS file into an LRF file.

Whenever you pass arguments to **lrs2lrf** that have spaces in them, enclose the arguments in quotation marks. For example "C:some path with spaces"

[options]

--help, -h
    show this help message and exit

--lrs
    Convert LRS to LRS, useful for debugging.

--output, -o
    Path to output file

--verbose
    Verbose processing

--version
    show program's version number and exit

web2disk

```
web2disk URL
```

Where URL is for example http://google.com

Whenever you pass arguments to **web2disk** that have spaces in them, enclose the arguments in quotation marks. For example "C:some path with spaces"

[options]

--base-dir, -d
    Base directory into which URL is saved. Default is .

--delay
    Minimum interval in seconds between consecutive fetches. Default is 0 s

--dont-download-stylesheets
    Do not download CSS stylesheets.

--encoding
    The character encoding for the websites you are trying to download. The default is to try and guess the encoding.

--filter-regexp
    Any link that matches this regular expression will be ignored. This option can be specified multiple times, in which case as long as any regexp matches a link, it will be ignored. By default, no links are ignored. If both filter regexp and match regexp are specified, then filter regexp is applied first.

--help, -h
    show this help message and exit

--match-regexp
    Only links that match this regular expression will be followed. This option can be specified multiple times, in which case as long as a link matches any one regexp, it will be followed. By default all links are followed.

--max-files, -n
    The maximum number of files to download. This only applies to files from <a href> tags. Default is 9223372036854775807

--max-recursions, -r
    Maximum number of levels to recurse i.e. depth of links to follow. Default 1

--timeout, -t

> Timeout in seconds to wait for a response from the server. Default: 10.0 s

--verbose

> Show detailed output information. Useful for debugging

--version

> show program's version number and exit

1.11.2 Undocumented Commands

- ebook-device

- markdown-calibre

You can see usage for undocumented commands by executing them without arguments in a terminal.

1.12 Setting up a calibre development environment

calibre is completely open source, licensed under the GNU GPL v3[116]. This means that you are free to download and modify the program to your heart's content. In this section, you will learn how to get a calibre development environment set up on the operating system of your choice. calibre is written primarily in Python[117] with some C/C++ code for speed and system interfacing. Note that calibre is not compatible with Python 3 and requires at least Python 2.7.9.

Contents

---

[116] http://www.gnu.org/copyleft/gpl.html
[117] https://www.python.org

1.12.1 Design philosophy

calibre has its roots in the Unix world, which means that its design is highly modular. The modules interact with each other via well defined interfaces. This makes adding new features and fixing bugs in calibre very easy, resulting in a frenetic pace of development. Because of its roots, calibre has a comprehensive command line interface for all its functions, documented in Command Line Interface (page 271).

The modular design of calibre is expressed via `Plugins`. There is a *tutorial* (page 236) on writing calibre plugins. For example, adding support for a new device to calibre typically involves writing less than a 100 lines of code in the form of a device driver plugin. You can browse the built-in drivers[118]. Similarly, adding support for new conversion formats involves writing input/output format plugins. Another example of the modular design is the *recipe system* (page 125) for fetching news. For more examples of plugins designed to add features to calibre, see the plugin index[119].

Code layout

All the calibre python code is in the `calibre` package. This package contains the following main sub-packages

- devices - All the device drivers. Just look through some of the built-in drivers to get an idea for how they work.
    - For details, see: `devices.interface` which defines the interface supported by device drivers and `devices.usbms` which defines a generic driver that connects to a USBMS device. All USBMS based drivers in calibre inherit from it.
- ebooks - All the ebook conversion/metadata code. A good starting point is `calibre.ebooks.conversion.cli` which is the module powering the **ebook-convert** command. The conversion process is controlled via `conversion.plumber`. The format independent code is all in `ebooks.oeb` and the format dependent code is in `ebooks.format_name`.
    - Metadata reading, writing, and downloading is all in `ebooks.metadata`
    - Conversion happens in a pipeline, for the structure of the pipeline, see *Introduction* (page 55). The pipeline consists of an input plugin, various transforms and an output plugin. The code that constructs and drives the pipeline is in `plumber.py`. The pipeline works on a representation of an ebook that is like an unzipped epub, with manifest, spine, toc, guide, html content, etc. The class that manages this representation is OEBBook in `ebooks.oeb.base`. The various transformations that are applied to the book during conversions live in `oeb/transforms/*.py`. And the input and output plugins live in `conversion/plugins/*.py`.
    - Ebook editing happens using a different container object. It is documented in *API Documentation for the ebook editing tools* (page 363).
- db - The database back-end. See *API Documentation for the database interface* (page 356) for the interface to the calibre library.
- content server: `library.server` is the calibre Content Server.
- gui2 - The Graphical User Interface. GUI initialization happens in `gui2.main` and `gui2.ui`. The ebook-viewer is in `gui2.viewer`. The ebook editor is in `gui2.tweak_book`.

If you want to locate the entry points for all the various calibre executables, look at the `entry_points` structure in linux.py[120].

If you need help understanding the code, post in the development forum[121] and you will most likely get help from one of calibre's many developers.

---

[118] https://github.com/kovidgoyal/calibre/tree/master/src/calibre/devices

[119] http://www.mobileread.com/forums/showthread.php?p=1362767#post1362767

[120] https://github.com/kovidgoyal/calibre/blob/master/src/calibre/linux.py

[121] http://www.mobileread.com/forums/forumdisplay.php?f=240

1.12.2 Getting the code

You can get the calibre source code in two ways, using a version control system or directly downloading a tarball[122].

calibre uses Git[123], a distributed version control system. Git is available on all the platforms calibre supports. After installing Git, you can get the calibre source code with the command:

```
git clone git://github.com/kovidgoyal/calibre.git
```

On Windows you will need the complete path name, that will be something like `C:\Program Files\Git\git.exe`.

calibre is a very large project with a very long source control history, so the above can take a while (10 mins to an hour depending on your internet speed).

If you want to get the code faster, the source code for the latest release is always available as an archive[124].

To update a branch to the latest code, use the command:

```
git pull --no-edit
```

Submitting your changes to be included

If you only plan to make a few small changes, you can make your changes and create a "merge directive" which you can then attach to a ticket in the calibre bug tracker[125]. To do this, make your changes, then run:

```
git commit -am "Comment describing your changes"
git format-patch origin/master --stdout > my-changes
```

This will create a `my-changes` file in the current directory, simply attach that to a ticket on the calibre bug tracker[126]. Note that this will include *all* the commits you have made. If you only want to send some commits, you have to change `origin/master` above. To send only the last commit, use:

```
git format-patch HEAD~1 --stdout > my-changes
```

To send the last *n* commits, replace *1* with *n*, for example, for the last 3 commits:

```
git format-patch HEAD~3 --stdout > my-changes
```

Be careful to not include merges when using `HEAD~n`.

If you plan to do a lot of development on calibre, then the best method is to create a GitHub[127] account. Below is a basic guide to setting up your own fork of calibre in a way that will allow you to submit pull requests for inclusion into the main calibre repository:

- Setup git on your machine as described in this article: Setup Git[128]
- Setup ssh keys for authentication to GitHub, as described here: Generating SSH keys[129]
- Go to https://github.com/kovidgoyal/calibre and click the *Fork* button.
- In a Terminal do:

---

[122] http://code.calibre-ebook.com/dist/src
[123] http://www.git-scm.com/
[124] http://code.calibre-ebook.com/dist/src
[125] https://bugs.launchpad.net/calibre
[126] https://bugs.launchpad.net/calibre
[127] https://github.com
[128] https://help.github.com/articles/set-up-git
[129] https://help.github.com/articles/generating-ssh-keys

```
git clone git@github.com:<username>/calibre.git
git remote add upstream https://github.com/kovidgoyal/calibre.git
```

Replace <username> above with your github username. That will get your fork checked out locally.

- You can make changes and commit them whenever you like. When you are ready to have your work merged, do a:

```
git push
```

and go to `https://github.com/<username>/calibre` and click the *Pull Request* button to generate a pull request that can be merged.

- You can update your local copy with code from the main repo at any time by doing:

```
git pull upstream
```

You should also keep an eye on the calibre development forum[130]. Before making major changes, you should discuss them in the forum or contact Kovid directly (his email address is all over the source code).

1.12.3 Windows development environment

Note: You must also get the calibre source code separately as described above.

Install calibre normally, using the Windows installer. Then open a Command Prompt and change to the previously checked out calibre code directory. For example:

```
cd C:\Users\kovid\work\calibre
```

calibre is the directory that contains the src and resources sub-directories.

The next step is to set the environment variable `CALIBRE_DEVELOP_FROM` to the absolute path of the src directory. So, following the example above, it would be `C:\Users\kovid\work\calibre\src`. Here is a short guide[131] to setting environment variables on Windows.

Once you have set the environment variable, open a new command prompt and check that it was correctly set by using the command:

```
echo %CALIBRE_DEVELOP_FROM%
```

Setting this environment variable means that calibre will now load all its Python code from the specified location.

That's it! You are now ready to start hacking on the calibre code. For example, open the file `src\calibre\__init__.py` in your favorite editor and add the line:

```
print ("Hello, world!")
```

near the top of the file. Now run the command **calibredb**. The very first line of output should be `Hello, world!`.

You can also setup a calibre development environment inside the free Microsoft Visual Studio, if you like, following the instructions here[132].

---

[130]http://www.mobileread.com/forums/forumdisplay.php?f=240
[131]https://docs.python.org/2/using/windows.html#excursus-setting-environment-variables
[132]http://www.mobileread.com/forums/showthread.php?t=251201

1.12.4 OS X development environment

Note: You must also get the calibre source code separately as described above.

Install calibre normally using the provided .dmg. Then open a Terminal and change to the previously checked out calibre code directory, for example:

```
cd /Users/kovid/work/calibre
```

calibre is the directory that contains the src and resources sub-directories. Ensure you have installed the calibre commandline tools via *Preferences->Advanced->Miscellaneous* in the calibre GUI.

The next step is to create a bash script that will set the environment variable CALIBRE_DEVELOP_FROM to the absolute path of the src directory when running calibre in debug mode.

Create a plain text file:

```
#!/bin/sh
export CALIBRE_DEVELOP_FROM="/Users/kovid/work/calibre/src"
calibre-debug -g
```

Save this file as /usr/bin/calibre-develop, then set its permissions so that it can be executed:

```
chmod +x /usr/bin/calibre-develop
```

Once you have done this, run:

```
calibre-develop
```

You should see some diagnostic information in the Terminal window as calibre starts up, and you should see an asterisk after the version number in the GUI window, indicating that you are running from source.

1.12.5 Linux development environment

Note: You must also get the calibre source code separately as described above.

calibre is primarily developed on Linux. You have two choices in setting up the development environment. You can install the calibre binary as normal and use that as a runtime environment to do your development. This approach is similar to that used in Windows and OS X. Alternatively, you can install calibre from source. Instructions for setting up a development environment from source are in the INSTALL file in the source tree. Here we will address using the binary as a runtime, which is the recommended method.

Install calibre using the binary installer. Then open a terminal and change to the previously checked out calibre code directory, for example:

```
cd /home/kovid/work/calibre
```

calibre is the directory that contains the src and resources sub-directories.

The next step is to set the environment variable CALIBRE_DEVELOP_FROM to the absolute path of the src directory. So, following the example above, it would be /home/kovid/work/calibre/src. How to set environment variables depends on your Linux distribution and what shell you are using.

Once you have set the environment variable, open a new terminal and check that it was correctly set by using the command:

```
echo $CALIBRE_DEVELOP_FROM
```

Setting this environment variable means that calibre will now load all its Python code from the specified location.

That's it! You are now ready to start hacking on the calibre code. For example, open the file `src/calibre/__init__.py` in your favorite editor and add the line:

```
print ("Hello, world!")
```

near the top of the file. Now run the command **calibredb**. The very first line of output should be `Hello, world!`.

1.12.6 Having separate "normal" and "development" calibre installs on the same computer

The calibre source tree is very stable and rarely breaks, but if you feel the need to run from source on a separate test library and run the released calibre version with your everyday library, you can achieve this easily using .bat files or shell scripts to launch calibre. The example below shows how to do this on Windows using .bat files (the instructions for other platforms are the same, just use a shell script instead of a .bat file)

To launch the release version of calibre with your everyday library:

calibre-normal.bat:

```
calibre.exe "--with-library=C:\path\to\everyday\library folder"
```

calibre-dev.bat:

```
set CALIBRE_DEVELOP_FROM=C:\path\to\calibre\checkout\src
calibre.exe "--with-library=C:\path\to\test\library folder"
```

1.12.7 Debugging tips

Python is a dynamically typed language with excellent facilities for introspection. Kovid wrote the core calibre code without once using a debugger. There are many strategies to debug calibre code:

Using print statements

This is Kovid's favorite way to debug. Simply insert print statements at points of interest and run your program in the terminal. For example, you can start the GUI from the terminal as:

```
calibre-debug -g
```

Similarly, you can start the ebook-viewer as:

```
calibre-debug -w /path/to/file/to/be/viewed
```

The ebook-editor can be started as:

```
calibre-debug -t /path/to/be/edited
```

Using an interactive python interpreter

You can insert the following two lines of code to start an interactive python session at that point:

```
from calibre import ipython
ipython(locals())
```

When running from the command line, this will start an interactive Python interpreter with access to all locally defined variables (variables in the local scope). The interactive prompt even has TAB completion for object properties and you can use the various Python facilities for introspection, such as `dir()`, `type()`, `repr()`, etc.

Using the python debugger as a remote debugger

You can use the builtin python debugger (pdb) as a remote debugger from the command line. First, start the remote debugger at the point in the calibre code you are interested in, like this:

```
from calibre.rpdb import set_trace
set_trace()
```

Then run calibre, either as normal, or using one of the calibre-debug commands described in the previous section. Once the above point in the code is reached, calibre will freeze, waiting for the debugger to connect.

Now open a terminal or command prompt and use the following command to start the debugging session:

```
calibre-debug -c "from calibre.rpdb import cli; cli()"
```

You can read about how to use the python debugger in the python stdlib docs for the pdb module[133].

Note: By default, the remote debugger will try to connect on port 4444. You can change it, by passing the port parameter to both the set_trace() and the cli() functions above, like this: `set_trace(port=1234)` and `cli(port=1234)`.

Note: The python debugger cannot handle multiple threads, so you have to call set_trace once per thread, each time with a different port number.

Using the debugger in your favorite python IDE

It is possible to use the builtin debugger in your favorite python IDE, if it supports remote debugging. The first step is to add the calibre src checkout to the `PYTHONPATH` in your IDE. In other words, the directory you set as `CALIBRE_DEVELOP_FROM` above, must also be in the `PYTHONPATH` of your IDE.

Then place the IDE's remote debugger module into the `src` subdirectory of the calibre source code checkout. Add whatever code is needed to launch the remote debugger to calibre at the point of interest, for example in the main function. Then run calibre as normal. Your IDE should now be able to connect to the remote debugger running inside calibre.

Executing arbitrary scripts in the calibre python environment

The **calibre-debug** command provides a couple of handy switches to execute your own code, with access to the calibre modules:

```
calibre-debug -c "some python code"
```

is great for testing a little snippet of code on the command line. It works in the same way as the -c switch to the python interpreter:

```
calibre-debug myscript.py
```

---

[133]https://docs.python.org/2/library/pdb.html#debugger-commands

can be used to execute your own Python script. It works in the same way as passing the script to the Python interpreter, except that the calibre environment is fully initialized, so you can use all the calibre code in your script. To use command line arguments with your script, use the form:

```
calibre-debug myscript.py -- --option1 arg1
```

The -- causes all subsequent arguments to be passed to your script.

1.12.8 Using calibre in your projects

It is possible to directly use calibre functions/code in your Python project. Two ways exist to do this:

Binary install of calibre

If you have a binary install of calibre, you can use the Python interpreter bundled with calibre, like this:

```
calibre-debug /path/to/your/python/script.py -- arguments to your script
```

Source install on Linux

In addition to using the above technique, if you do a source install on Linux, you can also directly import calibre, as follows:

```
import init_calibre
import calibre

print calibre.__version__
```

It is essential that you import the init_calibre module before any other calibre modules/packages as it sets up the interpreter to run calibre code.

1.12.9 API documentation for various parts of calibre

API Documentation for recipes

The API for writing recipes is defined by the *BasicNewsRecipe* (page 324)

class calibre.web.feeds.news.**BasicNewsRecipe** (*options*, *log*, *progress_reporter*)
> Base class that contains logic needed in all recipes. By overriding progressively more of the functionality in this class, you can make progressively more customized/powerful recipes. For a tutorial introduction to creating recipes, see Adding your favorite news website (page 125).

> **abort_article** (*msg=None*)
> > Call this method inside any of the preprocess methods to abort the download for the current article. Useful to skip articles that contain inappropriate content, such as pure video articles.

> **abort_recipe_processing** (*msg*)
> > Causes the recipe download system to abort the download of this recipe, displaying a simple feedback message to the user.

> **add_toc_thumbnail** (*article*, *src*)
> > Call this from populate_article_metadata with the src attribute of an <img> tag from the article that is appropriate for use as the thumbnail representing the article in the Table of Contents. Whether the thumbnail is actually used is device dependent (currently only used by the Kindles). Note that the referenced image must be one that was successfully downloaded, otherwise it will be ignored.

classmethod adeify_images (*soup*)

If your recipe when converted to EPUB has problems with images when viewed in Adobe Digital Editions, call this method from within *postprocess_html ()* (page 327).

canonicalize_internal_url (*url, is_link=True*)

Return a set of canonical representations of `url`. The default implementation uses just the server hostname and path of the URL, ignoring any query parameters, fragments, etc. The canonical representations must be unique across all URLs for this news source. If they are not, then internal links may be resolved incorrectly.

> **Parameters is_link** – Is True if the URL is coming from an internal link in an HTML file. False if the URL is the URL used to download an article.

cleanup ()

Called after all articles have been download. Use it to do any cleanup like logging out of subscription sites, etc.

clone_browser (*br*)

Clone the browser br. Cloned browsers are used for multi-threaded downloads, since mechanize is not thread safe. The default cloning routines should capture most browser customization, but if you do something exotic in your recipe, you should override this method in your recipe and clone manually.

Cloned browser instances use the same, thread-safe CookieJar by default, unless you have customized cookie handling.

default_cover (*cover_file*)

Create a generic cover for recipes that don't have a cover

download ()

Download and pre-process all articles from the feeds in this recipe. This method should be called only once on a particular Recipe instance. Calling it more than once will lead to undefined behavior. :return: Path to index.html

extract_readable_article (*html, url*)

Extracts main article content from 'html', cleans up and returns as a (article_html, extracted_title) tuple. Based on the original readability algorithm by Arc90.

get_article_url (*article*)

Override in a subclass to customize extraction of the *URL* that points to the content for each article. Return the article URL. It is called with *article*, an object representing a parsed article from a feed. See feedparser[134]. By default it looks for the original link (for feeds syndicated via a service like feedburner or pheedo) and if found, returns that or else returns article.link[135].

get_browser (**args, ***kwargs*)

Return a browser instance used to fetch documents from the web. By default it returns a mechanize[136] browser instance that supports cookies, ignores robots.txt, handles refreshes and has a mozilla firefox user agent.

If your recipe requires that you login first, override this method in your subclass. For example, the following code is used in the New York Times recipe to login for full access:

```
def get_browser(self):
    br = BasicNewsRecipe.get_browser(self)
    if self.username is not None and self.password is not None:
        br.open('http://www.nytimes.com/auth/login')
        br.select_form(name='login')
        br['USERID']   = self.username
```

---

[134] https://pythonhosted.org/feedparser/
[135] https://pythonhosted.org/feedparser/reference-entry-link.html
[136] http://wwwsearch.sourceforge.net/mechanize/

```
              br['PASSWORD'] = self.password
              br.submit()
          return br
```

get_cover_url()

> Return a *URL* to the cover image for this issue or *None*. By default it returns the value of the member *self.cover_url* which is normally *None*. If you want your recipe to download a cover for the e-book override this method in your subclass, or set the member variable *self.cover_url* before this method is called.

get_feeds()

> Return a list of *RSS* feeds to fetch for this profile. Each element of the list must be a 2-element tuple of the form (title, url). If title is None or an empty string, the title from the feed is used. This method is useful if your recipe needs to do some processing to figure out the list of feeds to download. If so, override in your subclass.

get_masthead_title()

> Override in subclass to use something other than the recipe title

get_masthead_url()

> Return a *URL* to the masthead image for this issue or *None*. By default it returns the value of the member *self.masthead_url* which is normally *None*. If you want your recipe to download a masthead for the e-book override this method in your subclass, or set the member variable *self.masthead_url* before this method is called. Masthead images are used in Kindle MOBI files.

get_obfuscated_article(*url*)

> If you set *articles_are_obfuscated* this method is called with every article URL. It should return the path to a file on the filesystem that contains the article HTML. That file is processed by the recursive HTML fetching engine, so it can contain links to pages/images on the web.
>
> This method is typically useful for sites that try to make it difficult to access article content automatically.

classmethod image_url_processor(*baseurl*, *url*)

> Perform some processing on image urls (perhaps removing size restrictions for dynamically generated images, etc.) and return the precessed URL.

index_to_soup(*url_or_raw*, *raw=False*, *as_tree=False*)

> Convenience method that takes an URL to the index page and returns a BeautifulSoup[137] of it.
>
> *url_or_raw*: Either a URL or the downloaded index page as a string

is_link_wanted(*url*, *tag*)

> Return True if the link should be followed or False otherwise. By default, raises NotImplementedError which causes the downloader to ignore it.
>
> **Parameters**
>
> - **url** – The URL to be followed
> - **tag** – The Tag from which the URL was derived

javascript_login(*browser*, *username*, *password*)

> This method is used to login to a website that uses javascript for its login form. After the login is complete, the cookies returned from the website are copied to a normal (non-javascript) browser and the download proceeds using those cookies.
>
> An example implementation:

```
def javascript_login(self, browser, username, password):
    browser.visit('http://some-page-that-has-a-login')
    form = browser.select_form(nr=0) # Select the first form on the page
```

---

[137] http://www.crummy.com/software/BeautifulSoup/bs3/documentation.html

---

```
        form['username'] = username
        form['password'] = password
        browser.submit(timeout=120) # Submit the form and wait at most two minutes for lc
```

Note that you can also select forms with CSS2 selectors, like this:

```
    browser.select_form('form#login_form')
    browser.select_from('form[name="someform"]')
```

parse_feeds()
> Create a list of articles from the list of feeds returned by *BasicNewsRecipe.get_feeds()*
> (page 326). Return a list of Feed objects.

parse_index()
> This method should be implemented in recipes that parse a website instead of feeds to generate a list
> of articles. Typical uses are for news sources that have a "Print Edition" webpage that lists all the
> articles in the current print edition. If this function is implemented, it will be used in preference to
> *BasicNewsRecipe.parse_feeds()* (page 327).

> It must return a list. Each element of the list must be a 2-element tuple of the form ('feed title',
> list of articles).

> Each list of articles must contain dictionaries of the form:

```
{
'title'       : article title,
'url'         : URL of print version,
'date'        : The publication date of the article as a string,
'description' : A summary of the article
'content'     : The full article (can be an empty string). Obsolete
                do not use, instead save the content to a temporary
                file and pass a file:///path/to/temp/file.html as
                the URL.
}
```

> For an example, see the recipe for downloading *The Atlantic*. In addition, you can add 'author' for the
> author of the article.

> If you want to abort processing for some reason and have calibre show the user a simple message instead
> of an error, call *abort_recipe_processing()* (page 324).

populate_article_metadata(*article*, *soup*, *first*)
> Called when each HTML page belonging to article is downloaded. Intended to be used to get arti-
> cle metadata like author/summary/etc. from the parsed HTML (soup). :param article: A object of
> class calibre.web.feeds.Article. If you change the summary, remember to also change the
> text_summary :param soup: Parsed HTML belonging to this article :param first: True iff the parsed HTML
> is the first page of the article.

postprocess_book(*oeb*, *opts*, *log*)
> Run any needed post processing on the parsed downloaded e-book.

> **Parameters**

> - **oeb** – An OEBBook object

> - **opts** – Conversion options

postprocess_html(*soup*, *first_fetch*)
> This method is called with the source of each downloaded *HTML* file, after it is parsed for links and
> images. It can be used to do arbitrarily powerful post-processing on the *HTML*. It should return *soup* after
> processing it.

> **Parameters**
>
> - **soup** – A BeautifulSoup[138] instance containing the downloaded *HTML*.
>
> - **first_fetch** – True if this is the first page of an article.

preprocess_html (*soup*)

This method is called with the source of each downloaded *HTML* file, before it is parsed for links and images. It is called after the cleanup as specified by remove_tags etc. It can be used to do arbitrarily powerful pre-processing on the *HTML*. It should return *soup* after processing it.

soup: A BeautifulSoup[139] instance containing the downloaded *HTML*.

preprocess_raw_html (*raw_html*, *url*)

This method is called with the source of each downloaded *HTML* file, before it is parsed into an object tree. raw_html is a unicode string representing the raw HTML downloaded from the web. url is the URL from which the HTML was downloaded.

Note that this method acts *before* preprocess_regexps.

This method must return the processed raw_html as a unicode object.

classmethod print_version (*url*)

Take a *url* pointing to the webpage with article content and return the *URL* pointing to the print version of the article. By default does nothing. For example:

```
def print_version(self, url):
    return url + '?&pagewanted=print'
```

skip_ad_pages (*soup*)

This method is called with the source of each downloaded *HTML* file, before any of the cleanup attributes like remove_tags, keep_only_tags are applied. Note that preprocess_regexps will have already been applied. It is meant to allow the recipe to skip ad pages. If the soup represents an ad page, return the HTML of the real page. Otherwise return None.

soup: A BeautifulSoup[140] instance containing the downloaded *HTML*.

sort_index_by (*index*, *weights*)

Convenience method to sort the titles in *index* according to *weights*. *index* is sorted in place. Returns *index*.

index: A list of titles.

weights: A dictionary that maps weights to titles. If any titles in index are not in weights, they are assumed to have a weight of 0.

classmethod tag_to_string (*tag*, *use_alt=True*, *normalize_whitespace=True*)

Convenience method to take a BeautifulSoup[141] *Tag* and extract the text from it recursively, including any CDATA sections and alt tag attributes. Return a possibly empty unicode string.

use_alt: If *True* try to use the alt attribute for tags that don't have any textual content

tag: BeautifulSoup[142] *Tag*

articles_are_obfuscated = False

Set to True and implement *get_obfuscated_article()* (page 326) to handle websites that try to make it difficult to scrape content.

---

[138] http://www.crummy.com/software/BeautifulSoup/bs3/documentation.html
[139] http://www.crummy.com/software/BeautifulSoup/bs3/documentation.html
[140] http://www.crummy.com/software/BeautifulSoup/bs3/documentation.html
[141] http://www.crummy.com/software/BeautifulSoup/bs3/documentation.html
[142] http://www.crummy.com/software/BeautifulSoup/bs3/documentation.html

auto_cleanup = False

> Automatically extract all the text from downloaded article pages. Uses the algorithms from the readability project. Setting this to True, means that you do not have to worry about cleaning up the downloaded HTML manually (though manual cleanup will always be superior).

auto_cleanup_keep = None

> Specify elements that the auto cleanup algorithm should never remove. The syntax is a XPath expression. For example:

```
auto_cleanup_keep = '//div[@id="article-image"]' will keep all divs with
                                            id="article-image"
auto_cleanup_keep = '//*[@class="important"]' will keep all elements
                                          with class="important"
auto_cleanup_keep = '//div[@id="article-image"]|//span[@class="important"]'
                    will keep all divs with id="article-image" and spans
                    with class="important"
```

center_navbar = True

> If True the navigation bar is center aligned, otherwise it is left aligned

compress_news_images = False

> Set this to False to ignore all scaling and compression parameters and pass images through unmodified. If True and the other compression parameters are left at their default values, jpeg images will be scaled to fit in the screen dimensions set by the output profile and compressed to size at most (w * h)/16 where w x h are the scaled image dimensions.

compress_news_images_auto_size = 16

> The factor used when auto compressing jpeg images. If set to None, auto compression is disabled. Otherwise, the images will be reduced in size to (w * h)/compress_news_images_auto_size bytes if possible by reducing the quality level, where w x h are the image dimensions in pixels. The minimum jpeg quality will be 5/100 so it is possible this constraint will not be met. This parameter can be overridden by the parameter compress_news_images_max_size which provides a fixed maximum size for images. Note that if you enable scale_news_images_to_device then the image will first be scaled and then its quality lowered until its size is less than (w * h)/factor where w and h are now the *scaled* image dimensions. In other words, this compression happens after scaling.

compress_news_images_max_size = None

> Set jpeg quality so images do not exceed the size given (in KBytes). If set, this parameter overrides auto compression via compress_news_images_auto_size. The minimum jpeg quality will be 5/100 so it is possible this constraint will not be met.

conversion_options = {}

> Recipe specific options to control the conversion of the downloaded content into an e-book. These will override any user or plugin specified values, so only use if absolutely necessary. For example:

```
conversion_options = {
  'base_font_size'   : 16,
  'tags'             : 'mytag1,mytag2',
  'title'            : 'My Title',
  'linearize_tables' : True,
}
```

cover_margins = (0, 0, '#ffffff')

> By default, the cover image returned by get_cover_url() will be used as the cover for the periodical. Overriding this in your recipe instructs calibre to render the downloaded cover into a frame whose width and height are expressed as a percentage of the downloaded cover. cover_margins = (10, 15, '#ffffff') pads the cover with a white margin 10px on the left and right, 15px on the top and bottom. Color names defined at http://www.imagemagick.org/script/color.php Note that for some reason, white does not always work on windows. Use #ffffff instead

---

delay = 0

Delay between consecutive downloads in seconds. The argument may be a floating point number to indicate a more precise time.

description = u''

A couple of lines that describe the content this recipe downloads. This will be used primarily in a GUI that presents a list of recipes.

encoding = None

Specify an override encoding for sites that have an incorrect charset specification. The most common being specifying `latin1` and using `cp1252`. If None, try to detect the encoding. If it is a callable, the callable is called with two arguments: The recipe object and the source to be decoded. It must return the decoded source.

extra_css = None

Specify any extra *CSS* that should be added to downloaded *HTML* files. It will be inserted into *<style>* tags, just before the closing *</head>* tag thereby overriding all *CSS* except that which is declared using the style attribute on individual *HTML* tags. For example:

```
extra_css = '.heading { font: serif x-large }'
```

feeds = None

List of feeds to download. Can be either `[url1, url2, ...]` or `[('title1', url1), ('title2', url2),...]`

filter_regexps = []

List of regular expressions that determines which links to ignore. If empty it is ignored. Used only if is_link_wanted is not implemented. For example:

```
filter_regexps = [r'ads\.doubleclick\.net']
```

will remove all URLs that have *ads.doubleclick.net* in them.

Only one of *BasicNewsRecipe.match_regexps* (page 331) or *BasicNewsRecipe.filter_regexps* (page 330) should be defined.

ignore_duplicate_articles = None

Ignore duplicates of articles that are present in more than one section. A duplicate article is an article that has the same title and/or URL. To ignore articles with the same title, set this to:

```
ignore_duplicate_articles = {'title'}
```

To use URLs instead, set it to:

```
ignore_duplicate_articles = {'url'}
```

To match on title or URL, set it to:

```
ignore_duplicate_articles = {'title', 'url'}
```

keep_only_tags = []

Keep only the specified tags and their children. For the format for specifying a tag see *BasicNewsRecipe.remove_tags* (page 332). If this list is not empty, then the *<body>* tag will be emptied and re-filled with the tags that match the entries in this list. For example:

```
keep_only_tags = [dict(id=['content', 'heading'])]
```

will keep only tags that have an *id* attribute of *"content"* or *"heading"*.

language = 'und'

The language that the news is in. Must be an ISO-639 code either two or three characters long

masthead_url = None

> By default, calibre will use a default image for the masthead (Kindle only). Override this in your recipe to provide a url to use as a masthead.

match_regexps = []

> List of regular expressions that determines which links to follow. If empty, it is ignored. Used only if is_link_wanted is not implemented. For example:

```
match_regexps = [r'page=[0-9]+']
```

> will match all URLs that have *page=some number* in them.
>
> Only one of *BasicNewsRecipe.match_regexps* (page 331) or *BasicNewsRecipe.filter_regexps* (page 330) should be defined.

max_articles_per_feed = 100

> Maximum number of articles to download from each feed. This is primarily useful for feeds that don't have article dates. For most feeds, you should use *BasicNewsRecipe.oldest_article* (page 331)

needs_subscription = False

> If True the GUI will ask the user for a username and password to use while downloading. If set to "optional" the use of a username and password becomes optional

no_stylesheets = False

> Convenient flag to disable loading of stylesheets for websites that have overly complex stylesheets unsuitable for conversion to ebooks formats. If True stylesheets are not downloaded and processed

oldest_article = 7.0

> Oldest article to download from this news source. In days.

preprocess_regexps = []

> List of *regexp* substitution rules to run on the downloaded *HTML*. Each element of the list should be a two element tuple. The first element of the tuple should be a compiled regular expression and the second a callable that takes a single match object and returns a string to replace the match. For example:

```
preprocess_regexps = [
    (re.compile(r'<!--Article ends here-->.*</body>', re.DOTALL|re.IGNORECASE),
     lambda match: '</body>'),
]
```

> will remove everything from *<!–Article ends here–>* to *</body>*.

publication_type = 'unknown'

> Publication type Set to newspaper, magazine or blog. If set to None, no publication type metadata will be written to the opf file.

recipe_disabled = None

> Set to a non empty string to disable this recipe. The string will be used as the disabled message

recursions = 0

> Number of levels of links to follow on article webpages

remove_attributes = []

> List of attributes to remove from all tags. For example:

```
remove_attributes = ['style', 'font']
```

remove_empty_feeds = False

> If True empty feeds are removed from the output. This option has no effect if parse_index is overridden in the sub class. It is meant only for recipes that return a list of feeds using *feeds* or *get_feeds()* (page 326). It is also used if you use the ignore_duplicate_articles option.

---

remove_javascript = True

> Convenient flag to strip all javascript tags from the downloaded HTML

remove_tags = []

> List of tags to be removed. Specified tags are removed from downloaded HTML. A tag is specified as a dictionary of the form:

```
{
 name      : 'tag name',   #e.g. 'div'
 attrs     : a dictionary, #e.g. {class: 'advertisment'}
}
```

> All keys are optional. For a full explanation of the search criteria, see Beautiful Soup[143] A common example:

```
remove_tags = [dict(name='div', attrs={'class':'advert'})]
```

> This will remove all *<div class="advert">* tags and all their children from the downloaded *HTML*.

remove_tags_after = None

> Remove all tags that occur after the specified tag. For the format for specifying a tag see *BasicNewsRecipe.remove_tags* (page 332). For example:

```
remove_tags_after = [dict(id='content')]
```

> will remove all tags after the first element with *id="content"*.

remove_tags_before = None

> Remove all tags that occur before the specified tag. For the format for specifying a tag see *BasicNewsRecipe.remove_tags* (page 332). For example:

```
remove_tags_before = dict(id='content')
```

> will remove all tags before the first element with *id="content"*.

requires_version = (0, 6, 0)

> Minimum calibre version needed to use this recipe

resolve_internal_links = False

> If set to True then links in downloaded articles that point to other downloaded articles are changed to point to the downloaded copy of the article rather than its original web URL. If you set this to True, you might also need to implement *canonicalize_internal_url()* (page 325) to work with the URL scheme of your particular website.

reverse_article_order = False

> Reverse the order of articles in each feed

scale_news_images = None

> Maximum dimensions (w,h) to scale images to. If scale_news_images_to_device is True this is set to the device screen dimensions set by the output profile unless there is no profile set, in which case it is left at whatever value it has been assigned (default None).

scale_news_images_to_device = True

> Rescale images to fit in the device screen dimensions set by the output profile. Ignored if no output profile is set.

simultaneous_downloads = 5

> Number of simultaneous downloads. Set to 1 if the server is picky. Automatically reduced to 1 if *BasicNewsRecipe.delay* (page 329) > 0

---

[143] http://www.crummy.com/software/BeautifulSoup/bs3/documentation.html#Searching%20the%20Parse%20Tree

summary_length = 500
> Max number of characters in the short description

template_css = u'\n .article_date {\n color: gray; font-family: monospace;\n }\n\n .article_description {\n text
> The CSS that is used to style the templates, i.e., the navigation bars and the Tables of Contents. Rather than overriding this variable, you should use *extra_css* in your recipe to customize look and feel.

timefmt = ' [%a, %d %b %Y]'
> The format string for the date shown on the first page. By default: Day_Name, Day_Number Month_Name Year

timeout = 120.0
> Timeout for fetching files from server in seconds

title = u'Unknown News Source'
> The title to use for the ebook

use_embedded_content = None
> Normally we try to guess if a feed has full articles embedded in it based on the length of the embedded content. If *None*, then the default guessing is used. If *True* then the we always assume the feeds has embedded content and if *False* we always assume the feed does not have embedded content.

use_javascript_to_login = False
> If you set this True, then calibre will use javascript to login to the website. This is needed for some websites that require the use of javascript to login. If you set this to True you must implement the *javascript_login()* (page 326) method, to do the actual logging in.

API Documentation for plugins

Defines various abstract base classes that can be subclassed to create powerful plugins. The useful classes are:

Plugin

class calibre.customize.**Plugin**(*plugin_path*)
> A calibre plugin. Useful members include:
>
> > • **self.plugin_path: Stores path to the zip file that contains** this plugin or None if it is a builtin plugin
> >
> > • **self.site_customization: Stores a customization string entered** by the user.
>
> Methods that should be overridden in sub classes:
>
> > • *initialize()* (page 334)

- *customization_help()* (page 335)

Useful methods:

- *temporary_file()* (page 335)

- *__enter__()*

- *load_resources()* (page 335)

supported_platforms = []
> List of platforms this plugin works on. For example: ['windows', 'osx', 'linux']

name = 'Trivial Plugin'
> The name of this plugin. You must set it something other than Trivial Plugin for it to work.

version = (1, 0, 0)
> The version of this plugin as a 3-tuple (major, minor, revision)

description = u'Does absolutely nothing'
> A short string describing what this plugin does

author = u'Unknown'
> The author of this plugin

priority = 1
> When more than one plugin exists for a filetype, the plugins are run in order of decreasing priority i.e. plugins with higher priority will be run first. The highest possible priority is sys.maxint. Default priority is 1.

minimum_calibre_version = (0, 4, 118)
> The earliest version of calibre this plugin requires

can_be_disabled = True
> If False, the user will not be able to disable this plugin. Use with care.

type = u'Base'
> The type of this plugin. Used for categorizing plugins in the GUI

initialize()
> Called once when calibre plugins are initialized. Plugins are re-initialized every time a new plugin is added. Also note that if the plugin is run in a worker process, such as for adding books, then the plugin will be initialized for every new worker process.
>
> Perform any plugin specific initialization here, such as extracting resources from the plugin zip file. The path to the zip file is available as self.plugin_path.
>
> Note that self.site_customization is **not** available at this point.

config_widget()
> Implement this method and *save_settings()* (page 334) in your plugin to use a custom configuration dialog, rather then relying on the simple string based default customization.
>
> This method, if implemented, must return a QWidget. The widget can have an optional method validate() that takes no arguments and is called immediately after the user clicks OK. Changes are applied if and only if the method returns True.
>
> If for some reason you cannot perform the configuration at this time, return a tuple of two strings (message, details), these will be displayed as a warning dialog to the user and the process will be aborted.

save_settings (*config_widget*)
> Save the settings specified by the user with config_widget.
>
> > **Parameters config_widget** – The widget returned by *config_widget()* (page 334).

do_user_config (*parent=None*)

    This method shows a configuration dialog for this plugin. It returns True if the user clicks OK, False otherwise. The changes are automatically applied.

load_resources (*names*)

    If this plugin comes in a ZIP file (user added plugin), this method will allow you to load resources from the ZIP file.

    For example to load an image:

```
pixmap = QPixmap()
pixmap.loadFromData(self.load_resources(['images/icon.png']).itervalues().next())
icon = QIcon(pixmap)
```

        Parameters names – List of paths to resources in the zip file using / as separator

        Returns A dictionary of the form {name: file_contents}. Any names that were not found in the zip file will not be present in the dictionary.

customization_help (*gui=False*)

    Return a string giving help on how to customize this plugin. By default raise a NotImplementedError, which indicates that the plugin does not require customization.

    If you re-implement this method in your subclass, the user will be asked to enter a string as customization for this plugin. The customization string will be available as self.site_customization.

    Site customization could be anything, for example, the path to a needed binary on the user's computer.

        Parameters gui – If True return HTML help, otherwise return plain text help.

temporary_file (*suffix*)

    Return a file-like object that is a temporary file on the file system. This file will remain available even after being closed and will only be removed on interpreter shutdown. Use the name member of the returned object to access the full path to the created temporary file.

        Parameters suffix – The suffix that the temporary file will have.

cli_main (*args*)

    This method is the main entry point for your plugins command line interface. It is called when the user does: calibre-debug -r "Plugin Name". Any arguments passed are present in the args variable.

FileTypePlugin

class calibre.customize.**FileTypePlugin** (*plugin_path*)

    Bases: *calibre.customize.Plugin* (page 333)

    A plugin that is associated with a particular set of file types.

    file_types = set([])

        Set of file types for which this plugin should be run. For example: {'lit', 'mobi', 'prc'}

    on_import = False

        If True, this plugin is run when books are added to the database

    on_postimport = False

        If True, this plugin is run after books are added to the database

    on_preprocess = False

        If True, this plugin is run just before a conversion

on_postprocess = False
>> If True, this plugin is run after conversion on the final file produced by the conversion output plugin.

run (*path_to_ebook*)
>> Run the plugin. Must be implemented in subclasses. It should perform whatever modifications are required on the ebook and return the absolute path to the modified ebook. If no modifications are needed, it should return the path to the original ebook. If an error is encountered it should raise an Exception. The default implementation simply return the path to the original ebook.

>> The modified ebook file should be created with the `temporary_file()` method.

>>> **Parameters** **path_to_ebook** – Absolute path to the ebook.

>>> **Returns** Absolute path to the modified ebook.

postimport (*book_id*, *book_format*, *db*)
>> Called post import, i.e., after the book file has been added to the database.

>>> **Parameters**

>>> - **book_id** – Database id of the added book.

>>> - **book_format** – The file type of the book that was added.

>>> - **db** – Library database.

Metadata plugins

class `calibre.customize.`**MetadataReaderPlugin**(**args*, ***kwargs*)
>> Bases: *`calibre.customize.Plugin`* (page 333)

> A plugin that implements reading metadata from a set of file types.

file_types = set([])
>> Set of file types for which this plugin should be run For example: `set(['lit', 'mobi', 'prc'])`

get_metadata (*stream*, *type*)
>> Return metadata for the file represented by stream (a file like object that supports reading). Raise an exception when there is an error with the input data. :param type: The type of file. Guaranteed to be one of the entries in *file_types* (page 336). :return: A `calibre.ebooks.metadata.book.Metadata` object

class `calibre.customize.`**MetadataWriterPlugin**(**args*, ***kwargs*)
>> Bases: *`calibre.customize.Plugin`* (page 333)

> A plugin that implements reading metadata from a set of file types.

file_types = set([])
>> Set of file types for which this plugin should be run For example: `set(['lit', 'mobi', 'prc'])`

set_metadata (*stream*, *mi*, *type*)
>> Set metadata for the file represented by stream (a file like object that supports reading). Raise an exception when there is an error with the input data. :param type: The type of file. Guaranteed to be one of the entries in *file_types* (page 336). :param mi: A `calibre.ebooks.metadata.book.Metadata` object

Catalog plugins

class `calibre.customize.`**CatalogPlugin**(*plugin_path*)
>> Bases: *`calibre.customize.Plugin`* (page 333)

> A plugin that implements a catalog generator.

---

file_types = set([])
>   Output file type for which this plugin should be run For example: 'epub' or 'xml'

cli_options = []
>   CLI parser options specific to this plugin, declared as namedtuple Option:

```
from collections import namedtuple
Option = namedtuple('Option', 'option, default, dest, help')
cli_options = [Option('--catalog-title',
                    default = 'My Catalog',
                    dest = 'catalog_title',
                    help = (_('Title of generated catalog. \nDefault:') + " '" +
                    '%default' + "'"))]
cli_options parsed in library.cli:catalog_option_parser()
```

initialize ()
>   If plugin is not a built-in, copy the plugin's .ui and .py files from the zip file to $TMPDIR. Tab will be dynamically generated and added to the Catalog Options dialog in calibre.gui2.dialogs.catalog.py:Catalog

run (*path_to_output, opts, db, ids, notification=None*)
>   Run the plugin. Must be implemented in subclasses. It should generate the catalog in the format specified in file_types, returning the absolute path to the generated catalog file. If an error is encountered it should raise an Exception.
>
>   The generated catalog file should be created with the `temporary_file()` method.
>
>   **Parameters**
>
>   - **path_to_output** – Absolute path to the generated catalog file.
>
>   - **opts** – A dictionary of keyword arguments
>
>   - **db** – A LibraryDatabase2 object

Metadata download plugins

class calibre.ebooks.metadata.sources.base.**Source** (**args, **kwargs*)
>   Bases: *calibre.customize.Plugin* (page 333)

capabilities = frozenset([])
>   Set of capabilities supported by this plugin. Useful capabilities are: 'identify', 'cover'

touched_fields = frozenset([])
>   List of metadata fields that can potentially be download by this plugin during the identify phase

has_html_comments = False
>   Set this to True if your plugin returns HTML formatted comments

supports_gzip_transfer_encoding = False
>   Setting this to True means that the browser object will add Accept-Encoding: gzip to all requests. This can speedup downloads but make sure that the source actually supports gzip transfer encoding correctly first

cached_cover_url_is_reliable = True
>   Cached cover URLs can sometimes be unreliable (i.e. the download could fail or the returned image could be bogus. If that is often the case with this source set to False

options = ()
>   A list of `Option` objects. They will be used to automatically construct the configuration widget for this plugin

config_help_message = None
> A string that is displayed at the top of the config widget for this plugin

can_get_multiple_covers = False
> If True this source can return multiple covers for a given query

auto_trim_covers = False
> If set to True covers downloaded by this plugin are automatically trimmed.

prefer_results_with_isbn = True
> If set to True, and this source returns multiple results for a query, some of which have ISBNs and some of which do not, the results without ISBNs will be ignored

is_configured()
> Return False if your plugin needs to be configured before it can be used. For example, it might need a username/password/API key.

get_author_tokens (*authors*, *only_first_author=True*)
> Take a list of authors and return a list of tokens useful for an AND search query. This function tries to return tokens in first name middle names last name order, by assuming that if a comma is in the author name, the name is in lastname, other names form.

get_title_tokens (*title*, *strip_joiners=True*, *strip_subtitle=False*)
> Take a title and return a list of tokens useful for an AND search query. Excludes connectives(optionally) and punctuation.

split_jobs (*jobs*, *num*)
> Split a list of jobs into at most num groups, as evenly as possible

test_fields (*mi*)
> Return the first field from self.touched_fields that is null on the mi object

clean_downloaded_metadata (*mi*)
> Call this method in your plugin's identify method to normalize metadata before putting the Metadata object into result_queue. You can of course, use a custom algorithm suited to your metadata source.

get_book_url (*identifiers*)
> Return a 3-tuple or None. The 3-tuple is of the form: (identifier_type, identifier_value, URL). The URL is the URL for the book identified by identifiers at this source. identifier_type, identifier_value specify the identifier corresponding to the URL. This URL must be browseable to by a human using a browser. It is meant to provide a clickable link for the user to easily visit the books page at this source. If no URL is found, return None. This method must be quick, and consistent, so only implement it if it is possible to construct the URL from a known scheme given identifiers.

get_book_url_name (*idtype*, *idval*, *url*)
> Return a human readable name from the return value of get_book_url().

get_book_urls (*identifiers*)
> Override this method if you would like to return multiple urls for this book. Return a list of 3-tuples. By default this method simply calls *get_book_url ()* (page 338).

get_cached_cover_url (*identifiers*)
> Return cached cover URL for the book identified by the identifiers dict or None if no such URL exists.

> Note that this method must only return validated URLs, i.e. not URLS that could result in a generic cover image or a not found error.

identify_results_keygen (*title=None*, *authors=None*, *identifiers={}*)
> Return a function that is used to generate a key that can sort Metadata objects by their relevance given a search query (title, authors, identifiers).

> These keys are used to sort the results of a call to *identify ()* (page 339).

For details on the default algorithm see *InternalMetadataCompareKeyGen* (page 339). Re-implement this function in your plugin if the default algorithm is not suitable.

identify (*log, result_queue, abort, title=None, authors=None, identifiers={}, timeout=30*)
Identify a book by its title/author/isbn/etc.

If identifiers(s) are specified and no match is found and this metadata source does not store all related identifiers (for example, all ISBNs of a book), this method should retry with just the title and author (assuming they were specified).

If this metadata source also provides covers, the URL to the cover should be cached so that a subsequent call to the get covers API with the same ISBN/special identifier does not need to get the cover URL again. Use the caching API for this.

Every Metadata object put into result_queue by this method must have a *source_relevance* attribute that is an integer indicating the order in which the results were returned by the metadata source for this query. This integer will be used by compare_identify_results(). If the order is unimportant, set it to zero for every result.

Make sure that any cover/isbn mapping information is cached before the Metadata object is put into result_queue.

> **Parameters**
>
> * **log** – A log object, use it to output debugging information/errors
>
> * **result_queue** – A result Queue, results should be put into it. Each result is a Metadata object
>
> * **abort** – If abort.is_set() returns True, abort further processing and return as soon as possible
>
> * **title** – The title of the book, can be None
>
> * **authors** – A list of authors of the book, can be None
>
> * **identifiers** – A dictionary of other identifiers, most commonly { 'isbn':'1234...'}
>
> * **timeout** – Timeout in seconds, no network request should hang for longer than timeout.
>
> **Returns** None if no errors occurred, otherwise a unicode representation of the error suitable for showing to the user

download_cover (*log, result_queue, abort, title=None, authors=None, identifiers={}, timeout=30, get_best_cover=False*)
Download a cover and put it into result_queue. The parameters all have the same meaning as for *identify()* (page 339). Put (self, cover_data) into result_queue.

This method should use cached cover URLs for efficiency whenever possible. When cached data is not present, most plugins simply call identify and use its results.

If the parameter get_best_cover is True and this plugin can get multiple covers, it should only get the "best" one.

class calibre.ebooks.metadata.sources.base.**InternalMetadataCompareKeyGen** (*mi, source_plugin, title, au-thors, iden-ti-fiers*)
Generate a sort key for comparison of the relevance of Metadata objects, given a search query. This is used only

---

to compare results from the same metadata source, not across different sources.

The sort key ensures that an ascending order sort is a sort by order of decreasing relevance.

The algorithm is:

- Prefer results that have at least one identifier the same as for the query

- Prefer results with a cached cover URL

- Prefer results with all available fields filled in

- Prefer results with the same language as the current user interface language

- Prefer results that are an exact title match to the query

- Prefer results with longer comments (greater than 10% longer)

- **Use the relevance of the result as reported by the metadata source's search** engine

Conversion plugins

class `calibre.customize.conversion.`**InputFormatPlugin**(**args*)
   Bases: *calibre.customize.Plugin* (page 333)

   InputFormatPlugins are responsible for converting a document into HTML+OPF+CSS+etc. The results of the conversion *must* be encoded in UTF-8. The main action happens in *convert ()* (page 340).

   file_types = **set([])**
      Set of file types for which this plugin should be run For example: `set(['azw', 'mobi', 'prc'])`

   is_image_collection = **False**
      If True, this input plugin generates a collection of images, one per HTML file. This can be set dynamically, in the convert method if the input files can be both image collections and non-image collections. If you set this to True, you must implement the get_images() method that returns a list of images.

   core_usage = **1**
      Number of CPU cores used by this plugin A value of -1 means that it uses all available cores

   for_viewer = **False**
      If set to True, the input plugin will perform special processing to make its output suitable for viewing

   output_encoding = **'utf-8'**
      The encoding that this input plugin creates files in. A value of None means that the encoding is undefined and must be detected individually

   common_options = **set([<calibre.customize.conversion.OptionRecommendation object at 0x7f30cae00150>])**
      Options shared by all Input format plugins. Do not override in sub-classes. Use *options* (page 340) instead. Every option must be an instance of `OptionRecommendation`.

   options = **set([])**
      Options to customize the behavior of this plugin. Every option must be an instance of `OptionRecommendation`.

   recommendations = **set([])**
      A set of 3-tuples of the form (option_name, recommended_value, recommendation_level)

   get_images ()
      Return a list of absolute paths to the images, if this input plugin represents an image collection. The list of images is in the same order as the spine and the TOC.

---

convert (*stream, options, file_ext, log, accelerators*)

This method must be implemented in sub-classes. It must return the path to the created OPF file or an `OEBBook` instance. All output should be contained in the current directory. If this plugin creates files outside the current directory they must be deleted/marked for deletion before this method returns.

Parameters

- **stream** – A file like object that contains the input file.

- **options** – Options to customize the conversion process. Guaranteed to have attributes corresponding to all the options declared by this plugin. In addition, it will have a verbose attribute that takes integral values from zero upwards. Higher numbers mean be more verbose. Another useful attribute is `input_profile` that is an instance of `calibre.customize.profiles.InputProfile`.

- **file_ext** – The extension (without the .) of the input file. It is guaranteed to be one of the *file_types* supported by this plugin.

- **log** – A `calibre.utils.logging.Log` object. All output should use this object.

- **accelarators** – A dictionary of various information that the input plugin can get easily that would speed up the subsequent stages of the conversion.

postprocess_book (*oeb, opts, log*)

Called to allow the input plugin to perform postprocessing after the book has been parsed.

specialize (*oeb, opts, log, output_fmt*)

Called to allow the input plugin to specialize the parsed book for a particular output format. Called after postprocess_book and before any transforms are performed on the parsed book.

gui_configuration_widget (*parent, get_option_by_name, get_option_help, db, book_id=None*)

Called to create the widget used for configuring this plugin in the calibre GUI. The widget must be an instance of the PluginWidget class. See the builtin input plugins for examples.

class `calibre.customize.conversion.`**OutputFormatPlugin**(**args*)

Bases: `calibre.customize.Plugin` (page 333)

OutputFormatPlugins are responsible for converting an OEB document (OPF+HTML) into an output ebook.

The OEB document can be assumed to be encoded in UTF-8. The main action happens in *convert ()* (page 341).

file_type = None

The file type (extension without leading period) that this plugin outputs

common_options = set([<calibre.customize.conversion.OptionRecommendation object at 0x7f30cae002d0>])

Options shared by all Input format plugins. Do not override in sub-classes. Use *options* (page 341) instead. Every option must be an instance of `OptionRecommendation`.

options = set([])

Options to customize the behavior of this plugin. Every option must be an instance of `OptionRecommendation`.

recommendations = set([])

A set of 3-tuples of the form (option_name, recommended_value, recommendation_level)

convert (*oeb_book, output, input_plugin, opts, log*)

Render the contents of *oeb_book* (which is an instance of `calibre.ebooks.oeb.OEBBook` to the file specified by output.

Parameters

- **output** – Either a file like object or a string. If it is a string it is the path to a directory that may or may not exist. The output plugin should write its output into that directory. If it is a file like object, the output plugin should write its output into the file.

- **input_plugin** – The input plugin that was used at the beginning of the conversion pipeline.

- **opts** – Conversion options. Guaranteed to have attributes corresponding to the Option-Recommendations of this plugin.

- **log** – The logger. Print debug/info messages etc. using this.

specialize_css_for_output (*log*, *opts*, *item*, *stylizer*)
> Can be used to make changes to the css during the CSS flattening process.

> ### Parameters

> - **item** – The item (HTML file) being processed

> - **stylizer** – A Stylizer object containing the flattened styles for item. You can get the style for any element by stylizer.style(element).

gui_configuration_widget (*parent*, *get_option_by_name*, *get_option_help*, *db*, *book_id=None*)
> Called to create the widget used for configuring this plugin in the calibre GUI. The widget must be an instance of the PluginWidget class. See the builtin output plugins for examples.

Device Drivers

The base class for all device drivers is *DevicePlugin* (page 342). However, if your device exposes itself as a USBMS drive to the operating system, you should use the USBMS class instead as it implements all the logic needed to support these kinds of devices.

class calibre.devices.interface.**DevicePlugin** (*plugin_path*)
> Bases: *calibre.customize.Plugin* (page 333)

> Defines the interface that should be implemented by backends that communicate with an ebook reader.

> **FORMATS = ['lrf', 'rtf', 'pdf', 'txt']**
> > Ordered list of supported formats

> **VENDOR_ID = 0**
> > VENDOR_ID can be either an integer, a list of integers or a dictionary If it is a dictionary, it must be a dictionary of dictionaries, of the form:

```
{
 integer_vendor_id : { product_id : [list of BCDs], ... },
 ...
}
```

> **PRODUCT_ID = 0**
> > An integer or a list of integers

> **BCD = None**
> > BCD can be either None to not distinguish between devices based on BCD, or it can be a list of the BCD numbers of all devices supported by this driver.

> **THUMBNAIL_HEIGHT = 68**
> > Height for thumbnails on the device

> **THUMBNAIL_COMPRESSION_QUALITY = 75**
> > Width for thumbnails on the device. Setting this will force thumbnails to this size, not preserving aspect

ratio. If it is not set, then the aspect ratio will be preserved and the thumbnail will be no higher than THUMBNAIL_HEIGHT Compression quality for thumbnails. Set this closer to 100 to have better quality thumbnails with fewer compression artifacts. Of course, the thumbnails get larger as well.

WANTS_UPDATED_THUMBNAILS = False

Set this to True if the device supports updating cover thumbnails during sync_booklists. Setting it to true will ask device.py to refresh the cover thumbnails during book matching

CAN_SET_METADATA = ['title', 'authors', 'collections']

Whether the metadata on books can be set via the GUI.

CAN_DO_DEVICE_DB_PLUGBOARD = False

Whether the device can handle device_db metadata plugboards

path_sep = '/'

Path separator for paths to books on device

icon = '/home/kovid/work/calibre/resources/images/reader.png'

Icon for this device

UserAnnotation

alias of `Annotation`

OPEN_FEEDBACK_MESSAGE = None

GUI displays this as a message if not None. Useful if opening can take a long time

VIRTUAL_BOOK_EXTENSIONS = frozenset([])

Set of extensions that are "virtual books" on the device and therefore cannot be viewed/saved/added to library. For example: `frozenset(['kobo'])`

VIRTUAL_BOOK_EXTENSION_MESSAGE = None

Message to display to user for virtual book extensions.

NUKE_COMMENTS = None

Whether to nuke comments in the copy of the book sent to the device. If not None this should be short string that the comments will be replaced by.

MANAGES_DEVICE_PRESENCE = False

If True indicates that this driver completely manages device detection, ejecting and so forth. If you set this to True, you *must* implement the detect_managed_devices and debug_managed_device_detection methods. A driver with this set to true is responsible for detection of devices, managing a blacklist of devices, a list of ejected devices and so forth. calibre will periodically call the detect_managed_devices() method and if it returns a detected device, calibre will call open(). open() will be called every time a device is returned even is previous calls to open() failed, therefore the driver must maintain its own blacklist of failed devices. Similarly, when ejecting, calibre will call eject() and then assuming the next call to detect_managed_devices() returns None, it will call post_yank_cleanup().

SLOW_DRIVEINFO = False

If set the True, calibre will call the `get_driveinfo()` (page 345) method after the books lists have been loaded to get the driveinfo.

ASK_TO_ALLOW_CONNECT = False

If set to True, calibre will ask the user if they want to manage the device with calibre, the first time it is detected. If you set this to True you must implement `get_device_uid()` (page 347) and `ignore_connected_device()` (page 348) and `get_user_blacklisted_devices()` (page 348) and `set_user_blacklisted_devices()` (page 348)

user_feedback_after_callback = None

Set this to a dictionary of the form { 'title':title, 'msg':msg, 'det_msg':detailed_msg} to have calibre popup a message to the user after some callbacks are run (currently only upload_books). Be careful to not spam the user with too many messages. This variable is checked after *every* callback, so only set it when you really need to.

is_usb_connected (*devices_on_system*, *debug=False*, *only_presence=False*)
Return True, device_info if a device handled by this plugin is currently connected.

> **Parameters devices_on_system** – List of devices currently connected

detect_managed_devices (*devices_on_system*, *force_refresh=False*)
Called only if MANAGES_DEVICE_PRESENCE is True.

Scan for devices that this driver can handle. Should return a device object if a device is found. This object will be passed to the open() method as the connected_device. If no device is found, return None. The returned object can be anything, calibre does not use it, it is only passed to open().

This method is called periodically by the GUI, so make sure it is not too resource intensive. Use a cache to avoid repeatedly scanning the system.

> **Parameters**
>
> - **devices_on_system** – Set of USB devices found on the system.
>
> - **force_refresh** – If True and the driver uses a cache to prevent repeated scanning, the cache must be flushed.

debug_managed_device_detection (*devices_on_system*, *output*)
Called only if MANAGES_DEVICE_PRESENCE is True.

Should write information about the devices detected on the system to output, which is a file like object.

Should return True if a device was detected and successfully opened, otherwise False.

reset (*key='-1'*, *log_packets=False*, *report_progress=None*, *detected_device=None*)

> **Parameters**
>
> - **key** – The key to unlock the device
>
> - **log_packets** – If true the packet stream to/from the device is logged
>
> - **report_progress** – Function that is called with a % progress (number between 0 and 100) for various tasks If it is called with -1 that means that the task does not have any progress information
>
> - **detected_device** – Device information from the device scanner

can_handle_windows (*device_id*, *debug=False*)
Optional method to perform further checks on a device to see if this driver is capable of handling it. If it is not it should return False. This method is only called after the vendor, product ids and the bcd have matched, so it can do some relatively time intensive checks. The default implementation returns True. This method is called only on windows. See also *can_handle()* (page 344).

> **Parameters device_info** – On windows a device ID string. On Unix a tuple of (vendor_id, product_id, bcd).

can_handle (*device_info*, *debug=False*)
Unix version of *can_handle_windows()* (page 344)

> **Parameters device_info** – Is a tuple of (vid, pid, bcd, manufacturer, product, serial number)

open (*connected_device*, *library_uuid*)
Perform any device specific initialization. Called after the device is detected but before any other functions that communicate with the device. For example: For devices that present themselves as USB Mass storage devices, this method would be responsible for mounting the device or if the device has been automounted, for finding out where it has been mounted. The method

`calibre.devices.usbms.device.Device.open()` has an implementation of this function that should serve as a good example for USB Mass storage devices.

This method can raise an OpenFeedback exception to display a message to the user.

Parameters

- **connected_device** – The device that we are trying to open. It is a tuple of (vendor id, product id, bcd, manufacturer name, product name, device serial number). However, some devices have no serial number and on windows only the first three fields are present, the rest are None.

- **library_uuid** – The UUID of the current calibre library. Can be None if there is no library (for example when used from the command line).

`eject()`
> Un-mount / eject the device from the OS. This does not check if there are pending GUI jobs that need to communicate with the device.
>
> NOTE: That this method may not be called on the same thread as the rest of the device methods.

`post_yank_cleanup()`
> Called if the user yanks the device without ejecting it first.

`set_progress_reporter(report_progress)`
> Set a function to report progress information.
>
> > **Parameters report_progress** – Function that is called with a % progress (number between 0 and 100) for various tasks If it is called with -1 that means that the task does not have any progress information

`get_device_information(end_session=True)`
> Ask device for device information. See L{DeviceInfoQuery}.
>
> > **Returns** (device name, device version, software version on device, mime type) The tuple can optionally have a fifth element, which is a drive information dictionary. See usbms.driver for an example.

`get_driveinfo()`
> Return the driveinfo dictionary. Usually called from get_device_information(), but if loading the driveinfo is slow for this driver, then it should set SLOW_DRIVEINFO. In this case, this method will be called by calibre after the book lists have been loaded. Note that it is not called on the device thread, so the driver should cache the drive info in the books() method and this function should return the cached data.

`card_prefix(end_session=True)`
> Return a 2 element list of the prefix to paths on the cards. If no card is present None is set for the card's prefix. E.G. ('/place', '/place2') (None, 'place2') ('place', None) (None, None)

`total_space(end_session=True)`

> **Get total space available on the mountpoints:**
>
> 1. Main memory
>
> 2. Memory Card A
>
> 3. Memory Card B
>
> **Returns** A 3 element list with total space in bytes of (1, 2, 3). If a particular device doesn't have any of these locations it should return 0.

`free_space(end_session=True)`

Get free space available on the mountpoints:

1. Main memory

2. Card A

3. Card B

> **Returns** A 3 element list with free space in bytes of (1, 2, 3). If a particular device doesn't have any of these locations it should return -1.

books (*oncard=None, end_session=True*)
Return a list of ebooks on the device.

> **Parameters oncard** – If 'carda' or 'cardb' return a list of ebooks on the specific storage card, otherwise return list of ebooks in main memory of device. If a card is specified and no books are on the card return empty list.
>
> **Returns** A BookList.

upload_books (*files, names, on_card=None, end_session=True, metadata=None*)
Upload a list of books to the device. If a file already exists on the device, it should be replaced. This method should raise a `FreeSpaceError` if there is not enough free space on the device. The text of the FreeSpaceError must contain the word "card" if `on_card` is not None otherwise it must contain the word "memory".

> **Parameters**
>
> - **files** – A list of paths
>
> - **names** – A list of file names that the books should have once uploaded to the device. len(names) == len(files)
>
> - **metadata** – If not None, it is a list of `Metadata` objects. The idea is to use the metadata to determine where on the device to put the book. len(metadata) == len(files). Apart from the regular cover (path to cover), there may also be a thumbnail attribute, which should be used in preference. The thumbnail attribute is of the form (width, height, cover_data as jpeg).
>
> **Returns** A list of 3-element tuples. The list is meant to be passed to *add_books_to_metadata()* (page 346).

classmethod add_books_to_metadata (*locations, metadata, booklists*)
Add locations to the booklists. This function must not communicate with the device.

> **Parameters**
>
> - **locations** – Result of a call to L{upload_books}
>
> - **metadata** – List of `Metadata` objects, same as for *upload_books()* (page 346).
>
> - **booklists** – A tuple containing the result of calls to (`books(oncard=None)()`, `books(oncard='carda')()`, :meth'books(oncard='cardb')').

delete_books (*paths, end_session=True*)
Delete books at paths on device.

classmethod remove_books_from_metadata (*paths, booklists*)
Remove books from the metadata list. This function must not communicate with the device.

> **Parameters**
>
> - **paths** – paths to books on the device.

- **booklists** – A tuple containing the result of calls to (`books(oncard=None)()`, `books(oncard='carda')()`, :meth'books(oncard='cardb')').

sync_booklists(*booklists, end_session=True*)

> Update metadata on device.

> > **Parameters booklists** – A tuple containing the result of calls to (`books(oncard=None)()`, `books(oncard='carda')()`, :meth'books(oncard='cardb')').

get_file(*path, outfile, end_session=True*)

> Read the file at `path` on the device and write it to outfile.

> > **Parameters outfile** – file object like `sys.stdout` or the result of an *open()* (page 344) call.

classmethod config_widget()

> Should return a QWidget. The QWidget contains the settings for the device interface

classmethod save_settings(*settings_widget*)

> Should save settings to disk. Takes the widget created in *config_widget()* (page 347) and saves all settings to disk.

classmethod settings()

> Should return an opts object. The opts object should have at least one attribute *format_map* which is an ordered list of formats for the device.

set_plugboards(*plugboards, pb_func*)

> provide the driver the current set of plugboards and a function to select a specific plugboard. This method is called immediately before add_books and sync_booklists.

> **pb_func is a callable with the following signature::** def pb_func(device_name, format, plugboards)

> You give it the current device name (either the class name or DEVICE_PLUGBOARD_NAME), the format you are interested in (a 'real' format or 'device_db'), and the plugboards (you were given those by set_plugboards, the same place you got this method).

> > **Returns** None or a single plugboard instance.

set_driveinfo_name(*location_code, name*)

> Set the device name in the driveinfo file to 'name'. This setting will persist until the file is re-created or the name is changed again.

> Non-disk devices should implement this method based on the location codes returned by the get_device_information() method.

prepare_addable_books(*paths*)

> Given a list of paths, returns another list of paths. These paths point to addable versions of the books.

> If there is an error preparing a book, then instead of a path, the position in the returned list for that book should be a three tuple: (original_path, the exception instance, traceback)

startup()

> Called when calibre is is starting the device. Do any initialization required. Note that multiple instances of the class can be instantiated, and thus __init__ can be called multiple times, but only one instance will have this method called. This method is called on the device thread, not the GUI thread.

shutdown()

> Called when calibre is shutting down, either for good or in preparation to restart. Do any cleanup required. This method is called on the device thread, not the GUI thread.

1.12. Setting up a calibre development environment

get_device_uid ( )
> Must return a unique id for the currently connected device (this is called immediately after a successful call to open()). You must implement this method if you set ASK_TO_ALLOW_CONNECT = True

ignore_connected_device (*uid*)
> Should ignore the device identified by uid (the result of a call to get_device_uid()) in the future. You must implement this method if you set ASK_TO_ALLOW_CONNECT = True. Note that this function is called immediately after open(), so if open() caches some state, the driver should reset that state.

get_user_blacklisted_devices ( )
> Return map of device uid to friendly name for all devices that the user has asked to be ignored.

set_user_blacklisted_devices (*devices*)
> Set the list of device uids that should be ignored by this driver.

specialize_global_preferences (*device_prefs*)
> Implement this method if your device wants to override a particular preference. You must ensure that all call sites that want a preference that can be overridden use device_prefs['something'] instead of prefs['something']. Your method should call device_prefs.set_overrides(pref=val, pref=val, ...). Currently used for: metadata management (prefs['manage_device_metadata'])

set_library_info (*library_name*, *library_uuid*, *field_metadata*)
> Implement this method if you want information about the current calibre library. This method is called at startup and when the calibre library changes while connected.

is_dynamically_controllable ( )
> Called by the device manager when starting plugins. If this method returns a string, then a) it supports the device manager's dynamic control interface, and b) that name is to be used when talking to the plugin.

> This method can be called on the GUI thread. A driver that implements this method must be thread safe.

start_plugin ( )
> This method is called to start the plugin. The plugin should begin to accept device connections however it does that. If the plugin is already accepting connections, then do nothing.

> This method can be called on the GUI thread. A driver that implements this method must be thread safe.

stop_plugin ( )
> This method is called to stop the plugin. The plugin should no longer accept connections, and should cleanup behind itself. It is likely that this method should call shutdown. If the plugin is already not accepting connections, then do nothing.

> This method can be called on the GUI thread. A driver that implements this method must be thread safe.

get_option (*opt_string*, *default=None*)
> Return the value of the option indicated by opt_string. This method can be called when the plugin is not started. Return None if the option does not exist.

> This method can be called on the GUI thread. A driver that implements this method must be thread safe.

set_option (*opt_string*, *opt_value*)
> Set the value of the option indicated by opt_string. This method can be called when the plugin is not started.

> This method can be called on the GUI thread. A driver that implements this method must be thread safe.

is_running ( )
> Return True if the plugin is started, otherwise false

> This method can be called on the GUI thread. A driver that implements this method must be thread safe.

synchronize_with_db (*db*, *book_id*, *book_metadata*, *first_call*)

Called during book matching when a book on the device is matched with a book in calibre's db. The method is responsible for syncronizing data from the device to calibre's db (if needed).

The method must return a two-value tuple. The first value is a set of calibre book ids changed if calibre's database was changed or None if the database was not changed. If the first value is an empty set then the metadata for the book on the device is updated with calibre's metadata and given back to the device, but no GUI refresh of that book is done. This is useful when the calibre data is correct but must be sent to the device.

The second value is itself a 2-value tuple. The first value in the tuple specifies whether a book format should be sent to the device. The intent is to permit verifying that the book on the device is the same as the book in calibre. This value must be None if no book is to be sent, otherwise return the base file name on the device (a string like foobar.epub). Be sure to include the extension in the name. The device subsystem will construct a send_books job for all books with not- None returned values. Note: other than to later retrieve the extension, the name is ignored in cases where the device uses a template to generate the file name, which most do. The second value in the returned tuple indicated whether the format is future-dated. Return True if it is, otherwise return False. Calibre will display a dialog to the user listing all future dated books.

Extremely important: this method is called on the GUI thread. It must be threadsafe with respect to the device manager's thread.

book_id: the calibre id for the book in the database. book_metadata: the Metadata object for the book coming from the device. first_call: True if this is the first call during a sync, False otherwise

class calibre.devices.interface.**BookList** (*oncard*, *prefix*, *settings*)

Bases: list

A list of books. Each Book object must have the fields

1. title

2. authors

3. size (file size of the book)

4. datetime (a UTC time tuple)

5. path (path on the device to the book)

6. thumbnail (can be None) thumbnail is either a str/bytes object with the image data or it should have an attribute image_path that stores an absolute (platform native) path to the image

7. tags (a list of strings, can be empty).

supports_collections ()

Return True if the device supports collections for this book list.

add_book (*book*, *replace_metadata*)

Add the book to the booklist. Intent is to maintain any device-internal metadata. Return True if booklists must be sync'ed

remove_book (*book*)

Remove a book from the booklist. Correct any device metadata at the same time

get_collections (*collection_attributes*)

Return a dictionary of collections created from collection_attributes. Each entry in the dictionary is of the form collection name:[list of books]

The list of books is sorted by book title, except for collections created from series, in which case series_index is used.

> **Parameters** `collection_attributes` – A list of attributes of the Book object

USB Mass Storage based devices The base class for such devices is `calibre.devices.usbms.driver.USBMS` (page 351). This class in turn inherits some of its functionality from its bases, documented below. A typical basic USBMS based driver looks like this:

```python
from calibre.devices.usbms.driver import USBMS

class PDNOVEL(USBMS):
    name = 'Pandigital Novel device interface'
    gui_name = 'PD Novel'
    description = _('Communicate with the Pandigital Novel')
    author = 'Kovid Goyal'
    supported_platforms = ['windows', 'linux', 'osx']
    FORMATS = ['epub', 'pdf']

    VENDOR_ID   = [0x18d1]
    PRODUCT_ID  = [0xb004]
    BCD         = [0x224]

    VENDOR_NAME = 'ANDROID'
    WINDOWS_MAIN_MEM = WINDOWS_CARD_A_MEM = '__UMS_COMPOSITE'
    THUMBNAIL_HEIGHT = 144

    EBOOK_DIR_MAIN = 'eBooks'
    SUPPORTS_SUB_DIRS = False

    def upload_cover(self, path, filename, metadata):
        coverdata = getattr(metadata, 'thumbnail', None)
        if coverdata and coverdata[2]:
            with open('%s.jpg' % os.path.join(path, filename), 'wb') as coverfile:
                coverfile.write(coverdata[2])
```

class `calibre.devices.usbms.device.`**Device**(*plugin_path*)

> Bases: `calibre.devices.usbms.deviceconfig.DeviceConfig`, `calibre.devices.interface.DevicePlugin` (page 342)

This class provides logic common to all drivers for devices that export themselves as USB Mass Storage devices. Provides implementations for mounting/ejecting of USBMS devices on all platforms.

WINDOWS_MAIN_MEM = None
> String identifying the main memory of the device in the windows PnP id strings This can be None, string, list of strings or compiled regex

WINDOWS_CARD_A_MEM = None
> String identifying the first card of the device in the windows PnP id strings This can be None, string, list of strings or compiled regex

WINDOWS_CARD_B_MEM = None
> String identifying the second card of the device in the windows PnP id strings This can be None, string, list of strings or compiled regex

OSX_MAIN_MEM_VOL_PAT = None
> Used by the new driver detection to disambiguate main memory from storage cards. Should be a regular expression that matches the main memory mount point assigned by OS X

MAX_PATH_LEN = 250
> The maximum length of paths created on the device

NEWS_IN_FOLDER = **True**
> Put news in its own folder

windows_sort_drives (*drives*)
> Called to disambiguate main memory and storage card for devices that do not distinguish between them on the basis of *WINDOWS_CARD_NAME*. For e.g.: The EB600

sanitize_callback (*path*)
> Callback to allow individual device drivers to override the path sanitization used by create_upload_path().

filename_callback (*default, mi*)
> Callback to allow drivers to change the default file name set by create_upload_path().

sanitize_path_components (*components*)
> Perform any device specific sanitization on the path components for files to be uploaded to the device

get_annotations (*path_map*)
> Resolve path_map to annotation_map of files found on the device

add_annotation_to_library (*db, db_id, annotation*)
> Add an annotation to the calibre library

class calibre.devices.usbms.cli.**CLI**

class calibre.devices.usbms.driver.**USBMS** (*plugin_path*)
> Bases: *calibre.devices.usbms.cli.CLI* (page 351), *calibre.devices.usbms.device.Device* (page 350)

> The base class for all USBMS devices. Implements the logic for sending/getting/updating metadata/caching metadata/etc.

> **upload_cover** (*path, filename, metadata, filepath*)
> > Upload book cover to the device. Default implementation does nothing.

> > **Parameters**
> > - **path** – The full path to the directory where the associated book is located.
> > - **filename** – The name of the book file without the extension.
> > - **metadata** – metadata belonging to the book. Use metadata.thumbnail for cover
> > - **filepath** – The full path to the ebook file

> **classmethod normalize_path** (*path*)
> > Return path with platform native path separators

User Interface Actions

If you are adding your own plugin in a zip file, you should subclass both InterfaceActionBase and InterfaceAction. The load_actual_plugin() method of you InterfaceActionBase subclass must return an instantiated object of your InterfaceBase subclass.

class calibre.gui2.actions.**InterfaceAction** (*parent, site_customization*)
> Bases: PyQt5.QtCore.QObject

> A plugin representing an "action" that can be taken in the graphical user interface. All the items in the toolbar and context menus are implemented by these plugins.

> Note that this class is the base class for these plugins, however, to integrate the plugin with calibre's plugin system, you have to make a wrapper class that references the actual plugin. See the calibre.customize.builtins module for examples.

If two `InterfaceAction` objects have the same name, the one with higher priority takes precedence.

Sub-classes should implement the `genesis()`, `library_changed()`, `location_selected()` `shutting_down()` and `initialization_complete()` methods.

Once initialized, this plugin has access to the main calibre GUI via the `gui` member. You can access other plugins by name, for example:

```
self.gui.iactions['Save To Disk']
```

To access the actual plugin, use the `interface_action_base_plugin` attribute, this attribute only becomes available after the plugin has been initialized. Useful if you want to use methods from the plugin class like do_user_config().

The QAction specified by `action_spec` is automatically create and made available as `self.qaction`.

name = 'Implement me'
> The plugin name. If two plugins with the same name are present, the one with higher priority takes precedence.

priority = 1
> The plugin priority. If two plugins with the same name are present, the one with higher priority takes precedence.

popup_type = 1
> The menu popup type for when this plugin is added to a toolbar

auto_repeat = False
> Whether this action should be auto repeated when its shortcut key is held down.

action_spec = ('text', 'icon', None, None)
> Of the form: (text, icon_path, tooltip, keyboard shortcut) icon, tooltip and keyboard shortcut can be None shortcut must be a string, None or tuple of shortcuts. If None, a keyboard shortcut corresponding to the action is not registered. If you pass an empty tuple, then the shortcut is registered with no default key binding.

action_add_menu = False
> If True, a menu is automatically created and added to self.qaction

action_menu_clone_qaction = False
> If True, a clone of self.qaction is added to the menu of self.qaction If you want the text of this action to be different from that of self.qaction, set this variable to the new text

dont_add_to = frozenset([])
> Set of locations to which this action must not be added. See `all_locations` for a list of possible locations

dont_remove_from = frozenset([])
> Set of locations from which this action must not be removed. See `all_locations` for a list of possible locations

action_type = 'global'
> Type of action 'current' means acts on the current view 'global' means an action that does not act on the current view, but rather on calibre as a whole

accepts_drops = False
> If True, then this InterfaceAction will have the opportunity to interact with drag and drop events. See the methods, `accept_enter_event()`, :meth`:accept_drag_move_event`, `drop_event()` for details.

accept_enter_event (*event*, *mime_data*)
> This method should return True iff this interface action is capable of handling the drag event. Do not call accept/ignore on the event, that will be taken care of by the calibre UI.

accept_drag_move_event (*event*, *mime_data*)

This method should return True iff this interface action is capable of handling the drag event. Do not call accept/ignore on the event, that will be taken care of by the calibre UI.

drop_event (*event*, *mime_data*)

This method should perform some useful action and return True iff this interface action is capable of handling the drop event. Do not call accept/ignore on the event, that will be taken care of by the calibre UI. You should not perform blocking/long operations in this function. Instead emit a signal or use QTimer.singleShot and return quickly. See the builtin actions for examples.

create_menu_action (*menu*, *unique_name*, *text*, *icon=None*, *shortcut=None*, *description=None*, *triggered=None*, *shortcut_name=None*)

Convenience method to easily add actions to a QMenu. Returns the created QAction, This action has one extra attribute calibre_shortcut_unique_name which if not None refers to the unique name under which this action is registered with the keyboard manager.

> **Parameters**
>
> - **menu** – The QMenu the newly created action will be added to
>
> - **unique_name** – A unique name for this action, this must be globally unique, so make it as descriptive as possible. If in doubt add a uuid to it.
>
> - **text** – The text of the action.
>
> - **icon** – Either a QIcon or a file name. The file name is passed to the I() builtin, so you do not need to pass the full path to the images directory.
>
> - **shortcut** – A string, a list of strings, None or False. If False, no keyboard shortcut is registered for this action. If None, a keyboard shortcut with no default keybinding is registered. String and list of strings register a shortcut with default keybinding as specified.
>
> - **description** – A description for this action. Used to set tooltips.
>
> - **triggered** – A callable which is connected to the triggered signal of the created action.
>
> - **shortcut_name** – The test displayed to the user when customizing the keyboard shortcuts for this action. By default it is set to the value of `text`.

load_resources (*names*)

If this plugin comes in a ZIP file (user added plugin), this method will allow you to load resources from the ZIP file.

For example to load an image:

```
pixmap = QPixmap()
pixmap.loadFromData(self.load_resources(['images/icon.png']).itervalues().next())
icon = QIcon(pixmap)
```

> **Parameters names** – List of paths to resources in the zip file using / as separator
>
> **Returns** A dictionary of the form `{name : file_contents}`. Any names that were not found in the zip file will not be present in the dictionary.

genesis ()

Setup this plugin. Only called once during initialization. self.gui is available. The action specified by `action_spec` is available as `self.qaction`.

location_selected (*loc*)

Called whenever the book list being displayed in calibre changes. Currently values for loc are: `library`, `main`, `card` and `cardb`.

This method should enable/disable this action and its sub actions as appropriate for the location.

library_changed(*db*)

> Called whenever the current library is changed.
>
> > **Parameters db** – The LibraryDatabase corresponding to the current library.

gui_layout_complete()

> Called once per action when the layout of the main GUI is completed. If your action needs to make changes to the layout, they should be done here, rather than in `initialization_complete()`.

initialization_complete()

> Called once per action when the initialization of the main GUI is completed.

shutting_down()

> Called once per plugin when the main GUI is in the process of shutting down. Release any used resources, but try not to block the shutdown for long periods of time.
>
> > **Returns** False to halt the shutdown. You are responsible for telling the user why the shutdown was halted.

class calibre.customize.**InterfaceActionBase**(**args*, ***kwargs*)

> Bases: *calibre.customize.Plugin* (page 333)

> **load_actual_plugin**(*gui*)
>
> > This method must return the actual interface action plugin object.

Preferences Plugins

class calibre.customize.**PreferencesPlugin**(*plugin_path*)

> Bases: *calibre.customize.Plugin* (page 333)

A plugin representing a widget displayed in the Preferences dialog.

This plugin has only one important method `create_widget()`. The various fields of the plugin control how it is categorized in the UI.

config_widget = None

> Import path to module that contains a class named ConfigWidget which implements the ConfigWidgetInterface. Used by `create_widget()`.

category_order = 100

> Where in the list of categories the `category` of this plugin should be.

name_order = 100

> Where in the list of names in a category, the `gui_name` of this plugin should be

category = None

> The category this plugin should be in

gui_category = None

> The category name displayed to the user for this plugin

gui_name = None

> The name displayed to the user for this plugin

icon = None

> The icon for this plugin, should be an absolute path

description = None

> The description used for tooltips and the like

create_widget (*parent=None*)

Create and return the actual Qt widget used for setting this group of preferences. The widget must implement the `calibre.gui2.preferences.ConfigWidgetInterface` (page 355).

The default implementation uses `config_widget` to instantiate the widget.

class `calibre.gui2.preferences.`**ConfigWidgetInterface**

This class defines the interface that all widgets displayed in the Preferences dialog must implement. See `ConfigWidgetBase` for a base class that implements this interface and defines various convenience methods as well.

changed_signal = **None**

This signal must be emitted whenever the user changes a value in this widget

supports_restoring_to_defaults = **True**

Set to True iff the `restore_to_defaults()` method is implemented.

restore_defaults_desc = **u'Restore settings to default values. You have to click Apply to actually save the (**

The tooltip for the Restore to defaults button

restart_critical = **False**

If True the Preferences dialog will not allow the user to set any more preferences. Only has effect if `commit()` returns True.

genesis (*gui*)

Called once before the widget is displayed, should perform any necessary setup.

> **Parameters gui** – The main calibre graphical user interface

initialize ()

Should set all config values to their initial values (the values stored in the config files).

restore_defaults ()

Should set all config values to their defaults.

commit ()

Save any changed settings. Return True if the changes require a restart, False otherwise. Raise an `AbortCommit` exception to indicate that an error occurred. You are responsible for giving the user feedback about what the error is and how to correct it.

refresh_gui (*gui*)

Called once after this widget is committed. Responsible for causing the gui to reread any changed settings. Note that by default the GUI re-initializes various elements anyway, so most widgets won't need to use this method.

class `calibre.gui2.preferences.`**ConfigWidgetBase** (*parent=None*)

Base class that contains code to easily add standard config widgets like checkboxes, combo boxes, text fields and so on. See the `register()` method.

This class automatically handles change notification, resetting to default, translation between gui objects and config objects, etc. for registered settings.

If your config widget inherits from this class but includes setting that are not registered, you should override the `ConfigWidgetInterface` methods and call the base class methods inside the overrides.

register (*name, config_obj, gui_name=None, choices=None, restart_required=False, empty_string_is_None=True, setting=<class 'calibre.gui2.preferences.Setting'>*)

Register a setting.

> **Parameters**
>
> - **name** – The setting name
> - **config** – The config object that reads/writes the setting

- **gui_name** – The name of the GUI object that presents an interface to change the setting. By default it is assumed to be `'opt_'` + name.

- **choices** – If this setting is a multiple choice (combobox) based setting, the list of choices. The list is a list of two element tuples of the form: `[(gui name, value), ...]`

- **setting** – The class responsible for managing this setting. The default class handles almost all cases, so this param is rarely used.

Viewer plugins

class `calibre.customize.`**`ViewerPlugin`**(*plugin_path*)

   Bases: `calibre.customize.Plugin` (page 333)

   type = u'Viewer'

   These plugins are used to add functionality to the calibre viewer.

   load_fonts()

   This method is called once at viewer startup. It should load any fonts it wants to make available. For example:

```
def load_fonts():
    from PyQt5.Qt import QFontDatabase
    font_data = get_resources(['myfont1.ttf', 'myfont2.ttf'])
    for raw in font_data.itervalues():
        QFontDatabase.addApplicationFontFromData(raw)
```

   load_javascript(*evaljs*)

   This method is called every time a new HTML document is loaded in the viewer. Use it to load javascript libraries into the viewer. For example:

```
def load_javascript(self, evaljs):
    js = get_resources('myjavascript.js')
    evaljs(js)
```

   run_javascript(*evaljs*)

   This method is called every time a document has finished loading. Use it in the same way as load_javascript().

   customize_ui(*ui*)

   This method is called once when the viewer is created. Use it to make any customizations you want to the viewer's user interface. For example, you can modify the toolbars via ui.tool_bar and ui.tool_bar2.

   customize_context_menu(*menu*, *event*, *hit_test_result*)

   This method is called every time the context (right-click) menu is shown. You can use it to customize the context menu. event is the context menu event and hit_test_result is the QWebHitTestResult for this event in the currently loaded document.

API Documentation for the database interface

This API is thread safe (it uses a multiple reader, single writer locking scheme). You can access this API like this:

```
from calibre.library import db
db = db('Path to calibre library folder').new_api
```

If you are in a calibre plugin that is part of the main calibre GUI, you get access to it like this instead:

```
db = self.gui.current_db.new_api
```

class calibre.db.cache.**Cache** (*backend*)

An in-memory cache of the metadata.db file from a calibre library. This class also serves as a threadsafe API for accessing the database. The in-memory cache is maintained in normal form for maximum performance.

SQLITE is simply used as a way to read and write from metadata.db robustly. All table reading/sorting/searching/caching logic is re-implemented. This was necessary for maximum performance and flexibility.

add_books (*books,   add_duplicates=True,   apply_import_tags=True,   preserve_uuid=False,   run_hooks=True, dbapi=None*)

Add the specified books to the library. Books should be an iterable of 2-tuples, each 2-tuple of the form (mi, format_map) where mi is a Metadata object and format_map is a dictionary of the form {fmt: path_or_stream}, for example: {'EPUB': '/path/to/file.epub'}.

Returns a pair of lists: ids, duplicates. ids contains the book ids for all newly created books in the database. duplicates contains the (mi, format_map) for all books that already exist in the database as per the simple duplicate detection heuristic used by *has_book ()* (page 360).

add_custom_book_data (*name, val_map, delete_first=False*)

Add data for name where val_map is a map of book_ids to values. If delete_first is True, all previously stored data for name will be removed.

add_format (*book_id, fmt, stream_or_path, replace=True, run_hooks=True, dbapi=None*)

Add a format to the specified book. Return True of the format was added successfully.

> **Parameters**
>
> - **replace** – If True replace existing format, otherwise if the format already exists, return False.
>
> - **run_hooks** – If True, file type plugins are run on the format before and after being added.
>
> - **dbapi** – Internal use only.

all_book_ids (*type=<type 'frozenset'>*)

Frozen set of all known book ids.

all_field_for (*field, book_ids, default_value=None*)

Same as field_for, except that it operates on multiple books at once

all_field_ids (*name*)

Frozen set of ids for all values in the field name.

all_field_names (*field*)

Frozen set of all fields names (should only be used for many-one and many-many fields)

author_data (*author_ids=None*)

Return author data as a dictionary with keys: name, sort, link

If no authors with the specified ids are found an empty dictionary is returned. If author_ids is None, data for all authors is returned.

author_sort_from_authors (*authors*)

Given a list of authors, return the author_sort string for the authors, preferring the author sort associated with the author over the computed string.

books_for_field (*name, item_id*)

Return all the books associated with the item identified by item_id, where the item belongs to the field name.

Returned value is a set of book ids, or the empty set if the item or the field does not exist.

copy_cover_to (*book_id*, *dest*, *use_hardlink=False*)

Copy the cover to the file like object `dest`. Returns False if no cover exists or dest is the same file as the current cover. dest can also be a path in which case the cover is copied to it if and only if the path is different from the current path (taking case sensitivity into account).

copy_format_to (*book_id*, *fmt*, *dest*, *use_hardlink=False*)

Copy the format `fmt` to the file like object `dest`. If the specified format does not exist, raises `NoSuchFormat` error. dest can also be a path, in which case the format is copied to it, iff the path is different from the current path (taking case sensitivity into account).

cover (*book_id*, *as_file=False*, *as_image=False*, *as_path=False*)

Return the cover image or None. By default, returns the cover as a bytestring.

WARNING: Using as_path will copy the cover to a temp file and return the path to the temp file. You should delete the temp file when you are done with it.

Parameters

- **as_file** – If True return the image as an open file object (a SpooledTemporaryFile)
- **as_image** – If True return the image as a QImage object
- **as_path** – If True return the image as a path pointing to a temporary file

data_for_find_identical_books ()

Return data that can be used to implement *find_identical_books()* (page 358) in a worker process without access to the db. See db.utils for an implementation.

data_for_has_book ()

Return data suitable for use in *has_book()* (page 360). This can be used for an implementation of *has_book()* (page 360) in a worker process without access to the db.

delete_custom_book_data (*name*, *book_ids=()*)

Delete data for name. By default deletes all data, if you only want to delete data for some book ids, pass in a list of book ids.

embed_metadata (*book_ids*, *only_fmts=None*, *report_error=None*, *report_progress=None*)

Update metadata in all formats of the specified book_ids to current metadata in the database.

fast_field_for (*field_obj*, *book_id*, *default_value=None*)

Same as field_for, except that it avoids the extra lookup to get the field object

field_for (*name*, *book_id*, *default_value=None*)

Return the value of the field name for the book identified by `book_id`. If no such book exists or it has no defined value for the field name or no such field exists, then `default_value` is returned.

`default_value` is not used for title, title_sort, authors, author_sort and series_index. This is because these always have values in the db. `default_value` is used for all custom columns.

The returned value for is_multiple fields are always tuples, even when no values are found (in other words, default_value is ignored). The exception is identifiers for which the returned value is always a dict. The returned tuples are always in link order, that is, the order in which they were created.

field_ids_for (*name*, *book_id*)

Return the ids (as a tuple) for the values that the field name has on the book identified by `book_id`. If there are no values, or no such book, or no such field, an empty tuple is returned.

find_identical_books (*mi*, *search_restriction=u''*, *book_ids=None*)

Finds books that have a superset of the authors in mi and the same title (title is fuzzy matched). See also *data_for_find_identical_books()* (page 358).

---

format (*book_id, fmt, as_file=False, as_path=False, preserve_filename=False*)

Return the ebook format as a bytestring or *None* if the format doesn't exist, or we don't have permission to write to the ebook file.

> **Parameters**
>
> - **as_file** – If True the ebook format is returned as a file object. Note that the file object is a SpooledTemporaryFile, so if what you want to do is copy the format to another file, use *copy_format_to()* (page 358) instead for performance.
>
> - **as_path** – Copies the format file to a temp file and returns the path to the temp file
>
> - **preserve_filename** – If True and returning a path the filename is the same as that used in the library. Note that using this means that repeated calls yield the same temp file (which is re-created each time)

format_abspath (*book_id, fmt*)

Return absolute path to the ebook file of format *format*. You should almost never use this, as it breaks the threadsafe promise of this API. Instead use, *copy_format_to()* (page 358).

Currently used only in calibredb list, the viewer, edit book, compare_format to original format, open with and the catalogs (via get_data_as_dict()).

Apart from the viewer, open with and edit book, I don't believe any of the others do any file write I/O with the results of this call.

format_hash (*book_id, fmt*)

Return the hash of the specified format for the specified book. The kind of hash is backend dependent, but is usually SHA-256.

format_metadata (*book_id, fmt, allow_cache=True, update_db=False*)

Return the path, size and mtime for the specified format for the specified book. You should not use path unless you absolutely have to, since accessing it directly breaks the threadsafe guarantees of this API. Instead use the *copy_format_to()* (page 358) method.

> **Parameters**
>
> - **allow_cache** – If True cached values are used, otherwise a slow filesystem access is done. The cache values could be out of date if access was performed to the filesystem outside of this API.
>
> - **update_db** – If True The max_size field of the database is updates for this book.

formats (*book_id, verify_formats=True*)

Return tuple of all formats for the specified book. If verify_formats is True, verifies that the files exist on disk.

get_categories (*sort=u'name', book_ids=None, icon_map=None, already_fixed=None, first_letter_sort=False*)

Used internally to implement the Tag Browser

get_custom_book_data (*name, book_ids=(), default=None*)

Get data for name. By default returns data for all book_ids, pass in a list of book ids if you only want some data. Returns a map of book_id to values. If a particular value could not be decoded, uses default for it.

get_id_map (*field*)

Return a mapping of id numbers to values for the specified field. The field must be a many-one or many-many field, otherwise a ValueError is raised.

get_ids_for_custom_book_data (*name*)

Return the set of book ids for which name has data.

---

get_item_id (*field*, *item_name*)

> Return the item id for item_name (case-insensitive)

get_item_ids (*field*, *item_names*)

> Return the item id for item_name (case-insensitive)

get_item_name (*field*, *item_id*)

> Return the item name for the item specified by item_id in the specified field. See also *get_id_map()* (page 359).

get_metadata (*book_id*, *get_cover=False*, *get_user_categories=True*, *cover_as_data=False*)

> Return metadata for the book identified by book_id as a Metadata object. Note that the list of formats is not verified. If get_cover is True, the cover is returned, either a path to temp file as mi.cover or if cover_as_data is True then as mi.cover_data.

get_next_series_num_for (*series*, *field=u'series'*, *current_indices=False*)

> Return the next series index for the specified series, taking into account the various preferences that control next series number generation.
>
> **Parameters**
>
> * **field** – The series-like field (defaults to the builtin series column)
>
> * **current_indices** – If True, returns a mapping of book_id to current series_index value instead.

get_proxy_metadata (*book_id*)

> Like *get_metadata()* (page 360) except that it returns a ProxyMetadata object that only reads values from the database on demand. This is much faster than get_metadata when only a small number of fields need to be accessed from the returned metadata object.

get_usage_count_by_id (*field*)

> Return a mapping of id to usage count for all values of the specified field, which must be a many-one or many-many field.

has_book (*mi*)

> Return True iff the database contains an entry with the same title as the passed in Metadata object. The comparison is case-insensitive. See also *data_for_has_book()* (page 358).

has_format (*book_id*, *fmt*)

> Return True iff the format exists on disk

has_id (*book_id*)

> Return True iff the specified book_id exists in the db

init ()

> Initialize this cache with data from the backend.

multisort (*fields*, *ids_to_sort=None*, *virtual_fields=None*)

> Return a list of sorted book ids. If ids_to_sort is None, all book ids are returned.
>
> fields must be a list of 2-tuples of the form (field_name, ascending=True or False). The most significant field is the first 2-tuple.

pref (*name*, *default=None*)

> Return the value for the specified preference or the value specified as default if the preference is not set.

read_backup (*book_id*)

> Return the OPF metadata backup for the book as a bytestring or None if no such backup exists.

remove_books (*book_ids, permanent=False*)

Remove the books specified by the book_ids from the database and delete their format files. If `permanent` is False, then the format files are not deleted.

remove_formats (*formats_map, db_only=False*)

Remove the specified formats from the specified books.

> **Parameters**
>
> - **formats_map** – A mapping of book_id to a list of formats to be removed from the book.
>
> - **db_only** – If True, only remove the record for the format from the db, do not delete the actual format file from the filesystem.

remove_items (*field, item_ids, restrict_to_book_ids=None*)

Delete all items in the specified field with the specified ids. Returns the set of affected book ids. `restrict_to_book_ids` is an optional set of books ids. If specified the items will only be removed from those books.

rename_items (*field, item_id_to_new_name_map, change_index=True, restrict_to_book_ids=None*)

Rename items from a many-one or many-many field such as tags or series.

> **Parameters**
>
> - **change_index** – When renaming in a series-like field also change the series_index values.
>
> - **restrict_to_book_ids** – An optional set of book ids for which the rename is to be performed, defaults to all books.

restore_book (*book_id, mi, last_modified, path, formats*)

Restore the book entry in the database for a book that already exists on the filesystem

restore_original_format (*book_id, original_fmt*)

Restore the specified format from the previously saved ORIGINAL_FORMAT, if any. Return True on success. The ORIGINAL_FORMAT is deleted after a successful restore.

safe_read_lock

A safe read lock is a lock that does nothing if the thread already has a write lock, otherwise it acquires a read lock. This is necessary to prevent DowngradeLockErrors, which can happen when updating the search cache in the presence of composite columns. Updating the search cache holds an exclusive lock, but searching a composite column involves reading field values via ProxyMetadata which tries to get a shared lock. There may be other scenarios that trigger this as well.

This property returns a new lock object on every access. This lock object is not recursive (for performance) and must only be used in a with statement as `with cache.safe_read_lock`: otherwise bad things will happen.

save_original_format (*book_id, fmt*)

Save a copy of the specified format as ORIGINAL_FORMAT, overwriting any existing ORIGINAL_FORMAT.

search (*query, restriction=u'', virtual_fields=None, book_ids=None*)

Search the database for the specified query, returning a set of matched book ids.

> **Parameters**
>
> - **restriction** – A restriction that is ANDed to the specified query. Note that restrictions are cached, therefore the search for a AND b will be slower than a with restriction b.
>
> - **virtual_fields** – Used internally (virtual fields such as on_device to search over).

- **book_ids** – If not None, a set of book ids for which books will be searched instead of searching all books.

set_conversion_options (*options*, *fmt=u'PIPE'*)
> options must be a map of the form {book_id:conversion_options}

set_cover (*book_id_data_map*)
> Set the cover for this book. data can be either a QImage, QPixmap, file object or bytestring. It can also be None, in which case any existing cover is removed.

set_field (*name*, *book_id_to_val_map*, *allow_case_change=True*, *do_path_update=True*)
> Set the values of the field specified by name. Returns the set of all book ids that were affected by the change.

> **Parameters**

>> - **book_id_to_val_map** – Mapping of book_ids to values that should be applied.

>> - **allow_case_change** – If True, the case of many-one or many-many fields will be changed. For example, if a book has the tag tag1 and you set the tag for another book to Tag1 then the both books will have the tag Tag1 if allow_case_change is True, otherwise they will both have the tag tag1.

>> - **do_path_update** – Used internally, you should never change it.

set_metadata (*book_id*, *mi*, *ignore_errors=False*, *force_changes=False*, *set_title=True*, *set_authors=True*, *allow_case_change=False*)
> Set metadata for the book *id* from the *Metadata* object *mi*

> Setting force_changes=True will force set_metadata to update fields even if mi contains empty values. In this case, 'None' is distinguished from 'empty'. If mi.XXX is None, the XXX is not replaced, otherwise it is. The tags, identifiers, and cover attributes are special cases. Tags and identifiers cannot be set to None so then will always be replaced if force_changes is true. You must ensure that mi contains the values you want the book to have. Covers are always changed if a new cover is provided, but are never deleted. Also note that force_changes has no effect on setting title or authors.

set_pref (*name*, *val*)
> Set the specified preference to the specified value. See also *pref()* (page 360).

tags_older_than (*tag*, *delta=None*, *must_have_tag=None*, *must_have_authors=None*)
> Return the ids of all books having the tag tag that are older than the specified time. tag comparison is case insensitive.

> **Parameters**

>> - **delta** – A timedelta object or None. If None, then all ids with the tag are returned.

>> - **must_have_tag** – If not None the list of matches will be restricted to books that have this tag

>> - **must_have_authors** – A list of authors. If not None the list of matches will be restricted to books that have these authors (case insensitive).

user_categories_for_books (*book_ids*, *proxy_metadata_map=None*)
> Return the user categories for the specified books. proxy_metadata_map is optional and is useful for a performance boost, in contexts where a ProxyMetadata object for the books already exists. It should be a mapping of book_ids to their corresponding ProxyMetadata objects.

API Documentation for the ebook editing tools

The ebook editing tools consist of a *calibre.ebooks.oeb.polish.container.Container* (page 363) object that represents a book as a collection of HTML + resource files, and various tools that can be used to perform operations on the container. All the tools are in the form of module level functions in the various `calibre.ebooks.oeb.polish.*` modules. You obtain a container object for a book at a path like this:

```
from calibre.ebooks.oeb.polish.container import get_container
container = get_container('Path to book file', tweak_mode=True)
```

If you are writing a plugin for the ebook editor, you get the current container for the book being edited like this:

```
from calibre.gui2.tweak_book import current_container
container = current_container()
if container is None:
    report_error # No book has been opened yet
```

The Container object

class `calibre.ebooks.oeb.polish.container.`**Container** (*rootpath, opfpath, log, clone_data=None*)

A container represents an Open EBook as a directory full of files and an opf file. There are two important concepts:

- The root directory. This is the base of the ebook. All the ebooks files are inside this directory or in its sub-directories.

- Names: These are paths to the books' files relative to the root directory. They always contain POSIX separators and are unquoted. They can be thought of as canonical identifiers for files in the book. Most methods on the container object work with names. Names are always in the NFC unicode normal form.

- Clones: the container object supports efficient on-disk cloning, which is used to implement checkpoints in the ebook editor. In order to make this work, you should never access files on the filesystem directly. Instead, use *raw_data ()* (page 365) or *open ()* (page 365) to read/write to component files in the book.

When converting between hrefs and names use the methods provided by this class, they assume all hrefs are quoted.

abspath_to_name (*fullpath, root=None*)

Convert an absolute path to a canonical name relative to `root`

> **Parameters** `root` – The base directory. By default the root for this container object is used.

add_file (*name, data, media_type=None, spine_index=None*)

Add a file to this container. Entries for the file are automatically created in the OPF manifest and spine (if the file is a text document)

add_name_to_manifest (*name*)

Add an entry to the manifest for a file with the specified name. Returns the manifest id.

book_type = u'oeb'

The type of book (epub for EPUB files and azw3 for AZW3 files)

commit (*outpath=None, keep_parsed=False*)

Commit all dirtied parsed objects to the filesystem and write out the ebook file at outpath. :param output: The path to write the saved ebook file to. If None, the path of the original book file is used. :param keep_parsed: If True the parsed representations of committed items are kept in the cache.

commit_item (*name*, *keep_parsed=False*)

Commit a parsed object to disk (it is serialized and written to the underlying file). If `keep_parsed` is True the parsed representation is retained in the cache. See also: *parsed()* (page 365)

decode (*data*, *normalize_to_nfc=True*)

Automatically decode `data` into a `unicode` object.

> **Parameters** **normalize_to_nfc** – Normalize returned unicode to the NFC normal form as is required by both the EPUB and AZW3 formats.

dirty (*name*)

Mark the parsed object corresponding to name as dirty. See also: *parsed()* (page 365).

exists (*name*)

True iff a file corresponding to the canonical name exists. Note that this function suffers from the limitations of the underlying OS filesystem, in particular case (in)sensitivity. So on a case insensitive filesystem this will return True even if the case of name is different from the case of the underlying filesystem file. See also *has_name()* (page 364)

filesize (*name*)

Return the size in bytes of the file represented by the specified canonical name. Automatically handles dirtied parsed objects. See also: *parsed()* (page 365)

generate_item (*name*, *id_prefix=None*, *media_type=None*, *unique_href=True*)

Add an item to the manifest with href derived from the given name. Ensures uniqueness of href and id automatically. Returns generated item.

guess_type (*name*)

Return the expected mimetype for the specified file name based on its extension.

guide_type_map

Mapping of guide type to canonical name

has_name (*name*)

Return True iff a file with the same canonical name as that specified exists. Unlike *exists()* (page 364) this method is always case-sensitive.

href_to_name (*href*, *base=None*)

Convert an href (relative to base) to a name. base must be a name or None, in which case self.root is used.

insert_into_xml (*parent*, *item*, *index=None*)

Insert item into parent (or append if index is None), fixing indentation. Only works with self closing items.

is_dir = **False**

If this container represents an unzipped book (a directory)

iterlinks (*name*, *get_line_numbers=True*)

Iterate over all links in name. If get_line_numbers is True the yields results of the form (link, line_number, offset). Where line_number is the line_number at which the link occurs and offset is the number of characters from the start of the line. Note that offset could actually encompass several lines if not zero.

manifest_has_name (*name*)

Return True if the manifest has an entry corresponding to name

manifest_id_map

Mapping of manifest id to canonical names

manifest_type_map

Mapping of manifest media-type to list of canonical names of that media-type

mi

The metadata of this book as a Metadata object. Note that this object is constructed on the fly every time this property is requested, so use it sparingly.

name_to_abspath (*name*)

Convert a canonical name to an absolute OS dependant path

name_to_href (*name*, *base=None*)

Convert a name to a href relative to base, which must be a name or None in which case self.root is used as the base

names_that_must_not_be_changed

Set of names that must never be renamed. Depends on the ebook file format.

names_that_must_not_be_removed

Set of names that must never be deleted from the container. Depends on the ebook file format.

names_that_need_not_be_manifested

Set of names that are allowed to be missing from the manifest. Depends on the ebook file format.

open (*name*, *mode=u'rb'*)

Open the file pointed to by name for direct read/write. Note that this will commit the file if it is dirtied and remove it from the parse cache. You must finish with this file before accessing the parsed version of it again, or bad things will happen.

opf

The parsed OPF file

opf_get_or_create (*name*)

Convenience method to either return the first XML element with the specified name or create it under the opf:package element and then return it, if it does not already exist.

opf_version

The version set on the OPF's <package> element

opf_xpath (*expr*)

Convenience method to evaluate an XPath expression on the OPF file, has the opf: and dc: namespace prefixes pre-defined.

parsed (*name*)

Return a parsed representation of the file specified by name. For HTML and XML files an lxml tree is returned. For CSS files a cssutils stylesheet is returned. Note that parsed objects are cached for performance. If you make any changes to the parsed object, you must call `dirty()` (page 364) so that the container knows to update the cache. See also `replace()` (page 366).

raw_data (*name*, *decode=True*, *normalize_to_nfc=True*)

Return the raw data corresponding to the file specified by name

Parameters

- **decode** – If True and the file has a text based mimetype, decode it and return a unicode object instead of raw bytes.

- **normalize_to_nfc** – If True the returned unicode object is normalized to the NFC normal form as is required for the EPUB and AZW3 file formats.

relpath (*path*, *base=None*)

Convert an absolute path (with os separators) to a path relative to base (defaults to self.root). The relative path is *not* a name. Use `abspath_to_name()` (page 363) for that.

remove_from_spine (*spine_items*, *remove_if_no_longer_in_spine=True*)

Remove   the   specified   items   (by   canonical   name)   from   the   spine.   If remove_if_no_longer_in_spine is True, the items are also deleted from the book, not just from the spine.

remove_from_xml (*item*)

Removes item from parent, fixing indentation (works only with self closing items)

remove_item (*name, remove_from_guide=True*)

Remove the item identified by name from this container. This removes all references to the item in the OPF manifest, guide and spine as well as from any internal caches.

rename (*current_name, new_name*)

Renames a file from current_name to new_name. It automatically rebases all links inside the file if the directory the file is in changes. Note however, that links are not updated in the other files that could reference this file. This is for performance, such updates should be done once, in bulk.

replace (*name, obj*)

Replace the parsed object corresponding to name with obj, which must be a similar object, i.e. an lxml tree for HTML/XML or a cssutils stylesheet for a CSS file.

replace_links (*name, replace_func*)

Replace all links in name using replace_func, which must be a callable that accepts a URL and returns the replaced URL. It must also have a 'replaced' attribute that is set to True if any actual replacement is done. Convenient ways of creating such callables are using the LinkReplacer and LinkRebaser classes.

serialize_item (*name*)

Convert a parsed object (identified by canonical name) into a bytestring. See *parsed ()* (page 365).

set_spine (*spine_items*)

Set the spine to be spine_items where spine_items is an iterable of the form (name, linear). Will raise an error if one of the names is not present in the manifest.

spine_items

An iterator yielding canonical name for every item in the books' spine. See also: *spine_iter* (page 366) and *spine_items* (page 366).

spine_iter

An iterator that yields item, name is_linear for every item in the books' spine. item is the lxml element, name is the canonical file name and is_linear is True if the item is linear. See also: *spine_names* (page 366) and *spine_items* (page 366).

spine_names

An iterator yielding name and is_linear for every item in the books' spine. See also: *spine_iter* (page 366) and *spine_items* (page 366).

Managing component files in a container

calibre.ebooks.oeb.polish.replace.**replace_links** (*container, link_map, frag_map=<function <lambda>>, replace_in_opf=False*)

Replace links to files in the container. Will iterate over all files in the container and change the specified links in them.

Parameters

- **link_map** – A mapping of old canonical name to new canonical name. For example: {'images/old.png': 'images/new.png'}

- **frag_map** – A callable that takes two arguments (name, anchor) and returns a new anchor. This is useful if you need to change the anchors in HTML files. By default, it does nothing.

- **replace_in_opf** – If False, links are not replaced in the OPF file.

calibre.ebooks.oeb.polish.replace.**rename_files** (*container*, *file_map*)
> Rename files in the container, automatically updating all links to them.

> **Parameters file_map** – A mapping of old canonical name to new canonical name, for example:
> {'text/chapter1.html': 'chapter1.html'}.

calibre.ebooks.oeb.polish.replace.**get_recommended_folders** (*container*, *names*)
> Return the folders that are recommended for the given filenames. The recommendation is based on where the majority of files of the same type are located in the container. If no files of a particular type are present, the recommended folder is assumed to be the folder containing the OPF file.

Pretty printing and auto fixing parse errors

calibre.ebooks.oeb.polish.pretty.**fix_html** (*container*, *raw*)
> Fix any parsing errors in the HTML represented as a string in raw. Fixing is done using the HTML5 parsing algorithm.

calibre.ebooks.oeb.polish.pretty.**fix_all_html** (*container*)
> Fix any parsing errors in all HTML files in the container. Fixing is done using the HTML5 parsing algorithm.

calibre.ebooks.oeb.polish.pretty.**pretty_html** (*container*, *name*, *raw*)
> Pretty print the HTML represented as a string in raw

calibre.ebooks.oeb.polish.pretty.**pretty_css** (*container*, *name*, *raw*)
> Pretty print the CSS represented as a string in raw

calibre.ebooks.oeb.polish.pretty.**pretty_xml** (*container*, *name*, *raw*)
> Pretty print the XML represented as a string in raw. If name is the name of the OPF, extra OPF-specific prettying is performed.

calibre.ebooks.oeb.polish.pretty.**pretty_all** (*container*)
> Pretty print all HTML/CSS/XML files in the container

Managing book jackets

calibre.ebooks.oeb.polish.jacket.**remove_jacket** (*container*)
> Remove an existing jacket, if any. Returns False if no existing jacket was found.

calibre.ebooks.oeb.polish.jacket.**add_or_replace_jacket** (*container*)
> Either create a new jacket from the book's metadata or replace an existing jacket. Returns True if an existing jacket was replaced.

Splitting and merging of files

calibre.ebooks.oeb.polish.split.**split** (*container*, *name*, *loc_or_xpath*, *before=True*, *totals=None*)
> Split the file specified by name at the position specified by loc_or_xpath. Splitting automatically migrates all links and references to the affected files.

> **Parameters**

> - **loc_or_xpath** – Should be an XPath expression such as //h:div[@id="split_here"]. Can also be a *loc* which is used internally to implement splitting in the preview panel.

> - **before** – If True the split occurs before the identified element otherwise after it.

1.12. Setting up a calibre development environment

- **totals** – Used internally

calibre.ebooks.oeb.polish.split.**multisplit** (*container, name, xpath, before=True*)

Split the specified file at multiple locations (all tags that match the specified XPath expression. See also: *split()* (page 367). Splitting automatically migrates all links and references to the affected files.

Parameters before – If True the splits occur before the identified element otherwise after it.

calibre.ebooks.oeb.polish.split.**merge** (*container, category, names, master*)

Merge the specified files into a single file, automatically migrating all links and references to the affected files. The file must all either be HTML or CSS files.

Parameters

- **category** – Must be either ′text′ for HTML files or ′styles′ for CSS files
- **names** – The list of files to be merged
- **master** – Which of the merged files is the *master* file, that is, the file that will remain after merging.

Managing covers

calibre.ebooks.oeb.polish.cover.**set_cover** (*container, cover_path, report=None, options=None*)

Set the cover of the book to the image pointed to by cover_path.

Parameters

- **cover_path** – Either the absolute path to an image file or the canonical name of an image in the book. When using an image in the book, you must also set options, see below.
- **report** – An optional callable that takes a single argument. It will be called with information about the tasks being processed.
- **options** – None or a dictionary that controls how the cover is set. The dictionary can have entries: **keep_aspect**: True or False (Preserve aspect ratio of covers in EPUB) **no_svg**: True or False (Use an SVG cover wrapper in the EPUB titlepage) **existing**: True or False (cover_path refers to an existing image in the book)

calibre.ebooks.oeb.polish.cover.**mark_as_cover** (*container, name*)

Mark the specified image as the cover image.

calibre.ebooks.oeb.polish.cover.**mark_as_titlepage** (*container, name, move_to_start=True*)

Mark the specified HTML file as the titlepage of the EPUB.

Parameters move_to_start – If True the HTML file is moved to the start of the spine

Working with CSS

calibre.ebooks.oeb.polish.fonts.**change_font** (*container, old_name, new_name=None*)

Change a font family from old_name to new_name. Changes all occurrences of the font family in stylesheets, style tags and style attributes. If the old_name refers to an embedded font, it is removed. You can set new_name to None to remove the font family instead of changing it.

calibre.ebooks.oeb.polish.css.**remove_unused_css** (*container, report=None, remove_unused_classes=False*)

Remove all unused CSS rules from the book. An unused CSS rule is one that does not match any actual content.

Parameters

- **report** – An optional callable that takes a single argument. It is called with information about the operations being performed.

- **remove_unused_classes** – If True, class attributes in the HTML that do not match any CSS rules are also removed.

calibre.ebooks.oeb.polish.css.**filter_css** (*container*, *properties*, *names=()*)
Remove the specified CSS properties from all CSS rules in the book.

Parameters

- **properties** – Set of properties to remove. For example: {'font-family', 'color'}.

- **names** – The files from which to remove the properties. Defaults to all HTML and CSS files in the book.

Working with the Table of Contents

calibre.ebooks.oeb.polish.toc.**from_xpaths** (*container*, *xpaths*)
Generate a Table of Contents from a list of XPath expressions. Each expression in the list corresponds to a level of the generate ToC. For example: ['//h:h1', '//h:h2', '//h:h3'] will generate a three level table of contents from the <h1>, <h2> and <h3> tags.

calibre.ebooks.oeb.polish.toc.**from_links** (*container*)
Generate a Table of Contents from links in the book.

calibre.ebooks.oeb.polish.toc.**from_files** (*container*)
Generate a Table of Contents from files in the book.

calibre.ebooks.oeb.polish.toc.**create_inline_toc** (*container*, *title=None*)
Create an inline (HTML) Table of Contents from an existing NCX table of contents.

Parameters title – The title for this table of contents.

Edit Book Tool

class calibre.gui2.tweak_book.plugin.**Tool**
Bases: object   The base class for individual tools in an Edit Book plugin. Useful members include:

- **self.plugin**: A reference to the *calibre.customize.Plugin* (page 333) object to which this tool belongs.

- self. *boss* (page 370)

- self. *gui* (page 370)

Methods that must be overridden in sub classes:

- *create_action ()* (page 370)

- *register_shortcut ()* (page 370)

name = None
Set this to a unique name it will be used as a key

allowed_in_toolbar = True
If True the user can choose to place this tool in the plugins toolbar

allowed_in_menu = True
If True the user can choose to place this tool in the plugins menu

toolbar_button_popup_mode = u'delayed'

    The popup mode for the menu (if any) of the toolbar button. Possible values are 'delayed', 'instant', 'button'

boss

    The *calibre.gui2.tweak_book.boss.Boss* (page 371) object. Used to control the user interface.

gui

    The main window of the user interface

current_container

    Return the current *calibre.ebooks.oeb.polish.container.Container* (page 363) object that represents the book being edited.

register_shortcut (*qaction, unique_name, default_keys=(), short_text=None, description=None, **extra_data*)

    Register a keyboard shortcut that will trigger the specified qaction. This keyboard shortcut will become automatically customizable by the user in the Keyboard section of the editor preferences.

    Parameters

- **qaction** – A QAction object, it will be triggered when the configured key combination is pressed by the user.

- **unique_name** – A unique name for this shortcut/action. It will be used internally, it must not be shared by any other actions in this plugin.

- **default_keys** – A list of the default keyboard shortcuts. If not specified no default shortcuts will be set. If the shortcuts specified here conflict with either builtin shortcuts or shortcuts from user configuration/other plugins, they will be ignored. In that case, users will have to configure the shortcuts manually via Preferences. For example: default_keys=('Ctrl+J', 'F9').

- **short_text** – An optional short description of this action. If not specified the text from the QAction will be used.

- **description** – An optional longer description of this action, it will be used in the preferences entry for this shortcut.

create_action (*for_toolbar=True*)

    Create a QAction that will be added to either the plugins toolbar or the plugins menu depending on for_toolbar. For example:

```
def create_action(self, for_toolbar=True):
    ac = QAction(get_icons('myicon.png'), 'Do something')
    if for_toolbar:
        # We want the toolbar button to have a popup menu
        menu = QMenu()
        ac.setMenu(menu)
        menu.addAction('Do something else')
        subaction = menu.addAction('And another')

        # Register a keyboard shortcut for this toolbar action be
        # careful to do this for only one of the toolbar action or
        # the menu action, not both.
        self.register_shortcut(ac, 'some-unique-name', default_keys=('Ctrl+K',))
    return ac
```

    See also:

    Method *register_shortcut()* (page 370).

Controlling the editor's user interface

The ebook editor's user interface is controlled by a single global *Boss* object. This has many useful methods that can be used in plugin code to perform common tasks.

class calibre.gui2.tweak_book.boss.**Boss** (*parent, notify=None*)

> **add_savepoint** (*msg*)
> > Create a restore checkpoint with the name specified as msg
>
> **apply_container_update_to_gui** (*mark_as_modified=True*)
> > Update all the components of the user interface to reflect the latest data in the current book container.
> >
> > > **Parameters mark_as_modified** – If True, the book will be marked as modified, so the user will be prompted to save it when quitting.
>
> **close_editor** (*name*)
> > Close the editor that is editing the file specified by name
>
> **commit_all_editors_to_container** ()
> > Commit any changes that the user has made to files open in editors to the container. You should call this method before performing any actions on the current container
>
> **currently_editing**
> > Return the name of the file being edited currently or None if no file is being edited
>
> **edit_file** (*name, syntax=None, use_template=None*)
> > Open the file specified by name in an editor
> >
> > > **Parameters**
> > >
> > > - **syntax** – The media type of the file, for example, 'text/html'. If not specified it is guessed from the file extension.
> > >
> > > - **use_template** – A template to initialize the opened editor with
>
> **open_book** (*path=None, edit_file=None, clear_notify_data=True, open_folder=False*)
> > Open the ebook at path for editing. Will show an error if the ebook is not in a supported format or the current book has unsaved changes.
> >
> > > **Parameters edit_file** – The name of a file inside the newly opened book to start editing. Can also be a list of names.
>
> **rewind_savepoint** ()
> > Undo the previous creation of a restore checkpoint, useful if you create a checkpoint, then abort the operation with no changes
>
> **save_book** ()
> > Save the book. Saving is performed in the background
>
> **set_modified** ()
> > Mark the book as having been modified
>
> **show_current_diff** (*allow_revert=True, to_container=None*)
> > Show the changes to the book from its last checkpointed state
> >
> > > **Parameters**
> > >
> > > - **allow_revert** – If True the diff dialog will have a button to allow the user to revert all changes
> > >
> > > - **to_container** – A container object to compare the current container to. If None, the previously checkpointed container is used

show_editor (*name*)
> Show the editor that is editing the file specified by `name`

sync_preview_to_editor ()
> Sync the position of the preview panel to the current cursor position in the current editor

1.13 Glossary

RSS **RSS** *(Really Simple Syndication)* is a web feed format that is used to publish frequently updated content, like news articles, blog posts, etc. It is a format that is particularly suited to being read by computers, and is therefore the preferred way of getting content from the web into an ebook. There are many other feed formats in use on the Internet, and calibre understands most of them. In particular, it has good support for the *ATOM* format, which is commonly used for blogs.

recipe A recipe is a set of instructions that teach calibre how to convert an online news source, such as a magazine or a blog, into an ebook. A recipe is essentially Python[144] code. As such, it is capable of converting arbitrarily complex news sources into ebooks. At the simplest level, it is just a set of variables, such as URLs, that give calibre enough information to go out onto the Internet and download the news.

HTML **HTML** *(Hyper Text Mark-Up Language)*, a subset of Standard Generalized Mark-Up Language (SGML) for electronic publishing, is the specific standard used for the World Wide Web.

CSS **CSS** *(Cascading Style Sheets)* is a language used to describe how an *HTML* document should be rendered (visual styling).

API **API** *(Application Programming Interface)* is a source code interface that a library provides to support requests for services to be made of it by computer programs.

LRF **LRF** The ebook format that is read by the SONY ebook readers.

URL **URL** *(Uniform Resource Locator)* for example: `http://example.com`

regexp **Regular expressions** provide a concise and flexible means for identifying strings of text of interest, such as particular characters, words, or patterns of characters. See regexp syntax[145] for the syntax of regular expressions used in Python.

---

[144]https://www.python.org
[145]https://docs.python.org/2.7/library/re.html

C

H

I